SPORTSMANLIKE DRIVING

Fifth Edition

by

AMERICAN AUTOMOBILE ASSOCIATION
Washington, D.C.

Webster Division

McGraw-Hill Book Company

St. Louis, New York, San Francisco, Dallas, Toronto, London

This book is dedicated to Helen K. Knandel, pioneer in driver education, major author of earlier editions and highly regarded AAA specialist.

Contents

Preface

The fifth edition of *Sportsmanlike Driving* includes new concepts and new illustrations which make it the most up-to-date textbook for high school driver education courses. It is designed to provide authoritative solutions to the driver education problems of the 1960s and the 1970s.

The content, format, and chapter arrangement reflect what teachers want in a comprehensive, easy-to-grasp textbook. Hundreds of teachers were queried, many by personal interview, as to the type of text needed for driver education in the sixties and seventies. This book takes into account their comments and suggestions.

The American Automobile Association, with its world-wide resources and three decades of pioneering and development in driver education techniques and materials, has applied both its resources and its experiences to this textbook. These, together with the Association's unparalleled experience in the fields of traffic operations and highway safety, give *Sportsmanlike Driving* unmatched authenticity.

The book is divided into two parts: *Getting Ready to Drive* and *In the Car*. This organization provides convenience for use in each of the two phases of a complete driver education course—classroom instruction and practice driving.

The teaching technique employed throughout the book is unique. Emotion-associated words are utilized to orient students to the factual material. This technique shapes the students' attitude toward safe and sportsmanlike driving. The effect is most apparent in the chapter, "The Psychology of the Driver."

There is an up-to-date chapter dealing with the increasingly important subject of freeway driving, and there is also a chapter describing how alcohol and drugs affect drivers. Many problems often encountered in teaching the effects of alcohol and drugs are simplified, since the approach is purely factual.

To help students understand how the automobile runs, a pictorial section shows simply and clearly how the various automobile systems work. There is also emphasis on buying, insuring, and operating a car. A compact but comprehensive reference list for students is included at the end of the book, and a glossary is one of the many useful features of this edition.

Sportsmanlike Driving has large pages, and two columns of type have been used for easy readability. There are about 400 illustrations and color is liberally used throughout the book.

Although there is some new material, approaches and concepts that have proved their appeal and value are retained. One of the most important of these is the time- and experience-tested step-by-step procedure used in the second part of the book, *In the Car*, for teaching driving skills. The over-all objective has also remained: to develop excellent, responsible drivers who, as citizens and voters, are well informed about the many traffic problems.

To the Student and the Teacher

By 1975 there will be more than 110 million drivers in this country. By 1975, there will be four cars on the road for every three now in use. Despite vast highway building programs, the future will bring extremely heavy traffic concentrations, especially in and around urban areas. Drivers will find themselves exposed to dangerous situations more frequently than ever before.

It is clear that in the decade ahead there will be a greater need for orderly, disciplined, careful, and safe driving. Indeed, the general level of driving skill must rise sharply if traffic is to be anything but chaotic. Our greatest hope for avoiding traffic chaos is driver education.

High schools have an extremely important role to play in the solutions to many of the problems we face today. The traffic problem is one which they can directly and forcefully attack. By 1975, four million young people will reach legal driving age each year. Through effective traffic and driver education courses, high schools can do a great deal to promote traffic efficiency and safety. In high school driver education courses, learning takes place in a climate favorable for thoughtful study.

Educators have an opportunity to provide young people with the knowledge, skills, and—most important—attitudes necessary to their well-being. Driver education has an important contribution to make to this basic purpose. It makes this contribution in the following ways:

1. *It promotes the safe, efficient, and rewarding use of the automobile.* Some forty studies indicate that high school–trained drivers have significantly fewer accidents than untrained drivers. As a greater proportion of new drivers complete high school courses, the tragic toll of highway casualties will be greatly reduced. Recognizing this fact, many insurance companies now provide insurance at reduced premiums to students who successfully complete state-approved courses.

2. *It fosters a strong sense of personal responsibility for traffic conditions and improvements.* It stresses mature and responsible attitudes. It conveys an early understanding of the reasons and the need for citizen support of effective laws and regulations dealing with traffic problems.

3. *It encourages cooperation in solving public problems.* For example, students in driver education courses cooperate with public officials and specialists in studying traffic conditions and in developing plans for solving problems of parking, congestion, and law enforcement. Such experiences help develop better-informed citizens.

4. *It develops pride in high standards of performance and conduct.* Through effective driver education, students develop high standards of conduct, both for driving and walking. These high standards are becoming increasingly necessary as the population grows and the volume of traffic rises.

Acknowledgments

The revision has been under the constant and direct supervision of W. L. Robinson, Associate Director of the Traffic Engineering and Safety Department of the American Automobile Association. As editor, he directed and coordinated the work of some seventy driver education teachers, engineers, and technical specialists who reviewed chapters of former editions, proposed changes, and submitted suggestions.

All those whose names appear in the following paragraphs have contributed greatly to *Sportsmanlike Driving,* and their work is much appreciated.

Dr. Arthur L. Mahony, Area Chairman, Fair Lawn (N.J.) Public Schools, formerly Senior Safety Education Representative, New Jersey Division of Motor Vehicles, is principally responsible for rewriting the text and for much original writing. He is the author of the doctoral thesis, *Teaching for Attitude Conducive to Safe Driving,* New York University, 1957, a neurological approach to the study of the nature and development of attitude.

Miss Grace Lyon, Driver Education Instructor, Ridgewood (N.J.) High School, prepared the *To Do* and *To Talk About* sections at the close of each chapter.

For critical review of the manuscript and for other valuable contributions, acknowledgment is made to associates on the Department staff: Earl Allgaier, Harold O. Carlton, W. L. Carson, Walter E. Morris, Amos E. Neyhart, Sam Yaksich, Jr., Mrs. Margaret Walker, and Mrs. Barbara Pixton.

We wish to express appreciation also to associates in other departments of the American Automobile Association: Charles N. Brady, Charles C. Collins, James L. Reardon, Kermit B. Rykken, Ross D. Netherton, Ira B. Priddy, Jr., Paul D. White, II, George Viverette, and Marjorie C. Dennin.

The splendid contributions of the late Helen K. Knandel are still apparent in the fifth edition, as is the constructive work in connection with earlier editions by Dr. Norman Key, Executive Secretary, National Commission on Safety Education of the National Education Association. The steps used for teaching practice driving are an outgrowth of the experiences of Amos E. Neyhart, Director of the Institute of Public Safety, The Pennsylvania State University, also Consultant on Driver Education, American Automobile Association, and those of Harold O. Carlton, Educational Consultant, American Automobile Association.

A number of special photographs were taken by Don Callander, District of Columbia Division, American Automobile Association. Acknowledgment is also freely given to school officials of the Montgomery-Blair High School, Silver Spring, Md., and especially Mrs. Cissie E. Gieda, Head of the Department of Driver Education, for their valuable help in arranging for suitable photographs.

From the beginning in the 1930s, the development of the *Sportsmanlike Driving* materials has been largely the result of the intensive and devoted work of Burton W. Marsh, former Director of the Department. The wide acceptance and successful use of *Sportsmanlike Driving* in all its editions are evidence of the foresight and insight of Mr. Marsh and his staff. Many ideas that Mr. Marsh originated and developed are retained in this edition.

For valued professional and technical suggestions, and for reviewing parts of the manuscript, acknowledgment is gratefully made also to those whose names appear on the next page.

Matthew C. Sielski, *Director*
Traffic Engineering and Safety Department
American Automobile Association

George D. Anderson, Driver Education Instructor, Herkimer (N.Y.) High School

Dr. Milton W. Beckmann, Supervisor of Mathematics, and Professor of Secondary Education, Teacher's College, University of Nebraska, Lincoln, Nebr.

Dr. Richard W. Bishop, Associate Professor, The Florida Institute for Continuing University Studies, Tallahassee, Florida

Edward W. Bonessi, Director of Driver Education and Safety, Southern Connecticut State College, New Haven, Conn., and West Haven (Conn.) High School

Dr. Harold Brandaleone, Associate Clinical Professor of Medicine, New York University, New York, N.Y.; Chairman, Committee on Standards for Motor Vehicle Drivers of the Industrial Medical Association; Chairman, Medical Advisory Committee, Motor Transport Conference, National Safety Council

William D. Cushman, Associate in Safety, National Commission on Safety Education, National Education Association, Washington, D.C.

William G. Eliot, III, Highway Engineer, U.S. Bureau of Public Roads, and Secretary of National Joint Committee on Uniform Traffic Control Devices, Washington, D.C.

Dr. A. E. Florio, Professor of Safety Education, University of Illinois, Urbana, Ill.

Dr. T. W. Forbes, Professor of Psychology & Engineering Research, Michigan State Univ., East Lansing, Mich.

Joseph Galvin, Formerly Head, Department of Driver Education and Accident Prevention, San Francisco Unified School District, San Francisco, Cal.

Dr. Jess L. Gardner, Driver Education Instructor, University of Kentucky, Lexington, Ky.

Mrs. Cissie E. Gieda, Safety Coordinator Department Head, Driver Education, Montgomery-Blair High School, Silver Spring, Maryland

Robert R. Grainger, Driver Education Instructor, Chester (Pa.) High School

Mrs. Devona Griffith, Driver Education Instructor, Wilbur Wright High School, Dayton, Ohio

Dr. Leslie V. Hawkins, Professor of Industrial Education and Driver Education, Texas A&M University, College Station, Tex.

Donald Healy, Driver Education Instructor, Shawnee Mission (Kans.) North High School

Dr. Herman A. Heise, Past Chairman of the Committee on Medico-legal Problems, American Medical Association, Milwaukee, Wisconsin

Robert R. Hume, National Academy of Sciences, National Research Council, Washington, D.C.

Joseph Intorre, Assistant Director, Institute of Public Safety, The Pennsylvania State University, University Park, Pa.

Ira Scott Johnson, Jr., Physics, Chemistry Instructor, Ocean City (N.J.) High School

Roy E. Jorgensen, Highway Engineering and Management Consultant, Gaithersburg, Maryland

Mrs. E'lise B. Kelly, Driver Training Instructor, Los Angeles (Calif.) City Schools

Mark M. Knoll, Instructor, Queen Anne High School, Seattle, Wash.

Dr. Bernard I. Loft, Associate Professor of Health and Safety, Indiana University, Bloomington, Ind.

J. Willard Lord, Fleet Safety and Motor Maintenance Consultant, Ithan-Villanova, Pa.

Dr. John W. McTigue, Chairman, Department of Ophthalmology, The George Washington University, Washington, D.C.

Alger F. Malo, Director, Department of Streets and Traffic, City of Detroit, Mich.

Monroe M. Mayo, Consultant in Safety Education, Jefferson County Public Schools, Lakewood, Colo.

Samuel P. Messer, Associate Professor of Physical Education, University of Miami, Coral Gables, Fla.

D. Grant Mickle, Executive Director, Highway Research Board, Washington, D.C.

J. B. Millsap, Head, Department of Driver Education, Lamar Senior High School, Houston, Tex.

Joseph M. Nelson, Supervisor of Driver Education, State Department of Education, Salem, Ore.

Robert D. Nesbitt, Jr., Formerly Associate Professor of Industrial Education, New Mexico Western College, Silver City, N.M.

Raymond M. Pecuch, Driver Education Instructor, California (Pa.) High School

Carlton C. Robinson, Traffic Engineering Division, Automotive Safety Foundation, Washington, D.C.

Truman S. Smith, Supervisor of Driver Training, Minneapolis (Minn.) Public Schools

Goley D. Sontheimer, Director, Department of Safety, American Trucking Assn., Inc., Washington, D.C.

Lewis Spears, Consultant in Health, Safety and Driver Education, Division of Program Development, Texas Education Agency, Austin, Texas.

Dr. John S. Urlaub, Counselor and Director of Driver Education, Berkeley (Calif.) High School

A. A. Vezzani, Professor, Driver Education, The University of Michigan, Ann Arbor, Mich.

Dr. Samuel A. Williams, Driver Education Instructor, Anacostia High School, Washington, D.C.

PART ONE

Getting Ready to Drive

You in the Driver's Seat

It is the evening rush hour. Traffic is heavy but moving steadily. Long lines of cars are carrying tired people home. Home. That is the magnet attracting nearly all the people in the traffic stream—family, a relaxed evening meal, and the simple enjoyment of home.

There is real drama in these streets and the houses along them. A doctor is in one of these lines, trying hard, in his cool way, to reach a critically ill patient. Nearby, a fire engine has just rushed out into the traffic, siren screaming, to begin a hazardous trip to do a dangerous job. If it and its crew are not delayed, the fire damage will be small and no one will suffer serious burns. *If.*

On a sidewalk and across intersections, a small boy walks home with his books and a large bag of groceries. His mother nervously glances at the clock and the street and wishes he were home. A father tries to concentrate on the car ahead as his mind keeps going back to a troublesome business conference. He wonders if the little boy on the corner will wait for the light; he slows down.

Two girls and a boy are being driven home in a friend's car. They are high school students—very happy ones. They chat gaily about the holidays: the game, the parties, the dance. They very much look forward to the days ahead.

And there is another person caught up in this drama. This person is the driver. What he does in the circumstances he meets may affect not only those persons whom we have just met but also many others. He can do things that will help speed them home. Or he can cause delays to tire them more or be responsible for an accident that may bring injury or even death. He has an important degree of control over the future of those around him.

Is he mature and skilled? Does he know the rules of the road? Is he *worthy* of his responsibility for the welfare of all these people? As you may have guessed, the answer lies with you. For *you* are in the driver's seat.

1

The Key

It is a small, flat piece of metal.
It weighs about half an ounce.
Its cost? Perhaps 25 cents.
It's a key to a car—*your* car—now or in the future.
What does it really represent?

The pictures on the next four pages suggest some things that come with a key. You undoubtedly have in mind still more plans for your driving future. Let's dream a moment of what lies ahead.

For You The moment you take the wheel for the first time alone, you have infinitely greater freedom—and responsibility to match. You have freedom to "be yourself," unsupervised by parents and teachers, away from home and school. You have reached full adulthood in your new responsibility for the lives and well-being of others. You are also approaching—and reaching—the age when so many young Americans enter the military services.

Probably the greatest significance of your age—*and of that car key*—is that it symbolizes the change that you, and adults, too, must recognize. You have cast off the sometimes annoying, sometimes comforting, status of being "boys and girls." You are now in fact young men and women.

The automobile can give you a great deal of pleasure. School games, dates, and dances were all fun when you and your friends walked or rode bicycles or buses to them. With a car, there is added a greater independence, comfort, con-

1
What Driving Means to You

2

venience, and range of travel. There is also the understanding of trust that your passengers place in you, a trust which assumes your maturity. The state assumes it, too, when it grants you your license.

Those of you who like camping, fishing, swimming, and other outdoor fun know what a car means to you. At times, as the years go by, you may take vacation trips by car. The forty-eight grouped states, Canada, Alaska, and Mexico are full of interesting places to visit. Inter-American highways are extending farther and farther "south of the border."

Right from your car windows you can see the Grand Canyon, the green-blue waters of the Gulf Stream, seals off the West Coast shore line, or skiing and tobogganing in the Adirondacks and the Rockies. You can sit in your car on a New York Harbor ferryboat and see the famous skyline of the city and the Statue of Liberty. You can drive across the country to visit a Spanish mission hundreds of years old, in the Southwest desert country. There is an almost unlimited number of places your car can take you. Best of all, a car makes trips by whole families convenient and economical. You can even tour our newest state, Hawaii, and Europe by car, if you make arrangements here at home before you start.

Pleasure trips are only part of the story of the Key in your future. There's an excellent chance that you will drive to and from your daily work, spending hours each week behind the wheel. Perhaps you will become a professional and earn your living as a commercial driver.

**Your
car
will
take
you. . .**

many interesting places. . .

Indeed, there are many other pleasant possibilities.

Were these the whole story, however, we'd have no book to write. You'd have no course to take. Here would be the "happy ending" of our story. *But there's much more to our story.*

You will have power! You will control the movement of thousands of pounds of steel, driven by hundreds of horsepower. You will be the brain of a powerful, modern "genie." You will have full *responsibility* for everything your car does.

You will have greater *mobility*, a freedom of movement unknown in man's history until very recently. All the enjoyable experiences pictured on pages 3 to 6 *may* be yours. In fact, you can make these things come true—*if you will.*

The Future   Most of you who read this book will enjoy over many years all the pleasure a car can provide. Some won't. Some will become impatient drivers, angry drivers, thoughtless drivers. They will always be unhappy drivers. Some will use this wonderful machine only as a means for showing off. Some will die as a result of their driving mistakes.

If today's accident rates continue,

with others to share the pleasure. . .

at home. . .

and abroad.

over 44,000 Americans now living will die in motor vehicle accidents before this date next year. Over 1½ million will receive disabling injuries, and probably twice that many will suffer minor injuries.

Your Future Because you who read this book are taking driver education courses, your chances of avoiding highway casualty are better than those of other people. ("Highway casualty" is a special term; look it up in the Glossary.)

You, as a group, may expect to be involved in less than one-half as many accidents. This is only a beginning, and there is still a long way to go. But driver education courses are an important breakthrough in the solution of the traffic-accident problem. Driver education is the best hope there is.

The Cost of Accidents   Infinitely less tragic than the loss of life, but of major importance in itself, is the annual economic loss of over 7 billion dollars ($7,300,-000,000) from highway accidents.

The amount is so large that we cannot grasp what the number means. Perhaps it will be more meaningful if we think of it in terms of these examples:

1. This $7,300,000,000 would buy *every* high school senior in the United States a $2,500 car!

2. *Devoted to additional research, this sum might bring about a cure for cancer.* It would certainly greatly increase our knowledge and improve our chances. It might mean years and lives saved and untold suffering avoided.

3. What does your family pay for automobile insurance? Certainly this is a necessary protection if there is a car in the family. *But if the traffic-accident loss were greatly reduced, insurance costs would*

Fig. 1–1. You will have power. What about *responsibility*?

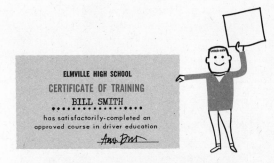

Fig. 1–2. The trained male driver under twenty-five years of age will benefit from lower insurance premiums.

go down in proportion. How could your family, or you, use the savings? For college expenses? Home improvements? Vacations?

The $7,300,000,000 is the annual cost of some people's bad driving! It is a wasteful, unnecessary loss.

Other facts concerning the cost of automobile accidents have a special interest for younger drivers. Although those under twenty-five years of age comprise only 17.7 percent of all licensed drivers, they are involved in about 30 percent of all highway accidents and over 29 percent of all fatal accidents.

Young male drivers have a higher-than-average accident rate. As a result, insurance rates for male drivers under twenty-five are especially high. However, young male drivers are usually allowed a premium reduction if they have had a high school driver education course. The reason is that trained male drivers under twenty-five do not have so high an accident rate as untrained male drivers in the same age group. Hence, the trained driver pays less for his automobile insurance.

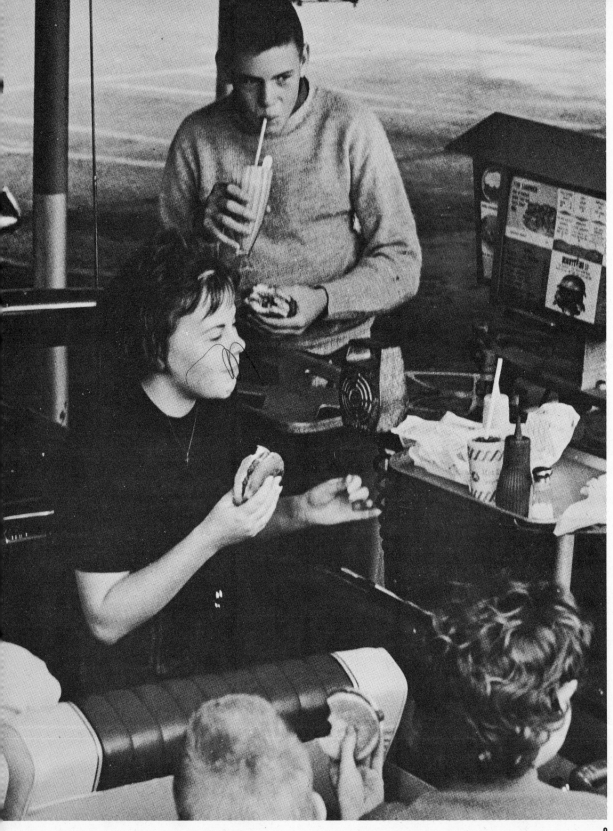

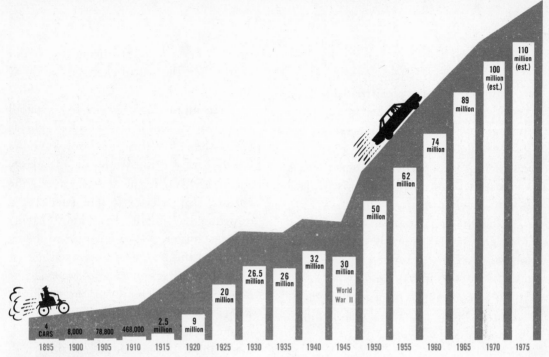

Fig. 1–4. We have rapidly taken to wheels.

So far, we have talked in terms of dollars and cents. But who would put a price on lives saved?

Gains from Driver Education   Increased mobility, better job opportunities, a better chance of staying alive, a smaller danger of injury, plus lower insurance costs—*all these can be yours.*

And your community gains, also. Despite uninformed claims to the contrary, study has shown that for every dollar spent for driver education, three dollars has been saved in accidents prevented.

These are facts that all citizens, young and old, should know.

Prediction   Statistics gathered over the years give us a good indication of what to expect in the future. By 1970, the number of drivers will probably pass the 105-million mark. Vehicles on the road will pass that mark by 1975, with the licensed drivers increasing to about 111 million. This is about 25 million more than we have today. What will be their future?

Unless driver education alters the statistical picture, the greater number of drivers and vehicles in the future will bring proportionate increases in traffic deaths, injuries, and economic loss. Individually, the story is different. We have no way of knowing the driving future of any one person. We do know that, to a great extent, his own driving behavior determines what that future will be.

What happens to people who travel on our highways? What can *you* look forward to as a driver?

Fig. 1–3. A part of your life today.

The Sign

Figure 1–5 is a typical roadside sign. You will see many like it scattered throughout the United States—except for one item. This sign has one place left blank. This particular sign, then, is an imaginary one. The unknown place is your driving future.

Others have passed this sign before—good drivers and poor ones, trained and untrained. Let's examine the cases of a few of these drivers and what each found at the unknown location or destination. These are actual happenings, *true stories of real people.*

Case One   Carol X, a seventeen-year-old high school girl, drove her parents' car with their permission. She was a careful, responsible, licensed driver. Hers was an average American family of moderate circumstances, owning their own home and planning for Carol to enter college in the fall. That is, this is the way it was

Fig. 1–5. Destination unknown.

up to a certain night during her senior year, when the world changed for the X family.

That night, Carol went to a school dance with a senior boy who had no car. Her father offered to let Carol drive the family car, and the young people gladly accepted. When the dance ended, the couple stopped for a late snack at a downtown all-night restaurant. Leaving the restaurant, Carol mentioned being tired and the boy, also a licensed driver, offered to drive home. Carol was glad he made the suggestion, and he took the wheel for the short ride home. A few moments later, a pair of headlights suddenly loomed from an intersecting road. Tires screeched, then came a crash.

For a while, everything was confusion. The police came, interviewed the drivers and passengers, and Carol and her friend went home in a cab. Both cars were badly damaged, but only one person complained of any injury—a wrenched back.

Carol's father received legal notice that he was being sued as the owner of the car involved in the crash in accordance with the law of that state. The suit was for an amount several times the cost of their home.

In court the jury decided against Mr. X. He had a $10,000–$20,000 liability insurance policy. The judgment against him was for $45,000! The injury was more serious than was at first believed. The insurance company paid the injured person $10,000; Mr. X was ordered to pay the remaining $35,000. The family sold their home and used the proceeds of the sale, plus all the money they had saved, toward settlement of the damages. They are now paying off the balance from Mr. X's salary and will be for years to come. Carol is working in a downtown store. For her, college is now far away.

One bit of carelessness ruined a lifetime of planning. Mr. X had never taken driver education in high school and had no knowledge of how important it is to have *adequate* automobile insurance. This is just one of the many subjects described in Chapter 17, "Buying, Insuring, and Operating Your Car."

Case Two A man was driving his car out of a large city along a wide, well-paved, through street. The weather was fair and warm, the pavement dry. The driver was experienced and well skilled.

Without warning, there suddenly came a thud and the driver got a glimpse of an arm at his left front fender. *There had been nobody in sight an instant before.*

The driver had hit a pedestrian, and soon after the accident the victim died. When the driver told the police that he had seen no one, they did not believe his story. They assumed that he had failed to yield to the man who had walked across the street, even though the pedestrian was in plain sight when he stepped off the left-hand curb. The driver, however, had told the truth. He hadn't seen anyone. What was wrong? Do you know? Very few drivers, even experienced drivers, know the answer to this question.

The driver had made one mistake in equipping his car. Knowing the need in modern highway traffic for seeing the blind spot at the left rear of his car, he had bought an outside mirror. When he mounted it, he made a serious error in mounting it *at his own eye level*. Had he placed it above or below his eye level, it would have been a helpful safety device. At eye level, it created a *permanent blind spot*. A coincidence in timing and circumstances did the rest, and he killed a man. Seldom thought about, this matter is one of the important items of information you will learn in Chapter 20, "Before You Start the Engine."

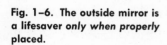
Fig. 1–6. The outside mirror is a lifesaver *only when properly placed.*

Case Three A woman was driving her new station wagon in a line of vehicles across a railroad grade crossing. The cars were moving slowly and close together.

As she was crossing the tracks the line of cars stopped. Almost immediately, the warning bell rang and the warning lights flashed. With cars close in front and in back, she couldn't move off the tracks. She sounded the car horn, but the driver ahead only motioned that he couldn't

move his car either. She saw the train rounding a curve a short distance away, left her car, and ran to safety.

At that moment, the line of cars started to move on. Hers was left alone, standing on the track. The locomotive struck the car and carried it a considerable distance along the track before the train could stop. The new car was completely wrecked.

She not only lost her car but also had to pay for disposal of the wreck. The greatest blow came later, when she learned that she had to pay for repairs to the locomotive!

Fortunately, there was no personal injury resulting from the accident, yet she still suffered considerable loss. Why? Do you know what she did wrong? She was one of those untrained drivers who just happened to have blank areas in her knowledge of good driving practices. One of the things she did not know was how to cross a railroad grade crossing, as described on pages 149 and 150 in Chapter 10, "Driving in the Country."

Case Four This case and the following two are taken from a report of an investigation conducted by a staff writer of the *Washington* (D.C.) *Star*.

A young couple decided to trade in their old car on another used one, several years newer. They had been attracted to a sleek convertible in a used-car lot and were told by the salesman that it would cost "only a few hundred dollars" to make the trade.

Fig. 1–7. Be careful never to get trapped at a railroad grade crossing.

They wanted to take a ride in the car before buying, but the salesman was unable to locate the keys of another car parked in front of it. They were told that if they didn't find the car perfectly satisfactory, they could always return it after a trial.

While someone went to look for the key to the car that was in the way, they were taken into the office. The boss filled out a sales contract form, and they gave him the $100 down payment he required. Told that they would need security to obtain a loan for the balance and that they were already committed to the deal, they agreed.

The key was still missing when the salesman drove them home to get the deed to their small home for security. Returning to the used-car lot, they signed the contract. The key to the car that had been blocking their car was then found, and they started home in their new car.

They hadn't driven it more than a few blocks before they realized that they had been "taken." The car was obviously no good. They drove back to the lot. The boss was gone and the salesman "too busy" to talk to them. They were told to go to a downtown office the next day and see the boss.

They did. The boss wasn't there, but a lawyer was. He pointed out that a clause in the long contract form they had signed called for a cash payment of $1,884 within six days. He told them that, since they had signed the contract but didn't have that much money, they would have to sign a deed of trust on their home as security. Stunned by the sudden turn of events and the amount of money they had unwittingly agreed to pay in six days, they signed.

For the next few days, while the husband had to be at work, the young wife went to the car lot, asking for their old car back. They told her it had been junked. She said it ran much better than the one they had just bought, but was told, "You've bought the other car. It's yours. We have no more to do with it."

The couple finally gave up and started paying off their large debt.

This, of course, is not the way legitimate dealers do business. Unfortunately, the actions of within-the-law swindlers affect the reputations of honest dealers. In many cases the uninformed buyer does not distinguish between the two. He accepts at face value the "bait" advertising and "bargains" that no reputable dealer could possibly offer and stay in business. The victim had never learned about this aspect of car purchasing.

Case Five A woman made a $400 down payment on a car. The salesman told her that he could not arrange for the insurance on it that night and did not have a spare tire or jack available for it at that time. He said he would take care of those things the next day. Meanwhile, he suggested that she take another car for transportation that night. The salesman wrote out a car order and bill of sale for the loaned car for the woman to sign "in case she was picked up by the police." The next day she attempted to return the car he had lent her and asked for the car she was buying. She was told, "You didn't buy any other car, you bought this one."

Case Six   Finding a car he liked in a used-car lot, a man agreed to buy it. He read the contract very carefully before signing it—and still got trapped.

There were a number of "copies" of the contract, one on top of another. The salesman folded back the "original" just far enough for the man to sign the others. His "copy" was mailed to him.

It was not a duplicate of the one he had read. The cash price had been raised $400 and the payments just about doubled. He called the dealer, who told him that the finance company was the one to deal with. When he tried to explain to them what had happened, he was told it would cost him another $500 to get the contract canceled. He was "hooked."

These last three cases, in which the car buyer was victimized, did not involve stupid people. They were just ordinary people who had never been told how to buy a car or how important it is to deal with a legitimate dealer. These are important items covered in Chapter 17, "Buying, Insuring, and Operating Your Car."

Case Seven   The next case comes from the Traffic Institute of Northwestern University, where a careful individual case study of a number of accidents was undertaken to learn their real causes.

A young man was driving about 45 miles per hour on a boulevard in a city park. A couple on foot had waited a long time for a gap in the traffic in order to cross. Finding one ahead of this driver's car, they started to run across. The girl hesitated to run when the boy did, but then followed him. She had lost so much time that she could not make it across the street. The oncoming car hit her with a terrific impact.

The peculiar thing about this accident is that the driver applied his brakes, skidded about 20 feet, and then took his foot off the brake. He again hit the brake just before striking the girl. The car did not swerve, and he did not know why he took his foot off the brake.

The fact was that being a new driver, he had never skidded before. The new sensations were rather frightening and, by reflex action, he reversed the action that had made him uncomfortable. He released the brake without realizing what he did.

He hadn't known two things. First, he had never read, nor had he been told, to expect the unexpected (see Chapter 12, "The Pedestrian and the Driver," page 166). A pedestrian may do the unexpected, and the driver must be ready for it. Second, the young driver didn't realize that experience counts a great deal in driving safely. *Quick reflexes and muscular strength and skill are not enough.* They must be accompanied by experience and judgment before they can be depended upon in an emergency. Even though the young driver was driving skillfully down the boulevard, his speed was too great for his driving experience. It did not give him enough time to react correctly in a difficult situation.

Case Eight   This case also comes from the Northwestern University study. Two boys taking two girls home in a car approached a fork in the road. The girl next to the driver told him to take the right fork. The couple in the rear seat didn't hear it. The girl in back thought that she was to go home first and that the driver was making a mistake. She called, "No! The other way!"

The driver, thinking he had misunderstood the original directions, whipped the wheel to the left. The car started to skid, the driver applied the brakes, and the car slid into a utility pole at the fork of the road. Result: Four persons were in a hospital. Causes: The passenger's sudden action and the driver's abrupt turning movement. Neither had any idea of the dangerous nature of what he—or she—did. A trained driver would.

Case Nine This case, also from the Northwestern University files, points out a common, but seldom realized, hazard. A driver was involved in an accident when his view to the right was cut off at a crucial moment. As the driver leaned forward to look to the right, his wife, who was sitting beside him, also leaned forward and blocked his view.

Seated beside a driver, one is often tempted to lean forward to see down a side street, or even to open the glove compartment. At the wrong time, this is like putting a screen before the driver's eyes in that direction. It shouldn't be done entering an intersection or at any other critical place. Most passengers just don't think of the hazards which their movements might create.

Case Ten This is the case, of which you may have read, in which five young people were killed returning from a game. They had met the driver, an acquaintance

of all five, at the game and had accepted his offer of a ride home. The ride would have been about 2 miles.

There is no mystery about what happened. Police investigating the head-on crash had no doubt as to *how* it happened. There were many witnesses. He had attempted to pass a long line of vehicles at high speed on a two-lane road. A heavily loaded truck approaching from the opposite direction, in its proper lane, came around a curve. The young driver's speed was far too great for him to be able to avoid the collision.

One of the victims' parents had warned her against riding with that driver. The state had previously suspended his license for traffic violations and only recently had restored it to him.

Young people who knew him could have recognized the pattern of behavior, described under the Show-off in Chapter 2, "The Psychology of the Driver." Every one of his driving acts followed

Fig. 1–8. The car of Case Ten.

the Show-off pattern. Unfortunately, the danger of that pattern was not realized by five young people. Here is a case in which a lack of understanding cost the five nondrivers their lives. This was a high price for a 2-mile ride. There are too many cases like this. Know your driver—and don't gamble. When you do gamble, the stakes are high and the odds are very much against you.

Price of Ignorance

Each of these cases concerned a driver or passenger who happened to have a gap, or probably blank spots, in his knowledge. Prior to the unfortunate experience, none realized his shortcomings. The average untrained driver, who hasn't been trapped by his ignorance, is unaware of it. He believes that he is a keen driver, that he knows the score, and that he drives accordingly.

All "Superior"?

A recent study, sponsored by an oil company and a nationwide trucking association, revealed a startling fact. *Nine out of ten adults* (and 100 percent of those with a record of traffic violations) rated themselves *above average* in driving skill. They said that they were better than average at obeying traffic laws, too. (This "they" included the violators!)

Physical condition, knowledge, skill, and attitude toward law and toward *learning* to own and operate a car safely and well are vitally important, for automobile driving will be an important part of your life. Carol's family, the driver who hit the pedestrian, the young couple who unwittingly mortgaged their home— these and others would tell you that they could have avoided their mistakes if they had completed a driver education course. They would tell you how much it would have meant to them to have known what you are learning and to have learned it in school, instead of by bitter experience.

Three Goals

Driver education is planned and taught in the modern high school with three main goals in mind: safety, a smooth flow of traffic, and enjoyable driving.

Safety Driver education stresses safety. Over 40,000 people die in traffic accidents each year, some after months of intense suffering following an accident. Over 1½ million people suffer disabling injuries, and we all pay over 7 billion dollars annually in costs. The major rea-

Fig. 1-9. Most drivers (including violators) think they are superior.

Fig. 1–10.
Training future
good citizens
of the highway.

Fig. 1–11. You will fit safely and enjoyably into
this smooth traffic.

son for all this is bad driving. Effective driver education can cut these tolls greatly.

Smooth Traffic In our country, everyone is dependent upon highway transportation for the essentials of life. Efficient movement of traffic is an absolute necessity. Delays or interruptions of that traffic are very costly. Constantly increasing numbers of vehicles make greater demands on the driver with each year. Yet smooth movement of the great volume of traffic depends on efficient, skillful driving of each vehicle on the highway.

Enjoyable Driving Driver education also aims at enjoyment of driving. You and all your family should be able to drive among other courteous, sportsmanlike people, free from the crowding, abuse, and even threats that are now sometimes a part of driving.

The automobile can be a source of real benefit and pleasure, as well as a convenience or necessity, if people will make it so. Isn't that what you want driving to mean to you?

17

To Talk About:

1. Tell how you think each of the following situations would affect your responsibilities as a driver: (*a*) You are driving a car belonging to someone else, perhaps a member of your family or a friend; (*b*) you have a number of passengers with you; (*c*) weather conditions are bad; (*d*) you are emotionally upset; (*e*) this is a long trip.

2. Discuss the advantages of driver education.

3. Discuss the reasons for male drivers under twenty-five years of age having to pay an extra automobile insurance premium when female drivers the same age do not. Report on comparative statistics of male and female driver accidents for all age groups.

4. Compare the number of traffic fatalities last year with all other types of fatal accidents in your state or community. Discuss what you believe to be the best answers to the traffic-accident problem.

5. Discuss the advantages of a dual-control driver education car.

6. Develop the relationship of another subject you are studying to driver education, particularly science, social studies, economics, or mechanics.

7. Discuss a driver's moral responsibility.

To Do:

1. Have each member of the group report briefly on one or two accidents. Bring newspaper clippings to class. State the situation and try to determine the causes of each accident: make a list of causes. Try to decide whether any of these accidents could *not* have been prevented. Discuss the significance of the fact that throughout your course you have an opportunity to learn how to avoid the mistakes these people made.

2. Make a survey among adults as to how they learned to drive. What probable relationship is there between the way they learned to drive and the number of traffic accidents there are today?

3. Find out about how much additional insurance premium per year must be paid by male drivers under twenty-five years of age who have not taken driver education. Multiply this by the number of years it must be paid. How far would this money go toward a college education?

4. Visit several local insurance agents. Make a report on their ideas about insurance for teen-age drivers.

5. Ask a member of the local police department to talk to the group about problems of teen-age drivers. Ask whether he has suggestions as to how the driver reputation of this group could be improved.

6. Write a letter to the editor of the local newspaper expressing appreciation for the action of the board of education in offering driver education to students. If possible, include statistics on reduction of accidents by driver education and the amount of money saved by this investment in your community.

With all the attention and material resources we rightly devote to the car, the highway, and the law, the basic problems of traffic safety lie deep within us, *the drivers*.

The good driver can successfully navigate our poorest roads under very bad conditions. The bad driver can kill himself—and others—in daylight on our safest superhighways.

If we study the driver and what "makes him tick," we will learn the answers to many of our most important traffic problems.

The Scientific Method

Just as the nuclear scientist in his laboratory carefully studies the problem at hand, other scientists about the country are closely studying the driver: his mind, his feelings, his senses, and his skills. What they learn about people who drive will help save lives—perhaps the lives of some people close to us, and possibly our own!

Scientists have found that drivers have some common patterns of behavior. These psychological characteristics are interesting, so let us take a close look at some driver types. Do any of the people you see driving around *your* school, or in *your* neighborhood, fit into these groups? It's a rare town that doesn't have some!

2 the
Psychology of the Driver

Bad Risks as Drivers

Traffic safety specialists, policemen, motor vehicle inspectors, highway patrolmen, truckers, and other professionals recognize people with certain psychological characteristics as highway hazards. Automobile insurance companies regard them as bad risks. In fact, these bad-risk drivers keep our insurance rates high.

For our own physical protection and for the protection of the lives of others who depend upon our driving, we should know all we can about these bad risks.

The Egotist   Babies are normally self-centered. They have not learned how to be unselfish; they have not learned how to share. They are good examples of the perfect egotist.

As babies grow into childhood, they learn that self is not the center of the universe. If they develop normally, they become more social; that is, they become concerned about the well-being of others. They become interested in the welfare of their community, their state, and their country. In short, they acquire *social attitudes*.

With his normal psychological make-up, the baby would make the worst possible driver. He would consider nothing but his own interest and immediate desires. The childish, self-centered adult makes a miserable driver for the same reason. He has never outgrown his babyish egotism. He has probably had the kind of childhood training that makes grown-ups act like babies.

When you see a driver who shows a complete disregard for others, who is aggressive, demanding, impatient, and thoroughly selfish in his actions affecting other drivers, you are looking at that fugitive from the nursery, the Egotist.

The Egotist is a psychological misfit in the traffic scene. He has not learned to share the highway with other people. He is easily spotted, and he is detested by other drivers, pedestrians, and traffic officers. The habit of thinking of others can keep you from being one of his kind.

The Overemotional Driver   Uncontrolled emotions are another sign of immaturity. A baby does not control his emotions; he merely expresses them. Your ability to control your emotions and to remain calm under pressure should develop as you grow older. This ability should be evident by the time you reach the later teens.

But some persons are never more than adult-sized babies so far as emotional control is concerned. They may take any word or glance as a personal offense. They show temper, or sulk, or whine. Trifles seem important to them. We say

Fig. 2–1. The Egotist.

Fig. 2–2. The Overemotional driver.

the shoulder? Have you watched him return for the next round or game period as coolly efficient as ever? There are no hysterics, no grinding of teeth, no name calling—only calm, cool determination.

Compare this champion athlete with the overtense, awkward, frightened, inexperienced competitor who believes he must get "fighting mad" to win. The latter cannot limit his nervous and muscular action to just what is necessary for efficient performance. Other muscle groups which should be relaxed and resting are contracted, working at the same time. They slow his movements, make them inaccurate, and exhaust him rapidly; he is "fighting himself." He will never be good until he overcomes this condition, and *neither will the overemotional driver.*

that they "make mountains out of mole-hills." They just haven't grown up.

Overemotional, immature drivers are apt to do any or all of the following things:

Get upset over trifles, or become nervous in unusual situations

Lose their tempers and, consequently, their judgment

Express anger by driving recklessly

Show impatience in traffic jams by useless horn blowing

Flash their high-beam lights in the eyes of approaching drivers

Talk loudly or use profanity

Resort to crowding and forcing others out of traffic lanes

Continually complain and find fault with others

Have you ever studied the champion athlete who, in action, moves faster and more accurately than the rest of his fellow athletes but at the end of the round or game period becomes perfectly relaxed and gives his opponent a friendly pat on

Fig. 2–3. The Rationalizer: "Well, it wasn't a U turn!"

The Rationalizer There is also the person who never learns to face facts squarely. He finds it easy to see a thing the way he wants to see it, rather than the way it really is. If he gets into an accident, he blames the driver of another car or anyone but himself. He will not admit his own errors, because he lacks the courage.

In the motor vehicle division of one state, there is an accident report that a typical rationalizer sent in. He had run into a big, slow, old-fashioned road roller with his shiny new convertible. He wrote, "I was proceeding south on Highway Number One at 30 miles an hour when this steam roller suddenly darted out from a side road."

The Show-off Here we have a driver who is one of our greatest problems. He may have any or all the faults of the other bad-risk drivers. *If he is a young person, he seems to be doing his best to give all young people a bad reputation as drivers.*

He may be older in years, but he continues to be childish no matter what his age. He hopes that all who see him will believe him to be a sort of daring story-book hero. Often he suffers from a feeling of inferiority, and he tries to cover it up by attempting to appear superior.

Unfortunately, there are many Show-offs. They threaten our lives so seriously, and the lives of the people dear to us, that they are a great problem. Indeed, the Show-off requires close study—like the mosquito. And like certain types of disease-carrying mosquitos, the Show-off can be extremely dangerous as well as a pest.

As in the case of the Egotist, the Show-off has never properly grown up. He has never managed, no matter what his age, to understand his real place among adult men and women. He doesn't stop to realize how ridiculous he looks to others.

He is easily recognizable by the things

Fig. 2–4. The Show-off.

he does. He gets satisfaction from making his tires squeal while "peeling rubber," braking, and turning. He ruins an expensive transmission (on his own car or that of his parents) and destroys perfectly good tires. He endangers you and your parents and friends merely to call attention to himself and his great "daring." He buys noisy gadgets to put on the exhaust system of his car, even though they are public nuisances and unlawful, and serve simply to call attention to his eccentricities. They also frequently bring him to the attention of officers of the law.

He never drives squarely *in* a line of traffic but is always nosing *out* of line a bit, ready to pounce on every possible chance to pass the car ahead. The speed of the line of traffic, or of the car ahead, has no bearing upon his urge to pass. When he cannot pass, he becomes what professional drivers call a "tailgater"—a dangerous road pest.

With every start the Show-off accelerates his car at the greatest possible rate. Approaching a red light, he continues his burst of speed until the last instant.

Then he jams on his brakes. You are never comfortable riding with him, and you cannot enjoy the ride. His rapid acceleration either plasters you against the back of your seat or his braking throws you forward out of your seat. The Show-off doesn't have the slightest appreciation or understanding of *smoothness* as a sign of driving skill. He tries to *force* the pace every moment he drives. He doesn't realize that even a child can floor the accelerator pedal.

When you ride with the Show-off, you are uncomfortable because you fight the force of inertia at every moment. In addition, you can plainly see that this driver cuts every margin of time and space too closely. You have the uncomfortable feeling that he is always taking chances, which in reality he does most of the time.

Taking chances—seeming to be a daredevil—is exactly the effect the Show-off is trying to create! He is trying to convince you, and all observers, that he is the heroic figure, the adventurer—a thrilling personality like his favorite television idol. He is living in a make-believe world of fiction, trying to give himself an aura of great courage to make up for the personal qualities he lacks.

Occasionally, you'll find individuals who apparently feel they can get greater public admiration by drag racing on a public highway. With no encouragement at all, this type of Show-off will explain at length what a daredevil he really is! If you are not pretty well informed on the subject or personally experienced in life-and-death situations, you may be fooled.

On the surface, he seems quite genuine.

There are people, however, who are not fooled. One of these people is the biological scientist. He tells us that *the human nervous system,* like those of other living things, *reacts violently against any recognized threat of its own destruction.* This is a major instinct of survival in the individual and in the species. The Show-off is no exception. His actions inspire in him the same unpleasant feeling as they do in his passengers or in anyone else—*fear.* If he claims that he recognizes the danger of his conduct and still enjoys it, he is simply not telling the truth. Sometimes he gives himself away to the keen observer when he finishes one of his drives, turns off the ignition, and unconsciously heaves an obvious sigh of relief. He is glad to get there alive, too!

Certainly there are times when a human being can force himself to do things which threaten, or actually bring about, his own destruction. Emergencies and war have brought out many such cases. The important point is that the individual *forced* himself to the deed and succeeded in overcoming the natural revulsion which *fear* brings within his own nervous system. He did not *enjoy* this experience.

Recognition of danger, of course, is part of the story. Anyone old enough and with sufficient intelligence to drive a car will easily recognize the danger in the Show-off's driving behavior. Even the Show-off cannot claim stupidity to an extent that he would be classed as feeble-minded instead of simply irresponsible. Strangely enough, police officers occasionally encounter one who attempts it.

Fig. 2–5.
Adventure
we can
enjoy.

We must admit that many of us like adventure, but we like it mild, as a thrill in which the shadow of maiming and death is not an immediate companion. Some like the rough sea (not quite rough enough to drown us, however). Some like a ski slope or a fast ride on water skis. Many enjoy a plane ride (though not when an engine quits, a storm hits, or heavy fog settles in), or maybe a controlled skid in a practice driving area off the highway. Such adventures promise a happy ending. But we do not knowingly invite imminent destruction.

We are all products of countless generations which survived by responding to the inborn drive of self-preservation. Heredity has carried and strengthened this drive for each of us. The Show-off's pretense of being a hero is pretty stupid in the light of science.

Do you recognize this person among the drivers you know in school or in the neighborhood of your home?

Stopping the Show-off   As long as there are Show-offs driving cars, thousands of innocent victims will die each year because these Show-offs want to be thought of as heroes. Their schoolmates and passengers and our families and friends are potential victims. Your immediate family is no exception! Is there anything we can do to stop them?

There are a number of things, and the best are those of prevention. *After* an accident, "cures" are too late to help the victim.

First, we can learn about the Show-off, what "makes him tick," and the kind of driving to expect from him. When we know and recognize him, we can always be sure that we never, even for a moment, show approval of any of his driving acts.

We have already seen the real motives of the Show-off as they are known to the scientist. Today, we have another source of information on the subject quite close at hand.

THE PSYCHOLOGY OF THE DRIVER

24

Some of our high school students have fathers, older brothers, or friends who have had combat experience either in World War II, in Korea, or both. Speak to someone who has been "through it"—one who was able to discipline himself to carry out his assignments under fire. Ask him if he *enjoyed* the "glorious adventure" of war, the "thrill of battle."

Choose an honest ex-serviceman and you'll get an honest answer, an answer you'll like because he will admit having the same revulsion to real, imminent danger as you have. The battle-tested soldier is no coward ("chicken," as the would-be heroes express it) and he has proved it. He knows the feeling a person experiences when facing danger. He knows, too, the sensation one gets on a high ladder or looking over the edge of a high roof. Nearly everyone remembers having had a bad dream about height. This very unpleasant feeling is nature's way of saying, "Don't." The soldier has proved that he could master that feeling when there was a good reason to do so. A desire to show off, risking the lives of others, cannot be considered a good reason by an intelligent person. In the history of our country, many people have overcome for very good reasons the natural, self-protective reaction to danger. You are different from them only if you have not had to. An intelligent person doesn't feel that he must continually put on an act to prove that he has courage or that he is a man.

The more of us who understand this, discuss it, and pass the word on, the fewer young people will feel *forced* by the taunts or acts of others to drive as "daredevils" to "prove" their courage. To yield to such pressure is to be ruled by ignorance. *It is a weakness and lack of courage in itself.* More importantly, ignoring such pressure will mean that fewer of us will experience the shock of a telephone call announcing the sad fact that a parent, sister, brother, or close friend has just been killed or maimed by a Show-off.

A Solution: Honesty Here is a problem that faces many young people today. One girl solved it by being frank and honest.

Linda, a high school senior, had been dating Jim, a boy in her class. They enjoyed the same things and the same places and had been looking forward to the day when Jim would be able to buy a second-hand car.

The big day finally came. Jim's car was an old gearshift model, but it was in good condition. It looked like a dream come true. They cleaned it, painted it, polished it, and even named it.

For a while it meant the happiest days of their school lives. At first Jim drove sensibly and well, taking good care of the cherished car. Gradually, however, his driving changed. As he gained self-confidence, he became more and more the typical Show-off. For Linda, the rides that had been so pleasant became first uncomfortable, and then more like nightmares.

Jim's old greeting of "Hi," when he called for her, was replaced by a poorly concealed boast of how quickly he had made it from his house to hers. His announced "time" for the trip had

25

dropped from 18 minutes to 11½ minutes. Each such announcement was accompanied by complaints about "slow-poke drivers" who blocked traffic.

Each time, there followed a wild ride to wherever they were going. Each time, the evening was spoiled for Linda by the ever-present dread of Jim's driving. She asked him many times to slow down, but he merely smiled that she, a nondriver, should tell him how to drive.

One evening, at Linda's request, Jim drove her to a shopping center on the edge of town. Now the situation came to a climax. After a bad ride and a particularly narrow escape (after which Jim, at fault, had shouted at the other driver), Linda reached the store nervous and shaking. When Jim asked how long she would be, she told him to go on back without her. She would go home on a bus.

Surprised, Jim asked why, and she told him, "I've asked you again and again *please* to take it easy in your driving. You just won't. Instead of enjoying the ride, we go through a sort of savage test of courage to and from every place we go.

"I'm being honest with you. I've tried to be a good sport, but I *am afraid.* I don't know why boys can't be honest, too. Any intelligent person knows that there's a strong drive of self-preservation in all of us. You don't enjoy close calls like we had on the way here. You were afraid, too. *Any sane person would be.* Nobody doubts your courage, but *why* must we continually risk both our lives to 'prove' it?"

Jim was uncomfortably conscious that Linda was telling the truth. A calm, frank talk at this point would have solved their problem. Linda, however, was too excited to choose her words carefully and said more. Angry words followed and Linda walked off to the bus stop.

A week passed, then another. They met in school without speaking. Linda knew she'd been right in inviting an honest understanding.

With the Senior Prom only three days off, Linda was reading at home in the evening when the phone rang. It was Jim. Basically an honest fellow, Jim had known all along that Linda was right. But her final, unconsidered words had angered him. However, they had planned all year to go to the Prom that was now at hand. Jim was calling to ask Linda to go with him.

A typical student telephone conversation followed, during which both families were cut off from telephone communication with the rest of the world for an hour and ten minutes. It ended with Linda asking Jim to come over so that they "could talk" about the Prom.

He agreed. "I'm starting now. See you in . . ." a moment's hesitation followed, and then, ". . . about twenty minutes."

Linda smiled happily. There was now one less Show-off driver, and lots of good times ahead.

The Mental Make-up of a Topnotch Driver

From a psychological point of view, the topnotch driver not only has skill but also *balance* and *self-control*. He has good social attitudes. Professional experts agree that the most important quality he possesses is *good driver attitude.* This quality is called "the driving conscience."

When the topnotch driver gets behind the wheel of a car, he shows certain excellent characteristics, such as:

Good sportsmanship
Acceptance of responsibility
Consideration for others, including car occupants
Good judgment
Controlled attention
Alertness
Foresight
A good attitude toward other highway users and toward law and law enforcement

It is difficult to distinguish among good sportsmanship, a sense of responsibility, and consideration for others. All are built on a sense of fairness and a desire for fair sharing. All reflect mental and emotional maturity.

Good Driving Judgment   Good judgment is not the mysterious gift that some people suppose. We think more soundly about things we understand thoroughly. The business of driving an automobile is no exception. A background of driver education is the *foundation* for good driving judgment. Experiences in well-supervised practice driving are good building blocks. Finally, many thousands of miles of careful driving under all sorts of road conditions are necessary before any person can truly claim to possess expert driving judgment.

A driver with good judgment is constantly sizing up the traffic situation well ahead and is not caught unawares. *Anticipation and recognition of danger are far more important than fast reaction time, skill in dodging, or bravery in emergencies.* One doesn't *have* to get out of situations one sees ahead of time and avoids. Also, it is often correct choice of reaction (which is built on judgment, developed through experience) more than speed of reaction which avoids the accident.

Controlled Attention   The person who cannot control his attention is not fit to drive a car. Imagine a man steering a fast-moving object on a highway with his attention ready to be caught by any accidental happening or circumstance! Unfortunately, there are many people like this—and hence many resultant tragedies. Attention has to be directed into place and held there.

The psychologically fit driver is able to attend to business. His business is the total traffic pattern. He "drives ahead," that is, considering everything that is happening in his whole field of vision that could possibly affect the driving picture. His attention is constantly centered on the path that his car should take, considering all the other factors in the situation.

How *long* a person can focus his attention on a subject is often called his "attention span." How *well,* how strongly, in spite of distractions, he can concentrate his attention is also very important in driving. Suppose we combine how long and how well he can concentrate and call the combination his *attention factor.*

The next time you have a chance to

observe other drivers in action, study their attention factors carefully. Decide how you would rate the following:

Some turn toward a passenger to speak to him, even if he is in the back seat.

Some take a hand (or two!) off the steering wheel to illustrate a point, or simply to talk with the hand, or even, it seems, to hold the car roof on.

Some "window-shop" while passing stores, used-car lots, etc.

Some fill their cars after a football or basketball game and join their cheering passengers in greeting friends along the way.

Some look for a particular store or a home address, almost completely ignoring the matter of driving.

Rate each, in your own mind, for attention factor. By the way, how's *yours?*

Attention and Controlled Eye Movements

One of the least excusable, but most frequent, types of accidents is that of the single vehicle running off the road. Most of these accidents result from a driver's failure to apply the principle of controlled attention.

There are many things that a driver should observe that are not in the road directly ahead, such as the position and speed of vehicles coming from left or right on intersecting or merging roadways, etc. There are still other things that capture his attention without his consent. In any case, there is one thing he should always remember: *No automobile will hold the road—even the straightest road—without constant steering corrections by the driver.* Slight differences in road surface, tire pressure, road crown, a side wind, or play in the steering wheel are likely to change the path of the momentarily unguided car.

When the driver's eyes are diverted from the road ahead for even a second or two, the car tends to wander. It may easily leave its intended path and move left or right without warning. In fact, it probably will!

The eyes of the driver normally should be centered on the road ahead, though moving and not "fixed," or stationary. When it is necessary to direct his attention elsewhere, the topnotch driver does it in a carefully controlled manner. He gives a *very brief* glance in the new direction and returns his eyes to the road ahead. He then has in his mind a "still" picture of the scene in that other direction. This does not tell him the speed of other objects there and may not give him all the other details he needs to have. He gives a second and perhaps a third, fourth, and fifth quick, short glance in the side direction, having a look at the road ahead between each two side glances.

Each glance to the side gives him a still picture, similar to the frames of a motion-picture film. His mind is able to piece together these still pictures to give him a motion picture of what is there. At the same time, when he looks ahead he gets a motion picture of the road ahead, enabling him to continue to steer his car and follow the road.

Alertness

The good driver is alert continuously while driving; that is, he is continuously vigilant as to what is happening and what is likely to happen. He is also on the lookout for danger and ready to act.

He does not allow himself to daydream or become drowsy. He gets enough sleep before starting on long trips. If he does find himself becoming sleepy or drowsy, he pulls well off to the side of the road and gets out for a breath of fresh air. He stops for a cold soft drink or a cup of coffee at the next opportunity.

Keeping alert involves more than just keeping awake. It means being vigilant concerning all factors in the driving situation. It is not always the easy thing to do, but it surely is one of the most important jobs the driver has.

Foresight The best drivers develop a high degree of *traffic imagination and foresight.* They see and think ahead. They keep control and avoid trouble by recognizing trouble-in-the-making. The latter may come in such forms as the following.

School children are walking or playing along the road. One is about to catch a ball. Suppose he misses it. Will he dart after it into the road? The driver who foresees this possibility may save a child's life. Even the sight of a ball alone in the road ahead should warn the driver that a child may dart out to get it.

A parked car some distance ahead has a person sitting in the driver's seat. Its tail or brake lights may or may not be lighted. Smoke may or may not be coming from the exhaust pipe. Will that driver pull out immediately in front of you? Some do! Will he open the car door and step out, just as you reach his car? That happens, too.

A pedestrian is crossing the street ahead. Will he stop for oncoming or turning traffic? Will he change his mind and turn back? The driver with foresight is prepared, no matter what he does.

You find yourself rapidly overtaking a vehicle ahead. You are accustomed to keeping a normally safe following distance. As an expert driver, however, you know that this is not enough here. Moving more slowly, the driver of that other vehicle *can and may stop* much more quickly than you possibly can at your faster pace. You slow down at once to allow an increased following distance, or "cushion." Whenever you find yourself rapidly overtaking the vehicle ahead and getting close, you are in danger.

A truck is stopped in the road ahead. You must stop, awaiting a break in the oncoming traffic. Although an inexperienced driver might approach very close to the truck before stopping, you stop some distance back. Then, when there is a sufficient break in the oncoming traffic, you can safely start to move left to pass. If you see another car approaching, you can quickly drop back into your lane. If you had stopped immediately behind that truck, you would have had to start left blindly, unable to see any oncoming vehicle until it was within a few feet of you. Then, you might have been too close to the truck to be able to pull back into your lane, providing there were sufficient time. The cars behind you might have moved up too close.

Some distance ahead you see a strip of icy road, or a section of wet or muddy pavement, or a large puddle of water.

Fig. 2–6. Can you spot these "Indian signs," or emergencies in the making? (1) School children walking or playing in the street. (2) A parked car with smoke coming from its tail pipe. (3) Ice under a bridge. (4) You are on a through street, but will the car on the cross street stop? (5) A gust of wind.

You anticipate what could happen if you were compelled suddenly to apply your brakes at that particular spot, or what effect there might be from hitting a deep puddle at your present speed. You brake to a safe speed *before* reaching the danger spot.

Approaching a bridge or culvert in cold weather, when the road is wet or has wet spots, you realize that ice forms more rapidly on bridges than on solid-based ordinary roads. You drive accordingly.

The road ahead is emerging from a deep cut through a hill. It is a windy day, and you know there will be a strong cross wind at the end of the cut. There may be a powerful sideward thrust on your car there because of the wind. Your foresight prepares you for it, and you will not be caught napping in your steering.

You are on a through-traffic street or highway. Ahead is an intersection with a STOP sign protecting you. You see a car on the crossroad moving quite rapidly toward the intersection. Will the driver be able to stop where he should? Does he even see the STOP sign? You are aware of the situation. Whatever the other driver does, you are prepared. You are showing foresight.

You are approaching a street intersection with a traffic light which has just turned green for you. It is a nearly blind corner. You can see but a very short distance to left or right on that cross street. Even though the light is green for you, as an experienced driver you know that people sometimes "run red lights," accidentally or purposely. You realize that

being legally right doesn't restore lives or make injuries less painful. You know, too, that just one second after the light changes it may be impossible to prove who *did* have the green light just before the accident. You approach cautiously, ready for any emergency.

Any one of these situations, without driver foresight, could result in tragedy. The topnotch driver will recognize all of them. Each one calls for traffic imagination and foresight.

The Driver's Attitude Toward Law

Most people have a deep respect for law. Most people we know would feel greatly insulted if accused of being dishonest. Most would refuse to associate with thieves, pickpockets, muggers, and other lawbreakers. In our way of life this is understandable. The laws are *our* laws, made for us by our representatives and observed by most people.

Strangely, however, there has grown up among too many people a somewhat different attitude toward traffic law. Many feel a strong dislike and distrust for law-breakers in general but vaguely sympathize with the traffic-law violator when he is given a ticket. They do not realize that traffic laws have two main purposes. One is efficient street and highway use. The other is prevention of accidents. Their own continuous violations of these laws defeat both of these purposes, inconveniencing them and involving them in accidents.

Fig. 2–8. The real reason for STOP signs.

You may know some people who are good, law-abiding citizens in all other respects, but who often exceed the speed limit, or who don't make a full stop at the STOP sign when "it's obviously perfectly safe." They unconsciously class some traffic laws as of minor importance and not morally wrong to violate.

But there are important factors which they fail to recognize. Violations which may seem minor are often factors in serious accidents. Moreover, violations of certain traffic laws tend to encourage some drivers to extend their violations to those laws which involve more serious offenses. Disobeying traffic laws becomes a common pattern of behavior. Then, too, one never knows where the power of example may lead someone else. Unquestionably, violations increase the likelihood of accidents and are the direct cause of many.

The man who picks your pocket steals money that can be replaced. The man who runs down and kills somebody dear to you takes away something irreplaceable and infinitely more important than money.

A Common Fallacy Many people have been summoned to court for traffic-law violations when they honestly believed that the particular provision of law they broke was either very minor or "silly."

Let us say that one man commits a stop-sign violation while driving at a speed of only 2 miles per hour. He tells the magistrate in court that the visibility was perfect, that there was no traffic on the other street, and that it was perfectly safe to proceed. He claims that it was "ridiculous" for the policeman to give him a summons.

Now, the next man to be brought in on the same charge was driving at only 4 miles per hour. He says visibility was "practically perfect." He, too, claims the police action was "ridiculous."

Then comes a man who was driving at only 6 miles per hour, then one at 8.

Are all these men right? If so, at just what point, at what speed, and at what condition of visibility should each policeman enforce the law? The man who was

Fig. 2–7. A "nicer" lawbreaker?

driving at only 1 or 2 miles per hour faster than *that* speed would still claim his arrest "ridiculous."

There is only one way to enforce the law fairly, and that is according to the way it is written. That is the policeman's duty. Varying degrees of seriousness of violations are provided for in the law, and the judge can give a penalty from minimum to maximum limits or even a suspended sentence, according to the circumstances. That is *his* duty.

It may be, in certain places, that a YIELD right of way sign would be more appropriate than a STOP sign. Persons holding that belief should request a traffic engineering and safety study and get the sign changed, if warranted. In the meantime, they should obey the legally posted regulations.

Speed   In speeding violations, some enforcement agencies recognize the mechanical limitations of speedometers and the sometimes unrealized effects of short downhill grades on the speed of cars. They allow a speed tolerance of perhaps 5 miles per hour above the legal speed limit.

This, however, is not universal, nor does it in any way protect the speeder if he is charged with a violation. It is a margin of error sometimes allowed for the driver's protection. It should not be used as a basis for determining one's driving speed.

If a speed limit is wrong or unrealistic,

then the proper thing to do is to get it changed legally. This can be done, and interested citizens have the right to request consideration of such change. The proper first step is to have the traffic engineer, in cooperation with the police, make a scientific study to determine reasonable speed.

In any case, the law should be respected as it exists.

Common Sense   In general, traffic laws as written represent the decisions of the legislative representatives of the people. The only way they can be enforced in fairness to all, and for the protection of all, is in just the way they are written.

If we allow one man to violate a certain law because he is "sure" it is safe to do so, then another has the right to do the same to another law, and another, and another. Soon, we would really have no effective law, would we?

The regular driver's license of one of the greatest racing drivers in the world was revoked for a violation of traffic law. No one doubts his judgment of time and distance. Yet even he made a serious mistake, for an accident resulted.

Compared with this expert, the amateur driver who thinks his skill and personal judgment are so good that he can safely violate the law seems pretty silly, doesn't he?

Our Problem

We know that the greater the number of traffic-law violations there are, the more accidents, and *fatal* accidents, there

will be. Do you sympathize with the violator, whoever he may be, who at this moment may be recklessly driving toward someone you care for? Would you grant him the right to drive as he pleases? Do you excuse *his* violation, sympathize with *him* on getting a ticket? Do you regard his violation as unimportant?

Isn't it a helpless feeling to *know*—statistically, of course—that he may *now* be heading for someone *you* love and that you can't stop him? Statistically he is in your town. He is in every town.

Well, you can't stop him at this moment. However, if enough of us realize what he is doing and insist that traffic laws be observed and enforced, not ignored or minimized, we can stop him, given time. Aroused public opinion is very powerful!

Somehow—and soon—we must make our personal and our public attitude toward traffic law just as strong and just as constructive as our attitude toward other laws that protect us and those we love.

If we don't? Then let's exercise our imagination for just a moment. Figure 2–9 shows some traffic victims of the future.

No faces? Well, *just imagine* the faces. Put in faces of people you care about—people you would be willing to sacrifice for the "right" of the selfish driver to drive as he pleases. But who among those you really care about would you sacrifice in excusing the violator from honest, impartial, and strict law enforcement? We all know our answer here: nobody!

Traffic laws are necessary to protect our

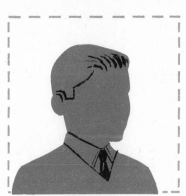

Fig. 2–9.
Who are these
traffic victims
of the
future?

people in this modern Motor Age. They set the pattern for voluntary observance and provide the basis for enforcement. The Constitution protects our rights. Traffic laws protect our property, our limbs, our *lives*. Nothing less than 100 percent support will do.

Power and People

It is not surprising that the automobile gives man a sense of power. Here is a modern miracle for personal transportation which, throughout past history, even the greatest kings on earth could not have. Yet, today even people with modest incomes can enjoy the increased personal

power and mobility which the automobile provides.

There are two things, however, for a man to remember when he uses power:

1. Power has constructive value only when in control. Out of control, it is dangerous and destructive.
2. How one uses power discloses just what kind of a person he is and the degree to which he has reached maturity.

Man is reduced to a weak and foolish-looking creature when the power he is supposed to direct runs away with him. He must face this fact at this point of history, since he now possesses weapons

35

of such power that they threaten his very existence. Either man controls power or it may destroy him. It is not simply power that man wants; it is *power under control.*

All drivers gain a sense of power. Only topnotch drivers develop the sense of power under control. This requires *self-control* and is clear evidence of maturity. Any power, whether through money, position, political prominence, or a fine car, makes a foolish man look more foolish and a wise man look wiser. How you use power shows the real you!

To Talk About:

1. Discuss the relative importance of driving skill and driver attitude.

2. Which driver types act the same way in everyday life and when driving? Which seem to take on new personalities when driving?

3. Discuss any responsibilities that passengers and observers have for the actions of "show-off" drivers.

4. Discuss the responsibility of a girl to tell her date if she does not like his driving. Suggest ways in which this might be done.

5. How would most boys react to frankness like Linda's? Why do some boys drive like Show-offs when they have girl passengers? Does this show interest in themselves or in the girl?

6. Discuss the idea that there is no such thing as a "minor violation."

7. To what extent do you think young people follow the examples set by their parents when they drive?

8. Report on accidents caused by small distractions.

9. Discuss: "Power in your hands shows up the real you."

10. Draw up rules of conduct for passengers in an automobile.

To Do:

1. Write an editorial about "The Teen-age Show-off Driver," suggesting some of the following ideas: (*a*) He is not creating the "hero" impression he is aiming for; (*b*) he is often ruining his car and, therefore, shows lack of intelligence; (*c*) he is endangering lives and property to satisfy his own ego; (*d*) he is damaging the reputation of other, sensible teen-age drivers; (*e*) he could improve his own reputation and self-esteem in many worthwhile activities; (*f*) other responsible, clear-thinking young people should sense their responsibility to show disapproval of the Show-off.

2. There are two important factors that the Show-off usually does not realize: (*a*) that with his planned "narrow escapes," he is putting other drivers who do not know his intentions into situations where they cannot act quickly enough; and (*b*) he may have very quick reactions, but he does not have the experience and mature judgment to make his quick reactions wise ones. Set up several situations to illustrate these points.

3. Have each member of the group write a description of a good driver and a poor driver whom they know. Include sex and age group. Record the number of males and females in each age group for the good drivers and also the poor ones. Discuss the totals of these lists and see whether they are what you would expect.

4. Write an editorial about "The Driver's Attitude Toward Law." Human lives depend upon the observance of traffic laws. Usually it is money, which is far less precious, that is involved in a theft. Why, then, do some people sympathize with the traffic-law violator and despise the thief?

5. Ask your local police department to set up a radar meter or other type of speed-checking device in the vicinity of your school so that the group can observe how such a device works.

6. Study your own responses in traffic situations. Do you show any of the characteristics of the "bad risks"? It is difficult to analyze yourself fairly, but if you intend to be the best driver you can, you will be alert to any bad tendencies you find and set up a program to correct them before they advance too far.

7. Draw two diagrams of the same traffic situation: (a) as it is first seen from a distance; (b) as it changes into a hazard by the time the driver reaches it. Show how proper foresight can, in such a case, avert trouble.

Fig. 2-10. Power under control.

3

the Eyes of
the Driver

We get most of our knowledge by using our eyes. In driving, we depend greatly on our sense of vision every moment we are behind the wheel. Through our eyes, we receive a flow of ever-changing new information. Our driving performance, enjoyment, and safety depend to a large extent on a clear, complete, and accurate picture of our surroundings.

Through sight, we learn:

The number, position, movement, and speed of other vehicles

Of the presence of pedestrians, animals, or other objects

Of the conditions ahead

Of the presence and meaning of traffic signs

The color of traffic signals

Of our speed and many aspects of our car's performance

Through sight, we also:

Judge distances

Estimate speed of other vehicles or of pedestrians

An eye test is required in all states prior to granting a new driver's license. Some states require a reexamination prior to renewal of the license. If the test shows it is necessary for a driver to wear glasses to see well, this condition may be entered upon his license. In this case, driving without glasses may be subject to penalty. But there is a great deal more to driving than whether or not you wear glasses.

**Fig. 3–1.
A restricted
license.**

The Sense of Vision

The sense of vision consists of a number of different and separate abilities or skills. A driver should be able to identify objects, colors on signs and signals, and relative distances to different objects. He should be able to see his way at night when there is little light by which to see —and in the face of glare. When looking straight ahead, he should be able to detect motion at the sides. The same person may be very efficient in some visual tasks and average or poor in others. It is highly desirable to have complete eye tests made. It is also interesting to take the various tests and to know how you rate on each and what to do about any weaknesses. This information may help keep you out of traffic trouble.

A person who has any reason to doubt the efficiency of any aspect of his vision

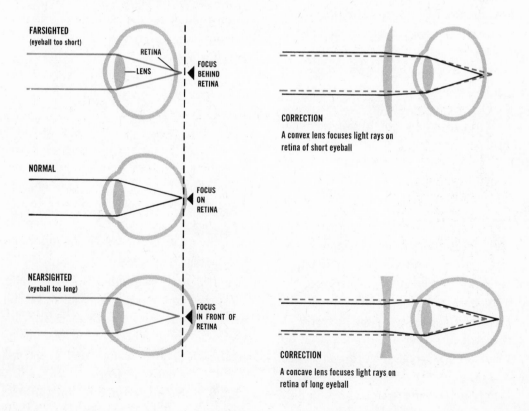

FARSIGHTED
(eyeball too short)
RETINA
LENS
FOCUS BEHIND RETINA

NORMAL
FOCUS ON RETINA

NEARSIGHTED
(eyeball too long)
FOCUS IN FRONT OF RETINA

CORRECTION
A convex lens focuses light rays on retina of short eyeball

CORRECTION
A concave lens focuses light rays on retina of long eyeball

Fig. 3–2. Two common defects of vision and correction by glasses.

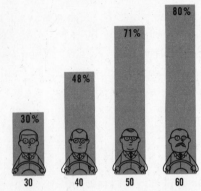

Fig. 3–3. The problems of vision increase with advancing age.

should take these precautions before attempting to drive a car:

1. Consult a competent eye specialist (ophthalmologist or optometrist).

2. Learn the nature and extent of his eye defects.

3. Have his faulty vision corrected as much as possible.

4. For uncorrectable eye defects, learn what kind of misjudgments he is likely to make.

5. Learn how to compensate for uncorrectable eye defects. Compensation for eye defects usually calls for *slower driving* and *greater alertness.*

The Motorists' Vision Committee of the American Optometric Association states that 30 percent of thirty-year-old drivers have visual problems, as do 48 percent of the forty-year-old drivers, 71 percent of fifty-year-old drivers, and 80 percent of sixty-year-old drivers. See Fig. 3–3.

Can you see the tremendous importance of an understanding of vision to (1) traffic and safety research, (2) licensing authorities, and (3) *you,* the driver?

Abilities and Skills of Vision

Every driver should know just how efficient each major aspect of his sense of vision is. The greatest danger lies in those weaknesses which are unknown to the driver himself.

Visual Acuity Clearness of vision is called *visual acuity.* People differ considerably in this quality. One person may be able to distinguish clearly a group of pedestrians and their movements 300 or 400 yards away. To another, the scene may appear as an indistinct or blurred picture. Accustomed to the latter condition, a person may not realize that his limited vision is not normal. He just believes that this is as much as anyone sees. He is badly in need of a test and information about his visual acuity.

An important point to remember here is that for many people visual acuity deteriorates (grows poor) in one's later years. This change is very gradual, and sometimes the person doesn't realize how far it has progressed. For this reason, a periodic recheck of vision is important.

Testing Acuity The most common test of visual acuity uses the Snellen chart. Most Snellen charts consist of several rows of letters of various sizes. Your visual acuity is scored by the size of the smallest letters you can read at a specified distance, usually 20 feet.

A person with normal vision can read standard Snellen letters about one-third of an inch high at a distance of 20 feet. This is called 20/20 vision, or normal

Fig. 3–4. Clear vision and poor vision.

vision. Many people have better than 20/20 vision and can see the same letters farther away. Good distance vision is very important in driving.

Try testing your visual acuity. Use the small chart in Fig. 3–5. Have a friend hold it in good light about 15 feet away. Cover one eye with a card, but don't press on it. Walk slowly toward the chart and read the letters aloud. Your partner can check for the accuracy of your reading. When you are close enough to the chart to read eight letters out of ten correctly, stop there. Carefully measure the distance from your eyes to the chart. Multiply this distance in feet by 10 and you will have your approximate visual-acuity rating in percent.

If you can read the letters at 10 feet, your vision for the eye tested is normal, or 20/20 vision. If you can read the letters at 12 feet, your rating is above normal. If 8.5 feet is as far away as you can read them, then your rating is below

average. Test the other eye in the same way. As you continue to read letters, change your direction of reading, left to right, right to left, up and down, and diagonally. To use the test correctly, avoid reciting them from memory.

This test is only an approximate measurement of your visual acuity. If it shows your vision to be much below normal in either eye (below 75 percent), further checking is indicated. Your school nurse may be able to help you, using the Snellen chart. Where any

Fig. 3–5. A scale-model chart for testing visual acuity.

41

doubt exists, consult a competent eye specialist. In addition to the value of good visual acuity to driving safety, early correction may prevent minor defects from becoming serious.

Desirable as good visual acuity is in driving, you don't have to have 20/20 vision to be entitled to a driver's license. Throughout the country, licensing authorities have established minimum visual-acuity requirements ranging from 20/30 to 20/70, as measured by the Snellen chart. Licensing standards are usually based on "corrected vision," that is, one's vision while wearing glasses, when such correction by use of glasses is indicated.

We say that 20/20 vision is normal. The most common minimum requirement for the driver's license is 20/40 vision. Any driver whose vision tests appreciably below normal should be referred to an eye specialist to learn whether his vision can be improved. Persons with less than the state minimum corrected vision should not drive.

Field of Vision You look directly at an object to see it sharply and in detail. Off to the side you see objects in less detail, that is, "out of the corner of your eye." The entire area which you can see to both sides while looking straight ahead is called your *field of vision*. Side, or peripheral, vision is very important in driving.

Detecting a moving object off to one side while looking straight ahead may bring it to your attention. You can then turn your eyes to focus your center vision on the object and see it in much greater detail.

Individuals differ in the extent of their field of vision. Some people have wider fields of vision than others. They see farther to the sides. It is a distinct advantage to a driver to be able to detect objects and especially motion over a wide field. It enables him to detect vehicles, persons, or animals approaching from the right or left.

Some persons have narrow visual fields. They are said to have *tunnel vision*. They see only a narrow field ahead—as though they were looking through a tunnel. They are at a great disadvantage when cars are overtaking them to pass, when ap-

Fig. 3-6. The *width* of your field of vision is important.

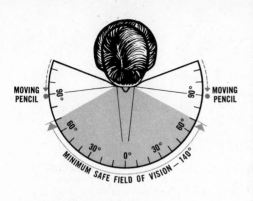

Fig. 3–7. You can make a field-of-vision testing device.

proaching intersections, and in many other circumstances on the highway.

Tunnel vision is another defect that a driver may have without realizing it. He may have unconsciously learned to compensate for it by continually moving his eyes to left and right.

Testing the Field of Vision You can make your own test equipment, using a cardboard protractor with a radius of 10 inches (see Fig. 3–7). At the midpoint of the curved edge, mark a zero. Then mark it on each side of the zero in 10-degree intervals to the 100-degree mark. Hold the protractor to the bridge of your nose with the zero directly ahead. Now look at a fixed point some distance straight ahead. Have someone move a pencil slowly from back to front along the edge of the protractor on one side. Remember to keep looking *straight ahead.* When you detect the movement of the pencil out of the corner of your eye, have him hold it still. That point where you first saw the movement of the pencil should be noted in degrees. Have several trials made for each side.

Most persons can see more than 90 degrees at each side, making a total field of vision of over 180 degrees. A field of

less than 70 degrees on each side is generally considered a serious handicap to safe driving. A person who knows he has such a handicap, however, can do much to compensate. He should:

1. Develop the habit of continually glancing left and right, by turning his head if necessary

2. Reduce speed to compensate for the brief intervals between side glances

Color Perception Special color cues are often used to give traffic information to the driver. Among these are:

1. Red signal lights for STOP, and green for GO

2. Red flags, lanterns, or flares at roadway hazards or obstructions

3. Red flags to show objects extended beyond vehicles

4. Red tail lights on cars

5. Flashing red directional signals on rear of cars, clear flashing lights in front

6. Red or yellow blinker lights at dangerous crossings

7. Colored road signs, route markings, and curb markings

Persons who are unable to distinguish the colors used to give traffic informa-

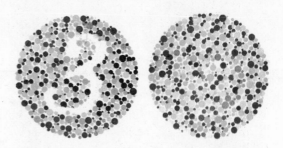

tion are handicapped. It is estimated that about one man in twenty-five has some difficulty in distinguishing certain colors. Defective color vision is about ten times as frequent among men as among women.

If tests show that you have a color-vision weakness, especially in red and green, learn to compensate for this deficiency. Here is what you can do:

1. Keep a sharper lookout for signals and signs at intersections.

2. Know the arrangements of signals at localities where you do your driving. Generally, signal positions' follow the national standard: red at the top, yellow in the center, and green below. Do not depend upon this position arrangement in unfamiliar localities. There are still some places with nonstandard arrangements.

3. Pay closer attention to the actions of other drivers at intersections.

4. Learn to interpret the shape of traffic markers and signs as a guide to what you may expect ahead. Learn what the different shapes (circle, octagon, diamond, triangle, and rectangle) signify.

Testing for Color Perception One color-vision test, the Ishihara, consists of several circular areas filled with spots and dots of various colors. Spots of a given color are arranged in patterns to form numbers. Persons with defective color vision cannot distinguish some of the figures from the background. The nature and extent of their color blindness are determined from their ability or inability to read the numbers (see Fig. 3–8).

The Ishihara test detects minor de-

Fig. 3–8. The Ishihara test. A normal eye sees a number emerge from dots of various colors filling the circle. The color-blind eye fails to distinguish that number because the colored dots in it look like the background.

grees of color blindness, some of which are not serious enough to interfere with driving. However, if this test indicates any degree of color blindness, you should be tested with actual traffic signals.

Some test patterns contain both differences in color and differences of shading. Differences of color form one number in a test pattern, and differences of shading form another number. The person with normal vision identifies the color-formed number. The color-blind person, on the other hand, cannot see the color-formed number, so he reads the other one.

A color-vision testing device which requires the same kind of color identification that a driver needs for reading

Fig. 3–9. The Colorator. The person being tested attempts to name each color as it shows through the opening in the box.

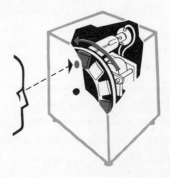

traffic signal lights is the Colorator, shown in Fig. 3–9. A small motor within the box turns a disk containing sections of traffic-signal glass. A light illuminates each section as it becomes visible through a small opening. Colors appear in random order, each exposed for about two seconds. To pass the test, you must name the colors correctly as they appear.

Depth Perception *Depth perception* refers to your ability to judge the distance between you and an object which you see. It is also concerned with the size and shape of the object in terms of depth.

A person with faulty depth perception usually cannot judge distances accurately. He may overestimate the distance of an approaching car and attempt to pass the car he is following when there is not enough clear space ahead. Also, he may stop suddenly, thinking the car ahead is closer than it really is.

Testing Depth Perception One of the several testing devices available for measuring depth perception is illustrated in Fig. 3–10. When you look into the eyepiece of this instrument you see miniature cars in a mirror. The mirror is placed 10 feet from the instrument, and the cars appear to be 20 feet away. As quickly as you can, you move the cars forward and backward until they appear to be side by side. When your depth perception is normal, you have an error of less than 1 inch in lining the cars up side by side.

If you find your ability in judging distances is below average, observe the following precautions:

1. Allow additional space between your car and other cars on the highway. Do not follow other cars closely.

2. When you overtake another car to pass, allow much more clear space ahead than you seem to need. If you know your distance judgment is faulty, allow for it.

3. Drive more slowly to reduce your stopping distance in an emergency.

4. Be more alert for emergency situations that might develop.

An infant learns to perceive depth by reaching. We do not know, however, to what extent depth perception can be learned and improved by experience. Read carefully the magazine and newspaper articles you may see in the future related to depth perception or other aspects of vision. There are many things yet to be learned through research in this area.

Fig. 3–10. Testing depth perception.

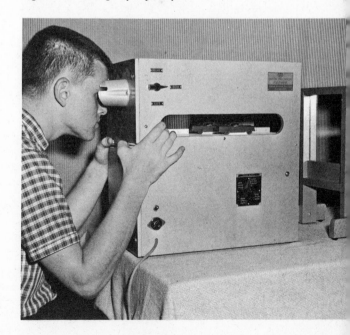

Night Vision

At night, the available light is very limited. In daylight, you often have some 10,000 foot-candles of light with which to see. At night, 100 feet from your car, you have only 7 or 8 foot-candles of light. Out ahead, at 1,000 feet, you have only one-fourteenth of a foot-candle.

The Mechanism of the Eyes   Your eyes make adjustments so that you can see under various levels of illumination. When the intensity of the light in front of your eyes changes, a reflex action occurs within the eye. This action opens and closes a kind of curtain, called the *iris,* at the front of the eye (see Fig. 3–11). The opening in the iris is called the *pupil.* The size of the opening, or pupil, controls the amount of light that enters the eye. The action resembles that of the diaphragm of a camera.

The sensitive area on the back of the eyeball which receives the light rays is known as the *retina.* The ends of the nerve fibers of the optic nerve which convey impulses to the brain are here. The retina adapts itself to various levels of light intensity.

When you first enter a dark theater in the daytime, it is very difficult to see, but gradually objects become visible. This is what happens. In the daylight, the pupil of your eye contracts to prevent too much light from falling on the retina (see Fig. 3–11). When you enter the dark theater, the pupil opens up fairly rapidly to allow more light to enter. But the sensitivity of your retina has become dulled by exposure to the brightness of day. Your vision is impaired, or lessened, during the time the retina recovers the sensitivity it needs for seeing in low illumination.

Eyes adjust much more slowly to darkness than to light. Although most of the adjustment takes place in the first few minutes after you enter the dark theater, there is still substantial adjustment taking place for as long as half an hour.

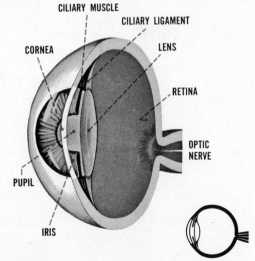

Fig. 3–11. Parts of the human eye.

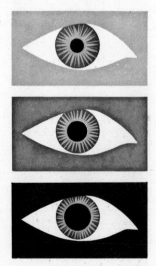

Fig. 3–12. The iris responds to the intensity of light on it. The less light on it, the larger its circular opening, or pupil, becomes.

Fig. 3–13. Driving at night is different.

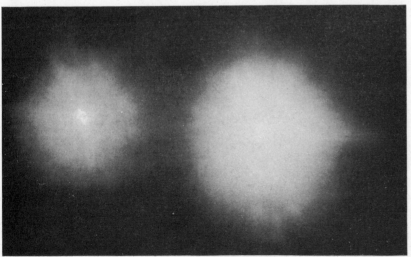

Fig. 3–14. Glaring headlights complicate night driving.

Exposure to very bright light makes subsequent adaptation to dim light considerably slower. The adaptation process may continue for several hours.

Your Eyes and Night Driving   Suppose that at dusk you have been driving toward the sun for some time, or sunbathing on the beach. Your visual adjustment to twilight and dark may be very poor. *This is a situation warranting special caution against accidents.*

Similarly, glaring headlights complicate night driving. The headlights of an approaching car greatly reduce your ability to see. When bright, high-beam headlights are about 100 feet away, it is very difficult to see objects beside or beyond the approaching car. Then, after the glaring lights have passed, your vision does not return to normal for some time. Hence, hazards are greatly increased.

These are times to slow down. Your stopping distance should never be greater than the distance in which you can see ahead clearly. Too many drivers try to drive at night at the same speed as in the daytime. *They overdrive their headlights.* They drive at a speed at which it is not physically possible to stop in the distance of their clear vision ahead. Then, in an emergency, they are unable to avoid trouble. Their stopping distance is longer than the beam of their headlights, so they do not see the danger in time. *Speed should always go down with the sun.* If people drive with the same *margin of safety* at night, instead of the same speed, there will be fewer night accidents. You may be aware that some states have lower speed limits after dark.

One very important fact should be noted here. *A person may have made normal scores in vision tests in good light and yet have definitely poor night vision.* Since so many eye examinations are given in daylight, this fact is important to remember. Routine visual-acuity and other tests performed only in daylight may easily lead to false confidence. Because so much driving is done at night, there is a need for separate testing for night vision.

Imagine yourself driving along a fairly busy highway at night. Vehicles are approaching with their headlights facing you. There's one with very bright lights. The next is dim, then there are a few about average. Here's a brief lull, none close right now. Now here comes one whose driver forgets to switch to his low-beam headlights. You are practically blinded for a moment!

What is happening during this period in the delicate and complex mechanism of your eyes? The iris in each eye opens and closes the pupil, or opening, to regulate the amount of light that enters the eye. The iris cannot operate fast enough, and the sensitive nerve structures in the retina are called upon to deal with varying light intensities.

Even the lights of a single vehicle cause complex eye adjustments between the time you first see them and the time they pass. The light intensity grows from dim to very bright. Then it suddenly disappears. Our eye structure, not by nature adapted to such conditions, now faces a new and unnatural brightness. Actually it adjusts quickly to the bright light, but

Fig. 3–15. Use tinted glasses only in bright light.

the adjustment back to dim light, after the vehicle has passed, is much slower. During that period, your night vision is definitely diminished.

This is the series of events when you meet only *one* car. Now, repeat that experience over and over for hours. Adjust —readjust—readjust. Fatigue sets in. Both nerve and muscle tissue must keep functioning.

We tend to take our vision for granted. Night is a common experience to mankind. The new demands on our night vision created by night driving conditions are too often overlooked.

Research in Night Vision   The Night Visibility Committee of the Highway Research Board has reported some significant findings of research in the field. For example, it has been found that individuals have different rates of adjustment to changing light conditions. People also differ in their *total ability to adjust*.

Various factors have been found to be related to a person's ability to adjust to night vision. One of these is age. A decrease in the ability to see satisfactorily at night is quite noticeable among older people tested.

Carbon monoxide from a faulty exhaust system lowers visual efficiency at night. Excessive smoking as well as high altitudes also tend to affect night vision adversely.

Tinted windshield glass also affects the ability to see at night. Since millions of cars are now equipped with it, we should be sure to note one fact. *The driver's vision ahead at night is impaired.* This is most evident when a driver approaches the bottom of one hill and faces another hill ahead. He is then looking through the darker portion of the tinted glass.

Research studies have brought out other data that are important to the motorist. For example, data indicate that using tinted eyeglasses at night decreases the already limited amount of light reaching the eyes and can be dangerous. Use of the same glasses to lessen glare in the daytime, as at the beach or when facing the setting sun, *aids night vision* and is wise if the person is going to drive after dark. Tests show that eyes not protected in brilliant sunlight require a very long period for the sensitive retina to become suitably adapted to darkness.

It has also been learned that the use of alcohol reduces the ability of a person to see in dim light.

49

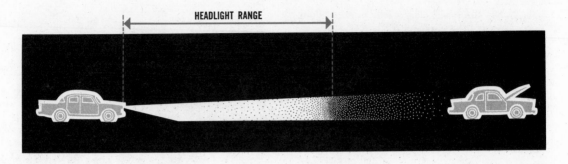

HEADLIGHT RANGE

Fig. 3–16. Beyond your headlights?

When You Drive at Night The difficulties and handicaps of night vision have to be taken seriously by people of all ages. *The fatal-accident rate, on the basis of miles driven, is 2½ times higher at night than during the day.* Inability to see well enough is a major contributing factor in the many serious accidents which occur after dark. Reduce the accident danger in your own driving in these ways:

1. Drive at night only after you have become a skilled driver.

2. Drive at a lower speed than in the daytime.

3. Drive at night only when rested. Fatigue impairs night vision and other vital factors of driving.

4. Know the range of your headlights and how well you can see at various distances. That is, be able to stop within the visibility range of your headlights. *Never overdrive your headlights.*

5. Avoid using dark or colored glasses at night.

6. When facing glare from approaching headlights, reduce speed; avoid looking directly at the lights.

7. Keep speed reduced until your eyes recover from the effects of the lights.

8. Always depress your headlights when meeting other cars. This common courtesy improves lighting on the road directly ahead and to the right, where you then most need the light. A driver "blinded" by your high-beam headlights may sideswipe your car.

9. Depress your lights when following another driver. The glare caused by your lights shining in his rear-view mirror can reduce his vision and cause an accident.

10. Keep your car's battery, lights, and electrical system in good condition.

11. Avoid lighting matches or using bright lights in the car. Keep bright interior lights off. You want to keep your eyes dark-adapted.

12. Keep headlights properly adjusted. Then the depressed beams are not high enough to hit the oncoming driver's eyes.

13. Keep the windshield and all lights clean.

14. Avoid excessive smoking.

15. Allow for lessening efficiency of night vision as you get older.

Testing Night Vision The ability to see at night varies greatly among individuals. Two persons may have the same visual acuity during the day, and yet one may see much better than the other at night.

The best tests of ability to see at night are those which most nearly duplicate night driving conditions. One test measures three things about ability to see at night: (1) vision under glare conditions, (2) ability to see objects in low illumination, and (3) recovery of vision after glare (see Fig. 3–17).

1. Glare vision. The subject looks through the eyepiece of the testing device at the target wheel and, as the wheel turns, reports the direction of the opening in the "C's," or broken circles, whether right, left, top, or bottom. Two small glaring lights shine directly into the subject's eyes. The examiner manipulates a shutter which controls the amount of light on the target wheel. He slowly reduces the illumination on the target until the subject can no longer identify the breaks in the circles correctly. The level of illumination at which the subject fails to give correct responses measures his glare vision.

2. Vision in low illumination. The glaring lights are turned off so that the subject no longer faces them. The light on the target wheel is slowly reduced until the subject cannot identify the breaks in the circles. This measures the degree of illumination required by the subject to see under low illumination—and this is by far the major visual task in night driving.

3. Glare recovery. The subject identifies the breaks in the circles while facing glaring lights similar to the glare he faces

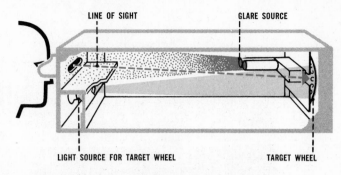

Fig. 3–17. A device for testing night vision under highway conditions of dim light and glare.

on the highway. The glaring lights are turned off, and the examiner reduces the illumination on the target to the amount required by the subject in test 2 above. A built-in timer then measures in seconds the time required for the subject to recover from the glare enough to be able to identify the breaks in the circles. There are very large differences in this time among individuals.

Some persons are so seriously handicapped by poor night vision that they should never drive at night.

Danger of Eye Fatigue

Continuous use for long periods of time puts a heavy strain on the eyes and results in eye fatigue. This is especially true in driving. A headache after a long drive is often a symptom of eye fatigue or deficient vision. Fatigue can cause poor driving for the following reasons:

1. Tired eyes tend to make a driver drowsy. Dozing at the wheel causes many accidents.

2. The ability to judge distance is often reduced by eye fatigue. When

this occurs, the dominant eye may well take over the main burden of seeing, resulting in something like one-eyed vision. The ability to judge depth and distance is then greatly reduced.

3. A driver's field of vision is likely to be greatly decreased. Objects approaching from the side are not so likely to be seen.

4. It is more difficult to keep your attention active and focused on the road ahead.

Never risk driving when your eyes are tired. On long drives, occasionally give your eyes a rest. Stop the car off the roadway and close your eyes. This helps relieve eye fatigue.

Keeping your eyes steadily in a fixed position tends to bring on drowsiness. Learn to shift your eyes easily over the whole area of your vision while driving. See quickly, accurately, and broadly. This is efficient use of your eyes. Take a moment here to review "Attention and Controlled Eye Movements" in Chapter 2, "The Psychology of the Driver."

Always remember this: a person often does not detect a weakness which exists in his vision. *It must be discovered by testing.*

As *you* grow older *your* vision will deteriorate. Although you may notice it in reading, you may not notice that it affects your driving vision—but it does! Keep rechecking!

Fig. 3–18. The ability to recover from glare while driving at night decreases with age.

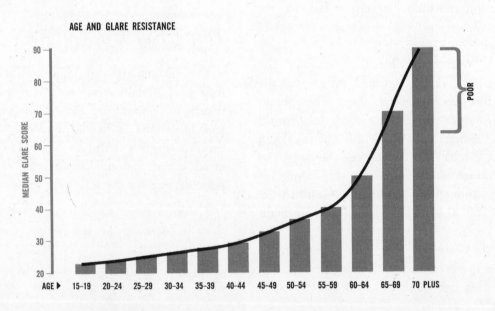

AGE AND GLARE RESISTANCE

To Talk About:

1. Discuss whether testing of night vision should be required in your state.

2. Discuss ways in which visual requirements for drivers might be improved.

3. Discuss the possibility of standardizing visual requirements throughout the country. Is it logical that states should vary in their requirements?

4. In what way do outside mirrors aid you in driving?

5. How would a bright light on your instrument panel or inside your car affect your vision of the road ahead at night?

6. When do sunglasses aid in driving? When are they undesirable?

7. Discuss the effect of oncoming bright headlights on a driver's vision.

To Do:

1. Find out the vision requirements and tests given for a license in your state. Set up what you consider to be sensible licensing procedures in relation to vision, including a recheck at certain intervals. Support your recommendations with facts.

2. Set up a number of situations which will clearly illustrate the hazard of overdriving your headlights and indicate what the results might be.

3. Have someone report to the class on the significance of color blindness in driving.

4. Some cars today have electronic eyes to dim headlights automatically. Have someone give a report on how these work and how effective they are. Do they prevent the driver in front of you from being blinded by your lights in his mirror? Discuss whether or not you think they should be standard equipment on all cars.

5. Have each member of the class take as many vision tests as are available. Record the results of each test and have each person write out exactly what compensations the tests indicate should be made.

6. Make a cardboard protractor, as illustrated on page 43, and measure the field of vision of each member of the class. Make a chart showing the range. How wide is a one-eyed person's range of vision? What should such a person do when driving?

7. Seeing with two eyes, or so-called "binocular vision," is a great help in depth perception. To illustrate this fact, ask someone to hold a pencil with the point up, about 30 inches in front of you. With your arm outstretched, hold your hand a few inches above the pencil; then attempt to touch the point with your index finger: (a) with your right eye closed; (b) with your left eye closed; and (c) with both eyes open. Describe what happens.

8. Measure the distance your car headlights on high beam reach ahead at night (on an object the size of a man). Then measure them on low beam. Figure the distance it would take to stop from various speeds and relate to these lighting distances.

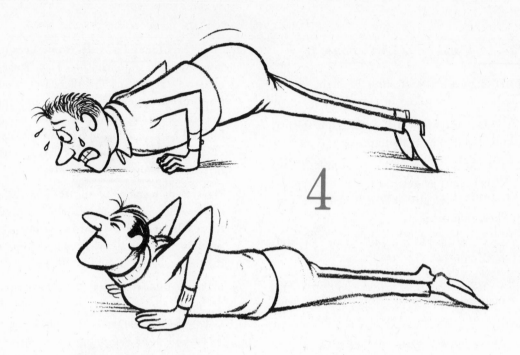

Physical Fitness and Safety

Human failure overshadows all other factors in producing highway accidents. Enjoyment, efficiency, and safety on the highway depend upon the driver. We know that his intelligence, his sense of responsibility, and his reaction under stress affect his performance. To these factors we must also add *the state of his physical health*. A driver, like a car, performs much better when he is in first-class condition.

Physical fitness means the proper working together of sound muscles, nerves, and all other body organs. Under such conditions, a person is much more likely to be at his best and safest as a driver.

Illness, such as influenza, infections, upset stomach, fever, and allergies, can reduce or even destroy one's ability to drive safely. Alertness may be decreased, clearness of vision reduced, judgment lessened, and reaction time slowed. Worry, headache, indigestion, a sore throat, or an aching tooth can be so distracting that they may affect driving ability and contribute to accidents.

No person who is seriously worried or in a state of health which might distract his mind from the important task at hand should drive. Under such conditions he should drive only if it becomes absolutely necessary. Only conscious and continuous control of attention, exceptional caution, and appropriately reduced speed can help compensate for the driver's poor physical state.

Disabilities: Correction and Compensation

There are some physical disabilities which permit correction. Certain sight defects can be corrected by wearing glasses. Vision may frequently be corrected so that the person sees quite normally.

Some disabilities, though perhaps *not correctable*, can be minimized in their effect, and therefore made less disabling, by procedures we call *compensations*. A deaf person, for example, may learn to use his eyes in such a way that he can compensate for his lack of hearing. Learning to read lips, though it would not correct his condition, would enable him to understand other people's speech, and in this respect it would compensate for his condition.

Among all these physical disabilities there are some which only temporarily disqualify persons from driving. Some people have physical handicaps for which neither correction nor compensation is possible and which definitely make them unfit to drive an automobile.

Permanent Disabilities: Correction or Compensation Possible

Vision Defective vision can greatly handicap a driver, as pointed out in Chapter 3, "The Eyes of the Driver." Adequate vision is essential for the proper and safe

Fig. 4–1. If cars could talk.

Fig. 4–2. Testing visual acuity.

operation of a motor vehicle. There are instruments to test vision and also to determine to what extent a person's visual defects may be corrected.

State departments of motor vehicles have established standards of visual acuity, or clearness and accuracy in seeing. Persons who do not meet these standards are denied licenses to drive.

The standards are usually based on "corrected vision"; that is, if a person requires glasses, his vision should be measured while wearing his glasses. Where glasses are found by test to be needed, it is usually noted on the person's license as a condition of his driving privilege.

Regulations for licensing drivers of commercial and passenger transport vehicles (trucks and buses) should require higher standards of vision than for drivers of private vehicles. Can you think of reasons why this should be so?

In addition to visual acuity, other factors of vision are important in driving. The width of one's field of vision determines how well one can detect objects on either side. Many people with a very limited field of vision, called *tunnel vision,* learn to compensate for it by continually glancing left and right.

Some drivers have normal vision in good light, but see very poorly at night. This is frequently a factor in serious motor vehicle accidents (see "Night Vision," Chapter 3, "The Eyes of the Driver," page 46).

Hearing Poor hearing handicaps a driver. It can prevent him from hearing other vehicles or horn signals from cars that are about to pass. Sometimes the first warning a driver has of a car about to pass is the noise of an engine, or sound of tires on the pavement. Rear-view mirrors do not ensure perfect awareness in all directions at all times.

Railroad crossings, especially if unprotected, offer a hazard to the deaf. It is difficult, too, for some people who are either deaf or who have impaired hearing to hear the sirens of emergency vehicles. Such drivers have less warning of danger. Proper hearing aids correct the condition in a great many cases.

Many deaf persons learn to compensate for their disability by:

Effective use of peripheral, or side, vision, aided by frequent, sweeping eye movements

Additional rear-view and side mirrors

Being exceptionally alert and watchful

The person who is unaware of his handicap, or refuses to admit or understand the dangers, creates a serious driving hazard.

A Simple Test of Hearing Many schools test the hearing acuity of students by means of a device called the *audiometer.* Where such a device is not available, students can conduct their own tests, using a watch that ticks loudly.

Hold the watch up to the ear of the person to be tested. Move it away and then back toward his ear until you can measure the farthest distance from the ear at which the person can hear the tick. Write his name and score on paper.

Test a number of people. Make note of the average distance from the ear at

Fig. 4–3. You can test hearing ability with a watch.

nature of these changes and how they affect us as drivers. Certain facts should be understood:

1. There are great individual differences in the physical and mental effects of aging. Men of about seventy years of age have been known to run marathon races in successful competition against opponents of all ages! Each person's fitness to drive should be determined *individually*.

2. Reaction time grows longer as one grows older. This does not mean that all young drivers have faster reaction times than all older drivers. They do not. Each person's own reaction time tends to lengthen as he grows older.

RELATION OF AGE TO REACTION TIME

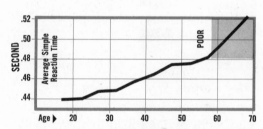

Fig. 4–4. Reaction time lengthens with age, but most rapidly near and after age sixty.

which those with good hearing can detect the sound of the same watch.

Each person's rating, in percent, is found by dividing that average hearing distance into the person's score and multiplying by 100.

Advancing Age   Ponce de Leon sought a means of *correcting* the disabilities which accompany advanced age. The legendary Fountain of Youth would simply make people young again.

Today, we have a much better understanding of the changes which accompany the aging process and how they affect driving. Though many of these disabilities are not correctable, a high degree of *compensation* is very often possible. Science is making it possible for more and more people to live longer. Persons past sixty are an important and sizable segment of our society.

The Nature of Changes   Although people realize that we change with advancing age, not very many understand the

3. Degenerative changes that accompany old age are usually due to arteriosclerosis, or hardening of the arteries. They affect the heart, blood vessels, hearing, vision, and nervous system. Sometimes they impair the mental processes.

4. Vision frequently changes between the ages of forty and fifty years. For this reason, it has been recommended that people of this age have periodic eye examinations. Such examinations detect

PHYSICAL IMPAIRMENTS BY AGE GROUPS

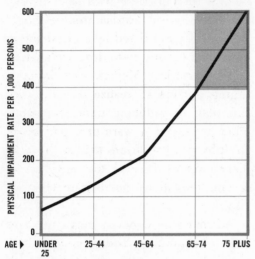

PHYSICAL IMPAIRMENT RATE PER 1,000 PERSONS

AGE ▶ UNDER 25 — 25–44 — 45–64 — 65–74 — 75 PLUS

Fig. 4–5. Physical impairments mount with age, but most rapidly after sixty-five.

abnormalities and permit prescriptions for corrective lenses.

The older driver has certain advantages which may compensate for his handicaps. He usually has driving experience, judgment, a sense of responsibility, and a tendency toward caution.

Physical Handicaps War, accidents, and disease have left many people with physical handicaps which, at first glance, would seem to disqualify them as drivers.

Under proper conditions, however, many of them have become skillful and safe drivers. Automotive engineers and car manufacturers have designed special levers and switches which have given handicapped people full control of cars. Automatic transmission cars have been a great help, especially to amputees.

Some states grant handicapped persons restricted, or conditional, licenses which permit them to drive an appropriately equipped car. With good training, proper equipment, and desirable driving attitudes, the physically handicapped person can be a highly efficient and safe driver.

Permanent Disabilities: Fitness Determined by Physician

A few disabilities may impair the driving skill of some, but not all, persons. Each requires an individual case study.

Diabetes Patients suffering from diabetes of a degree that can be controlled adequately by diet and/or oral drugs may drive any type of motor vehicle. In cases where insulin is required and the diabetes is well controlled, the individual may drive a private vehicle. He should

Fig. 4–6. Handicapped persons can become skillful and safe drivers.

be advised not to drive a commercial or passenger transport vehicle because of the possibility of sudden attack of unconsciousness due to an excess of insulin. The uncontrolled diabetic should be advised not to drive any type of motor vehicle.

Convulsive Disorders (Epilepsy) Any person suffering from a convulsive disorder resulting in loss of consciousness should be prevented from driving. Under certain conditions, persons under treatment for epilepsy whose seizures are controlled may, in some states, be granted restricted licenses following detailed examination by qualified specialists.

Disorders Affecting Muscular Control Multiple sclerosis, some cases of poliomyelitis, and other diseases affecting the nervous system pose special problems. People with any such disease should be carefully evaluated by a physician before attempting to drive.

Mental Diseases There are various types of mental diseases that may make a person unsafe as a driver. Persons suffering from serious mental illness are usually patients in a hospital. However, mental-illness patients who are not hospitalized should be permitted to drive only after very careful evaluation.

Organic Brain Diseases There are some other disorders, such as brain tumors or syphilis, that may cause a person to become paralyzed or to be unable to drive safely. A physician should determine the status of each such person.

Heart Disease There are many types of heart disease. Some cardiac conditions may incapacitate a driver; some may not in any way interfere with safe driving. Each person with cardiac trouble should be carefully evaluated by a physician to determine his ability to drive with safety.

The American Medical Association is urging doctors to realize the role they can play in reducing traffic accidents. They are urged to warn their patients of any physical conditions that might make them unfit to drive or that might make certain limitations on their driving advisable.

Advances in modern medicine have been phenomenal. Today, doctors help people recover and regain their health from diseases that just a few years ago were considered crippling. Because of this, it is important to emphasize the necessity of constant evaluation of health abnormalities by competent physicians. Policies of licensing authorities should also be constantly reevaluated in the light of advances in medical science.

Fatigue—a Temporary Disability

For a variety of reasons, we are not certain of the total number of accident cases in which drivers have fallen asleep at the wheel. It is known, however, that a great many accidents do occur as a result of fatigue.

Cars involved in accidents caused by a sleepy driver are generally very badly wrecked. An unconscious driver makes no effort either to prevent or to decrease the impact of the crash.

The person who finds himself getting sleepy at the wheel should consider himself fortunate. He has had warning! He must pull over to the side of the road and rest before driving again.

The state of being drowsy, or "half asleep," is in some ways similar to a drugged condition. A person would normally be horrified at the realization that he was at the wheel of a car that at any moment might turn directly into a head-on crash with a vehicle in the next lane. *He does not have this realization nor self-protective reaction when "half asleep."*

Suppose you are caught "in the middle of nowhere" when you become very sleepy. Don't wait for the next restaurant for coffee—pull off the road and stop! Go to sleep; when you awaken, walk or run around the car a few times. Do a couple of "setting up" exercises. Get back in your car, arrange windows and vents to get plenty of fresh air, and then drive on until (1) you come to a place where you can stop at a motel or hotel, (2) you reach the restaurant where you can get

some strong coffee or tea as a temporary "lift," or (3) you have just begun to feel "settled" (not drowsy) after your little exercise—and then stop again. Repeat this procedure if necessary.

Neither of these two latter devices will substitute for sleep. They will merely serve to get you to a place where it is safe to get some sleep—*the only real cure for the condition.* A person should not try to go on indefinitely by means of these "refresher stops."

Taking turns at driving is a good practice, but remember that if a driver is sleepy, it is while he is driving and while his companion or companions are sleeping that the danger is greatest. People starting a trip while tired face this danger even though they intend to take turns driving.

Sometimes people succumb to a condition commonly called "highway hypnosis." Monotonous, uninterrupted,

Fig. 4–7. Fatigue and darkness spell danger.

HOURS OF OCCURRENCE OF FATAL ACCIDENTS

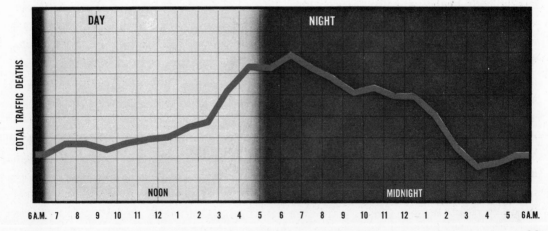

Fig. 4-8. Many highways provide special off-the-road areas for rest stops.

steady driving, usually on superhighways, tends to bring it on. Sleepiness may come only a few miles after starting to drive under such conditions.

When this "hypnosis" affects a driver, he should make a refresher stop. This condition can be avoided to some extent, however, by regularly moving the eyes away from a fixed, or "set," position, by talking, singing, chewing gum, fruit, or candy, and by keeping the temperature within the car quite cool with plenty of fresh air.

Avoid Fatigue and Be Safe
Many commercial concerns limit the number of consecutive hours their bus or truck drivers are allowed to drive. As early as 1939, the Interstate Commerce Commission limited the hours of driving by bus and truck drivers under their jurisdiction to ten hours, after which eight hours must be taken off duty.

Considering ten hours as maximum for a professional driver, what do you think of the practice of the amateur driver who works all day at his job and then starts on a long trip? He intends to drive all that night "to avoid traffic." Not well planned, is it?

Many accidents involving truck and bus drivers have occurred within a few hours after the start of a trip. Authorities believe that, in many of these cases, the drivers had neglected to get proper rest during their preceding off-duty hours.

One situation in which the armed services and traffic-safety authorities have become very much interested is that of servicemen-drivers on weekend passes. Many serious accidents, some with multiple fatalities, have occurred when groups of servicemen have attempted to travel too great distances in too short a time. Any person about to start a trip should make certain he is ready. This means rest and sleep, not starting out after a day's work or following late hours and insufficient sleep the night before.

Carbon Monoxide Poisoning Driving along a highway, a man suddenly heard a crash and felt a bump. He put his hand to his head and felt moisture. He looked at his hand and saw blood. He looked about and discovered, to his confusion, that he was sitting in his car in the middle of a creek. How he got there he never knew. The doctor found that he had been poisoned by carbon monoxide.

A family was wakened by the blowing of a horn. They found their young son sitting in the car in the garage slumped unconscious over the steering wheel. He had driven in and kept the engine running while he sat reviewing the events of the evening. The wind had blown the door shut. As he lapsed into unconsciousness, his body fell on the horn button. The horn brought the puzzled family to the garage. Artificial respiration saved his life. Few cases of carbon monoxide poisoning end so fortunately.

Carbon monoxide is in the exhaust gases of all automobiles, produced by the incomplete combustion of gasoline. Excessive amounts come from poor ignition and faulty carburetor adjustment. It is a *colorless, tasteless, odorless* gas and can be deadly even in small amounts. In a very short time, it can impair a person's mental reactions. He loses coordination of muscles and cannot safely operate a car.

A motor running at idling speed in a closed garage generates enough of this gas in a few minutes to cause death. Cues to the presence of carbon monoxide may be mental dullness, absent-mindedness, sudden perspiration, headache, drowsiness, dizziness, or nausea. The odor of exhaust gas is one of the cues to the presence of carbon monoxide, *but the odor may not be present.*

Fig. 4–9. Carbon monoxide—a colorless, tasteless, and odorless gas.

21 Children in Church Bus Overcome by Exhaust Gas

Plain Dealer Bureau

AKRON, O. — Twenty-one children from 11 to 16 years old and members of the [illegible] Church, were overcome by carbon monoxide fumes while riding in a church bus on their way to a skating party here last night.

Sgt. Frank Zepko of the Summit County sheriff's department said all were treated and released to their parents.

Sgt. Zepko said the children were overcome by fumes which seeped up through holes which had rotted in the floor of the former school bus.

Car Fumes Kill 4 At Drive-In Show

COLUMBUS, Ga., Dec. 18 (AP)—Four persons watching a drive-in movie with their car heater going died of carbon monoxide poisoning.

An attendant found the bodies after other cars had left the drive-in theater near here last night.

Simple rules to prevent carbon monoxide poisoning:

1. Run your engine as little as possible inside a garage and then only with the garage doors open.
2. Always have plenty of fresh air in the car.
3. Have the entire exhaust system inspected periodically to discover carbon monoxide leaks—from the car floor, heater system, muffler, exhaust and tail pipes, and the "seal" between the body of the car and the engine.
4. Be sure there is adequate ventila-

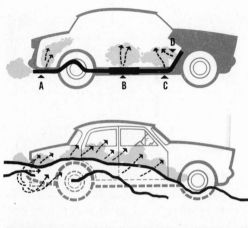

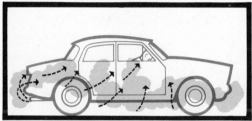

Fig. 4–10. Carbon monoxide can leak into your car . . . if there is a hole in the tail pipe (A), the muffler (B), or the exhaust pipe (C). The gas can enter the car through the floor or through a defective seal (D). Running the engine with snow surrounding the car can "pocket" the carbon monoxide gas and cause it to seep into the body of the car. Running the engine in an enclosed space invites carbon monoxide poisoning.

tion if you run the engine to keep warm while the car is standing still at any time. In a snowbank, the snow around the car may "pocket" the gas and cause it to seep into the body of the car. If you must keep the engine running, shovel the snow away from an area of about 2 feet all around the car *and keep it clear.* There have been cases where *drifting* snow formed the fatal pocket.

5. If ventilators are at the front, close them if you are kept waiting behind cars with engines running. Otherwise, the vents act as funnels, conducting the ex-

haust gases from the cars in front into your car.

6. Replace muffler or exhaust or tail pipe if clogged or damaged by corrosion. Have bent or broken exhaust or tail pipe straightened, repaired, or replaced.

7. If holes are drilled in the fire wall between the engine and the passenger compartment to install new accessories, be sure an adequate seal prevents engine fumes from entering the car.

8. Keep the car engine in proper condition to reduce the amount of carbon monoxide produced.

Carbon monoxide may be a greater factor in causing accidents than is commonly realized.

The cells of your brain have to be well supplied with oxygen to function properly. Carbon monoxide in the body rapidly robs the blood stream of its oxygen. The brain cells are then not supplied, and your brain operates inefficiently. You become groggy. Your reaction time is slowed down. You may drive off the road or into oncoming traffic.

The first thing to do with a carbon monoxide victim is to get him into *fresh air.* Send for a doctor. In the meantime, apply artificial respiration if needed.

The Winning Team

Many championship games and contests have been lost by the stronger team or competitor. How fit one is at most times, how fit for other sports—these do not determine the outcome. Fitness for the thing one is doing and fitness *at that moment* determine the final score. Your test as a driver starts at the moment you get behind the wheel and does not end until you stop driving. During that time, you must be ready, wide awake, free from strain of poor health or stress of worry. During that time you must be *fit*.

To Talk About:

1. Discuss some famous people (or others) who have had physical handicaps to overcome and tell how they have compensated for these handicaps.

2. Discuss the desirability of requiring drivers who reach a certain age to pass periodic eye and road tests in order to renew their operators' licenses. At what age? Why?

3. Discuss some of the ways people react, or foolish things that they do, when they are worried or tired. How might these lead to disaster if the person were driving a car?

4. Compare the effects of loss of hearing and visual defects. Discuss which would handicap the driver more.

5. Discuss the qualities of carbon monoxide that make it so dangerous. What can the driver do to prevent carbon monoxide poisoning?

6. Discuss the effects of smoking too much during long drives.

To Do:

1. Plan a trip of at least 1,000 miles, including rest and overnight stops: (*a*) driving the entire distance yourself; (*b*) with two or more licensed drivers in the car. Consider the element of fatigue carefully.

2. By means of an audiometer, or the test given on page 56, test and rate the hearing of all members of the group.

3. Interview a number of drivers and report on the methods they use to ward off fatigue. Can all of them be recommended for common use? Which would you not recommend?

4. The Bureau of Motor Carriers of the Interstate Commerce Commission has set up regulations placing restrictions on the number of hours companies are permitted to allow their drivers to operate. Secure a copy, study the regulations carefully, and summarize them. Then determine a set of regulations which you think your state should adopt. Report to the group for discussion, making sure you can defend your proposals.

R esearch studies conducted in various countries are focusing ever-increasing attention on the problem of people who drink and then drive. Post-mortem tests (tests made after death) for alcohol in body tissues of traffic-accident victims disclose that a startlingly high percentage took some alcohol before the accident.

National Safety Council figures, based on accident reports, give the following information:

Nearly one out of every three fatal motor vehicle accidents involved a drinking driver. Indeed, special studies indicate almost one out of every two.

One out of every four adult pedestrians killed in a motor vehicle accident had been drinking.

Over half the Christmas-season fatal accidents involved a drinking driver.

State traffic-safety officials, reporting to the Association of Casualty and Surety Companies, said that in one year drinking drivers were involved in over 130,000 reported accidents. The most significant statement of the report follows: "These figures reveal only *some* of the drivers who, because of an accident, were found by police to have been drinking."

5

the

Sneak Attack

of Alcohol and Drugs

Man, Alcohol, and Science

Recognizing the nature of a problem is the first step in solving it. It is known that alcohol does certain things to the person who drinks it:

1. Alcohol is absorbed into the blood stream almost immediately, and it impairs the functions of the central nervous system.

2. The effects of alcohol differ widely among different individuals and in the same individual at different times.

3. Alcohol interferes with vision, weakening the driver's "first line of defense."

4. Alcohol lessens control of nerve and muscle tissues. Driving skill is impaired.

5. Alcohol slows the reaction time of the drinking driver.

6. Alcohol is not the stimulant it was once believed to be. Quite the opposite, we now know it to be a depressant.

Scientists have known these facts for years, and many school generations have heard them. Yet the problem of the drinking driver persists, and today's research identifies it as a major concern to everyone interested in traffic orderliness and safety. Why?

"The Other Fellow"   Though most people who drive are at least vaguely aware of these facts, there is an almost unbelievably strong tendency to ignore them. Even to the person studying them, these facts are considered to apply only to "someone else"—never to "me."

This would be understandable if it applied only to young people. Actually, this is the sincere belief of many older people. They believe that alcohol, at least in the quantity and manner they use it, does not adversely affect them. They just do not know two important facts on the subject:

1. There are effects, other than the physical ones they have learned in the past, which cannot be felt.

2. There is a tendency for alcohol to affect the brain so as to mask from the person his own condition.

People can often recognize the effects of alcohol in others, but they do not as a rule see these same effects in themselves. For example, there is the story of

Fig. 5–1. The "unseen companion."

EFFECTS OF ALCOHOL

two men on a spree: One says, "Shay Jim, you've had enough! You're gettin' all fuzzhy."

This is why the drinking-and-driving problem is almost always thought to apply to "the other fellow"—it is more obvious in others.

The Obvious Cases   People who drink heavily, stagger to cars, and then weave recklessly in and out through traffic are obvious cases. All the obvious effects of alcohol are present and can be easily recognized. Sight, coordination, and judgment are badly impaired. These people are not fit to drive. This is the *obvious* danger. In the past, states and communities first directed their attack only at these obvious cases.

The Not-so-obvious Cases   Today, scientists who study the nervous system have found that even the first few drinks often have a dangerous effect on our behavior. The entire problem must now be viewed in a different light.

The "heavy drinker," "the drunk," numbers but a very small proportion of all drivers. His victims therefore are a small proportion of the total. He is easily detected. There are tests to prove that he is under the influence of alcohol. The public doesn't want him driving a car, and public opinion is against him. When found, he is arrested and prosecuted, and often his driving license is revoked.

We have tended to direct our attention to such persons as the whole of the drinking-and-driving problem. This has diverted our attention from an unrealized greater danger.

67

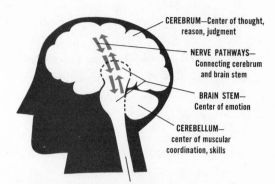

SPINAL CORD—Consists of many nerve fibers which carry stimuli ("messages") between the brain and all parts of the body.

In the early stages of drinking, with a low blood-alcohol concentration, the "higher" centers of judgment and reason are impaired. Inhibitions are lessened or wiped out.

Witn continued drinking, all parts of the nervous system are affected, impairing vision, skill, reaction time, etc.

Fig. 5–2. The destructive "sneak attack" of alcohol is the unrealized effect it has on the driver's behavior.

Hidden Danger!

Wherein *does* the greater danger lie? If not in the "drunk," then in whom? Let us remember this question so that we may answer it later.

Figure 5–2 is a diagram which will help us understand how the brain functions. In the long biological history of animals and man, some parts of the central nervous system developed earlier than others. The newer parts are most prominent in the higher forms of life. Here we are concerned with the *cerebrum*, which is best developed in man. It contains the areas called the "higher" centers of the brain. *This is the center of thought and reason.*

Note the arrows, which represent nerve pathways between the cerebrum (where reason and judgment are centered) and the brain stem, where scientists say emotion resides.

Fig. 5-3. Alcohol affects inhibitions.

A System of Control These pathways carry a tremendously complex interchange of nerve impulses, or "messages," between the cerebrum and the brain stem. This normally gives reason and judgment an important place in total brain activity. Our intelligence is given a system of control over our behavior.

Danger! Under the influence of alcohol and drugs, the higher centers of the brain are first and most affected. Their control system starts to break down with the first drink. The centers of emotion, daytime vision, and coordination are not much affected at this time.

However, *inhibitions* are affected. This is an important word to understand and remember. Inhibitions are restraints, restrictions, or limits imposed on our behavior by our intelligence, judgment, reason, conscience, or training.

An interesting point is that one of the inhibitions dulled or lost at this time is the very important inhibition against further drinking!

After the first drink, the light-to-moderate drinker has no physical evidence to cause him to doubt his ability to drive. He is a person with impaired judgment whose emotional drives are as strong as ever. He may become angry with other drivers. He may want to get home quickly. He may become impatient. His uncontrolled emotion may lead to many foolish and dangerous driving acts.

Formula for Danger The seriousness of the situation in which the light-to-moderate user of alcohol finds himself is not obvious. However, he is affected in several ways.

The effects of alcohol on a person add up as follows:

$$
\begin{array}{r}
\text{weakened judgment} \\
+ \ \text{weakened inhibitions} \\
+ \ \text{unimpaired emotional drives} \\
+ \ \text{ignorance of his condition} \\
\hline
= \qquad \text{danger} \qquad\quad
\end{array}
$$

Think of the person who normally refuses to dance or sing because he does both poorly. After "a few drinks," he dances or sings with gusto. But alcohol improves neither his skill nor his voice. He may even be making a fool of himself. His inhibitions, or controls, no longer safeguard him. This is just one example of how alcohol affects human behavior. Actually, alcohol affects all kinds of human behavior.

Later Changes If a person continues drinking, all areas of his nervous system eventually become affected.

Here is where the obvious effects of alcohol make themselves known. Alcohol does interfere with vision, especially night vision. His coordination becomes impaired. The driving skill of which he may be very proud progressively leaves him. To complicate this situation, he almost always believes he is handling his car even better than usual. On the contrary, among other effects his reaction time is lengthened considerably. Often a driver, returning home after drinking too much, has an accident with his garage door because he lacks his normal skill at the wheel and doesn't realize it. Even such a slight error in judgment, occurring on a highway, could cause a fatal accident.

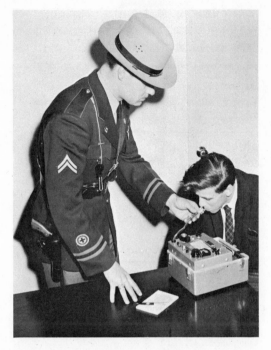

Fig. 5–4. A breath test for alcohol.

Sobriety Tests The effects of alcohol differ considerably with the individual. This leads to two problems: First, the lack of any sensation in the early stages of drinking gives many people the troublemaking idea that "It doesn't affect me. I can take it; let's have another." Second, individual differences in resistance to alcohol cause too many people to doubt scientific tests as to the significance of various amounts of alcohol in the blood. They think it impractical to set limits as to the percentage of alcohol in the blood to determine whether a person is legally "under the influence."

Studies by doctors and other competent specialists years ago gave assurance that this can be done. The most commonly used test does this through a

Table 5-1. Blood alcohol concentrations.
Medico-legal interpretations as to whether persons tested are "under the influence" of an intoxicant*

Alcohol Concentrations in the Blood	Medico-Legal Interpretation
0 to 0.05%	Not evidence of being "under the influence" of an intoxicant.
0.05% to 0.10%	Inadequate evidence requiring further support. Possibly "under the influence."
0.10% or more	Presumed to be "under the influence."

* Standards recognized by the American Medical Association, the American Bar Association, the National Safety Council, and other organizations. Also found in the Uniform Vehicle Code, Chapter 11, Sec. 11–902.

Fig. 5–5. "One for the road."

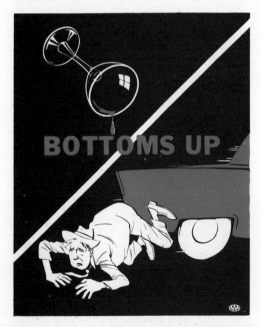

BOTTOMS UP

chemical analysis of that person's breath. There is a reliable relationship of this analysis to alcohol in the blood (see Fig. 5–4).

As a principle of our system of law, the individual is given a safe margin of protection from unjustified legal penalty. The American Medical Association, the American Bar Association, the National Safety Council, and other organizations have devised a set of standards to assist in the legal handling of drinking-and-driving cases. Table 5–1 shows these standards, which are also found in the Uniform Vehicle Code.

In some states and cities, courts accept the equivalent of fifteen-hundredths of one percent (0.15 percent) of alcohol by volume in a driver's blood as evidence of his being under the influence of alcohol. Some have recently changed their standard to 0.10 percent, believing that any person with that lesser alcohol concentration has his faculties sufficiently impaired to be legally "under the influence." The truth is that even the 0.10 percent allows the accused driver a considerable margin for his individual resistance to the drugging effect. He *has been* influenced, if that 0.10 percent point has been reached.

In Europe, an even lower concentration is being used as the criterion of legally being "under the influence." Recently the Traffic Conference of the National Safety Council voted to advocate nationally the 0.10 figure. In some Scandinavian countries, a driver is considered guilty if a blood test for alcohol shows 0.05 percent or more, even if there are no obvious signs of intoxication.

Some recent research studies have indicated that there is a measurable impairment of driving ability in some persons with a blood alcohol level as low as 0.03 percent. Even before that stage is reached, there are subtle personality changes in the individual, unfelt and as yet *unmeasurable!*

The effects of alcohol are not directly proportional to the amount in the body. They increase as the *square* of the blood alcohol concentration, according to Dr. Herman A. Heise, the chairman of the Committee on Medicolegal Problems of the American Medical Association. For example, a person may have a blood alcohol concentration of 0.05 percent (about two drinks) and be affected to a degree. At 0.10 percent, the effects are not merely doubled; they are four times as great. At 0.20 percent, the effects are increased sixteen times. Death occurs at 0.60 percent.

A Protection Scientific blood alcohol tests constitute a real protection for everyone, drinker or not. When we read of them in the newspapers, we should remember these facts:

1. They aid in removing the dangerous drinking driver from the highway.

2. They allow an accused driver a wide margin of leeway in his defense, requiring either 0.15 percent or 0.10 percent as evidence of being "under the influence." Any concentration lower than 0.05 percent is considered proof of innocence—with the range from 0.05 percent to 0.15 percent now generally considered inconclusive. In most cases, the test is used in addition to other testimony of a police officer.

3. They protect the driver who may be unjustly suspected or accused by establishing *that he has not been drinking,* or that so small a blood alcohol concentration exists that he cannot be legally considered "under the influence."

The Drinking Driver

Research has yielded very valuable information about the relationship between alcohol and driving behavior. The best scientific evidence known today supports the following conclusions:

1. The effects of alcohol begin with the first drink.

2. The first effects are impairment of judgment and reason and weakening of self-control and normal inhibitions. A driver's normal cautions begin to desert him.

3. After one drink, a person often has little or no feeling or sensation to warn him of these changes.

4. The "drunk," although dangerous, constitutes a very small proportion of all drivers. Much more common are "social

71

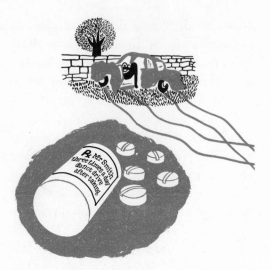

Fig. 5–6. Drugs and the driver.

Drugs and the Driver

The noun "drug" has two quite different meanings. When we think of a drug store, we think of drugs being used in medicine. In the following discussion, we are thinking of certain drugs which, taken internally, produce marked changes in the individual. These changes are as follows: reduction of the ability to reason; reduction or removal of inhibitions, causing "hopped-up" feelings; easing of pain; relaxation; or inducing of drowsiness.

Today, some people take drugs to ease the tensions and worries of their everyday lives. At times, people who work or drive long hours—or who drive after long hours without sleep—take drugs to help them stay awake. Certain benzedrine compounds relieve the feeling of sleepiness.

Many individuals who take such medication to keep awake believe that it will keep them awake for long periods of time, in spite of marked fatigue. This introduces a *very serious danger,* for no drug can be depended upon in this way. They may cause a driver to believe he has protected himself for further hours of driving.

Some drugs are habit forming, and those addicted to them become slaves to their use. As in the problem of the heavy drinkers, drug addicts constitute a very small number among drivers.

The great number of drivers who use "tranquilizing" drugs should concern all of us. Those who seek to keep awake without rest on long trips by means of

drinkers"—those who limit themselves to a few drinks. They are usually not thought of as part of the drinking-and-driving problem. The National Safety Council, however, says, "Social drinkers are the big menace. Their critical judgment is impaired with a fairly low alcohol concentration. Car weavings of obvious drunks can be avoided. But the social drunk appears normal until his wits fail him in an emergency."

5. Each drink leads more easily to the next.

6. All driving skills, senses, and capabilities are lowered with each additional drink.

7. Dr. Heise also concluded that the "harboring of about three ounces of alcohol in your body increases your chances of having an accident by more than 1,000 percent."

drugs should also concern all of us. We share the highway with these people.

There are popular brands of drugs on the market that can be bought without a doctor's prescription, including certain remedies for colds. Hearing about them, seeing them advertised, many people are inclined to use them. How do they affect those people as drivers?

A Similar Pattern Some of the effects are like those learned in the study of alcohol. The person is usually not conscious of any impairment of his ability to cope with any driving situation. He senses no impairment of his driving skills, alertness, capability, vision, or reactions.

There is great similarity between the drinking driver and the "drugged" driver. Both may be said to be "under the influence" and unfit to drive. The higher brain and nerve centers are first affected. Reason, judgment, self-control, and normal inhibitions are impaired, but the

driver cannot know it. He feels fine. In the same way as alcohol, certain drugs soon bring on advanced symptoms. His skills, senses, and the quality and timing of reactions are impaired.

The kinds of drugs involved have a number of basic names: narcotics, barbiturates, tranquilizers, antihistamines, amphetamines. Some of these are widely sold under various trade names, but others must be prescribed by a physician. The driver should, however, be thoroughly aware of *the danger of using any of them and then driving a car.*

More and more, we are learning to accept the description "under the influence of alcohol or drugs." The effect of either on the driver, in terms of results, may often be much the same.

Combining one of these drugs with alcohol may produce a dangerous condition. A person who takes a drug may happen to take a drink or two later.

Fig. 5–7. 1 + 1 = ?

One + One = ? In simple arithmetic, the result of adding 1 to 1 is, of course, always 2. However, in biological science, due to the many factors which are not expressed in the numbers, the results of adding one substance to another substance may vary. The result depends upon the amounts of the substances used and the conditions under which they are combined. The results of combining drugs and alcohol may vary, depending upon the person, his physical condition, his activities, and the amounts of the drug and alcohol consumed.

Though the intensity of the reaction cannot be predicted in each case, the effect of the amount of alcohol consumed plus the effect of the drug may be *greatly* intensified or complicated when they are combined. Very small amounts of each may add up to an unexpected and dangerous result.

Facts to Pass On

1. Drugs, even the popular "mild" varieties, should be avoided as potentially dangerous when the person who takes them drives, or is soon going to drive.

2. A combination of *any* quantity of a drug and *any* quantity of alcohol may produce serious results.

3. Drugs are safely used only under the direction of a physician. Anyone who takes a drug should get his doctor's approval before attempting to drive a vehicle.

When these basic truths about drugs are widely known we will all be less threatened by drug-affected drivers on the highways.

To Talk About:

1. Discuss the penalty in your state for driving while under the influence of alcohol. Do you think it is severe enough? Too severe?

2. Discuss the handicaps resulting from the drunken-driving penalty in relation to: (*a*) a high school- or college-age person; (*b*) a businessman; (*c*) a housewife.

3. Discuss the use of sobriety tests from the point of view of convicting the guilty and protecting the innocent.

4. Suppose you are at a party and the person who is to drive you home has been drinking. Discuss: (*a*) Do you have any moral or legal responsibility as to whether he drives or not? (*b*) If you ride with him and are injured in an accident, is the fault entirely his?

5. On what basis can you, personally, decide how you will cope with the problem of drinking and driving?

6. List arguments which might be used to discourage a person from combining alcohol and driving.

7. Even a fine car may be turned into an instrument of destruction if placed in the hands of the wrong person. Explain why the drinking driver makes it such an instrument.

8. How would you explain the difference between the "drinking driver" and the "drunken driver?" Discuss the danger of each to society.

9. What effect may alcohol have on the attitude of the driver which could prove to be more disastrous than his physical limitations?

10. Discuss the use of so-called "pep pills," tranquilizers," "stay-awake pills," and "cold medicines" on the actions of a driver. Point out any dangers there might be in their use.

11. Discuss the implications of "Drugs and the Driver" for: (*a*) a physician prescribing medication for a patient, (*b*) the patient, and (*c*) any driver who uses *any* kind of drug.

To Do:

1. Find out what percentage of alcohol in a driver's blood is accepted as evidence of being "under the influence of alcohol" in your state. How does this compare with the table on page 70?

2. Find out the number of persons convicted of drunken driving in your state and in your community during the latest year for which figures are available. How many of these drivers were in traffic accidents?

3. Write an article for your school or local paper warning drivers about the dangers of driving after the use of certain drugs.

4. Have the chemistry instructor demonstrate how the addition of alcohol changes the color of a solution of sulfuric acid and potassium permanganate, as in the breath test for alcohol.

5. Look up and report on the state regulations concerning driving under the influence of drugs.

Controls on Your Driving

Man has labored for many years to understand the forces of nature which govern his earth. As he learned, he recognized certain principles which hold true under all circumstances. He called these "laws of nature." He learned that he cannot change them.

We know today that as drivers we are subject to these laws of physics and chemistry and, if we are to survive, we must respect them. Man cannot break nature's laws, and he is often severely punished for trying to do so. The intelligent person *learns* about those laws of nature which affect him. He then governs his actions according to his knowledge.

As society developed, man found that laws of another kind were necessary. He had to establish codes of behavior to make possible the high degrees of civilization he sought. Thus, there came about a system of man-made laws. These can be broken, of course, so man devised codes of punishment for those who do break them. Their purpose is to discourage people from doing so.

As the motor vehicle became an important part of our lives, special man-made laws became necessary for efficient, safe, and convenient motor transportation. Traffic laws were devised.

The understanding person who drives an automobile today knows that he will be vitally affected by both kinds of law—nature's and man-made. Being intelligent, he makes certain to learn about both. Understanding their importance, he obeys willingly.

As a driver, both kinds of law affect you: they are controls on your driving!

11

6

Traffic Laws
Made by Nature

Many traffic accidents result from the driver's ignorance of natural laws. Some of nature's laws affect driving so seriously that you cannot drive intelligently without knowing how they work. You must know how to deal with friction, the effect of inertia on driving on curves (centrifugal force), the pull of gravity, and force of impact. You must understand the effect of these factors on driving. Superior drivers recognize that nature's laws must be obeyed.

Friction

When two bodies are in contact they resist motion which would cause the surface of one to slide over the surface of the other. This resistance is called *friction*.

The entire control of a moving automobile depends on the grip which four small areas of tire surface have on the road. This grip results from friction. Friction between the road and the four wheels is important; it enables an automobile to start, stop, turn, or keep moving. When this friction is reduced, driver control is also reduced, and an accident is more likely to result.

The friction between two surfaces sliding across each other can change. Anyone who has skated or pulled a sled or a wagon remembers and recognizes the conditions that result in differences in friction. Some surfaces grip, or hold fast to, each other. Some surfaces slide very easily across each other. These facts are very important for car control.

When the pavement is dry and your tires are in good condition, you have maximum friction and better control of your car. When, on the other hand, the pavement is slippery or the tires are worn, the friction is greatly reduced. The tires slide or spin on the pavement, and driver control is reduced accordingly.

Here is one of nature's laws at work. Try as he will, no driver can exercise complete car control unless there is adequate friction. Keeping tires and brakes in first-class condition assures that maximum friction is available whenever it is needed.

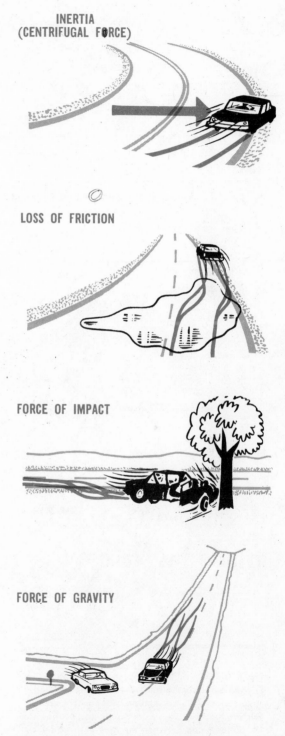

INERTIA (CENTRIFUGAL FORCE)

LOSS OF FRICTION

FORCE OF IMPACT

FORCE OF GRAVITY

Fig. 6–1. Nature's laws enforce themselves.

Fig. 6–2. The areas of friction between the tires and the road surface are small.

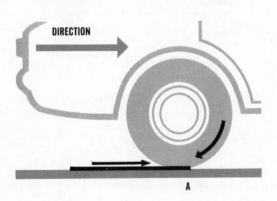

DIRECTION

A

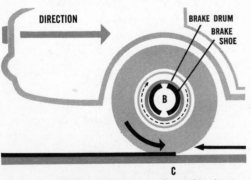

DIRECTION

BRAKE DRUM
BRAKE SHOE

B

C

Fig. 6–3. Starting and stopping depend on friction. Friction between the rear wheels of the car and road surface (A, top) enables the car to start. Friction between the brake drums and brake shoes (B, bottom) and between the tires and road surface (C, bottom) enables the car to stop.

Friction in Starting and Stopping   The friction between the tires on the rear wheels of the car and the road surface enables the car to start. Without friction the wheels would merely spin as on ice or in mud.

Friction is equally important in stopping. When you apply the brakes, friction comes into play in two ways: (1) between the brake shoes and brake drums, and (2) between tires and road surface (see Figs. 6–2 and 6–3).

The stopping forces which you have at your command when you want to stop your car depend almost entirely on these two sources. A driver's ability to stop the car at any time is limited by the weaker of these two sources of friction. Even if the tires are in good condition and the pavement is dry, worn or greasy brake linings give little braking force. Brakes in the best of condition will not provide much stopping force if the road pavement is so slippery that friction between it and the tires is small.

The amount of friction available for car control varies, therefore, with the condition of (1) brakes, (2) tires, and (3) road surface.

If the string breaks
the rock flies off

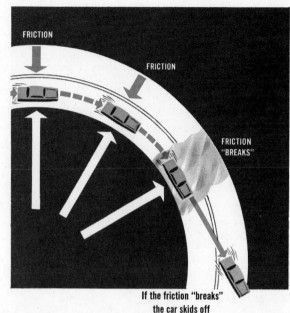

FRICTION

FRICTION

FRICTION
"BREAKS"

If the friction "breaks"
the car skids off

Fig. 6–4. When inertia overcomes friction, the car slides.

Effects of Bumps and Hollows on Friction   On a smooth, level road, free from bumps and hollows, the tires press fairly evenly against the road. On uneven or bumpy roads, the wheels bounce up and down. One or another of the wheels barely touches the road surface at times. This results in unequal friction under the various wheels. It produces difficult steering, unevenness in braking, and reduced stopping control for the driver. Skids can then easily occur.

At high speeds, a bumpy road surface makes driving difficulties greater by further reducing the friction between the tires and the road. The driver can control this situation only by choosing a lower driving speed. In fact, drivers who know the facts of friction know that it is important to *reduce speed* on a dry, bumpy road surface, just as it is on a slippery, smooth one.

Soft springs, shock absorbers, and low-pressure tires all add to riding comfort. They help to reduce the bouncing effects of bumps and hollows. They help to maintain uniform friction between tires and road. This makes braking more effective.

Control on Curves

When your car is rounding a curve, there is another factor to consider. This factor is inertia. The inertia of a moving body tends to keep it moving in a straight line at a constant speed. The object, for example, a car, moves in a curved path only when some force pulls or pushes it out of the straight path.

If you were to whirl a rock above your head on the end of a string, the pull of the string would force the rock to move in a curved path. You can feel the force needed to pull the rock away from a straight path. If the string breaks, the rock leaves the curved path and flies off in a straight line. Every driver must contend with this tendency to leave a curved path and fly off in a straight line, sometimes called centrifugal force, when his car rounds a curve (see Fig. 6–4).

When you steer around a curve you control the direction in which friction acts. The car tends to go off in a straight line at every point along the curve. However, the steered car is constantly kept to a curved path by means of the friction between its tires and the surface of the road.

Road-surface friction counteracts the inertia of the car. Without this road-surface friction, or gripping between the tires and the road, a car would be unable to make a turn.

If the car hits a slippery spot on a curve, there is a lessening of the friction between tires and road surface. Accurate steering then becomes impossible. The car will obey nature's law and leave the curve to follow a straight path, just as the whirled rock does when the string suddenly breaks.

The seriousness of such an accident depends to a great extent on the speed at which the car was traveling when friction was reduced. The presence of ditches, trees, large rocks, or other vehicles may cause great damage.

Friction and Motion on Curves The control which a driver has when his car rounds a curve depends on these four factors:

1. Speed of the car

2. Sharpness of the curve

3. Road and tire conditions

4. Side slope of the road surface

Of the four factors listed above, car speed is usually the most important. Fortunately, it is also the one over which the driver has full control as he approaches a curve.

When you drive you must take the road as you find it. You cannot redesign the curve. Nor can you, at the moment, change the tires you have on the car. You can, however, *control car speed.*

Car Speed on Curves The faster a car moves around a curve, the greater the tendency for the car to skid off the road. Doubling the speed of a car more than doubles the tendency to skid. This is an inescapable natural law.

Entering any curve at too high a speed can be dangerous. The car is likely to slide off the curve or roll over before you can reduce speed. Enter the curve at

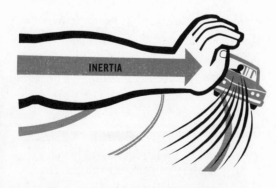

INERTIA

Fig. 6–5. You control inertia by controlling your speed.

a speed that does not overtax the available friction. Never round curves with the car on the verge of a skid. Drive a curve at a speed that allows a generous factor of safety.

When you round curves, keep your car speed well below the point at which friction ceases to hold. Safe speeds on curves depend to a large extent on the sharpness of the curve and the slope of the road surface.

Sharpness of Curve The sharper the curve, the greater the tendency to skid for a given speed and the easier it is for the car to leave the road. This is why sharp curves especially need correct banking and can be rounded intelligently only at reduced speeds.

A driver who reduces speed approaching a sharp curve shows an intelligent understanding of nature's laws. He is reducing the tendency to skid. Because it is difficult for a driver to sense the sharpness of curves on sight, safe speeds for curves are often posted, and they should always be observed.

Road and Tire Condition Frictional forces on a curve depend also on the condition of tires and road surfaces. If a curve is free from bumps and hollows, if the tires have ample tread, and if the road surface is not slippery, there will usually be good traction. On bumpy, muddy, wet, or icy roads, or with smooth, worn-out tires, traction is considerably less.

Side Slope of Road Surface If a driver makes it a practice to observe the kind of side slope of the road on a curve, he is in a position to determine the speed at which he can safely round it.

There are three principal kinds of road surfaces on curves:

(1) Banked

(2) Flat

(3) Crowned

Imagine cutting straight across a roadway with a huge saw to make a road "cross section." The three types of roadway would look somewhat like the cross sections in Fig. 6–6.

1. The *banked* curve is the best type of construction. Banking toward the inside of the curve helps keep the car toward the center, assisting in preventing skids and helping to keep the car on the road.

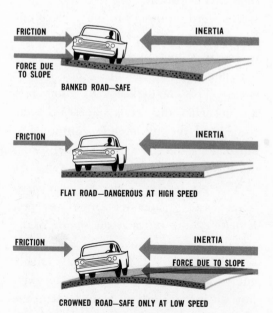

Fig. 6–6. Three types of road curves.

2. On *flat* curves, the road is of very little help in keeping the car on the inside of the curve. Friction easily gives way and skidding occurs. High speeds add to the difficulty in holding your car on a curve constructed with a flat surface instead of a banked surface.

3. On *crowned* curves, a car in the outside lane tends to slide down the crown and away from the center of the curve toward the road shoulder. Car weight actually increases the tendency to skid by helping to pull the car off the road. Only by reducing speed can a driver keep a car moving safely on a crowned curve.

Kinetic Energy

The energy of motion is called *kinetic energy*. The word *kinetic* comes from a Greek word meaning "to move." All objects in motion have kinetic energy, that is, energy of motion.

A moving automobile has kinetic energy. This energy keeps an automobile moving when the driver releases the gas pedal, and the automobile continues to move along the street with no help from the engine.

The greater the speed of a moving object, the greater its kinetic energy. Kinetic energy varies as the *square* of the speed. This means that when you double a car's speed, you increase its kinetic energy by four times. This is a very important fact when you want to stop the car.

Stopping the Car

The only way you can stop a moving car is to change its kinetic energy to another form, or forms, of energy. The greater the speed, the more kinetic energy you have to change before you can stop a moving car.

How can you change the car's kinetic energy? One way is by merely coasting to a stop. The kinetic energy decreases little by little because of air resistance, action between tires and road surface, and the friction between moving parts.

But this method of overcoming kinetic energy takes too long for driving purposes, so you apply brakes to do it quickly. Through friction, brakes rapidly change the kinetic energy to heat. The heat is radiated into the surrounding atmosphere. You can readily detect this heat in the vicinity of the brake drums after braking. If the tires skid, the tire surfaces become hot.

If you are on a smooth, straight, clean, dry road and have good brakes, you can apply the brakes, change the kinetic energy to heat, and stop the car rapidly.

If the road is slippery and the tires are smooth, no matter how hard you apply the brakes you develop only a little braking force. Then kinetic energy is not transformed into heat and dissipated so rapidly. It is impossible to stop quickly.

Under the same road and tire conditions, a greater distance is always required to slow down from high speeds than from low speeds. A driver must understand the relationship among speed, kinetic energy, and stopping distances.

The Effect of Gravity on Downgrades

With the same stopping force at his command, a driver cannot stop so quickly on a downgrade as he can on a level surface. Part of the stopping force is needed to overcome the pull of gravity on the automobile. Therefore, the braking distance required on a downgrade is greater than the braking distance on a level surface.

The steeper a hill is, the greater is the pull of gravity and the longer is the braking distance that the driver must allow (see Fig. 6–9). Add the factor of speed, and a situation is built up which makes it difficult to dissipate the kinetic energy of the automobile and bring it to a stop. This is another case in which a law of nature sets up a condition that every driver must take into consideration.

As you drive your automobile over the crest of a hill, your danger zone lengthens even if you do not increase speed. The only way that you can prevent your danger zone from lengthening is to decrease the speed of your automobile at the crest of the hill.

Remember also that, when you are driving downhill, you must start braking earlier than is necessary when you wish to stop or slow down on level ground or on an upgrade. A good practice is to decrease your foot pressure on the accelerator when you reach a downgrade. Far less power is needed to keep the automobile in motion on the downgrade.

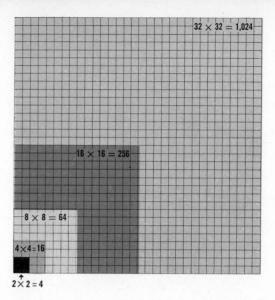

Fig. 6–7. How numbers increase by squaring.

Force of Impact

By *force of impact,* we mean the force with which objects meet. It comes into play, for example, when cars collide.

Force of impact is measured in pounds and is determined by:

1. The speed of the moving object

2. The distance within which the object is stopped after hitting

3. The weight of the object

Speed is very important, since force of impact varies as the *square* of the speed. If speed is doubled, the force of impact is four times as great. If speed is tripled, the force of impact is nine times as great. The damages resulting from collisions increase in the same proportion. The greater the speed, the more severe the damages are likely to be in case of a collision accident.

 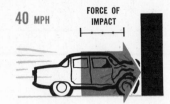 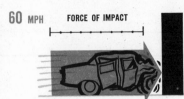

Fig. 6–8. If you double the speed of a car, you increase its force of impact four times. If you triple its speed, you increase its force of impact nine times.

Force of impact varies *inversely* as the distance it takes an object to stop after it hits something, if other factors remain constant.

Suppose that an automobile being driven at 40 miles per hour is forced off the road and is stopped by small trees and bushes. If there is enough "give" to the bushes, the automobile may continue moving through them for a distance of 10 feet before finally stopping.

The greater the distance within which the automobile is brought to a stop, the less is the force of impact. The amount of damage to the automobile and injury to the occupants are, of course, less also.

Suppose that another automobile, also being driven at 40 miles per hour, hits an object, such as a parked vehicle, which has less "give" than the bushes, and is stopped within 2 feet after hitting. In this collision, the force of the impact would be five times as great as that in the first example. Damage to the automobile and injury to the occupants would be correspondingly increased.

In the event that a collision accident is inevitable, an alert driver may be able to lessen the impact. He may have the opportunity to steer away from rigid objects which would stop his automobile in a very short distance.

Fig. 6–9. Braking distances lengthen on downgrades.

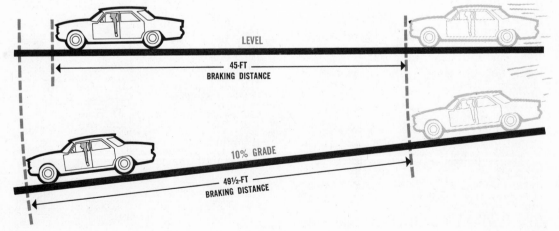

LEVEL

45-FT
BRAKING DISTANCE

10% GRADE

49½-FT
BRAKING DISTANCE

TRAFFIC LAWS MADE BY NATURE

86

Fig. 6-10. A place to slow down!

To test the value of roadside planting of small trees and bushes for cushioning a crash, automobiles have been driven into a heavy growth of specially chosen shrubbery. Other automobiles have been driven, at the same speed, into a heavy bus. The latter automobiles were greatly damaged, but the former were relatively undamaged.

The "give" in the bushes was so effective that the force of impact was cushioned, and only minor damage was done to the car. This demonstrates an important value for well-placed plantings on median strips between roadways. Similarly, they serve well along road edges

where there are special dangers of skidding or running off the road and hitting solid objects.

The distance traveled while stopping after hitting an object is important to passengers in a car. The greater the distance, the less the force of impact. In a sudden stop, a passenger's head may be thrown against the dashboard. If the dashboard has a "give" amounting to only one-eighth of an inch, the person's head is stopped in that distance. Some dashboards are padded with an energy-absorbing material with enough "give" to let the head cover a distance of 1 inch before stopping. This difference is ex-

Fig. 6–11. Impact is reduced when stopping distance is longer. (A) The bushes provide a longer stopping distance after hitting. (B) The solid bus shortens the stopping distance after hitting.

tremely important. The force of impact then is only one-eighth as great, and the likelihood of injury is correspondingly reduced.

Double the weight of one object colliding with another, and you double the force of impact, if the velocity and the stopping distance remain the same. This is an important fact to the pedestrian. No wonder he always comes out "second best" when colliding with cars twenty or twenty-five times his weight!

In driving, as well as in other activities of life, we should remember one important principle. Some people violate man's laws. Many of them are punished; some escape penalty. The violator takes a gambling chance. But we *cannot* escape nature's laws! We may try, though people have suffered severe penalties even for *trying*. We can't possibly win. It's a losing game. What kind of a person—even a gambler—would play that kind of game?

To Talk About:

1. Discuss the condition of tires in relation to available friction.

2. How do different types of road surfaces affect friction? Which types supply the greatest amount? The least? How do different weather conditions alter available traction on the various surfaces?

3. What is the advantage of snow tires? Chains? Do these supply more traction than regular tires in all situations? How do they affect stopping distances?

4. Consider the problem of driving on an icy pavement and why it is easier to maintain traction if you can keep your car moving, even very slowly, than if you stop and have to start up again.

5. As you approach a curve in the road there usually will be a diamond-shaped warning sign. Explain exactly what the skillful driver will do from this point on around the curve.

6. Explain why it is important to reduce speed approaching a downgrade.

7. Discuss the statement that "nature's laws enforce themselves." Illustrate the significance of this statement to drivers.

8. Explain how speed and kinetic energy are related and their effect on stopping.

To Do:

1. Turning a corner is similar to rounding a curve, except that it is sharper. Many drivers have not learned to do this smoothly and accurately. Observe various drivers and make note of their errors. Tell what they do that is wrong and how it can be corrected.

2. To illustrate the tendency of a car to slide off the road on a curve, lay a bicycle flat on the ground. Let one tire represent a miniature circular roadway. Place a penny on the tire to represent a car on the road. Turn the wheel slowly, then faster and faster, until the coin slides off the tire. To illustrate the effects of "banking" and "crowning," lay three coins on the tire a few inches apart. Lay one on the highest part of the tire (as on a flat curve); one in toward the axle (as on a banked curve), and one on the edge near the tread (as on a crowned curve). Now rotate the wheel, starting slowly and speeding up. Note the order and relative speeds at which the coins slide off the rotating wheel.

3. Devise ways of demonstrating graphically to a group: (a) why the danger zone lengthens at a hill crest; (b) why excessive speed is more serious on a curve than on a straight road; (c) how much farther it takes to slow down from 60 miles per hour to 45 miles per hour than from 30 miles per hour to 15 miles per hour.

Stopping Distances and the Driver

Sometime you may hear a driver claim, "Best brakes on the market. I can stop her on a dime."

He can't. It would be best not to ride with him. He doesn't understand braking at all.

If he were driving at 50 miles per hour, applied those brakes fully, and could stop on a dime, and you were riding in the car, one of two things would happen. You would either be thrown through the windshield to the roadway beyond or you would be flattened against the structure of the car itself with a force of some *109 tons.*

Brakes *do not* stop cars on dimes. Strictly speaking, brakes do not stop *cars* at all. They stop only the *wheels.* The car tends to continue its forward motion, and the tires rub along the surface of the road.

Brakes are only one factor involved in bringing your car to a halt. There are three other factors that are important:

1. Tires—their material, design, and condition

2. Pavement—its kind, surface, covering, and condition

3. Driver—his reaction time and braking skill

The Emergency Stop

Let's set up and carefully analyze a possible highway situation.

This time, you are driving along a highway at the speed limit of 50 miles per hour. This road has just one traffic lane for each direction, and there is a solid line of cars moving toward you in the other lane. The shoulder of the road on your side is narrow, and there isn't room for you to turn out to the right.

Suddenly, a farm vehicle comes out of a hidden driveway on the right side of the road ahead of you and starts across the road. Its driver stops for oncoming traffic on his right. The farm vehicle completely blocks your lane. You can't move left or right; your brakes are your only chance of avoiding a collision. Let's see what will happen.

Conditions To analyze this situation with reasonable accuracy, there are several factors we must know. Let's assume that the following situation exists:

1. This is a level, hard-surfaced highway. The pavement is dry.

2. You have very efficient brakes.

3. Your tires are good, new ones of standard design and composition.

4. The farm vehicle comes out on the road just 200 feet in front of where you are at the moment (200 feet is two-thirds the length of a football playing field).

5. You are Mr. Average Driver.

6. In this emergency stop, you will use brakes at their maximum efficiency. (Mr. Average Driver is not always so skillful.)

A Frequent Occurrence In the near future, you may find yourself in a serious driving emergency. It may be a farm vehicle. It may be a child running out between two parked cars in a city or village. It may be one of countless things that happen to force a driver to bring his car to a stop as quickly as he can. It is a *real* and *frequent* occurrence. Here is what happens!

Reaction Time and Distance

Before you can realize that you must stop your car to avoid an object ahead, you must see it. Because of inattention, poor vision, or low visibility conditions, you may travel some distance toward a dangerous situation before you see it. Even after you see an object in your path, you may go an additional distance before recognizing it as a hazard which would require a stop.

Fig. 7–1. Fact and fallacy: far from being able to "stop on a dime," a car going 50 miles per hour needs a braking distance of 133 feet to come to a safe stop.

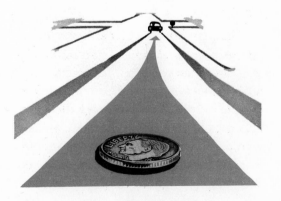

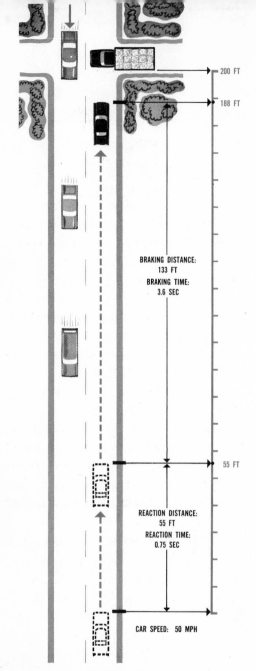

BRAKING DISTANCE:
133 FT
BRAKING TIME:
3.6 SEC

REACTION DISTANCE:
55 FT
REACTION TIME:
0.75 SEC

CAR SPEED: 50 MPH

Fig. 7–2. You stopped less than a car length away.

Realizing you must stop, you move your foot from the accelerator, or gas pedal, to the foot brake. As Mr. Average Driver, you take a part of a second to do this. During that time, your car consumes some more of your available clear dis-

tance ahead. At 50 miles per hour, your car is moving 73⅓ feet per second.

Using a reaction-time testing device or the detonator test, the average driver would take 0.44 second to "hit the brake" (see pages 97 and 99). These are prearranged tests, with the driver anticipating a certain signal and fully prepared and "keyed up" for his quickest movement. This time is, therefore, called *simple reaction time.*

A driver is not so fast under normal driving conditions. In these conditions, he frequently takes three-quarters of a second or more to react after a hazard comes into view. If his attention happens to be distracted at the moment, this three-quarters of a second may be doubled, to 1½ seconds. Since we have decided that you are Mr. Average Driver, we will use the three-quarters of a second as your reaction time.

So far, then, you as the driver have seen and recognized a hazard and have hit the brake pedal with your foot. In other words, you have *reacted.*

The *time* it took you, from the moment you recognized the farm vehicle as a hazard, to depress the brake pedal with your foot (to react) is called your *reaction time.* The 55 feet (73.3 feet per second × 0.75 second) that the car covered during this time is called your *reaction distance.*

Braking Time and Distance   As your foot hit the pedal, the brakes acted and, depending on how well the tires gripped the road surface, your car came to a stop.

On the hard-surfaced road, with your good, new tires and your good job of braking, it took about 3.6 seconds for the brakes and friction to stop the car. This is called *braking time.* During that time, your car traveled *133 feet farther* before stopping. This is called your *braking distance.*

The Stop   You made a successful stop. You avoided hitting that farm vehicle by quick, appropriate action. You had 200 feet ahead of you when it appeared, about two-thirds the length of a football playing field. A comfortable safety margin, it would seem, at 50 miles per hour.

But look where you are (see Fig. 7–2). That was a close one. You stopped *just 12 feet short of hitting it; less than a car length away!* These are actual distances. You used 55 feet in *reaction distance* and 133 feet in *braking distance,* a total of 188 feet of your 200-foot margin of safety to stop after you sighted the vehicle. This is the way it really *would* happen under the conditions described.

The Stopping Distance

Suppose you had been a little slower in reacting. Suppose your brakes hadn't been perfect. Suppose you hadn't used your brakes *perfectly.* This is what happens in thousands of cases. People usually do not realize how great a distance a car will travel before it can be stopped. It depends upon car speed, the driver's speed of reaction, the braking distance of the car as determined by its braking power, the tires, and the road surface. *It is much longer than most people think it is!*

93

Let's put this trial case into a formula for determining stopping distance:

Reaction distance
+ Braking distance
= Stopping distance

In Table 7–1, the column under *Braking distance* shows how greatly braking distance lengthens as car speed increases. Although this distance depends also on the braking force available, the speed of the car is the most important factor in determining its length.

Braking distance does not increase at the same rate as the speed of the vehicle. It would seem logical, from simple arithmetic, that if the braking distance is *33* feet at 25 miles per hour, it would become 66 feet at 50 miles per hour. It would seem logical that doubling the speed would double the braking distance. This is not the case. Braking distance increases much more rapidly.

Computing Braking Distances   The procedure for computing the increase in braking distance that accompanies an increase in speed is based on the rule: *Braking distances are roughly proportional to the square of the driving speeds.* If the speed is two times as great, the braking distance is four times as great $(2 \times 2 = 4)$. Therefore, if the braking distance is *33* feet at 25 miles per hour, it will be about 132 feet at 50 miles per hour. This increase of 25 miles per hour raises the braking distance from *33* to about 132 feet $(4 \times 33 = 132)$.

It should be remembered that braking distances vary with different pavement

TABLE 7-1

MINIMUM STOPPING DISTANCES AT DIFFERENT SPEEDS (DANGER ZONE) (TO NEAREST HALF FOOT) REACTION TIME 0.75 SEC

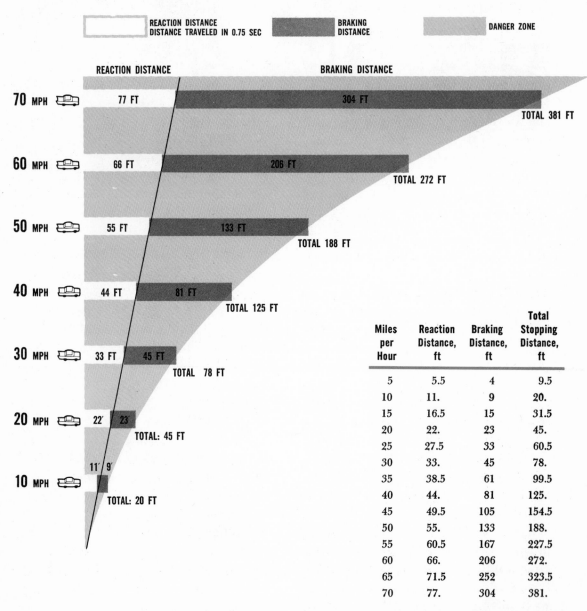

Miles per Hour	Reaction Distance, ft	Braking Distance, ft	Total Stopping Distance, ft
5	5.5	4	9.5
10	11.	9	20.
15	16.5	15	31.5
20	22.	23	45.
25	27.5	33	60.5
30	33.	45	78.
35	38.5	61	99.5
40	44.	81	125.
45	49.5	105	154.5
50	55.	133	188.
55	60.5	167	227.5
60	66.	206	272.
65	71.5	252	323.5
70	77.	304	381.

These distances are based on tests made by the Bureau of Public Roads. The chart shows how greatly braking distances and danger zones increase when you increase your speed.

Fig. 7–3. Will he make it?

surfaces and with the type, composition, and condition of tires. Those shown in Table 7–1 are based on actual tests made by the U.S. Bureau of Public Roads. Improvements in tires and pavement surfaces undoubtedly will shorten those braking distances we know today.

The rule that braking distances are proportional to the *square* of the speeds holds true at speeds between 20 and 50 miles per hour. At lower speeds, the increase is not so pronounced. *At higher speeds, the braking distances increase even faster.* The really good driver never forgets this fact.

Study Table 7–1 and the interesting diagram with it. The curve that shows the relationship of minimum stopping distances to car speed rises sharply. Every 10 miles per hour added to your speed gives you a far more serious emergency stopping problem than you had at 10 miles per hour slower.

The Danger Zone   How could you tell an untrained driver about the importance of the stopping distance? You could explain to him that the stopping distance, at any moment, is a *danger zone.* It is always in front of him when he drives. The slower his reaction time, the poorer the road traction, the less the braking power of his car, or the faster his speed, *the longer the danger zone becomes.*

He should always drive with full realization that the danger zone ahead of him is a stretch of road *within which he cannot stop.* Its length depends upon him. His life may depend on it!

You could also tell him that at 60 miles per hour (which is common on major highways) on good, dry pavement, with perfect tires, he would need 272 feet, nearly the length of a football playing field, to stop his car.

On roads made slippery by rain, he could not stop his car in the full length

Fig. 7–4. A danger zone always stretches out in front of your car.

of that field; he would need *nearly twice that distance.*

The next time he drives 50 or 60 miles per hour, his danger zone should be a part of his driving thought. If he cannot stop his car in the distance he can see ahead of his car, what does that mean? What may happen? What should he do?

One of the basic principles of good driving is this:

Always drive at a speed at which you can stop within the clear, visible distance ahead. You must be able to see beyond your danger zone.

That same untrained driver might be very much shocked to learn one other fact.

Speed and Impact   If, at 60 miles per hour, his car were to strike a solid wall, it would strike with the same force as if he had driven it off the roof of a nine-story building and it fell to the sidewalk below.

If we were to look over the edge of the roof of that nine-story building, most of us would get a frightening sense of height and danger. Unfortunately, modern car speeds are so new in the history of the human race that we haven't developed a corresponding reaction to them. Hence, your car is equipped with a speedometer. It's a good friend if wisely used.

Testing Reaction Time

A great deal of scientific research has been done in relation to reaction time, braking distance, and the force with which a car strikes an object. Professional safety men study these matters and apply the principles they learn to increase the safety and efficiency of cars, equipment, and highways.

The Test Machine: One Choice   Test machines are built (you may have one in your school) with a brake pedal and an accelerator pedal, just as in a car. The machine also has a clock with a dial reading in hundredths of a second, and a red light is used as a signal to the person taking the test. The clock has a timing hand which makes 1 revolution per second.

The person being tested is seated at the machine and told that when the light flashes, he should take his foot off the accelerator and depress the brake pedal *as quickly as he can.*

When the light flashes, the clock starts. It continues to run until the brake pedal is depressed. It shows the elapsed

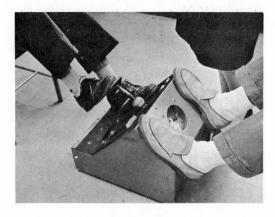

Fig. 7–5. Testing simple reaction time.

What effect would there be on his reaction time if he followed directions and reacted to the red light but not to the green? How do you think it would affect *you*?

Reaction Time on the Highway

time between the flashing of the light and the pressing down of the brake—how long it took to "hit the brake." This is a measurement of *simple reaction time.*

The average driver stops the clock in 0.44 second. Because a driver's reaction time varies from trial to trial, the test should be given at least ten times to each person, and the time scores should be averaged.

Some machines show a green signal light when the person being tested presses down on the accelerator. This is an additional check that ensures that his foot is in the proper position while he is taking the test.

A Variation: Two Choices Suppose, however, the machine were wired so the operator giving the test could press a button (preferably with his hands out of sight) and could choose to light either the red or the green light. The person taking the test would be told to "hit the brake" when the red light flashed but to keep his foot on the accelerator if the green light flashed. He has been given two choices.

Now, consider a real driving situation. A driver is not given only two choices; there are a tremendous number of possibilities. He must see and recognize any situation that suddenly faces him, not just two lights. He may have to turn the steering wheel. Which direction he chooses to turn it, and how much, could be very important. It may be that by sounding his horn he can warn the driver of another vehicle so that the other driver can take proper action to prevent an accident.

On the highway there may also be many distractions not present during the machine test. Examples of such distractions are daydreaming, worry, sorrow, business, social planning, or concentration on a radio program or on a conversation taking place in the car.

It is also very important to remember the fact that the test machine almost always makes a person as alert and attentive as he can be. On the highway, unfortunately, there are many times when drivers for many reasons are not so alert as they are during tests.

Fig. 7–6. A special traffic camera, mounted in a car, "caught" this accident situation.

Is Reaction Time Always the Same?

A driver's normal reaction time may be lengthened by any one or more of the following factors:

1. Alcohol
2. Fatigue
3. Drugs
4. Eyestrain
5. Low visibility
6. Carbon monoxide
7. Age
8. Distractions

Test Scores and Your Driving

Testing your brake reaction time is a worthwhile project. However, in the interest of safety there are two important things to remember:

1. Your reaction time on the road will almost always be *slower*—reactions will take a *longer* time—than those you scored on a testing machine.

2. Your reaction time—*no matter how fast*—is only one factor in your ability to stop your car. It is less important than such other factors of driving as your *alertness, foresight, recognition of hazards,* and *choice of reaction.*

Be glad of your fast reaction time. Most young people have it, and it's good. Don't *depend* upon it, though—ever!

The next step is to test reaction time and braking distance with a real automobile on a real road.

The Detonator Test

A test unit was devised for this purpose, called the *brake reaction detonator* (see Fig. 7–7). It is mounted on the front bumper. Two blank cartridges, loaded with yellow marking powder, are inserted into the two miniature gun barrels which point downward toward the pavement.

Conducting the Test

The test should be given in a restricted area that is free of other traffic. The person who is testing you sits beside you and tells you to drive at a given speed, such as 20 miles per hour. You are to stop as quickly as possible when you hear a shot fired.

He watches the speedometer. When it holds steady at 20 miles per hour, out of your sight he pulls a string to fire the first shell in the detonator.

The explosion shoots the yellow marking powder to the pavement, where it leaves a yellow spot. This shows the exact position of your front bumper when you heard the signal shot directing you to brake.

You React

At the sound of the shot, you take your foot off the accelerator and press down on the brake pedal as quickly as you can. This pressure not only begins

How would you analyze it?

the braking but also fires another shot, this one from the second barrel of the detonator. If you are an average driver, your reaction time will be 0.44 second.

This second mark shows where your front bumper was when you began to brake. The distance between these two marks is your *reaction distance*.

The Brakes Act   A white chalk mark is placed at the point where the front bumper of your car stops. From the second yellow mark to this white one is your *braking distance*. Applying the formula shown on page 93 to this detonator

Fig. 7–7. The brake reaction detonator.

Fig. 7–8. How to use a brake reaction detonator.

test, your *reaction distance* + your *braking distance* = your *stopping distance*.

Limitations of the Test   It should be remembered that you were "tipped off" beforehand as to what to expect and exactly

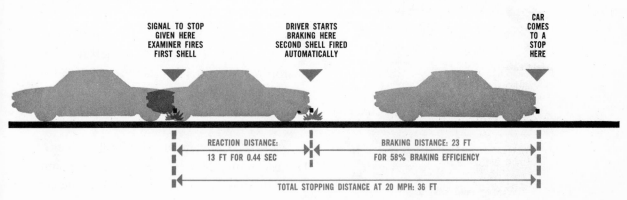

SIGNAL TO STOP
GIVEN HERE
EXAMINER FIRES
FIRST SHELL

DRIVER STARTS
BRAKING HERE
SECOND SHELL FIRED
AUTOMATICALLY

CAR
COMES
TO A
STOP
HERE

REACTION DISTANCE:
13 FT FOR 0.44 SEC

BRAKING DISTANCE: 23 FT
FOR 58% BRAKING EFFICIENCY

TOTAL STOPPING DISTANCE AT 20 MPH: 36 FT

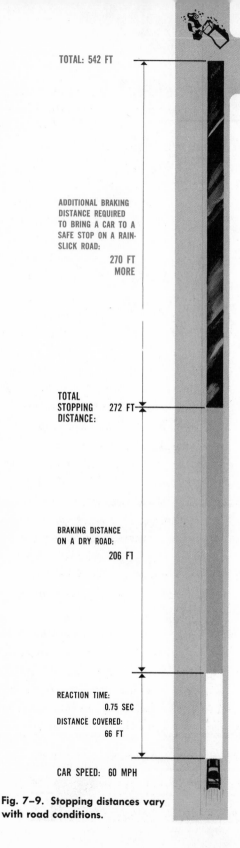

TOTAL: 542 FT

ADDITIONAL BRAKING
DISTANCE REQUIRED
TO BRING A CAR TO A
SAFE STOP ON A RAIN-
SLICK ROAD:
270 FT
MORE

TOTAL
STOPPING   272 FT
DISTANCE:

BRAKING DISTANCE
ON A DRY ROAD:
206 FT

REACTION TIME:
0.75 SEC
DISTANCE COVERED:
66 FT

CAR SPEED: 60 MPH

Fig. 7–9. Stopping distances vary with road conditions.

what to do. You did not have to see and recognize a hazardous situation. Also, you needed no time to make a *choice* of reactions, since braking was all you were required to do.

This test, therefore, is called a "simple" brake reaction test. In actual highway situations, your stopping distance will be *considerably greater* than in the test. On the highway, you must *see* and *recognize* a situation, then *choose* your reaction— possibly you will have to react several ways at once.

The greater your speed when you hear the detonator shot, the greater will be your reaction distance, your braking distance, and your stopping distance.

What Shall We Conclude?   Here we should remember one very important fact. The purpose of these tests is to discover our own limitations and the limitations of the car. We should *never* assume that making a good score in a test means that we are better or safer drivers. There are other important factors, *not measured by tests,* which may prove otherwise!

At 50 miles per hour, it takes two-thirds of the length of a football playing field to stop on *dry pavement*. This is *after* you see the danger.

If a car is going 50 miles per hour when its driver sees a hazard and tries to stop as quickly as possible, the car will still be going 42 miles per hour after traveling 100 feet (one-third the length of a football playing field).

Rain on pavement increases the braking distance to as much as *twice* that on dry pavement. What would be the effects of snow or ice?

Safe Following Distances

Accident investigators have found that one of the most common causes of accidents is following the vehicle ahead too closely. Most enforcement authorities believe that whatever the leading driver may or may not have done to cause an accident, any driver who hits a car from the rear was negligent. They assume that he was following too closely and so couldn't stop in time.

The Chain Reaction   On a congested highway, a driver's act of braking involves more than himself, his car, and whatever lies in the danger zone ahead of him.

All other drivers behind him are affected by the necessity of avoiding him by either stopping or driving around him. Frequently, traffic and road conditions permit no choice. An emergency stop is necessary.

There have been accidents in which ten, twenty, thirty, or even more vehicles have crashed in a chain reaction after the leading driver used his brakes. How did this happen? What preceded the crash? What caused it?

Let's assume that Car B is following Car A at an interval of about 60 feet. Both cars are moving at 50 miles per hour in the same traffic lane. There is no clear space on either side of A for B to pass, even if he so desires.

Suddenly, Driver A sees a hazard in front of him. It is perhaps a sharp break in the pavement, an animal bounding onto the road from nearby brush, or any one of a great number of common occurrences. Driver A brakes forcibly.

The Time Lag   A's stop light flashes a warning to B. The latter sees the light, recognizes the danger, cannot pass, and must stop, and so moves his right foot from accelerator to brake. This normally requires a reaction time of about three-quarters of a second *after* A *has braked.*

During that three-quarters of a second, B's car has traveled 55 feet, his reaction distance at 50 miles per hour.

Figure 7–10 shows the relative braking positions of the two cars.

Although B had been following A at a distance of 60 feet, the time it took him to react and brake *after* A had braked used 55 feet of that interval. *Allowing the same braking distance for both cars, B would reach a point only 5 feet behind A's halted car before he, B, could stop.* Normally, B would not be concentrating on the stop lights of the car ahead. His reaction time might be substantially greater than three-quarters of a second.

This is the reason that an understanding of following distances is so important. The following car travels its full *stopping* distance *after the car ahead brakes.* The car ahead moves *only its braking distance* beyond that point.

A Good Rule   It is not expected that each driver will recognize these distances in terms of numbers of feet. A good formula for remembering and applying the principle of maintaining a minimum safe following distance is this:

Allow at least 1 car length between your car and the car ahead for each 10 miles per hour of your car's speed! This is the minimum for safety.

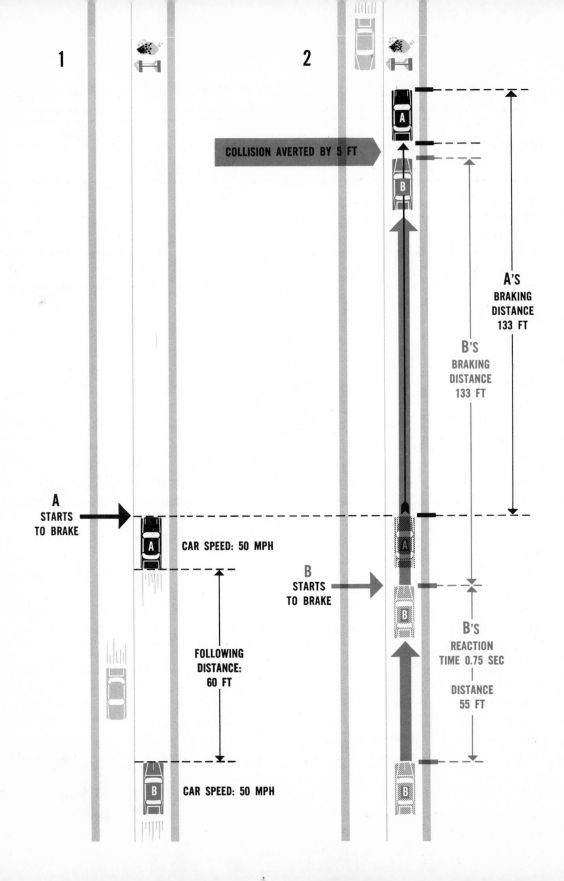

1

2

COLLISION AVERTED BY 5 FT

A
STARTS
TO BRAKE

CAR SPEED: 50 MPH

B
STARTS
TO BRAKE

A'S
BRAKING
DISTANCE
133 FT

B'S
BRAKING
DISTANCE
133 FT

B'S
REACTION
TIME 0.75 SEC

DISTANCE
55 FT

FOLLOWING
DISTANCE:
60 FT

CAR SPEED: 50 MPH

Fig. 7–11. Following distance: Allow at least 1 car length between you and the car ahead for each 10 miles per hour of your speed.

If at any time you find yourself rapidly overtaking the car ahead, this minimum is *not enough*. Moving more slowly, that car's braking distance is now *shorter* than yours. Slow down at once *before* an emergency develops.

That "Other Fellow" It is true, as some drivers have said, that maintaining a safe following distance ahead of you is difficult on some busy highways. Other drivers sometimes cut into that space. It is difficult, but it is still the intelligent, safe thing to do to drop back to a safe distance again. The poor driving of others does not excuse your getting into trouble. You know better.

Similarly, when moving back into line after passing another vehicle, do not cut in too near him. He needs a following distance, too! Check his position with your rear-view mirror before cutting in.

Many drivers do not understand the necessity for a safe following distance.

Fig. 7–10. Five feet—a narrow margin of safety.

They have not had an opportunity to study the facts about stopping distances as you have.

A safe "cushion" of clear space in front of your car allows you to stop less abruptly when the driver ahead "crash stops." This greatly lessens *your* chance of being hit from behind by any close-following vehicle.

Should you find someone "tailgating" your car, that is, driving very close to your back bumper, allow an *extra* margin of safety in front.

The further you are behind the vehicle ahead, the less of your field of vision is screened by that vehicle. A safe following distance gives you better visibility.

How You Can Help Sometimes, when you are chatting with friends who are not trained drivers, explain to them *stopping distance* (or danger zone) and the *minimum safe following distances*. You'll be doing them a big favor. Also, the more who know this, the safer highways will be for all.

To Talk About:

1. Define reaction time and discuss what the driver does during this time.

2. Define braking distance and list factors which determine this distance.

3. A driver should always be able to stop his car in the assured clear distance ahead. What is meant by the term "assured clear distance?"

4. Describe the danger zone and decide how you will think of this as you drive.

5. Describe situations which make an accident certain because of the reaction times and braking distances involved.

6. Show that the danger zone is flexible, and explain how the driver controls it.

7. How do you account for the fact that reaction times differ in the same person at different times?

8. If you notice that the vehicle behind you is much too close, should this knowledge in any way affect the distance you keep from the car in front of you?

9. Would it be possible for a person with extremely quick reactions to be a menace as a driver in some situations?

10. Discuss power brakes and whether or not they shorten braking distances.

11. Discuss factors which increase the danger zone.

12. Discuss the fact that any driver who hits a car in front of him is considered to be negligent.

To Do:

1. Secure a brake reaction detonator and make stopping-distance tests at 20 and 30 miles per hour in a place where there is no other traffic, or have someone come and give such a demonstration.

2. Measure along a curb the total stopping distances shown in Table 7–1 for 20 through 60 miles per hour so you will realize how far a car travels at these speeds before you can stop it.

3. If a reaction-time machine is available, test members of the class. Determine the average reaction time for the group. Discuss reasons why your reactions in actual driving situations would take considerably longer. What is the difference between simple and complex reactions?

4. Using a scale of 1 inch for every 60 feet of road, make a chart showing the danger zones at 20, 30, 40, 50, and 60 miles per hour. Indicate how many parallel-parked cars you would pass in this distance if one parked car requires 20 feet.

5. Assemble clippings of accidents in which following too closely was the cause. What happened and how many cars were involved?

6. Make a chart showing stopping distances at 20 miles per hour on various surfaces: dry pavement, wet pavement, snow, ice.

7. When you are a passenger in a car or bus, watch the speedometer and the road ahead. Learn to spot hazards *before* they enter your danger zone.

Two ships approach each other at night. A single, hoarse, mournful sound comes from one. It is echoed by a similar sound from the other. Each directs its course slightly to starboard (right), and a port-to-port passing is made. The left side of one ship passes nearest to the left side of the other. They "keep to the right."

On each ship, hundreds of passengers sleep peacefully on. They have confidence in the professional competence of the officers on watch and the time-tested "rules of the road" at sea. Their confidence is fully justified.

Those who ride with us in our cars should be able to have similar confidence in our driving competence. They are entitled to expect that we have learned *our* rules of the road. Also, other drivers and pedestrians who share the highways with us are entitled to expect us to conform to traffic rules. The significant point is this: *Whether piloting ships or driving motor vehicles, it is our responsibility to know the rules of the road and to obey them.*

Who Makes Traffic Laws?

Each state has the power to control those actions of people which strongly affect public safety. This is fundamental to our system of government. Adoption of laws controlling motor vehicles and their drivers is the responsibility of the state legislatures. On some traffic subjects, such as parking, one-way streets, and certain pedestrian regulations, the states share their powers with cities and towns.

Traffic Laws
Made by Man

As a result, municipal ordinances supplement state vehicle codes.

Alternatives to state responsibility would have been to vest such authority in either the Federal or the local government.

Fig. 8–1. An early Vermont law required a mature person to precede an automobile by one-eighth of a mile to warn persons traveling on the road of the car's approach.

If We Had Federal Control   Suppose we consider the possibility of having the Federal government enact our traffic laws. This would be undesirable for a number of reasons. Consider the following:

1. The enactment of traffic laws is a logical state function under our division of governmental powers.

2. Developing traffic laws requires large amounts of legislators' time. Members of the Congress would have to devote much time to studying state and local needs in addition to passing the laws. These activities would take time away from work which only a national legislative body can perform.

3. Federal traffic legislation would logically result in Federal enforcement. It would be very costly to employ the necessary number of Federal officers to enforce a Federal vehicle code.

There are two matters over which the Federal government appropriately exercises authority. It has certain controls over commercial vehicles transporting passengers or goods across state lines. The Federal government also exercises certain controls relating to bridges which cross navigable waters.

If We Had Local Control   Local control of traffic legislation would have serious disadvantages, as well. Local legislative bodies would not want to have this responsibility. If they nonetheless were given it, entirely different traffic regulations would exist among the many local communities. Chaos would result. Drivers who travel from place to place could not possibly know all the regulations they would be expected to obey. Vehicle codes are extensive publications which are costly to print, and most local communities would not wish to make such expenditures.

Even with present limited local authority to regulate traffic, difficulties often arise. Drivers proceeding from one municipality to another often encounter different speed limits for conditions which seem practically the same. Fortunately, many state and local authorities are working to establish realistic and reasonable speed limits. They are based on principles and methods proved by experience to be practical. As this process is extended, sections of highway with the same characteristics will have the same speed limit.

State vehicle codes provide uniformity in many traffic laws. Examples are general speed limits, right of way, and rules concerning overtaking and passing. Moreover, there is steadily increasing uniformity among the states on many basic traffic laws, or "rules of the road." Probably the greatest aid to the development of such uniformity is the Uniform Vehicle Code.

The Uniform Vehicle Code

We Americans traveling in our cars now pay little attention to state lines. Not so long ago, crossing state lines often meant encountering considerable differences in rules of the road. The more differences there are, the greater the chance is of misunderstanding, unintentional law violations, and accidents.

The need for agreement on uniform traffic laws has grown with increases in interstate motor vehicle travel. Out of this need developed the Uniform Vehicle Code, which is a guide for states in adopting their vehicle codes. A companion guide for municipalities is the Model Traffic Ordinance. It aids them in developing their traffic ordinances and properly relating them to their state vehicle code. Many states and cities have used these guides, and we drivers have been greatly benefited by the resulting sound and uniform traffic laws.

In general, the state vehicle code includes all the basic rules of the road for the entire state. The state vehicle code usually permits municipalities to regulate such local matters as parking, stops at intersections, and designation of one-way streets.

Motorists who travel from state to state are finding more uniformity in the rules of the road. However, this is not the only way the Uniform Vehicle Code helps. The Code also includes numerous other kinds of guide material for state vehicle codes. Examples are proposals for state legislation on vehicle registration, driver licensing, and vehicle equipment (such as brakes and lights).

Today, traffic laws receive very careful attention in our state legislatures and city councils. Such laws are vital to public safety. Every person who drives a car is responsible for knowing and obeying them.

Fig. 8–2. Our people often cross state lines.

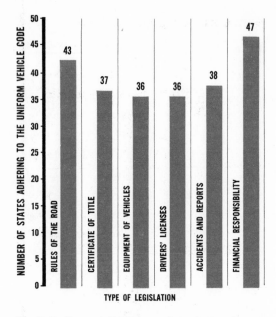

TYPE OF LEGISLATION

Fig. 8–3. Progress is being made in the number of states that conform to the Uniform Vehicle Code.

Rules of the Road

The following general rules for good driving are based on the *Uniform Vehicle Code* and the *Model Traffic Ordinance.* Regulations in your state or locality may differ from them. If so, you must be governed by the laws of the area in which you drive. If you plan to drive in *other* states and communities, be sure you know and obey their laws and regulations.

Many states publish well-illustrated digests of their rules of the road, written in a simple, nontechnical style. Without such rules, traffic conditions would be chaotic. No one could depend on being able easily to go where he wishes; vehicles would repeatedly be in hopeless tangles; there would be great delays. The number of accidents would be unbelievable!

Rules of the road—when obeyed by all —mean order in the traffic pattern. Here are seven common-sense rules of the road:

1. **Drive to the right of the road center.**

2. **Pass to the right of vehicles you meet.**

3. **Pass to the left of vehicles going in the same direction.**

4. **Allow overtaking vehicles to pass.**

5. **If driving slowly, keep to the right-hand lane.**

6. **Signal your intention to reduce speed, stop, turn, change lanes, or pass.**

7. **Always drive at a speed that is reasonable and prudent under existing conditions.**

Any direction given by a traffic officer or indicated by an official sign, signal, or road marking takes precedence over the customary rules of the road. Where there is no special direction, the rules of the road are proper guides.

These rules of the road are so fundamental that we scarcely think of them as laws. We observe them because of their obvious importance to avoiding accidents.

First Basic Principle   With so many drivers sharing the highways today, certain fundamental principles of procedure are necessary. One of the most basic of these is the following:

You as a driver must always obey right-of-way laws.

"Right of way" means the right to immediate use of the roadway, but use only in such a manner as will assure the safety of other drivers and pedestrians. A fundamental part of the right-of-way rule is the duty to drive in such a way as to avoid accidents.

In general, right-of-way rules indicate who shall yield when there is a potential conflict between vehicles or between a vehicle and a pedestrian. In other words, *they establish traffic priority.* You must always remember that you do not permanently have the right of way. You are required to *yield* it under certain circumstances.

The driver of an emergency vehicle, for instance, warns he is coming by use of a siren and/or flashing red light. He has immediate priority. It is the duty of all other drivers to yield the right of way to him. They must get out of an intersection, move as far to the right as possible and stop, or take any other needed action to clear the way for the emergency vehicle. The driver of an emergency vehicle, too, is responsible for knowing and obeying the traffic laws of his state.

Right-of-way Rules Keep in mind that you, as a driver, are required to know and obey the rules of the states and communities in which you drive. Here, from the Uniform Vehicle Code, are five right-of-way rules which, in most places, you will find in effect:

1. The driver approaching an intersection shall *yield* the right of way to a vehicle which has already entered the intersection from a different highway.

2. If two vehicles reach an uncontrolled intersection at the same time, the driver on the left shall *yield* the right of way to the driver on his right.

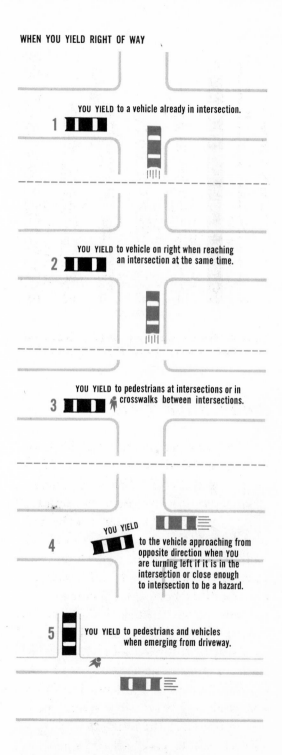

WHEN YOU YIELD RIGHT OF WAY

1 YOU YIELD to a vehicle already in intersection.

2 YOU YIELD to vehicle on right when reaching an intersection at the same time.

3 YOU YIELD to pedestrians at intersections or in crosswalks between intersections.

4 YOU YIELD to the vehicle approaching from opposite direction when YOU are turning left if it is in the intersection or close enough to intersection to be a hazard.

5 YOU YIELD to pedestrians and vehicles when emerging from driveway.

Fig. 8–4. Know your right-of-way rules.

3. Drivers shall *yield* the right of way to pedestrians crossing *at* intersections in accordance with regulations and crossing on marked crosswalks *between* intersections.

4. The driver within an intersection and intending to turn left shall *yield* the right of way to vehicles approaching from the opposite direction and within the intersection or so close to it as to constitute an immediate hazard.

5. A vehicle emerging from a driveway shall *yield* the right of way to vehicles on the street or highway and to pedestrians on the sidewalk.

Second Basic Principle   We are morally and legally obligated to do more than merely fulfill the letter of the law where danger to others may be involved. Whatever the circumstances, or whatever the actions of others, we are always bound by the following principle:

The driver of an automobile must always do everything he can to protect another driver or a pedestrian.

Even when the actions of another motorist or of a pedestrian are foolish or illegal, a driver has no right to let such actions result in an accident which he has the *last clear chance* to prevent. He may be held accountable for an accident which he did not directly cause but which *he could have helped avoid.*

When a driver shares the roadway with pedestrians, he has a special duty to drive so that he will not endanger them. He must realize that pedestrians may easily misjudge the speed and movement of cars. Also, some pedestrians have handicaps which sometimes prevent motorists from being able correctly to anticipate their movements. The law places a special responsibility on motorists to drive with care near pedestrians.

Fig. 8–5. The driver must protect the pedestrian.

Signs, Signals, and Markings

1 The *colors, shapes, sizes, and legends* of traffic signs, signals, and markings have been standardized so that they can be recognized quickly and easily throughout the country. The *Manual on Uniform Traffic Control Devices for Streets and Highways* sets forth the standards for states and municipalities to follow. For the driver, the result of this standardization is that he receives the vital messages of these signs, signals, and markings in one "language" instead of many. Adoption of these uniform standards has been a significant contribution to the safety and convenience of all who use the highways.

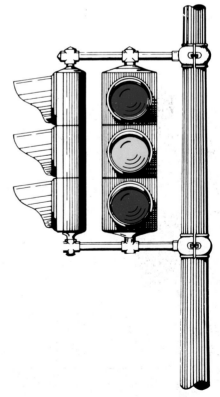

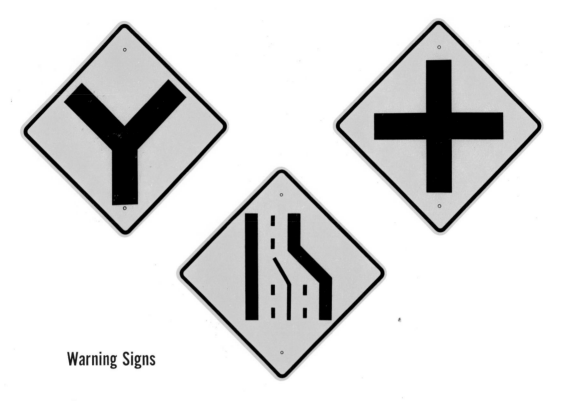

Warning Signs

❷ Drivers must be warned of hazardous conditions either on or adjacent to roadways and know what they are in time to take appropriate action. For this purpose *warning* signs are placed where drivers can easily see them well in advance of these hazardous conditions.

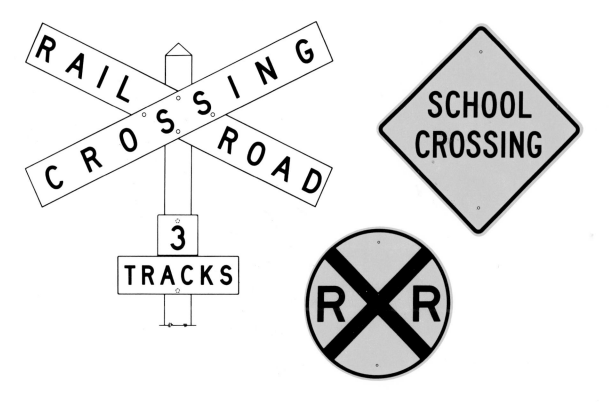

The legend or symbol of each warning sign clearly shows the driver what to expect. Warning signs call for *caution* and usually a reduction in speed. The intelligent, well-trained driver looks upon them as his good friends of the highway, not as restrictions upon his freedom of movement. They are warnings that arm him against dangers ahead.

Guide Signs

❸ Guide signs are of three principal types:

1. Route markers, identifying the highway by number and symbol as part of a national, state, or local network. Auxiliary markers point the direction of the route.

2. Destination and distance signs, showing directions and mileage to cities, towns, or other places ahead.

3. Informational signs, giving items of interest to travelers on the highway.

INTERSTATE

(STATE)

75

④ Interstate Highway System

This distinctive red, white, and blue route marker is used on the National System of Interstate and Defense Highways.

A green guide sign indicates the routes and names the most important places to be reached by leaving the highway at the nearby interchange.

Blue signs direct the traveler to rest areas and to service facilities.

**REST AREA
2 MILES**

DO NOT PASS

SPEED LIMIT 50

KEEP → RIGHT

ONE HOUR PARKING 9AM-7PM ←→

Regulatory Signs

5 This type of road sign informs highway users of certain traffic laws or regulations which apply to those sections of roadway where the signs are placed. Failure to comply with the directions indicated on such signs constitutes a violation of law. The primary purpose of these signs is to promote safe and efficient use of streets and highways.

YIELD

NO PARKING ANY TIME ←→

NO U TURN

NIGHT 45

PEDESTRIANS PROHIBITED

Pedestrian Signs and Signals

6 Standard signs and signals promote vehicular safety and efficiency. Pedestrian signs and signals are designed to protect and assist people on foot.

CROSS ON WALK SIGNAL ONLY

WALK ON LEFT FACING TRAFFIC

Road Markings

7 Markings are used either to supplement highway signs or signals or independently. They are used because sometimes the road conditions the driver must be aware of can best be indicated by markings on the pavement. Also, the driver can see them without diverting his attention from the roadway. Other markings are helpful in making obstructions or similar hazards more conspicuous.

A THREE-LANE ROAD

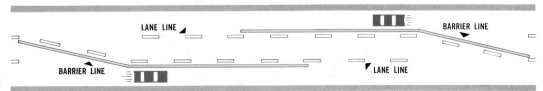

These markings define traffic lanes with broken white lane lines. They also show places where drivers are forbidden to pass other vehicles. A solid yellow barrier line on the driver's side of the broken line means that he may not cross.

FIRST AID STATION

FILLING STATION

RIGHT (LEFT) CURVE

MECHANICAL HELP

TELEPHONE

UNEVEN ROAD

ROAD INTERSECTION

DANGEROUS CURVE (Curves)

Double Curve, First to Right (Left)

TRAFFIC CIRCLE

DIRECTION TO BE FOLLOWED

UNSPECIFIED DANGER

COMPULSORY CYCLE TRACK

TRAFFIC CIRCLE

FIRST AID STATION

No Parking Fig. 1 Side Uneven Dates, Fig. 2 Even Dates

STOP AT INTERSECTION

End of Prohibition to Overtake

International Road Signs

8 Standard danger, regulatory, and informational road signs have been adopted internationally; they are used in European countries and elsewhere. A triangular shape is used to denote danger, circular signs give definite instructions, and rectangular signs give information. Although the colors used are not always uniform, the signs can easily be recognized by their shapes and symbols.

END OF SPEED LIMIT

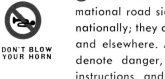
CUSTOMS, STOP

DON'T BLOW YOUR HORN

Restricted Stopping Or Waiting

Give Way To Approaching Traffic

Fig. 8–6.
Who had
the last
clear chance?

Speed Control

In general, state laws establish one of two types of speed limits: fixed (or absolute) speed limits, and flexible speed limits, called *prima facie* limits, which involve consideration of existing conditions.

Fixed Speed Limits Under such a speed-control law, certain selected speeds must not under any condition be exceeded. "Absolute" limits are set in terms of miles per hour, and motorists who exceed these limits can be arrested and penalized for speeding, regardless of how favorable conditions may be. Motorists who drive below such fixed limits cannot be arrested for "speeding," although they may be arrested for reckless driving or for driving at a speed which *under existing conditions* is unreasonable or imprudent.

Flexible Speed Limits These are legally known as *prima facie* speed limits. This type of speed-control law recognizes the fact that no one fixed speed limit is correct for a particular place all the time under all conditions. Whether or not a maximum speed limit is appropriate depends on highway, traffic, weather, light, and other conditions at the time. Hence, a flexible speed limit, or prima facie limit, is set. The court must decide whether or not a motorist is guilty of the charge against him after hearing all the conditions.

Suppose, for example, you are arrested for exceeding the prima facie speed limit of 50 miles per hour. You have a chance to prove to the court that, even though you were exceeding the prima facie limit, you were not driving too fast for existing conditions. This is not true in the case of the common, fixed, "absolute" speed limit. Suppose, on the other hand, an officer arrests you when you are driving at a speed lower than the prima facie limit. The officer must then convince the court that you were driving too fast for conditions—for example, because the road was icy or because traffic was exceptionally heavy.

The Basic Speed Rule   Drivers should always control their speed to comply with this basic rule: *Always drive at a speed which is reasonable and proper for existing conditions,* even where the law permits a higher speed in miles per hour.

Such a basic speed rule (generally having additional descriptive wording) is included in the law of every state. It holds good no matter what kind of speed limit is set by law. Following this basic rule and posted speed limits assures you of the best possible protection. Intelligent drivers always impose the basic rule on themselves, regardless of whether there are fixed or prima facie limits where they are driving.

Fig. 8–8. Speed zoning is based on traffic engineering.

Safe, prudent speeds vary with the type of highway, the driver's physical condition, brake efficiency, condition of pavement, weather, and traffic conditions. A speed which is reasonable when there are few persons or vehicles on the street may be excessive in heavy traffic. It may be dangerous at hours when school children are crossing the streets. Lower speed limits are sometimes set for nighttime driving (see Fig. 8–7). On the same stretch of roadway, speeds that are proper at certain times are foolish at others. Thus you can understand the great importance of always adhering to the basic speed rule!

Speed Zoning   There is now, fortunately, widespread recognition of the fact that no one numerical speed limit can possibly suit all stretches of all highways. Flexible speed limits constitute one way to help take account of this. Another constructive idea is that of *speed zoning.*

This means that studies and field observations are first made by traffic engineers to determine reasonable and proper speeds for certain stretches of highway under normal conditions. Then signs are installed to inform drivers of such a

Fig. 8–7. *Conditions determine safe speeds.*

speed limit for each "zone" (see Fig. 8–8). Whole sections of highway may be speed-zoned. Or, such special limits may be set for specific residential or business districts, or for curves, intersections, or school zones.

Your Responsibilities if You Are Involved in an Accident

If you are so unfortunate as to be involved in an accident, your character, judgment, and sense of social responsibility are put to the test. Everyone involved has certain obligations.

Your first obligation is to "stand by" and render assistance, if needed. Running away from an accident is cowardly and irresponsible. There may be an injured person who needs attention. Hit-and-run

drivers are held in the lowest esteem by their fellow men and are subject to very heavy penalty under the law. Your obligations, if involved in an accident, are to:

Stop immediately

Render assistance

Obtain medical help, if needed

Call an ambulance, if one is required

Give your name and address and the license number of your car. Ask the other driver for similar information

If possible, obtain the names and addresses of witnesses

Remain at the scene of the accident until your help is no longer needed

Make accident reports promptly to the police, the motor vehicle department, if required, and your insurance company or representative

Careful! Use extreme care in assisting an injured person. Doctors and Red Cross first-aid experts warn that unskilled handling, particularly when there are

Fig. 8–9. Everyone should have first-aid training.

broken bones, may increase the seriousness of the injury and even cause death.
For example, a fracture of the neck or
spine may often heal quite readily when
properly treated. The same injury, aggra-
vated by improper movement of the victim, may result in permanent paralysis or
death. *Avoid moving an injured person
carelessly or hurriedly, or lifting him into
a passenger car to rush him to the hospital.*
Unless you have completed a standard
first-aid course and know what is safe to
do, confine first aid to keeping the victim
warm and controlling his bleeding.

Every one should have first-aid training.
Immediate, intelligent aid can save a life
or make the doctor's later care more
effective. A first-aid kit should be carried
in your car, and you should know how
to use it. Why not contact your Red
Cross to organize a first-aid course?

The Aftermath   The legal results of a traffic
accident can be very serious. They are
even more serious if you have an accident
while breaking a traffic law. In that case,
you may be fined, or you may be put in
jail. You will have points assessed against
your record if your state uses a "point
system" (see Chapter 9, "Observance
and Enforcement"). Finally, your driver's
license may be suspended or revoked.
Thus, having an accident while violating
a traffic law *can involve you in a criminal
case.*

There can be other serious results. If
someone is injured in the accident, you
may be held responsible and sued for
damages. Where there is no injury but
there is property damage in an accident
in which you are involved, you may also
be sued. Whether you have to pay for
property damages or not is a matter for
decision in court. If you have an accident
while driving another person's car, both
you and the owner may be sued, and in
court you may be held responsible for
personal injury or property damage. Such
court cases are known as *civil cases.* You
may have to pay the other party the
amount of money which the judge or
jury decides, plus court costs. This sum
may be many thousands of dollars. It
may be much more than your insurance
policy covers! (See Chapter 17, "Buying,
Insuring, and Operating Your Car.") To
make the payments, you may be forced
to give up your own car and other possessions. You may also be required by the
court to pay part of your wages or salary
for many years!

But that's not all. In most states, if you
are involved in an accident you must
satisfy requirements of the "financial-responsibility," or "safety-responsibility,"
law (see page 118) in order to retain your
driving privilege. Usually, you must
satisfy court-imposed judgments against

THE JURY AWARDS
$47,000 DAMAGES

Fig. 8–10. Years of payment may follow an accident.

you, that is, pay an amount ordered by the court. You must also make provision (usually by insurance) for future payment of any damages against you in any future accident.

Nor is even *that* all, where insurance merit rating is in effect. In such places, you will have to pay more for your insurance if you have been involved in an accident. And the only way that you can again earn the merit rating is to maintain a record clear of accidents and of major violations for (usually) three years.

Indeed, being found responsible in an accident can have serious consequences —yet it is obvious that laws concerning traffic accidents must be strong and even severe.

Your Responsibilities if You Approach the Scene of an Accident

Suppose you come upon an accident (you are not involved) where the police have taken charge. Unless directed to do so, do not stop nearby. Police have plenty to do to aid the injured, to investigate the accident, and to keep other traffic safe and moving freely. Unnecessary onlookers are a nuisance and add to the hazards.

Suppose you witness an accident or come upon one that has just happened. What should you do? That depends. If you are qualified to render assistance and the accident appears serious, you should stop well out of the way and off the road and offer help. You might offer to obtain police and medical aid, possibly using the nearest telephone. You should note as accurately as possible the location of the accident so as to be able to direct the police, doctor, or ambulance correctly. If you witnessed the accident, you should give your name and address if requested in order to assist the innocent party. If *you* had the accident, you would want the witnesses to assist *you* in court.

Car Ownership, License, and Responsibility

As a car owner, you must meet certain legal requirements. You must obtain a certificate of title (or similar proof of ownership) when you buy a car. This is a legal paper, properly witnessed, which states that you purchased the car from its former owner and that you are now the proper owner. Then you must secure a vehicle registration card and license plates from your state motor vehicle department.

Certificate of Title   When you purchase a new car, the dealer signs a bill of sale and registers the purchase with the state authorities. Most states retain this bill of sale and issue a certificate of title which describes the car and names you as its owner. Those states which do not issue a certificate of title provide in some other way for you to have a paper indicating vehicle ownership.

Guard this certificate or paper carefully. You will need it if you sell your car. Certificates of title are of great value to

Fig. 8–11. Happy day! The state grants your privilege to drive.

both car owner and the state. A bona fide certificate of title generally assures you that you are not purchasing a stolen car. A thief does not possess the certificate of title unless the owner has been foolish enough to leave it in the car. Certificate-of-title requirements discourage thieves from stealing cars for the purpose of reselling them.

Vehicle Registration

Vehicle registration cards and vehicle registration tags or license plates protect an owner. Police frequently detect stolen automobiles through vehicle registration data. The license plates on your car can prove of unexpected value in helping the police locate you in emergencies when you are on a trip.

Your vehicle registration card must always be carried in the car or in your possession to show at the request of the police or motor vehicle department representative. This is required by law, so guard this card carefully.

Your Driver's License

Before you drive a car on the public highway, you must secure permission from the state. This is an important legal requirement. The state grants the driving privilege and determines what qualifications a person must have to obtain it. Your driver's license is the legal evidence that the state has granted you this privilege.

When you want to obtain a license, secure an application form. Fill it out and return it with the required fee to your state licensing authority.

If you want to learn to drive, in most states you must get a learner's permit. This allows you to practice driving for a designated period, provided a licensed driver is in the front seat beside you. You must then take an examination and secure a regular driver's license before the learner's permit expires, or you must renew the permit.

The state examiner will test you in various ways, depending on your state regulations. Here are items that may be included:

1. Your knowledge of motor vehicle regulations in your state
2. Tests of your vision
3. Your understanding of traffic signs, signals, and markings
4. A driving test in your car to check your skill, including such acts as starting, stopping, turning, signaling, starting on an upgrade, and parking

You must carry your driver's license at all times when operating a motor vehicle. You must show it to the police or a representative of the motor vehicle department upon request. When you change your address, you must notify the proper state office.

A good license test can provide a valuable "weeding-out" process. It can keep off the road persons who cannot drive properly, who are physically or mentally unqualified, or who are ignorant of traffic laws.

No doubt there will be important improvements in the reexamination of licensed drivers—especially of accident repeaters, violation repeaters, and the aged. Whether we like it or not, society will undoubtedly become stricter in controlling the driving privilege.

Some states require students under eighteen years of age who want a driver's license to pass an approved driver education course first. At least one state issues to new drivers under twenty-one years of age a provisional license. To earn a regular license, the driver must keep his record clear of major violations or accidents for two years. Some states require all applicants under twenty-one years of age to have a paid-up liability-

insurance policy or other evidence of their ability to pay damages if judged responsible for an accident. What do *you* think about the following questions?

Are our states too liberal in granting the right to operate motor vehicles and in permitting certain drivers to continue to drive? Are we paying more attention to the keen desire of individuals to operate cars than to the welfare and safety of the general public? Should there be more thorough and more strict licensing requirements and tests? Should there be more restricted or conditional licenses?

In carefully planned licensing programs, drivers of motorcycles, motorized bicycles, and motor scooters are required to have drivers' licenses. Special tests must be passed on a motorized cycle of the type the driver will operate before he is granted a license. Drivers of small powered vehicles can cause serious accidents. They should be licensed only if they have the necessary driving skills and are old enough to realize the need for careful driving and to accept full responsibility.

Fig. 8–12. Something to think about.

If a driver is convicted of any of certain serious offenses, some states require that his license be suspended or revoked for a period of time. In states which have a point system (as described in Chapter 9, "Observance and Enforcement") licenses are suspended or revoked for repeated violations of law or for a single violation of a serious nature. All states retain the right to suspend or revoke a driver's license for due cause.

Financial-responsibility Laws All states and the District of Columbia have enacted financial-responsibility, or "safety-responsibility," laws. These require a driver, under certain conditions, to pay any damages which a court has assessed against him for an accident and to provide proof of his ability to pay the costs (up to stated limits) of any future accident for which he is responsible.

Such laws require that a driver's license and registration certificate be suspended under certain circumstances. Following are the conditions under which this action may be taken by the state:

1. If he has a criminal conviction for certain serious violations of motor vehicle law and fails to show proof of financial responsibility for any future accidents.

2. If he is involved in an accident resulting in death, bodily injury, or substantial property damage *and* does not submit proof that he is able to pay the damages for which he may be held legally responsible.

Generally speaking, a driver must pay damages arising out of an accident for which he is responsible. Then he must prove, before he is permitted to drive a car again, that he can pay the costs of any future accident in which he may become involved. This is called *future proof.* He may give this proof by means of a suitable insurance policy. Most drivers choose this method. He may instead, however, provide a bond or deposit sufficient money or securities with the state.

Accident Compensation Funds Some states and Canadian provinces have established special funds from which accident victims can receive compensation for injuries caused by drivers who are financially irresponsible. These funds are often maintained by additional fees imposed on car owners who do not carry liability insurance.

Financial-responsibility laws help greatly to assure payment of accident-caused damages. They help to keep financially irresponsible drivers off our streets and highways.

Regulations Concerning Equipment

The Uniform Vehicle Code includes regulations as to equipment on all motor vehicles. These regulations are intended to benefit traffic safety or traffic movement. As more states adopt provisions consistent with those in the Code, we all gain because of its protective and other features. Chiefly, these regulations cover:

Lights on motor vehicles; their number, type, intensity, and use

Brakes, and the performance standards of braking equipment

Warning devices required or permitted on different kinds of vehicles

Mufflers and their condition

Mirrors and their placement

Windshields and windshield wipers, and their condition

Safety-glass requirements for windshields and side and rear windows

Condition of tires

Warning devices to be used on disabled vehicles

Passenger automobiles, trucks, and buses are supplied by the manufacturer with at least the minimum safety equipment required by law. It is your responsibility as a driver to keep these devices in good working order and to use them legally.

Small Motorized Vehicles

Small two-wheeled and three-wheeled vehicles with motors, such as motor scooters and motorized bicycles, are defined by traffic regulations as motor vehicles. They must be registered and are subject to the same rules of the road as motorcycles—and to some of the same equipment requirements. If you drive one of these vehicles, be sure you know what the law requires of you and your machine.

Too often, small motorized vehicles are not legally equipped. This is especially true with respect to lights and brakes. When a motor is added to an ordinary bicycle, the normal brake is no longer safe for the increased weight and speed. Whether hand or foot brake, it must be adequate to permit stopping safely at higher speeds. Many bicycle lights are not adequate when the bicycle is motorized and can go much faster. When there is no storage battery, the lights may fail to give clear vision for the longer stopping distances.

These are matters which warrant more attention as traffic and the numbers of such small motorized vehicles increase. Parents and the general public should insist on sound regulations and precautions as to use of such vehicles. What measures would *you* advocate?

The Driver and the Law

Traffic laws are made for our benefit to prevent accidents and to make traffic movement efficient. We know that violations of law defeat both objectives. As drivers, we are both legally and morally obliged to obey the law. Moreover, it makes good sense!

By "the law" we mean the rules and regulations which legally apply to us *in any location in which we may be driving*. To *obey* means we must *know*. A good motto for the new driver to adopt would be, "Learn and obey—and enjoy driving."

To Talk About:

1. Explain the principle of "last clear chance." Give examples of situations in which it might apply.

2. Discuss the idea that "nobody ever *has* the right of way, but someone is expected to *yield* it." How should this interpretation of the right of way affect your actions?

3. What are the advantages and disadvantages of fixed speed limits and prima facie speed limits?

4. What is the difference between a criminal- and a civil-court case resulting from an automobile accident?

5. To what extent does a financial-responsibility law protect innocent victims of accidents?

6. Does your state have some kind of point system under which licenses may be suspended or revoked? Discuss its merits.

7. Discuss a driver's moral obligation to obey the law.

8. The basic speed law is that a driver must always drive at a speed that is reasonable and proper for existing conditions. What should you consider in deciding what this speed should be?

9. What do you think should be the minimum legal driving age? Discuss this with a traffic-police official, judge, or representative of the state motor vehicle department or highway patrol.

To Do:

1. Study the Uniform Vehicle Code as to (*a*) right of way; (*b*) overtaking and passing; (*c*) speed; and (*d*) traffic signals.

2. Examine your own state motor vehicle code. Find out any important ways in which it differs from the provisions set forth in the Uniform Vehicle Code. Make a list of changes which you think should be made in your state's traffic laws to make them consistent with the Uniform Vehicle Code. Discuss this list with your group. What practical steps could be taken by interested citizens to secure such changes?

3. On a traffic board, or the blackboard, set up various right-of-way situations. Indicate which driver should yield. Study these until you understand them and see how they help to make traffic move safely and smoothly.

4. Find out the procedure for obtaining a certificate of title in your state. When you buy a car, exactly what should you do? Does it make any difference whether you buy a new or a used car? Where should you keep this document? When you sell your car, what do you do with the certificate of title?

5. Find out about the driver licensing requirements in as many states as possible. In what ways do they differ? Suggest any changes you would make in your state licensing program. What types of drivers would you eliminate by the program you have set up?

6. Find out how many states now require applicants under eighteen years of age to complete a driver education course before being granted a license? Would you recommend that all applicants for an original license, regardless of age, be required to complete a driver education course? Is this preferable to raising the age for obtaining a license?

Observance and Enforcement

In studying the psychology of the driver in Chapter 2, his attitude toward law was considered. Although that attitude is appropriately included there, it is very closely related to this chapter, as well. Review "The Driver's Attitude Toward Law," page 31, and return to this point. Then, how would you answer the following questions? (1) What is the relationship between a person's *attitude* toward law and his *observance* of law? (2) When does *enforcement* of law become necessary for our protection?

In speaking of obedience or conformance to law, the term *observance* is often used. In this sense, observance means voluntary obedience to law. Let's consider what observance of law and enforcement of law mean to us.

Safety and Efficiency Are the Goals

The best possible situation on our streets and highways would be this: every person would always drive and walk according to existing laws, rules, and regulations. Ideally, everyone would do this *voluntarily*.

It is voluntary observance that makes laws effective. If the great majority of people were not law abiding, enforcement efforts would be futile. Law would have little real meaning. Traffic-law enforcement alone would need an officer in every vehicle on the highway.

Our traffic laws, rules, and regulations were adopted because experience proved them to be necessary for traffic safety and efficiency. Obeying them is not only our duty as citizens, it is also common sense. They are for our protection.

The Three E's

There are several basic approaches to achieving safety and efficiency on our streets and highways. Three of the more important approaches are "The Three E's"; they are Education, Engineering, and Enforcement.

Your driver education course is the best example there is of the first "E." Press, radio, television, posters, and other means are also used to educate the public. The value of education in achieving our goals has been firmly established by careful research.

Engineers contribute significantly to traffic safety through their use of scientific principles in planning, design, construction, and operation of modern highways.

The word "enforcement" usually brings to mind the image of a policeman. When "rules of the road" are violated, it is the duty of the police to take appropriate action. They instruct or warn drivers, issue "tickets" ordering them to court, and occasionally take them in for immediate court action. These activities also can be considered a form of driver education.

It is difficult to draw a definite line between enforcement and education. Policemen are often called upon to instruct. Judges frequently inform and instruct people who come before them in court.

Many people who drive, lacking your opportunity for a course in driver educa-tion, receive some instruction in other ways. For example, they study the state driver's manual. Other publications, safety campaigns, newspaper and magazine articles, and radio and television programs all play a part in keeping the public informed.

The goals of both education and enforcement are to teach people to drive and walk safely and to promote efficient movement of traffic. The majority of people do a good job in driving and walking most of the time. Unfortunately, however, many of us knowingly or thoughtlessly violate some traffic regulation now or then, and a few persons are guilty of frequent violations. It is the job of enforcement officers to deal with all people whose actions constitute a violation of the law.

Rules of the Road

In any civilized society, it is necessary that there be rules of acceptable behavior. Without them there would be bad feelings, chaos, and many accidents. Traffic laws are a necessary basis for convenient, safe, and efficient use of our streets and highways. Unsafe drivers and careless pedestrians make the road hazardous for others. Most driving and walking rules, or "rules of the road," have been developed out of the customs and experience of many people. Drivers, traffic engineers, police, judges, lawyers, educators, and others with traffic responsibilities have contributed. Our laws represent their best thinking about what is necessary for efficiency and safety on the highway. Our only intelligent course as drivers is to understand these laws and to observe them.

Fig. 9-1.
High school
driver education
is one of the best
hopes we have
for brightening
our traffic future.

Fig. 9-2.
Traffic engineers
plan for the
safe and efficient
operation
of the highway.

Fig. 9-3.
Student cooperation
with police
helps the
community.

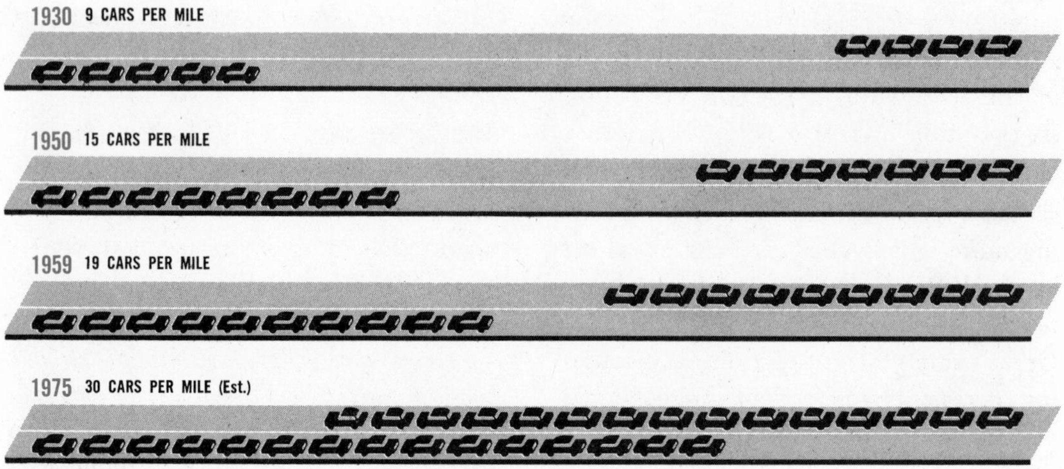

1930 9 CARS PER MILE

1950 15 CARS PER MILE

1959 19 CARS PER MILE

1975 30 CARS PER MILE (Est.)

Fig. 9–4. The number of cars per mile of road in the United States is growing.

Police Responsibility

Long before the automobile was on the scene, some traffic regulation was necessary. Growing numbers of automobiles emphasized the need for increasing supervision of street traffic. The police were the only existing group with sufficient organization and authority to meet the new problem. They were assigned the task.

Although most people are willing to observe traffic laws, police are still necessary. Foolish, selfish, unsafe acts, if allowed to go unchecked, would seriously endanger everyone. Those who would voluntarily obey the law do not always know what the law is. How many violations do you see committed by people *you know* who do not mean to break any law?

Another necessary aspect of police work is *direction* of traffic. This and the enforcement function make police operations vitally necessary.

A Major Problem In the early days of the automobile it found few buyers, and it was a rare thing to see one on the road. Roads were not yet ready for modern traffic. Today's finest cars might never succeed in making a cross-country tour under the highway conditions of those days. Traffic problems were unknown and undreamed of.

Today, motor vehicles are practically everywhere. You are almost never "the only one on the road." Cars seem to move in streams, whether rushing along a superhighway or crawling on a crowded city street.

There are few families without cars today, and nearly one out of every five automobile-owning families has more than one, a recent survey showed. This causes the traffic problem. There are over 82 million vehicles on our roads and over 92 million drivers! Averaging about 10,000 miles per year, they travel an almost incomprehensible 820 *billion*

124

miles per year. Nearly two-thirds of the automobiles and one-half of the trucks in the world are in the United States. Registration of motor vehicles in other countries has been increasing each year.

Our Needs Grow Manufacturers are building more and livelier cars. States, aided by the Federal government, are building many more miles of streets and highways. Great centers of population are becoming increasingly dependent upon the free movement of motor vehicles.

With this tremendous growth, a need is developing for better laws, more supervision, and more enforcement. Now more than ever, the practice of *voluntary observance* is clearly a necessity.

Police Traffic Direction Some people think of policemen as uniformed men who ride around in squad cars looking for violators to whom they can give tickets. Issuing tickets is only a small part of the work of most traffic officers. A main job is *directing* and *aiding* the movement of vehicles. The purpose of this work is to keep the road safe and open for the free movement of traffic. Sometimes the traffic officer stands in a busy intersection and directs vehicular and pedestrian traffic. So complex and variable are traffic movements at times that such traffic direction is needed in place of lights and signs.

Sometimes, the policeman "cruises" in a squad car, watching for dangerous or congested conditions. He must, at the same time, be ready to deal with any dangerous driving or illegal parking or loading which he may see. He is always subject to call in *any* kind of an emergency.

Whatever his tasks may be, he is *helping drivers* move as efficiently as possible. He is keeping the road *as safe as possible.*

Police as Enforcers Part of the traffic officer's job is, of course, enforcing the law. It is part of his bigger job of traffic supervision. His duty is to see that drivers and pedestrians obey traffic rules established for their benefit.

Accident records show that practically every traffic collision involves at least one violation. This fact alone demonstrates the protective nature of our traffic laws and regulations. It shows that violations are a hazard to everyone. Also, studies have proved that good programs of traffic-law enforcement reduce the numbers of accidents.

Fig. 9–5. Directing traffic is but one of the many duties of the policeman.

Fig. 9–6. Specter! The traffic-law violator lives under a shadow.

These facts permit only one conclusion: police supervision of traffic saves lives, prevents injuries, and greatly reduces property damage.

"Handing out tickets," as some express it, is not pleasant for the officer. In many places, he has to go to court *on his own time.* He has to testify effectively against the accused person, presenting the *facts* and letting the judge decide. He would much rather be home or out on the road helping and guiding traffic.

Accident Investigation You have heard the sirens and seen the flashing red lights of police vehicles. This often means that there has been an accident involving costly vehicle damage, frayed nerves, often injury—tragedy. This is another of the officer's duties which isn't easy or pleasant.

The police must reach the scene quickly, often giving first aid, fighting a gasoline fire, or directing traffic away from a dangling live wire caused by the accident. Often police must remove victims from dangerous situations. They must get doctors and ambulances when needed and occasionally transport injured persons to hospitals. These are immediate duties.

Then they must investigate the circumstances of each accident thoroughly and objectively. This, as well as the emergency actions, requires training and judgment. They must find out as much as possible about how and why the accident happened, who was involved, and whether or not a law was violated. As far as possible, they determine who was responsible. They make accurate, detailed reports.

Accident Analysis All the facts cited in the reports are collected and systematically analyzed. Sometimes this is done in the traffic engineer's office. Findings are used in evaluating the enforcement, control devices, traffic regulations, and supervision then in effect. Many improvements in existing programs are based to a great extent on the study of accidents. The better the reporting and analysis, the better the chance of preventing accidents in the future.

Planned Enforcement Many police departments record accident locations on large *spot maps* which show all streets and roads. Different-colored pins are used to indicate, for example, whether the accident involved fatality, personal injury, or property damage only. These pins are

Fig. 9-7. Spot maps show where accidents occurred.

placed at the exact location of each accident. Several spot maps may be maintained to show, for example, seriousness of accidents, pedestrian accidents, daylight versus darkness accidents.

Accident spot maps, with further data from accident reports, are used in planning action. They help assure that traffic officers are used to maximum effectiveness. Officer assignments take account of the violations and locations associated with the most and worst accidents. Thus the police are able to concentrate their activities to achieve smoothest traffic flow and fewest accidents. This is "selective enforcement" at its best. Accident data also help assure best use of traffic-control devices.

Traffic Court

Good traffic courts are also essential to observance and enforcement. Like the police, their broad objective is to prevent accidents and to help assure a smooth and efficient flow of traffic. To accomplish this, they:

1. *Educate drivers*. In part, this involves interpreting the law, in part producing a better understanding of why the law exists—what's behind it.

2. *Penalize violators*. This, in a sense, has educational value, also. It involves determining guilt and assigning appropriate penalties. Americans are entitled to a fair court trial when accused of violation of law.

Traffic judges generally study local traffic-safety problems and know the accident picture in their communities. Thus, they know the driving practices and violations that are causing traffic-safety troubles. They work to discourage these acts and hence to reduce the accident toll.

Like the police, our traffic-court judges want voluntary observance of traffic law. Most court procedures are directed to that end. In certain cases, the judge may

Fig. 9-8. A radar set used for enforcement and for traffic speed studies.

not impose a fine or jail sentence. He may require certain violators to attend an evening driver education school. These "driver-improvement" schools, to the extent which limited time permits, teach the same things you study.

Many judges begin each session of traffic court with a short talk on traffic safety. They point out the seriousness of the community's traffic problems and stress the importance of acceptance of individual responsibility in traffic.

In helping to enforce the law, the court must, in many cases, assign penalties. It is a means of impressing on the violator the importance of obeying the law in the future. The penalty frequently is a fine. For some violations, the fine for a first offense is usually not large. If the same person appears as a "repeat violator," the penalty is usually heavier. Sometimes a jail sentence is necessary to convince the violator that he must stop his dangerous

Fig. 9–9. Drivers should find this choice easy.

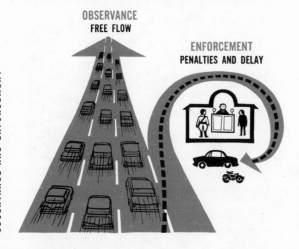

OBSERVANCE AND ENFORCEMENT

conduct. In very serious cases, the matter may be referred to the state motor vehicle administrator so that he can determine whether the violator's driving license should be suspended or revoked.

Point Systems

In some states, traffic convictions are reported to the state licensing authority. These violations then become a part of the driver's record. For each violation, a certain number of "points" is charged against him. Passing a STOP sign, violating a traffic signal, failing to signal, etc., are each assigned a standard number of points. Figure 9–10 shows a typical schedule of violation points.

Procedures vary, but a common one is to send a warning letter when a driver has accumulated a certain number of points in a two-year period. If his point score reaches a specified higher amount, he may be called in for an interview. He can then cite any extenuating circumstances (that is, circumstances that may lessen his guilt). One result of the interview may be suspension of his driving license. Or, the violator may be cautioned or may be given certain tests. The interviewer may seek to improve the driver's attitude. After a specified higher number of points has been accumulated, his driving license may be suspended—for a short or long time. Some states automatically revoke licenses on points, and this can result from *one* serious violation.

Typical point-system scale.*

Offense	Points charged
Driving, or permitting another to drive, under the influence of alcohol or drugs	12
Involvement in fatal accident (if held responsible)	12
Leaving the scene of an accident	8
Reckless driving	6
Exceeding speed limit	4
Other violations	3
Three convictions within 18-month period	additional 3

* A driver who is charged with 12 points in a three-year period is called before the director of motor vehicles to show cause why his driving privilege should not be revoked.

Fig. 9–10. Traffic violations are recorded as points against a driver.

Generally, a driver is entitled to a hearing before suspension or revocation if he requests one.

A well-planned and well-administered point system can be a very effective enforcement method. One basic merit is that each driver builds his own record and knows "where he stands" at all times. A good point system "catches up" with a persistent violator. It can help greatly to impress the violator who is not much affected by fines. Indeed, fines alone may mean little to some drivers who can easily afford them. But, suspension of his driving privilege is one of the most serious actions many violators can imagine! (For example, think what it could mean to a salesman with a large territory to cover by car.)

Some states charge appropriate points against an individual's record even though the driver was convicted of the violation in another state.

Central Driver Register

Some drivers whose licenses have been suspended or revoked have illegally obtained a driving license in another state. They withheld the information that their license had been suspended or revoked. Moreover, there is strong support for the idea that a driver guilty of a very serious offense in another state should have this information entered on his "home state" driving record. For such reasons, Congress authorized the establishment of a country-wide National Driver Register Service in the Bureau of Public Roads. This organization will maintain those records of revocations of licenses reported by participating states for drunken driving and for violation of a motor vehicle law resulting in the death of a person. This plan will help hold the individual responsible for his traffic actions wherever he may be.

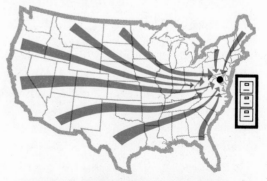

Fig. 9–11. The central driver register records violations involving fatalities and drunken driving.

Fig. 9–12. Most drivers voluntarily obey; a few don't.

Driving Is a Privilege

It is a recognized principle of our law that a state authority decides which residents of that state shall be licensed to drive. The state vehicle code specifies what qualifications the driver must have —his age, vision, physical fitness, knowledge, skill, etc. It also specifies the conditions of licensing and the cost and duration of the license.

Generally, most drivers voluntarily obey the law and drive safely. *This is the way in which a person earns the privilege of continuing to drive.* The process of ob- taining the first license is only a test of our initial fitness to drive. Our driving behavior from then on is actually what earns us the continuing driving privilege. Our licensing authorities and our courts uphold this principle.

You Can Help

The best guarantee of traffic orderliness and safety in any community is individual responsibility. This shows in how we drive and walk. It shows, too, in our support of sound traffic measures.

Police, court, and other responsible officials can do much when actively supported by the public—including you. And you don't even have to wait until you are a voter!

Effective traffic-improvement programs must have adequate personnel and facilities. Only the community can make them possible.

Police and court personnel should be selected and given responsibilities in relation to their qualifications and abilities. Political assignment of traffic jobs should not be tolerated by the citizens of any community. Specialized education and training courses should be encouraged as a sound means of improving traffic-law enforcement.

Police vehicles, equipment, and supplies should be adequate in amount, modern in design, and properly maintained. Traffic courtrooms should meet modern standards of adequacy of size and equipment, and of appearance.

When existing programs are not operating successfully, appropriate studies should be made. Outside experts are sometimes warranted, and their recommendations should be carefully considered.

All such things depend upon an alert, interested, and informed citizenry. You are one of the citizens. You, working actively with others, can make your community a safer and more pleasant place to live. You are preparing for it now.

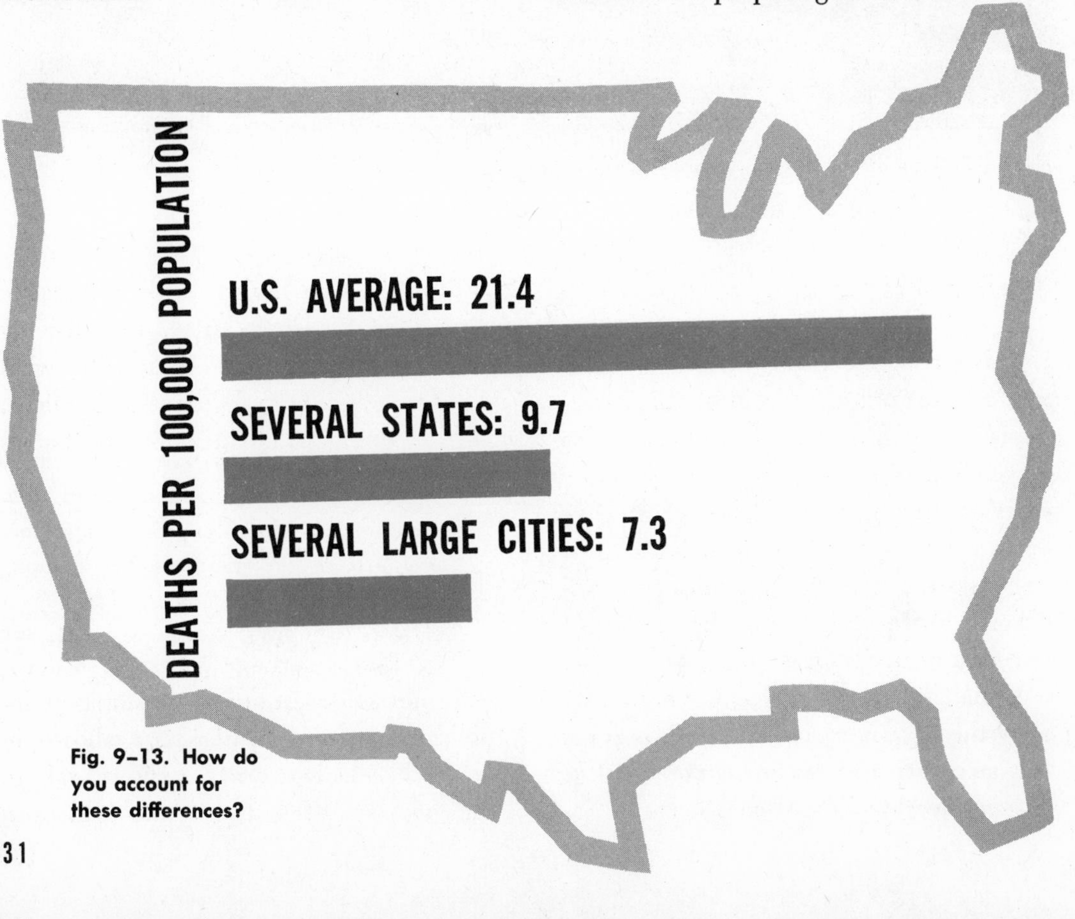

DEATHS PER 100,000 POPULATION

U.S. AVERAGE: 21.4

SEVERAL STATES: 9.7

SEVERAL LARGE CITIES: 7.3

Fig. 9–13. How do you account for these differences?

Fig. 9–14. "Well, officer, it was like this. . . ."

To Talk About:

1. After receiving your license, how will you keep informed of changes in traffic laws?
2. Discuss the probable effects of fines, jail sentences, and other penalties.
3. Discuss a sensible program for dealing with violation repeaters. What are the merits of a point system? Do you think drivers should be charged with points for violations in other states?
4. What do you think are the best ways of improving the traffic behavior of the general public? Explain.

5. What are the advantages and limitations of the following means of traffic education: (*a*) newspaper features and drawings; (*b*) radio announcements and radio programs; (*c*) television programs; (*d*) motion pictures; (*e*) a permanent community organization for safety work; (*f*) posters in store windows, service stations, and elsewhere; (*g*) meetings and lectures; (*h*) special campaigns, such as safety week and courtesy week; (*i*) a safe drivers' club; (*j*) adult education courses; (*k*) outdoor advertising?

6. Some people believe, "It's all right if you don't get caught!" How does this attitude make for trouble? How can it be changed?

7. In relation to voluntary observance of the law, talk about driving when underage and allowing unlicensed friends to drive.

8. The age at which one can obtain a license varies among the states. Consider why this is so.

9. Debate: "Resolved: That use of clearly marked police cars is more effective in traffic-law observance and enforcement than the use of unmarked cars."

10. Discuss the basic lack of morality shown by persistent traffic-law violators.

To Do:

1. Have some members of the group visit a session of the local traffic court and report to the class on the cases they heard. What were the most frequent violations? Did the judge do any "educating"?

2. Find out the procedure in your town for changing a traffic regulation. Is it an easy or difficult process?

3. Practically every traffic collision involves at least one violation. If you made a study of the causes of accidents in connection with Chapter 1, "What Driving Means to You," refer to these causes now and review the violations involved. If you did not make such a study, assemble clippings now and analyze them.

4. Secure several large maps of your local area. Use them in one or more of the following ways: (*a*) "spot" with pins the locations of accidents; (*b*) use special color for those involving pedestrians; (*c*) "spot" intersections or other areas which you have found to be particularly dangerous; (*d*) mark places where members of the class agree that some change in existing conditions is needed. After your study is completed, invite a local traffic officer to come and discuss the results with you.

5. Discuss the Driver Register authorized by Congress. Should it include only cases of drunken driving and fatalities?

6. There are a number of teen-age organizations which promote better driving. Find out about these and see if it would be desirable to join one and work on some of the projects. If you prefer, consider starting a local organization to promote voluntary observance and sound enforcement of traffic regulations.

7. Invite your traffic-court judge to talk to your class. Ask him to discuss his place both as educator and law-enforcement official. What does he think of fines? What does he think would help most to reduce traffic accidents?

8. Plan and put into effect ways for making traffic-law observance "the thing to do" among members of your group.

9. Find out what five types of violations produce the most convictions in your town. Do you think these are the violations which need most attention? If not, which violations should have more attention? Why don't they have it?

Mature Driving Practices

A newspaper reporter was talking to a blind man who operated a newsstand at a busy corner. The reporter was impressed by the wisdom of the blind man and enjoyed talking with him whenever possible. The stand was near the curb, and sounds of traffic were heard all day. When cars stopped for the traffic light, voices of drivers and pedestrians could often be distinguished.

This day, as the light changed, a vehicle near the curb came to a tire-screeching halt opposite the newsstand. The voices of the driver and another man with him could be heard. They were deep, hoarse, weary voices. They were angry, complaining voices—apparently displeased that so many other people were unreasonable enough to use "their" street. They called the traffic light "ridiculous" and "stupid."

As the light changed and the car roared away, the blind man said smilingly to his friend, "There go a couple of spoiled babies."

"Babies?" said his companion, "How old do you think those two are?"

"Oh, I'd guess about fifty-five," was the remarkably accurate answer.

With the very next change of the light, a car stopped at the same spot smoothly and quietly. The reporter noted that the driver and his companion, talking quietly after the car stopped, were quite young. He noted, too, that the blind man was listening to their young voices. As the light turned green for the driver, pedestrian footsteps could be heard completing an unhurried crossing in front of his car. The driver, then silent and concentrating on his task, started the car smoothly and quietly.

As it moved on, the reporter asked the blind man, "And who do you think those . . ."—he almost said "kids"—"two were?"

The blind man smiled. He knew. "A young man and a young woman," he said.

135

10 Driving in the Country

When we think of going for a country drive, the picture that first comes to mind is one of pleasant, relaxed, almost perfectly safe travel through fields, woods, and villages. The dangers of congested city traffic seem far away.

Facts the Driver Should Know

Does it come as a shock to learn that in just such a rural setting imminent, unrealized danger lurks? Almost three times as many motor vehicle deaths occur on rural roads as in urban areas. Most occur on straight, clear roads. A great many victims simply "ran off the road" and did not collide with another vehicle! Knowing that country roads have far fewer intersections, cars, trucks, buses, pedestrians, and bicycles, one naturally wonders why.

What are the factors that make this seemingly simple, safe car operation not so simple and sometimes dangerous?

The Illusion of Security   The modern car is a smooth-running, powerful, fast, and quiet machine. People riding in it do not have a feeling of its true speed and momentum. It is only when an emergency arises and the car must be stopped quickly—or actually hits something—that its real power shows. The quiet efficiency of the car sometimes lulls us into forgetting its speed, momentum, and the ever-present need for *control*. Our feeling of great need for alertness, foresight, and *constant* attention to driving may slip away as we ride.

There is no doubt that high speed makes rural-highway accidents more severe. Why do so many drivers continue to drive too fast for conditions when this fact is known? There is a reason. The human being becomes quickly adjusted to increased speed and loses his realiza-

Fig. 10–1. In the quiet of the country a driver often has an illusion of security.

tion of it. Experts say he becomes *velocitized.*

This condition is evident when a driver leaves a 50-mile-per-hour highway and enters a village street. He usually feels that he is "crawling" at 35 or 40. Many violators of 25-mile-per-hour village and town speed limits have been genuinely surprised when given summonses for speeding. Many, meeting with an emergency at an intersection, had no idea of their speed until they tried to stop.

Well-trained, experienced drivers know that they grow accustomed to high speed and become unaware of it. They compensate by *checking the speedometer frequently.*

Driving Ahead Under the heading "Foresight," in Chapter 2, "The Psychology of the Driver," the recognition of danger-in-the-making well ahead is shown to be extremely important. Sighting a *possible* emergency ahead, the good driver slows down and carefully analyzes the situation he is approaching. He decides just what he will do *if* the emergency develops. If he recognizes no alternative to an accident, should the threatened danger materialize, he slows down so he *can* stop. He stops well short of the point of a "crash stop." He is "driving ahead." This is the judgment that beginners should develop.

Lifesaving Tips How much pain and trouble could be avoided in life if we could see the future! How well we could live if we knew of certain events ahead of time!

The tips on the immediate future in driving are traffic *signs, signals,* and *markings.* They are called *traffic-control devices.*

Fig. 10–2. What do these sign shapes mean? (See color section following page 110.)

In our life as drivers we actually get clues to the future. The driver who ignores such "breaks" is woefully stupid! Here are the smart driver's tips on the *near* future.

Signs Traffic signs have three main purposes:

1. To regulate traffic
2. To warn of hazardous conditions
3. To guide or show direction

For quick identification, signs generally follow uniform standards of shape, color, wording, symbol, and position along streets and highways. To help drivers see these signs easily at night, traffic-control agencies have reflectorized or lighted many of them.

Even before you are close enough to read the message on a sign, you should recognize its general meaning by its standard shape and color.

Signals Commonly called "traffic lights," the traffic engineer usually refers to them as "traffic-control signals."

The standard light colors are given below, together with their meanings:

1. Red—Stop.
2. Yellow—Do not enter the intersection.
3. Green—Go, if roadway is clear.
4. Flashing red—Stop. Proceed only when safe.
5. Flashing yellow—Caution.
6. Green arrow—Traffic moving in the direction of the arrow may proceed.

The yellow signal precedes the red in standard signal operation.

For quick identification when partly

139

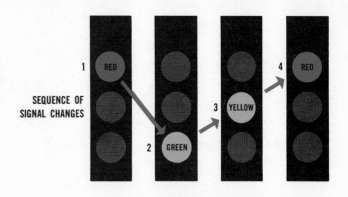

HORIZONTAL TRAFFIC-CONTROL SIGNAL

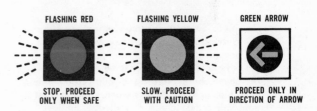

Fig. 10–3. Traffic signals—their arrangement and meanings.

screened from view, and for drivers who are color blind to any degree, signals are standardized as to position. When set vertically, the red should be on top, the yellow in the middle, and the green at the bottom. In horizontal installations of traffic signals, the red is at the left, the yellow is in the middle, and the green at the right.

Markings Important information is often given to the driver by lines, lettering, or symbols on the pavement. Traffic lanes on highways are shown in this way. Pedestrian crosswalks, vehicle stop lines, no-passing zones, and left, right, and straight-ahead lanes are among these instructions. Yellow curb markings show

Fig. 10–4. Road markings on a two-lane road.

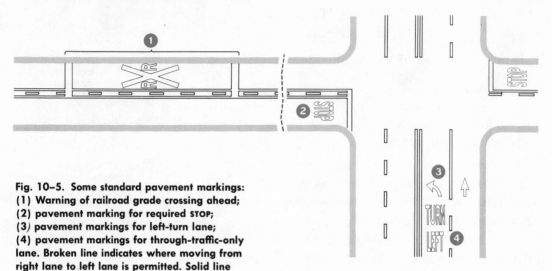

**Fig. 10–5. Some standard pavement markings:
(1) Warning of railroad grade crossing ahead;
(2) pavement marking for required STOP;
(3) pavement markings for left-turn lane;
(4) pavement markings for through-traffic-only
lane. Broken line indicates where moving from
right lane to left lane is permitted. Solid line
indicates where it is not.**

no-parking areas. Individual parking stalls are also outlined by painted lines. The good driver is alert for these pavement markings as well as for signs and signals.

Teamwork in Traffic

The inexperienced spectator tends to watch only the "stars" of the football game. He misses most of the play. He doesn't understand the signals being used, the carrying out of individual assignments, or even the real meaning of the word "team."

How futile would be the brilliance of a Napoleon, a Grant, or a Lee if it were not for the teamwork of thousands upon

thousands of "ordinary" soldiers! The even greater numbers of people involved and the complexity and speed of modern motor vehicle traffic make teamwork on the highway no less important. And teamwork, in turn, is completely dependent upon communication among drivers. This is accomplished by using hand and electrical turn signals.

Signaling Your Intentions Drivers must constantly adjust to the actions of other drivers. Each must know what the other will do. Chaos and tragedy follow when communication and teamwork break down. Highway communication depends upon a recognized system of signals.

Four common methods of signaling your driving intentions are:

1. By the lane position of the car.

2. With left hand and arm. See Fig. 10–6 for the standard hand signals recommended by the Uniform Vehicle Code. *Learn them well.* Using them correctly is one mark of a better driver.

3. With electrical turn signals. These are also known as "directional signals."

4. With the horn.

Consult your state and local regulations for approved methods of signaling. Observe them. Whenever you drive outside of your own area, *be sure you know what procedures are required where you will be driving.*

The lane position of a car on the road, especially at intersections, gives certain information about its driver's intentions. It is often the most important signal a driver can give. Many state laws require that turns be made only from the proper lanes. Right turns are made from the right traffic lane and left turns from the lane immediately to the right of the center line. The exception is the one-way road, where the left turn is made from the extreme left lane. Use lanes in such a way that other drivers can tell by the position of your car what you intend to do.

Whenever you see another driver's arm extended outside the car, be ready for anything. He may be a good driver. He may be, and probably is, giving you a proper hand and arm signal. He may be a poor, thoughtless driver, and what appears to be a signal may be merely an arm where it doesn't belong. Give him plenty of room. He may be about to make some unusual move, or he may be flicking the ashes from his cigarette.

Whether it is making a proper signal or not, that arm is still a *warning* to the good driver.

In protecting himself and his passengers, the good driver is said to drive *defensively.* Here is a term worth remembering: *defensive driving.*

The *electrical turn signal* operates a flashing clear or amber light on the front of a car and a flashing red light in back. These lights show that the driver intends to turn in the direction of the flashing light. A lever, usually on the left side of the steering post, operates the signal.

This is the type of signal most commonly used today for any change of direction. Lane changes, as well as intersection turns, are usually announced by the

Fig. 10–6. Hand signals, electrical directional signals, and stop lights.

Fig. 10–7. The Weaver.

flashing light of this device. Accept this as a warning of another driver's probable turning, but not blindly. Keep an eye on him. Sometimes these signals fail to stop after a turn is completed. The other driver may not have noticed that they are still operating. Once in a while a forgetful driver switches on the wrong lights and turns to the direction opposite to his signal!

The timing of signals is very important. They must be given soon enough and continued long enough to be observed and acted upon. The speed of modern rural traffic calls for earlier signaling than in the past. In some places, signaling in accordance with minimum legal require-ments may not be sufficient for today's conditions. Keep in mind the protective purpose of signaling.

The *horn* is a courtesy signal, to sound a warning or attract attention. It is for *emergency* warning. Excessive use of horns makes them practically meaningless in emergencies. This excessive use is also illegal in most places.

The Thoughtless Three The movement of traffic on the open highway is safer and more efficient when all vehicles travel at approximately the same speed. The "Weaver" who worms his way in and out, passing all other vehicles, is a hazard and a nuisance. Even if his skill were as great as he is attempting to prove, he would still seriously endanger others.

Similarly, another dangerous road pest is the selfish "Sight-seer" on the busy highway. He cruises along slowly, not caring about anybody else, and forces the rest of the traffic to go around him. His driving often causes accidents, while he continues on without being hit.

A third nuisance is the "Dead-foot Driver." His attention is usually not on his driving. His right foot maintains a

Fig. 10–8. The Sight-seer.

Fig. 10–9. The Dead-foot Driver.

steady, constant pressure on the accelerator. When he goes uphill, his car loses speed little by little, and all other traffic must line up behind him.

The downhill story is different. Keeping the same "dead" foot on the accelerator, he lets his car run itself and gravity plays its part. If he has unconsciously slowed down to 35 miles per hour on the upgrade, he may reach 70 before he arrives at the bottom of the following downgrade. This weird motion, slow and fast, fast and slow, continues mile after mile. Everybody else on the highway suffers inconvenience and increased danger.

Don't be a "Dead-foot." Check your speedometer. Unless conditions prevent it, maintain a consistent speed. Regulate power as needed. Do not let gravity drive your car.

The "Weaver," the "Sight-seer," and the "Dead-foot" haven't made the highway team. They stand out as obvious misfits. The truly expert driver doesn't stand out at all. He fits so smoothly and so well into the traffic picture that you rarely notice his presence.

Passing

Passing is a common maneuver, yet one of the most dangerous. A mistake may be costly. You must correctly judge every one of the following factors:

1. The speed of the car you are about to pass
2. Your own car speed
3. The distance both cars will travel before you can pull back into line

Fig. 10–10. Modern highway construction contributes greatly to safety and ease in passing.

4. The assured clear distance ahead
5. The speed of any oncoming vehicle
6. The space available to move back in line in front of the passed vehicle
7. The existence of any additional hazard

The combined speeds of two approaching vehicles make such judgments even more difficult. Suppose you are moving at 50 miles per hour and an oncoming vehicle is traveling at the same speed. The two are then approaching each other at a 100-mile-per-hour impact speed!

Two dangerous possibilities confront the driver who wants to pass: *error in judgment,* and *impatience.* Of the two, the latter is the greater hazard. You can wait to pass until it is *obviously* safe to do so, allowing a good margin for error. The impatient driver *does not* wait; he gambles. Consider what he stands to lose in comparison with the most he could possibly gain! Recognizing this, *make your own rule* about passing. Patience pays off!

143

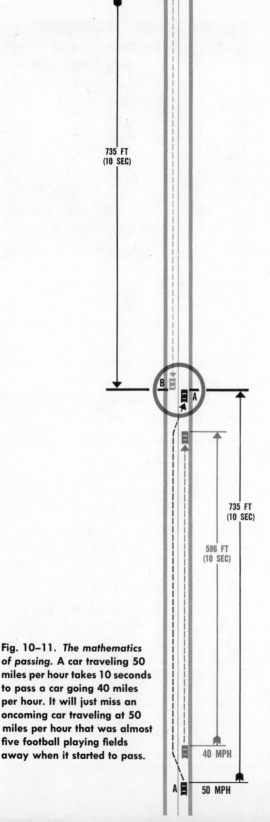

50 MPH

B

735 FT
(10 SEC)

B ↓ A
↑

735 FT
(10 SEC)

586 FT
(10 SEC)

40 MPH

A ▪ 50 MPH

Fig. 10–11. *The mathematics of passing.* A car traveling 50 miles per hour takes 10 seconds to pass a car going 40 miles per hour. It will just miss an oncoming car traveling at 50 miles per hour that was almost five football playing fields away when it started to pass.

Mathematics of Passing Assume that a car you are about to pass is 17 feet long. To pass it, it would seem that you would need only a few car lengths, starting from in back of the other car and pulling into line in front of it. The deceptive factor is the *forward movement of both cars* during the passing operation.

If you are traveling at 50 miles per hour and the driver ahead is at 40, you will need about 10 seconds to pass him safely. During this time, you will cover over 735 feet—about 43 car lengths. Remember that it will take you still longer to pass a long tractor-trailer. This means that both vehicles will travel farther during the passing. A longer assured clear distance is needed.

Now, suppose there is an oncoming vehicle approaching at 50 miles per hour. He will also travel 43 car lengths toward you while you are passing. Therefore, in order to have sufficient space to pass, you needed *at least 86 car lengths between you and the oncoming vehicle.* Even that would mean an extremely close call—much too close to estimate safely in advance.

To allow about 5 seconds for a margin of safety would mean another 43 car lengths needed, or 129 car lengths in all.

Imagine 129 cars lined up. They would cover 2,193 feet, or almost half a mile! This would mean five city blocks needed between you and the oncoming vehicle for a safe, reasonable passing. You may well be doubtful about estimating such a great distance. Experience will help you develop ability to judge when it is safe to pass and when it is not. The important

144

point to remember is: *When there is any doubt, do not pass.*

Precautions Before Passing   When you have overtaken and are about to pass another vehicle, be sure that you observe each of the following precautions:

1. *Watch for signs and pavement markings.* They are vital tips, as well as legal traffic controls. In passing on two-lane rural roads, for example, you may cross the broken white line when conditions permit. But a solid yellow line in your lane next to the center line means that it is unsafe and unlawful to do so. Wait.

2. *Look ahead before you decide to pass.* An intersection, a railroad, a narrow bridge, a partly screened side road, a hill, a curve, or any unusual situation may make passing dangerous!

3. *Know what is behind you.* Before you start to pass another vehicle, check in your rear-view and left outside mirrors. Be sure there is nothing in the lane you are about to enter and no vehicle about to pass you.

4. *Give the proper turn signal.* Do this before you move out of your lane to pass.

5. *Sound your horn.* Let the driver ahead know you intend to pass. Otherwise, he might speed up and start to pass a vehicle ahead of him as you pull out.

6. *Return to the proper lane.* After you have finished passing, put on the right-turn signal. Return to the proper lane only *after you can see the car you have passed* in your rear-view mirror.

Cooperation in Passing   When another vehicle is about to pass you, *cooperate.* Here teamwork is essential. Drivers judge the speed of cars they intend to pass just before starting to pass. If you increase your speed while another driver is alongside passing, he may never realize it. Some drivers cut in fairly closely in front of cars they have passed. If this passing driver happens to be one of them, he may unconsciously steer right into your left front fender. In most places, the law forbids increasing speed when being passed; if anything, reduce speed.

Some drivers insist on passing every person whose manner of driving they don't like. Some have an almost irresistible urge to avoid following any other vehicle. This sometimes leads to hazardous, unnecessary passing. With the numbers of vehicles on highways today, there will be vehicles ahead of you much of the time. Once you accept this undeniable fact, your driving life will be much more pleasant—and safer.

We have mentioned two things which are vital for safe country driving: *teamwork* and *defensive driving.* Many times the trained driver finds he is put "on the spot" by another driver, and it becomes necessary for him to protect himself and others by quick thinking and action.

For example, you are driving along a highway in a line of cars. You notice the driver behind you is anxious to pass. You keep a close watch on him because there are not many opportunities on this road, and he seems very eager. He pulls out to pass. His decision is a poor one because a car is now approaching from the opposite direction. You must help him out of his dilemma to protect him, yourself, and the approaching driver. If he has advanced too far to drop back in line behind you, you must slow down as much as necessary to give him a chance to fit his car safely back into the line in front of you. A situation like this calls for quick thinking and cooperation. Again, *foresight* will help you out. You had noticed his actions and anticipated what could happen; you were ready.

Meeting Other Cars

One lane of the roadway certainly is yours. But if an approaching driver is in it, there is no sense in risking a fatal or expensive accident by "standing your ground." For all you can tell, the approaching driver may be asleep, drowsy, inattentive, incompetent, ill, or drunk. If you are suspicious of the way he is approaching, be defensive in your driving. Warn him with your horn and pull to the right-hand side of the road as far as possible. Good driving on your part means yielding the road and protecting yourself against him. The defensive driver is the smart driver.

Anything that happens between cars that are meeting happens quickly. As noted before, two cars approach each other at a crash speed equal to the sum of their speeds. Be ready.

It is not surprising that so many accident victims report, "It was all over so quickly. I never knew just what happened."

Stopping Along the Highway

Always pull to the right, entirely off the pavement, to stop. Never stop on the road surface. If the shoulder is too narrow, keep going until you can pull off at a place where sight distances are good both front and back. Even in the case of a flat tire, it is better to ruin the tire than to have another car crash into yours.

Stopping entirely off the pavement is especially important at night. A driver who sees a tail light ahead may not realize soon enough that it is on a stopped car. This is particularly true if he is facing the lights of an approaching car. Put yourself in his place. Size up the situation from his view. Plan your stop and position accordingly.

In case you have to stop, as in certain emergencies, a little foresight is of great value. An emergency flare kit in your car is very cheap insurance!

Rounding Curves

Curves can show up good and bad driving practices. Forces acting on a car are more complex on curves than on straight roads, as you have learned in Chapter 6, "Traffic Laws Made by Nature." If you fail to slow down properly *before* entering a curve, your car may skid and leave the lane, or even the highway.

A good driver slows down before entering a curve, not while on it. Your car is steadier on a curve when the engine is pulling at a constant speed

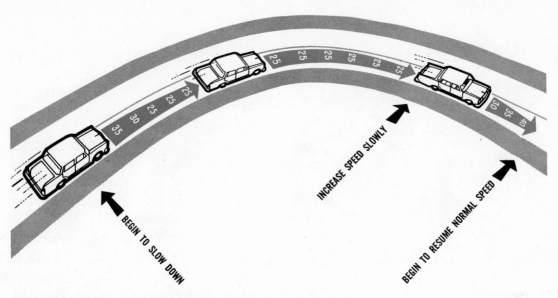

Fig. 10–12. **Practice good speed control on curves.**

than when the car is coasting or being braked. Therefore, enter the curve slowly enough so that you can accelerate while in it and your engine can continue pulling. For smoother, safer, more expert driving, brake before you are on the curve, if necessary, rather than braking on it. In the latter case, you would be attempting to correct an error of judgment.

Braking on a curve is a dead giveaway to unskillful driving. It means that a driver has given himself a difficult and needless struggle with physical forces. The struggle can result in squealing tires, a leaning car, lurching passengers, a skid, difficult steering, or worse trouble. When you take a curve so that passengers are not even "curve conscious," you are doing a "polished" piece of driving.

Curves usually shorten sight distance, so even in daylight the driver cannot see so far ahead. Emergency situations can develop very rapidly within these unseen-danger zones. *Always drive at such a speed that you can stop in the assured clear*

distance ahead. You should always be able to see your entire danger zone. Stay in your lane on your side of the road on curves.

Be ready also for the oncoming car which may appear on your side of the center line. Frequently, drivers who find they have entered a curve too fast move over into the wrong lane in attempting to turn more gradually. All you can do is to yield space to them, hoping they will mature as drivers before you meet them again.

Fig. 10–13. **At every curve assume there may be an obstruction in your path.**

Fig. 10-14. On curves, speeding drivers often use the wrong lanes to avoid skidding . . . and to avoid running off the road.

Hills and Hill Crests

Hill crests can be driving hazards on the open highway. You do not know what traffic conditions exist beyond the top.

Wreckage from a recent collision may be strewn across the road; a car may be stopped on the roadway; an approaching car may be in your lane. Be ready to meet any unexpected situation.

Don't pass a car near the crest of a hill. As you ascend, sight distance ends at the hilltop. Never cross the center line when approaching a crest. Observe closely any markings painted on the road surface.

It may be irritating to follow slow-moving vehicles up a long, winding hill. But where the only alternative is to pass with limited sight distance ahead, control your irritation and follow all the way over the crest before passing. This kind of caution, even though it delays you, is a necessary part of really intelligent motoring.

If a road has four lanes or more and a divider strip, too, and if your sight distance is adequate, you may pass near a hill crest. But even on a four-lane road, a wreck or other obstruction over the crest may be in your lane.

Reduce pressure on the accelerator as you approach the top of a hill. Bear in

Fig. 10-15. Reduce speed as you approach a hill crest. You never know what is just beyond your range of vision.

mind, as you go over the crest and start down, that sight distance increases, but so does braking distance. *Always drive at a speed that will let you stop within the assured clear distance ahead.* Otherwise, you are at the mercy of circumstances and can lose control. If the downgrade is at all steep, shift to a lower gear before starting down. Then the engine acts as a braking force and saves wear on the brakes.

Keep Control   On a long, steep downgrade, keep a light pressure on the brake pedal to keep the car from gaining speed. Less heat is built up in the brakes and tires by this method than when hard brake pressure is applied intermittently.

Never coast down hills with the gearshift or selector lever in neutral or with the clutch disengaged. (In many states, it is illegal to do so.) When the car is coasting, the engine is not helping to brake. The job of slowing down and stopping the car is thrown entirely on the brakes and tires. Stopping distance can become so greatly lengthened that you lose control.

Coasting in neutral can also be very hard on your car. In gearshift cars, there is a severe strain on mechanical parts if engine speed and car speed are not matched when the clutch is again engaged. In automatic transmission cars, the transmission can be seriously damaged.

A Good Tip   Professionals who drive the highways a great deal learn to "size up" other vehicles and drivers. One of the things they recognize is the variation in speed of heavily loaded commercial vehicles on hills.

149

If you overtake one of them and follow it to the crest of a hill, expect it to increase speed on the downgrade. Before you start to try to pass after topping the hill crest, stay behind a moment. See whether its driver will pick up speed rapidly on the downgrade.

If you wait a moment, you may avoid an inefficient and unnecessary passing and repassing operation. Observe his pickup and speed. If he is going to drive faster than you are, do not pass. Let him stay ahead. Judgments in passing a rapidly accelerating vehicle are very difficult to make. Let him reach his normal driving speed and *then* decide whether or not you want to pass.

Handling Special Situations

Some driving experiences do not occur often. Some we encounter only on trips away from home. Frequent or not, we should know about them.

Railroad Grade Crossings   Grade crossings are a very dangerous kind of "highway intersection." About 1,500 persons are killed and 4,000 injured each year on them. A study made by the Baltimore and Ohio Railroad Company showed that, in about one-third of the accidents involving cars and trains, the automobile struck the locomotive or even part of the train behind the locomotive.

There are many kinds of railroad-crossing warning devices. Some crossings have watchmen constantly on guard. Some have automatic warning and control devices such as lights, bells, gates, or wigwag signals. Always heed these warnings as well as the round advance-warning Railroad Crossing highway sign.

The best rule is this: *Treat a railroad crossing as you would any dangerous, uncontrolled intersection.* Heed all warnings and use all your defensive senses also. Approach the crossing *slowly, look* carefully, lower your car window in advance, and *listen.* Under adverse driving conditions, *stop* before entering the crossing. Never enter unless the vehicle ahead has cleared the tracks by enough to give you an "out" if it stops. Many automobiles have been *caught* on tracks in a stopped line of traffic.

Don't start across the tracks immediately after a train passes. People have done so only to be struck by a second train coming from the other direction. It just happened to be screened from view by the first train. Remember, the engineer can't dodge you. His stopping distance is usually a *very* long one! He also has the right of way!

Keep in mind that the law requires some vehicles, such as buses and certain types of trucks, to make a complete stop before crossing railroad tracks. When driving behind these vehicles, be prepared to stop even though there is no sign of a train approaching.

Pavement Edges   The edge of the road pavement sometimes causes very serious accidents. A ridge between the road pavement and the road shoulder easily throws a car into a skid. Keep all the wheels of your car always on the paved surface.

If the car's right-hand wheels do get off the paved surface, use the correct technique for getting them back on (study Fig. 10–17). Don't try to get back on the pavement at high speed. Avoid panic. Never "slam on the brakes." Drive straight ahead, with the right wheels off the pavement, and slow your car down gradually.

Fig. 10–16. A good rule: Approach a grade crossing with great caution.

Fig. 10-17. Slow down, then drive back on the pavement at a sharp angle.

Drive at a *slow speed* with the right wheels about 2 feet, if possible, out on the shoulder. Check the roadway behind you. Then cut back onto the pavement by turning the front wheels sharply to the left. If you jerk back at high speed, or attempt to get back while driving nearly parallel to the pavement edge, you can ruin tires, throw the car into a dangerous skid, or cause it to roll over.

Be aware of another danger along the edge of the road. Soft road shoulders, if you happen to drive on them, may "drag" your car off the road. They actually pull the car's wheels farther into the loose dirt. Stay away from soft shoulders. If you find yourself on one, grip your wheel strongly and firmly as you steer and move, at reduced speed, back onto the traveled part of the road.

If a Tire Blows Out There's a beginning and an end to every story. First, you may recognize a cut or "bubble" on a tire if you make it a practice to inspect your tires regularly. You may avoid having a blowout on the road. When the car is on a grease rack is a good time to check the tires.

If a tire blows out, it is extremely important to keep control of your car and yourself. This is a situation which requires presence of mind.

What follows a blowout? It depends on which tire blows out. A rear-tire blowout sways the rear end of your car from side to side. If the right front tire blows out, your car swerves to the right; if it is the left front tire, the car swerves to the left. In any case, steering is very difficult.

Steering is the important thing. Grip the steering wheel firmly and try to keep your car in as straight a path as possible. Do not brake, but let up on the accelerator. Only when your car is under complete control should you begin to brake.

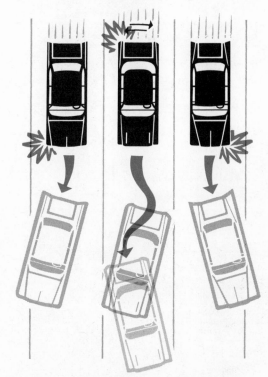

Fig. 10-18. Blowouts in tires shown will cause a car to move in the directions of the arrows.

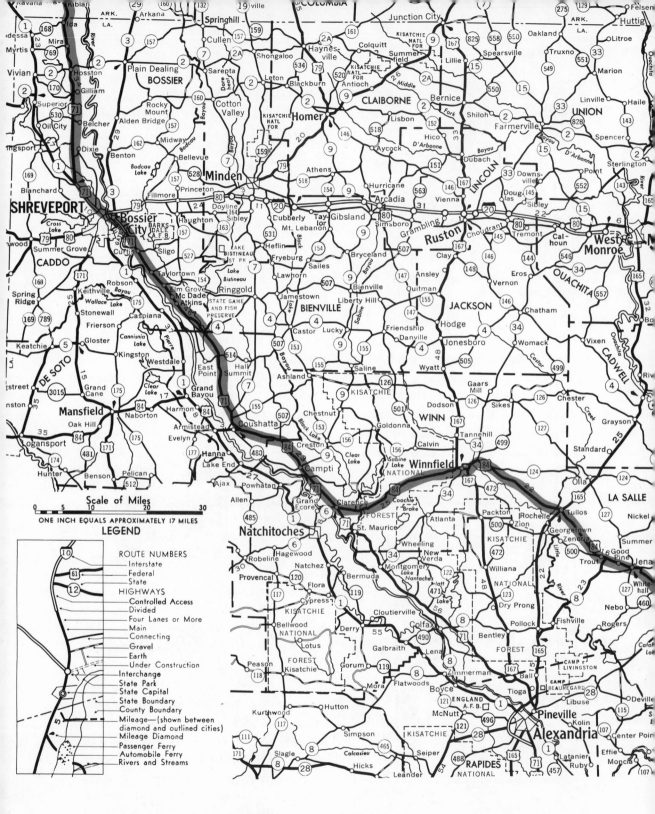

Fig. 10–19. Learn how to use a road map.

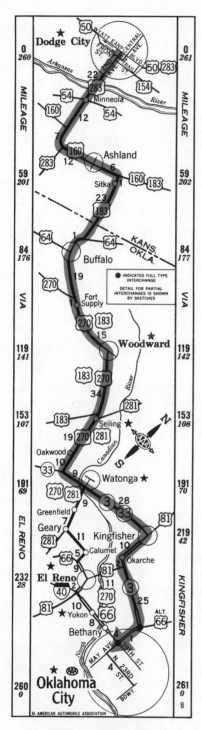

Fig. 10–20. Strip maps make it easier to follow planned routes.

Apply the brakes very gently and slowly, keeping the car in gear so that the engine helps slow down the car.

The end of this story? It was literally that for many motorists who stopped suddenly in trying to save tires that had gone flat. They did not drive their cars *off* the roadway to a safe spot to change a tire. They or their cars were hit by other vehicles. Important at any time, moving off the road to change a tire or to make other repairs is *vital* at night.

Road Maps

Your trip is more enjoyable and your driving more efficient if you make good use of road maps. The night before the trip is a good time for planning.

It is surprising how many drivers try to read and use road maps while their cars are moving. If you are alone, pull off the traveled roadway and stop the car when you want to consult your road map. If you have a passenger, let him or her be your navigator. If necessary, show him how to follow your intended course on the map. Give necessary instructions, however, while the car is standing still.

Today's road maps are excellent, easy to read and interpret. Study the "legend" —the explanation that accompanies the actual map picture (see Fig. 10–19). You can pick your route in advance and take advantage of the best roads and of other physical features shown on the map. Often, points of interest along your route are described.

From the map you can learn distances from place to place and plan your stops intelligently. This is a safety feature as well as a convenience.

A good procedure when planning a trip is to draw a heavy line along your proposed route (see Fig. 10–20). On your trip, when you check your progress and location, it is infinitely easier to find where you are. Your progress can be marked by X's at each check point.

A map can add interest as well as helping you to find your way. It is a useful and friendly fellow traveler.

To Talk About:

1. Discuss various hand signals you have seen. Are those required in your state the same as the Uniform Vehicle Code recommends?

2. Make a list of discourteous acts of some drivers on hills; on curves; on straight, level roads. Discuss these discourtesies and why they are serious.

3. What does it mean to drive "defensively"? Give several examples.

4. Mention places and situations where it would be illegal or unwise to use your horn. In what situations should the horn be used?

5. Discuss reasons why many accidents occur on straight, level, clear roads in good weather.

To Do:

1. To find out how much your engine really helps you to brake, try this experiment, or have someone do it for you: Find a level street with no traffic or parked cars, and at a certain speed (not over 20 miles per hour) shift to neutral and coast to a stop. Note the point where you shifted to neutral and the exact spot where you came to a stop. Drive around the block and at exactly the same speed and same starting point, release your accelerator, keeping your car in high gear, or in **Dr.** See how much sooner you stop. Repeat the experiment in second gear if you are driving a manual-shift car, and in **L** if you are driving an automatic transmission car. Note that the lower the gear, the more your engine will help to brake.

2. Find out what proportion of rural traffic fatalities in your state occurs on straight roads, on curves, on hill crests, in overtaking and passing. What driving faults or violations are most often involved in such accidents? Summarize your findings.

3. Prepare a list of ten sound driving practices for country driving, putting first the ones you consider most important. Watch drivers you ride with to see whether they follow these practices. Do different drivers follow the same driving practices?

4. Obtain samples of well-prepared state and sectional road maps and study them until you understand all they show. Then, plan a trip of about 300 miles and list the important things about this trip that you are able to learn from the maps.

City driving is a special skill in itself. Heavy traffic, narrow streets, the bewildering number of signs, signals, and markings, and the unpredictable movements of pedestrians often create a confusing picture in the eyes of the new driver. Before venturing into this new "world," he should make absolutely certain that he is *ready*.

While we are learning a skill, we perform each act *consciously*. As we become more adept, we accomplish much of the procedure below our level of consciousness. This frees our minds so that we can devote our attention to the scene about us. It is only after we have progressed this far, when we can perform our hand and foot movements automatically, that we are ready for driving in city traffic.

Getting the Car into the Street

The first demand on your city driving skills may be that of getting your car into the street from the garage. Frequently, you have to back your car into the street. Limited visibility often creates a major hazard.

Before you enter the car to back up, *walk around and look behind it.* A small child or an object directly in back of the car is not visible to a person in the driver's seat. Tragic accidents have resulted from neglect of this precaution. As you back out, take the following steps:

11 Driving in Cities and Towns

STOP BEFORE ENTERING THE STREET

STOP BEFORE CROSSING THE SIDEWALK

CHECK BEHIND CAR BEFORE GETTING IN

Fig. 11–1. Before backing a car into the street check behind the car. Check both right and left for pedestrians and vehicles. Make a double stop, as shown.

Step 1. *Look in all directions. Back your car slowly, looking over your shoulder.*

Step 2. *Be aware of people on foot, especially children, in a position where they may step into your path.*

Step 3. *Come to a stop before crossing the sidewalk. In some states, this stop is required by law. Always yield the right of way to pedestrians.*

Step 4. *As you start again to move into the roadway, yield the right of way to any approaching vehicle. This also is usually required by law.*

Step 5. *On a quiet residential street, back slowly and carefully into the lane for the direction in which you wish to go. Be aware of the position of any parked cars. One may remain in your blind spot as you back and turn.*

Step 6. *On a busy street, back into the nearest lane and proceed in the direction of the traffic flow. It is better to go around the block than to back across traffic.*

Driving in Traffic

Pedestrians, cross streets, traffic congestion, *reduced vision,* and many other factors require reduced speed in built-up areas.

If you happen to be driving into the city from the open highway, check your speedometer frequently. Keep within the posted speed limit. If there are no signs, assume that the limit is 25 miles per hour. Remember that after open-road speeds, you may seem to be "crawling" when you are still going too fast for city streets.

Fig. 11–2. Sportsmanlike driving is needed in situations like this.

City driving conditions make clear the great need for desirable attitudes, courtesy, and sportsmanship. While you, as a trained driver, will have and use these qualities, you cannot be sure that others, less informed, will do the same. You should make up your mind to drive *defensively* and be ready and willing to allow for the other fellow's mistakes.

Safe City Speeds   In city traffic, a normal rate of flow is set by the traffic conditions at the time. Traffic moves more smoothly when all drivers adjust to the normal rate. Constantly passing other cars, or moving so slowly that other cars must pass you, is both annoying and dangerous. Never let the impatient "tailgater" force you to an illegal or unsafe speed. Don't let him drive *your* car. Don't let the "horn blower" make you do something you should not do.

Don't forget your minimum following distance. This should be at least 1 car length for each 10 miles per hour of your speed.

Remember that as your speed increases, your danger zone lengthens. *Either pedestrians or vehicles may enter your danger zone from either side at any time* (see Fig. 11–3). Keep this possibility in mind as you drive in city traffic.

Speed and Traffic Signals   Never speed up to "beat" the change of a light. If the light does change as you approach, your increased speed simply makes what would be a normal stop a "crash stop." When approaching a red light, it is poor driving to continue at the same speed up to the last instant. When you see that you must slow down or stop, reduce pressure on the gas pedal and let the engine and nature's laws slow down the car. This saves wear and tear on brakes, tires, and the nerves of those around you.

As you approach a light which may be about to change, note carefully the speed and nearness of cars behind you. Then, if the light does change, you can make a quick decision as to whether it is safe to stop short, depending upon the distance to the intersection.

While waiting at an intersection for the light to change, keep your right foot on the foot brake. Don't creep. If pedes-

Fig. 11–3. In city driving, danger zones extend to the sides as well as straight ahead.

trians are passing in front of your car, you should move the selector or gearshift lever to neutral.

Don't let the change to green be your signal to go. Always check left and right to make sure no cars are coming through the intersection before starting.

A Progressive Signal System Many cities use a progressive system of traffic lights. The signals are so timed that a driver moving at a proper speed will find that each light turns green as he nears it. He will not have to stop. Driving too fast or too slowly simply means meeting red lights. You can't beat it; "join it."

Speed at Intersections How fast should you approach an intersection? The answer cannot be given in number of miles per hour. The conditions of the moment must govern your actions. It is obvious that you must adjust speed for any actual or potential hazard that you see and recognize. When no danger appears to threaten, you can protect yourself by making and keeping a good, sensible rule:

<u>Never enter an intersection at a speed from which you could not stop before striking any suddenly appearing object. The degree of visibility at that particular intersection at that moment should control your speed.</u>

In following this rule, the new driver sometimes worries that he may be slowing down too much and appear overcautious. To him, it seems that the experienced driver enters intersections without looking. This is not the case. If it were, he probably would not have lived to become an experienced driver. He has simply learned through experience to look in each direction more quickly than the new driver may and then to interpret the meanings of what he has seen in terms of what to do.

Never enter an intersection blindly. The width of the street, the distance of the buildings from the corner, and the presence of parked cars or other obstructions

Fig. 11–4. Always enter an intersection at a speed from which you could stop if you should find another moving vehicle about to enter it.

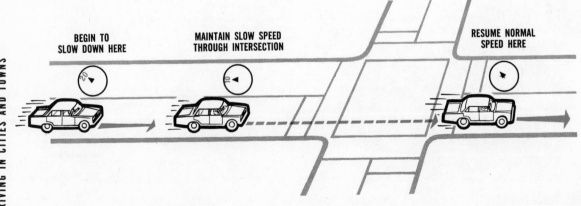

BEGIN TO SLOW DOWN HERE

MAINTAIN SLOW SPEED THROUGH INTERSECTION

RESUME NORMAL SPEED HERE

DRIVING IN CITIES AND TOWNS

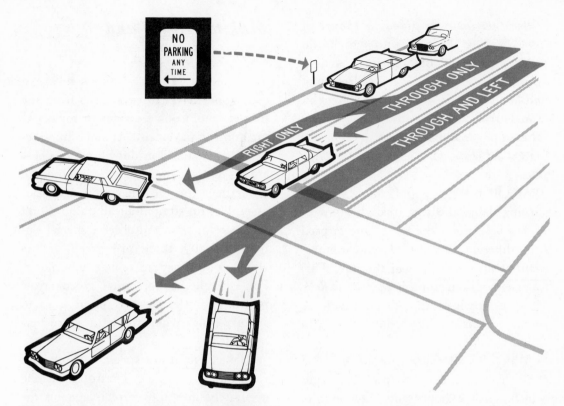

Fig. 11–5. Proper car positions on a multi-lane street.

to vision determine how much slowing down is necessary when approaching an intersection. A good pattern for reducing speed at intersections is shown in Fig. 11–4.

Driving in Lanes Many city streets are marked off into traffic lanes by lines painted on the pavement. Even when there are no markings, the skilled driver patterns his course as though there were. He assumes that the lanes would normally be parallel to the curb lines of the street. The better driver you become, the more you will pity the "wanderer" who strays from lane to lane. Sometimes he drives in part of each of two lanes. His life will never be happy. He will always be accompanied by danger and ridicule.

Choose your lane carefully. First, consider the provisions of law that govern the locality in which you are driving. Second, if you intend to turn, move into the proper lane well ahead of time. Third, if you intend to drive straight ahead, remember that turning vehicles often must stop before turning. They sometimes block traffic in their lanes at each intersection.

If you are driving in the lane next to parked cars, reduce speed so that you can stop very quickly. Pedestrians frequently appear suddenly from between parked cars. Because of this, and because people sometimes open car doors unexpectedly, it is wise not to drive too closely to parked cars.

159

Remember, always signal a change of lane. Be *sure* the lane into which you move is clear. Another driver, missing your signal, may be in your blind spot and about to pass you. Always check in your mirrors before making the change. The proper sequence is: *look, signal, look, wait until clear, then move into the other lane.*

Reversed Traffic Flow Avoid finding yourself turning dangerously against the flow of traffic. Sometimes the same lane is used for a different direction of vehicle movement at different times of the day. This system is called a *reversed traffic flow.* It is used where the heaviest volume of traffic changes direction at certain hours.

Watch for all markings, barriers, and traffic cones, and for arrows and signs which tell the hours and directions of traffic flow. Be especially alert for this control system in unfamiliar cities and towns.

Fig. 11–6. Traffic direction is sometimes changed to accommodate the "rush-hour" flow.

Making Right and Left Turns

A good driver always turns from the proper lane. Look for signs or for markings on the pavement. At some intersections, particularly in downtown business areas, certain turns may be prohibited. Sometimes specific lanes are marked for turning or for straight-ahead traffic. Don't forget to look for and observe special signals. Usually these are green arrows which control certain vehicle movements. For example, a horizontal green arrow pointing to the right is often used to specify times when right turns are permissible.

Make turns at low speed, keeping your car under complete control. Turning accurately into the correct lane on the new street requires careful timing. Remember that new drivers sometimes start to straighten the car's front wheels too late. This results in "oversteering," or continuing the turn too far. Be conscious of having your right foot ready for quick braking until your car is running straight ahead in the new direction. These turns, though strange at first, will become commonplace with experience.

Overtaking and Passing

You are expected to know and observe the laws and regulations governing each area in which you drive. Check state and local regulations. In many marked locations, passing another vehicle is forbid-

Fig. 11–7. These continuous lines move independently of each other.

den. Watch for pertinent signs and pavement markings, particularly the double lines painted on the street.

In general, you pass other vehicles on the left. There are two exceptions to this rule:

1. When two continuous lines of traffic are moving in the same direction, it is undesirable to require the right line to stop every time the left one does. In this case, each line of vehicles may move independently of the other. Under these conditions, no abrupt, unexpected, or unsignaled transfer from one lane to the other should be made. The driver who continually switches from lane to lane to gain a few car lengths is a hazard to others. It is possible that this will be called to his attention by an alert police officer.

2. When a vehicle is about to turn left at an intersection, it may be passed on the right-hand side. In some states, passing on the right is permitted under other specific conditions.

Some Common Hazards

Recognition of hazards is a mark of a good driver. The lucky driver gets out of dangerous situations as long as his luck holds out. The good driver *avoids* them.

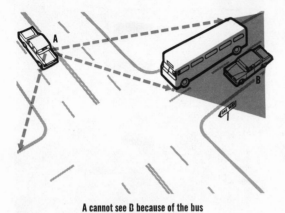

A cannot see B because of the bus

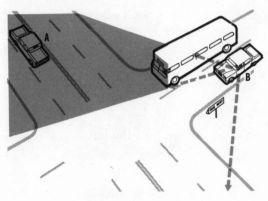

B cannot see A because of the bus

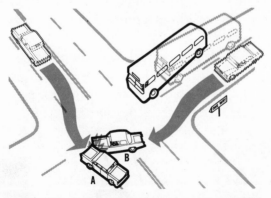

Result: A collision may occur if A and B both try to cross the intersection.

Fig. 11–8. A bus pulling out of a one-way street may hide other vehicles.

Remember that in Chapter 2, "The Psychology of the Driver," such hazards were described under "Foresight." Now, while you are learning to drive in traffic, is a good time to review situations which demand foresight. Read them again and be able to recognize *danger-in-the-making*.

Reduced Visibility   Remember that driving in the city means greatly reduced visibility. Slow-moving lines of traffic mean close intervals between vehicles. You may find yourself following a truck or a bus in a line of traffic at a very slow speed. Even though you are not afraid of running into it at that speed, there is another and important point to keep in mind. Following a truck or bus is like driving with a large screen in front of your eyes. Your entire danger zone and its margins are obscured. You may not even be able to see overhead traffic signals as you enter intersections. The greater your following distance, the smaller the screen.

The Stopped Bus   Passengers alighting from a public bus sometimes fail to wait for the bus to move on. Some hurry to cross the street in front of it; an approaching driver has no warning at all. Anticipating this, he must also realize that other persons may appear suddenly from any direction. When running to catch a bus, people often pay little attention to crosswalks.

The Manned Vehicle   Frequent starting and stopping are characteristic of city driving. We should try to anticipate every other driver's intended actions, but we can't ever be sure. The stopped vehicle, even the parked vehicle, is a possible threat *if there is a person at the wheel.*

If you see a car stopped ahead of you in the traffic lane, watch it carefully as you approach. You may see that the driver is about to back into a parking place next to the curb. Unless you can allow a full car width in passing, stop and wait for him to move out of the way. In backing into the right-hand curb, the front end of his car will swing wide *to the left*. He may apply considerable power to move out of the traffic lane quickly. Looking over his right shoulder, he may be completely unaware of the direction taken by the front of his car. Passing at that moment can be dangerous.

"Muscling In"

Marked or not, a crosswalk should be kept clear for pedestrians. When you stop at an intersection, stop short of the crosswalk and stay stopped. Usually 4 feet is the margin. Stopping in the crosswalk forces pedestrians to walk in dangerous territory. Remember, also, that a large truck or bus turning left from the street on your right needs considerable space. Don't be in it!

Fig. 11–9. Where a bus is stopped, drivers should be especially alert for pedestrians.

If any vehicle is turning in that manner in front of you, keep a close check on it as you start ahead. Some drivers cut their turns very sharply. If the left rear of his car and the left front of your car collide, it will be both his fault and yours. Picture this situation a moment. Who do you think would be most likely to be blamed when the police arrived to investigate?

Fig. 11–10. Stopping in the crosswalk forces pedestrians into dangerous territory . . . and can embarrass and endanger you as well.

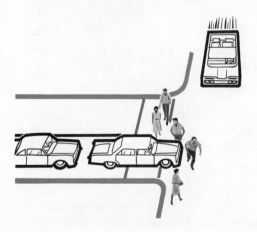
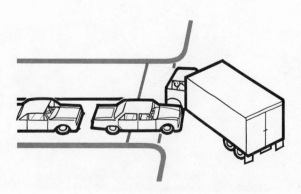

City Driving Means Cooperation

For the new driver, about to experience city traffic driving for the first time, the best start would be to do the following things:

1. Review and learn the situations described under "Foresight" in Chapter 2, "The Psychology of the Driver."

2. Carefully review Chapter 22, "Maneuvers." Practice maneuvers away from traffic until you have fully mastered them.

3. If there are streetcar or railroad tracks in your city, learn about their special hazards in Chapter 14, "Driving Under Adverse or Special Conditions."

In city driving, you will be sharing the highway with many other people. Your relationship with them should be *cooperative,* never competitive.

Fig. 11–11. Cooperation among drivers is essential.

To Talk About:

1. Note how frequently someone who has passed you in a dangerous place, such as just before an intersection with a traffic signal, is waiting just ahead of you at the same or the next red light. Is it worth taking this chance to be first instead of second in line?

2. If you are close to an intersection when the light changes from green to yellow, how will you decide whether or not you should go through? What should you have been noting as you approached the signal? What is the purpose and meaning of the yellow light?

3. Sometimes on busy city streets you will find vehicles that are double-parked. Discuss what your procedure should be as you come up behind such a vehicle. What part does foresight play here?

4. Discuss several intersections in your community with special driving hazards. Tell what precautions are needed in each case.

5. Do your local traffic regulations permit right turns on a red light? Should they permit or forbid them? Is a green turn arrow used? Discuss the advantages and disadvantages of green arrows, considering especially their effects on the safety of pedestrians.

6. Consider the places on the streets of your community where parking is prohibited. Explain these restrictions. Do they seem wise? Why are they needed?

7. Discuss some of the traffic markings on the pavement in your community. How do they help drivers? In what ways do they help to keep traffic moving freely and safely? Are there any places where these markings seem to be confusing?

8. Discuss (*a*) the advantages of the small or compact cars in maneuverability and economy, (*b*) the extra precautions the small-car driver must take *to be seen.*

To Do:

1. Make a study of blind corners in your community. In each case explain what interferes with vision and how each situation might be improved. Do you have a law limiting the height of bushes and hedges and their distance from the corner? Is it strict enough? Is it enforced?

2. Make a list of the special hazards involved in driving along streets where many cars are angle- or parallel-parked. List clues a driver should notice which may warn him of approaching danger.

3. Use a traffic board or a blackboard to set up a situation in which a car approaches an intersection where the driver intends to make a left turn. Indicate all possible interference he must consider from vehicles or pedestrians. Do this for an intersection with a traffic signal and another one without a signal. Repeat for a right turn.

4. Make a survey of vehicles turning corners. Have each member of your group observe a certain number of turning drivers. Note the number who fail to signal, turn from the wrong lane, complete the turn in the wrong lane, or disregard pedestrian rights. Tally the results and find out what percentage of the drivers turned properly. Discuss the errors noted and see if you can guess why they were made.

Although you are now in the very interesting process of becoming a driver—a really good driver—there is one fact that you should never forget. We are all pedestrians. Practically every man, woman, and child in this country spends part of his or her time on foot on street or highway.

When a pedestrian and an automobile collide, the pedestrian obviously is at a great disadvantage. The automobile has the advantage on all counts—size, weight, speed, momentum, and hardness of material. Flesh and bones are no match for steel, glass, and rubber tires under pressure. When car crashes into car, personal injury occurs in only about one out of every ten accidents. Almost every accident where car and pedestrian collide involves an injury (see Fig. 12–2).

A 140-pound pedestrian walking at 3 or 4 miles per hour has no chance against the impact of a ton or two of steel traveling at even 25 miles per hour. The latter speed is legal in most city traffic, and 40- to 50-mile-per-hour speeds are permitted in many suburban and rural areas.

Each year some 8,000 pedestrians are killed and 130,000 others are injured in traffic. About one out of every five traffic deaths in the U.S. is that of a pedestrian. In most large cities, pedestrian fatalities represent a high percentage of all traffic deaths. In some large cities, it is as high as 79 percent (see Fig. 12–3).

For these reasons, it is vital that all drivers understand their responsibility to people on foot and what can be done to avoid pedestrian accidents.

12 the Pedestrian and the Driver

A PEDESTRIAN IS NO MATCH FOR A CAR

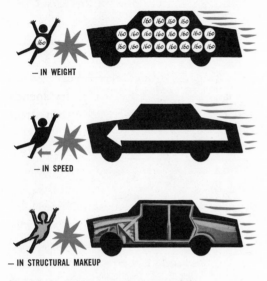

— IN WEIGHT

— IN SPEED

— IN STRUCTURAL MAKEUP

Fig. 12–1. Man versus the automobile.

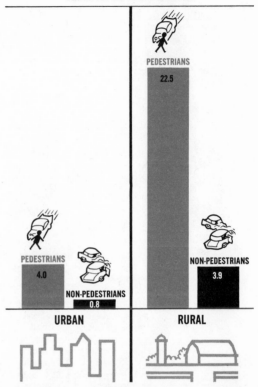

DEATHS PER 100 TRAFFIC CASUALTIES

PEDESTRIANS 22.5

PEDESTRIANS 4.0

NON-PEDESTRIANS 0.8

NON-PEDESTRIANS 3.9

URBAN

RURAL

Fig. 12–2. In both city and country, accidents involving pedestrians are likely to cause deaths.

Let us first study the pedestrian. Who is he? Why are pedestrians victims of so many accidents? What can the *driver* do to avoid these accidents?

Meet the Pedestrian

Who is he? Well, first, he is a thinking, feeling human being. He can be rudely shocked by a sudden, unexpected loud blast of a nearby horn. He can, at times, be bullied by a selfish, belligerent driver. He may be a fine, courteous person, or he may be as mean as some drivers we know.

He may be the first one at your side to help if you are in an accident or other trouble!

It's possible that he may be absentminded at times (who isn't), and sometimes he is in a hurry and careless. True, he shouldn't be, but these weaknesses don't warrant such punishment as a crippling injury.

He, or she, doesn't deserve sudden death, either, nor do members of his or her family deserve that shocking telephone call announcing tragedy in the home. That family could be yours; the victim your mother, father, sister, or brother. No one is free of this threat.

But we all *can* do something about it. We can learn about the pedestrian and what to be prepared for when we see him in traffic.

His Limitations In every place in our country, small or large, there are people walking the streets and roads who are old,

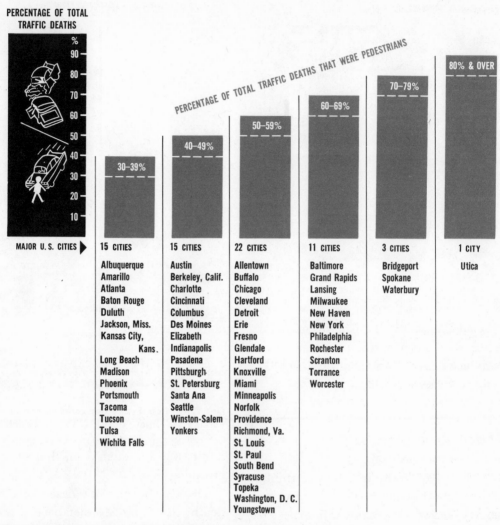

PERCENTAGE OF TOTAL TRAFFIC DEATHS

PERCENTAGE OF TOTAL TRAFFIC DEATHS THAT WERE PEDESTRIANS

MAJOR U. S. CITIES ▶	15 CITIES	15 CITIES	22 CITIES	11 CITIES	3 CITIES	1 CITY
	30–39%	40–49%	50–59%	60–69%	70–79%	80% & OVER
	Albuquerque	Austin	Allentown	Baltimore	Bridgeport	Utica
	Amarillo	Berkeley, Calif.	Buffalo	Grand Rapids	Spokane	
	Atlanta	Charlotte	Chicago	Lansing	Waterbury	
	Baton Rouge	Cincinnati	Cleveland	Milwaukee		
	Duluth	Columbus	Detroit	New Haven		
	Jackson, Miss.	Des Moines	Erie	New York		
	Kansas City,	Elizabeth	Fresno	Philadelphia		
	Kans.	Indianapolis	Glendale	Rochester		
	Long Beach	Pasadena	Hartford	Scranton		
	Madison	Pittsburgh	Knoxville	Torrance		
	Phoenix	St. Petersburg	Miami	Worcester		
	Portsmouth	Santa Ana	Minneapolis			
	Tacoma	Seattle	Norfolk			
	Tucson	Winston-Salem	Providence			
	Tulsa	Yonkers	Richmond, Va.			
	Wichita Falls		St. Louis			
			St. Paul			
			South Bend			
			Syracuse			
			Topeka			
			Washington, D. C.			
			Youngstown			

Fig. 12–3. Pedestrian fatalities are a major problem in many large cities.

weak, hard of hearing, crippled, mentally incapable of protecting themselves, or even partially or totally blind. Do you know that a pedestrian carrying a white cane is blind?

Also, many pedestrians who have never driven a car have little or no knowledge of how much distance is needed to stop one. They do not realize that a car cannot be stopped "on a dime." Several studies have shown that nine out of ten adults killed while walking in traffic were nondrivers. Such pedestrians just do not understand the operation of an automobile.

The Senior Citizen Accident records show that two-thirds of all pedestrians killed are over forty-five years of age (see Fig. 12–4). The death rate for pedestrians sixty-five years and older is higher than

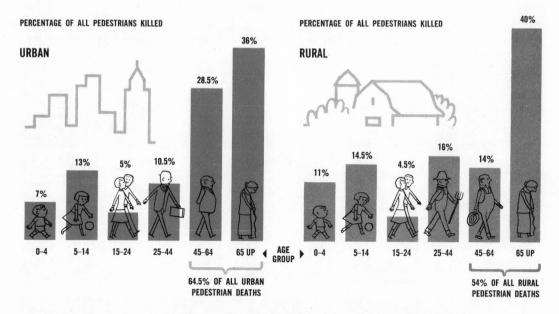

URBAN

36%

28.5%

7%

13%

5%

10.5%

0-4   5-14   15-24   25-44   45-64   65 UP

64.5% OF ALL URBAN
PEDESTRIAN DEATHS

◄ AGE
GROUP ►

RURAL

40%

16%

11%

14.5%

4.5%

14%

0-4   5-14   15-24   25-44   45-64   65 UP

54% OF ALL RURAL
PEDESTRIAN DEATHS

Fig. 12–4. Pedestrians over forty-five years of age are the ones most frequently killed in both the city and the country. The next most vulnerable pedestrian group is that from one to fifteen years of age.

that for all other ages combined. Physical handicaps probably are largely responsible. This senior-citizen group probably includes a *greater percentage of non-drivers* than all other adult groups. Also, older pedestrians developed walking habits in days when traffic was lighter, slower, and less congested.

The Very Young　At the other end of the life span, children, too, are highly liable as pedestrians to traffic injury and death. Several studies have shown that about 60 percent of all pedestrians injured in traffic were under fourteen years of age. Though children are physically active and have keen senses, they do not fully realize the speed and momentum of the automobile and the driver's limitations. Neither are they capable of concentrating on the dangers of street and highway while their minds are fully engaged with

the games they may be playing (see Fig. 12–4); the driver must do all he can to protect them.

The Pedestrian Accident

The alert driver should know what to expect and when and where a pedestrian accident is most likely to occur.

On City Streets　More pedestrians are killed on city streets than on rural roads, as you would expect, because of the greater traffic density of both motor vehicles and pedestrians (see Fig. 12–5).

Those Jaywalkers　Those who violate traffic laws in crossing streets are commonly called "jaywalkers." Probably the most obvious jaywalker is the one who crosses a street between intersections. A person leaves a store in the middle of a block on one side of the street and crosses to the

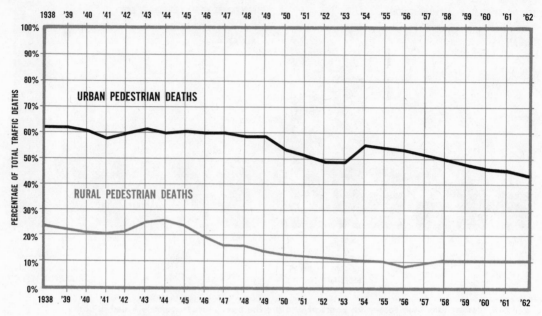

Fig. 12–5. The pedestrian-fatality problem is much worse in cities than in rural areas.

Table 12-1   Actions of Pedestrians Resulting in Death or Injury *

At intersections:	Pedestrians	Percentage
1. Crossing with signal	9,868	10.6
2. Crossing against signal	5,750	6.1
3. Crossing—no signal	8,823	9.4
4. Crossing diagonally	2,692	2.9
SUBTOTAL	27,133	29.0
Not at an intersection:		
5. Crossing between moving vehicles	24,380	26.1
6. Coming from between parked cars	11,293	12.1
7. Walking in roadway	4,383	4.7
8. Standing in safety zone	1,101	1.2
9. Getting on or off streetcar or bus	514	.5
10. Getting into or out of other vehicle	683	.7
11. Working in roadway	1,524	1.6
12. Playing in roadway	5,771	6.2
13. Hitching on vehicle	370	.4
14. Other in roadway	1,922	2.0
15. Not in roadway	3,612	3.9
16. Not stated	10,846	11.6
SUBTOTAL	66,399	71.0
TOTAL	93,532	100.0%

* Information from AAA Pedestrian Program Appraisal based on reports from 34 states and the District of Columbia. (1963)

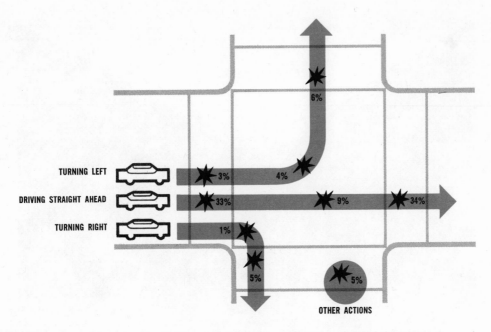

Fig. 12–6. At intersections, more pedestrians are killed by cars moving straight ahead than by those that are turning.

other side, often starting from between parked cars. If by chance a car approaches at that time, neither pedestrian nor driver can see the other until the very last minute. Note in Table 12–1 that the largest number of pedestrians struck in traffic were crossing streets between intersections.

While pedestrians are expected to cross streets always at crosswalks, as required by ordinance in many cities, the driver must always be on guard.

Pedestrian "Paths" A crosswalk is really a pedestrian path where the sidewalk would be if it were extended. Even at marked crosswalks, however, extreme alertness is necessary, for a substantial number of pedestrians disobey traffic signals and cross on red or DON'T WALK signals. Other pedestrians are struck by overanxious drivers who "jump the gun" as the traffic

signal is changing. Such thoughtless and unlawful action does not give those in the crosswalk ample time to clear the intersection.

In some states drivers must stop completely—even in midblock—when approaching a marked crosswalk in which any person is walking. Heavy fines may be imposed for failure to do so.

It may be generally thought that turning vehicles create the major hazard to pedestrians. But according to special studies made in Florida, Oregon, and Minnesota of the movements of vehicles involved in pedestrian fatalities at intersections, 76 percent of the vehicles were moving straight ahead (see Fig. 12–6).

This problem is further complicated by drivers parking cars so close to the intersection as to obstruct vision. Traffic laws in most cities forbid such parking.

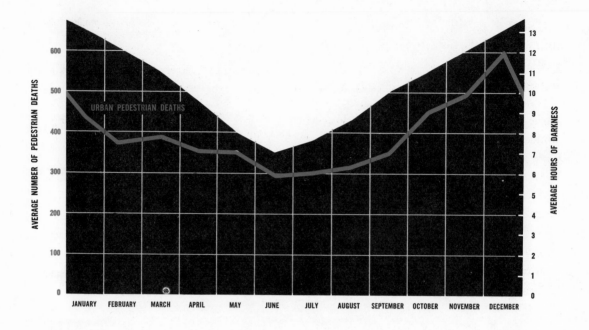

Fig. 12–7. The death toll of city pedestrians rises during the months having more hours of darkness.

Special traffic signals, including WALK and DON'T WALK, are used in many cities to reduce pedestrian-vehicle conflicts. Such signals as those shown in Fig. 12–15 provide exclusive time periods for those afoot and for drivers. As a driver, you must learn to recognize these signals and what is required of you.

That Rush-hour Traffic Pedestrian accidents reach a peak period between 4 and 8 P.M. Traffic congestion is greater at this time than any other. A study made in Washington, D.C., showed that nearly 40 percent of all pedestrian fatalities happened between those hours. This is typical of most city areas.

This is the time when weary drivers and pedestrians tend to relax and become careless. In addition, these hours include the hazardous dusk period, when visibility is poorest.

The Hidden Walker Darkness increases danger to the pedestrian. More than half of all pedestrians killed are struck during hours of darkness. Figure 12–7 shows how closely urban pedestrian deaths parallel the hours of darkness. Pedestrians are almost invisible to a driver at night until his car is dangerously close to them.

There are many conditions of visibility in which a person or an object on the road ahead cannot be seen. Sometimes a combination of darkness, bad weather, and roadside signs makes visibility very poor. The glare of approaching headlights may in itself obscure the driver's vision so that he cannot possibly see a person walking along the road.

172

The driver usually recognizes this condition but tends, unfortunately, to assume that any pedestrian will see his car and its lights and will step out of danger.

The pedestrian, however, seeing the car's lights and what in his eyes (accustomed to the darkness between passing cars) seems a perfectly clear picture, often assumes that the driver must see him. He does not step aside. Here are all the elements of tragedy.

Alcohol and Pedestrian Accidents

In Chapter 5, "The Sneak Attack of Alcohol and Drugs," we studied the drugging effects of alcohol. We must never forget that these same conditions apply to the person on foot in traffic. The person who drinks and then walks in traffic unknowingly takes abnormal risks. Depending on the amount of alcohol he has taken, his *judgment,* alertness, coordination, vision, and normal ability to react may have been slightly—or badly—impaired.

He is a person whose normal defenses are gone. Yet he walks in the paths of masses of steel machinery which move faster than he could at his best. One might believe that he is in greater danger of being killed than he would be if he mixed drinking and *driving.* According to statistics, he is! Look at Fig. 12–8.

The person who drinks and then walks in traffic might, at first thought, seem to be endangering only himself. Records show, however, that injuries and death have come to others when drivers swerved to avoid careless pedestrians.

It is just as dangerous to *walk* in traffic after drinking as it is to drive.

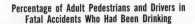

Percentage of Adult Pedestrians and Drivers in Fatal Accidents Who Had Been Drinking

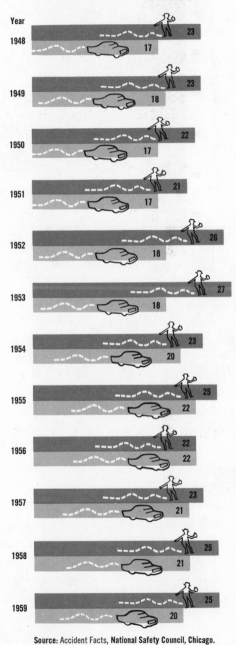

Source: Accident Facts, **National Safety Council, Chicago.**

Fig. 12–8. Accident statistics show that alcohol was a factor in a large percentage of pedestrian fatalities among adults.

Fig. 12-9. Be alert for midblock pedestrian crosswalks.

Fig. 12-10. Looking for a way to avoid old age, fellows?

Fig. 12-11. The pedestrian "speaks" for himself.

Fig. 12-12. A driver cannot see them.

Fig. 12-13. They must be taught to protect themselves.

Fig. 12-14. They are not thinking.

Fig. 12-15.
Do not ignore
the WALK signal;
it is there
to help you.

Fig. 12–16. This is all the driver could see. . . .

A flash bulb reveals what he failed to see:
a hidden pedestrian.

When You're Driving, Expect the Worst

Knowing the unsafe habits of many pedestrians and also the mechanical limitations of his car, the topnotch driver knows what to look for. He recognizes danger signals others would miss and knows what to do about them.

Good driving demands that you be ready for the most dangerous move "the other fellow" could make. If he doesn't make that move, you have lost nothing. If he does make it and you are *ready* for it, you control the situation and there is no accident. If you take for granted that he will not do anything surprising and dangerous, you can be caught completely off guard.

Here are some danger signs that help the best drivers anticipate trouble:

Suspicious Characters Children at play and small pets are recognized as a source of danger by an alert driver. Without warning, children intent on their games are apt to dart off in any direction. They may run directly into the street or roadway. Tragedy has struck many times without a moment's warning when a child darted in front of a car and was hit, or caused a driver to brake and other cars to swerve and crash. This is also true of dogs and other animals that are frequently present on streets and highways.

Those Parked Cars Whenever he sees a row of cars along a curb or roadside, the really good driver looks sharply for any sign of pedestrians in the vicinity. One may at any moment step out from between two parked cars directly in front of him.

There is another hazard in passing parked cars. A driver or passenger may open the door on the traffic side and step out immediately in front of your car. Many are injured or killed this way. Even if the person merely opens the door before looking, as many do, the inattentive driver may strike it. He sometimes finds himself with a "five-door sedan"—with one door of a color that doesn't match the rest of his car!

That Stopped Bus When passing a stopped bus, *look out* for people who may walk across the street from in front of the bus. Leave enough space between your car and the bus so that the person walking can see you and stop before getting directly into your path. This also gives you more chance to avoid him, possibly averting a swerve to the left and into another vehicle.

Children who ride school buses are taught to cross *in front* of the bus, since in most states a stopped school bus legally stops traffic. Sometimes when these same children ride in regular public buses they forget and start across the road *in front* of the bus before it starts again. Here, however, the law *does not* require traffic to stop for this stopped bus. Be alert!

Recognition of these hazards *well in advance of the danger* is a mark of the really excellent driver. When the hazard is recognized, a driver should immediately slow to a speed from which he can stop in time—if he must stop. He should

FIRST LOOK

THEN RELEASE LEVER

THEN LEAVE

Fig. 12–17. Remember the three L's before leaving your car.

also note the traffic condition in the lane next to him, in case an emergency "pull-out" to the left becomes necessary.

When You're Changing from Driver to Pedestrian

There comes a time when you've approached your destination as closely as you can with your car. You park. You are about to shed your identity as a driver to assume that of a pedestrian.

The Safer Way   If you always leave by the *curb-side* door you stand no chance of being struck by another vehicle. This is ideal for safety. For various reasons, however, most people do not do so. Almost everybody who drives simply opens the car door next to him and steps out into the roadway. Since most people do this, it is well worthwhile to develop a *habit* of looking over your left shoulder *before* opening the car door. The habit should be so strong that you cannot open the car door without first looking.

Bicyclists Move Quietly   We find a special kind of accident to be quite frequent and sometimes quite serious. Bicyclists tend to ride quite close to vehicles parked alongside the curb. Their obvious desire to give *moving* vehicles as much room as possible causes them to skim close to those not moving. Many a motorist has parked his car, opened his door to look out before getting out, and "caught" a bicyclist who was passing by. Many bicycle riders have been hurt this way. The probability of such an accident depends on whether the driver or passenger, in leaving the car, *looks first* or *opens the door first!*

A firm, self-taught habit of (1) *looking over his roadside shoulder* (*usually left*), (2) *opening the car door,* and then (3) *stepping out of the car* will eliminate those leaving-the-car accidents.

When You Are a Pedestrian

Many people do not realize that pedestrian traffic is governed by law in much the same way as vehicular traffic. Signals apply to the man on foot as well as to the driver. Various provisions of traffic law control the movements of those afoot. In an increasing number of cities, pedestrians are summoned to court for violations (see Table 12–2).

In City and Village Congested traffic in cities and towns seems to make the pedestrian's life hazardous. Actually, he does face danger frequently in his movements. The chief source of this danger, however, is not in the density of the traffic nor in the power and weight of the modern motor vehicle. It is within himself—his careless walking habits and his lack of appreciation of the importance of traffic laws and regulations as they apply to him.

Based on existing laws and sound practices, the following rules comprise an excellent safeguard for all pedestrians:

1. Always look carefully in all directions before crossing.
2. Continue giving short, quick glances in all directions until you have completely crossed the street. Don't forget to keep checking for cars turning left or right from *the street directly in back of you.*
3. Never step out into the street from between parked cars.
4. Cross streets only at intersections.
5. Obey traffic signals as rigidly as you expect drivers to obey them, crossing only with a green light or a pedestrian WALK signal.
6. Never cross a street by weaving in and out between cars.
7. After alighting from a public bus, wait until it has moved on before attempting to cross the street, except when protected by a traffic signal or a police officer.
8. The adult who cooperates with School Safety Patrol members on duty sets an excellent example for young children. He also gives the Patrol members themselves a feeling of being recognized and appreciated. Cooperate!
9. Never allow young children to play in the roadway!
10. No one would want to be responsible for the death or injury of a child. When an older person darts across a street against a traffic signal, who knows what big eyes in a small person may be watching? They see and follow examples. Some of our examples may be very costly!

On Rural Highways Out of town, the conditions are somewhat different. Traffic is less dense but moving faster. Highway lighting usually is not comparable to that of city streets. Lights on moving vehicles are usually the main, or only, aid to night vision. Stopping distances are much longer because of the much higher speeds.

Table 12-2 Enforcement of Pedestrian Ordinances in 32 Cities During One Year

City population class	PEDESTRIAN ARRESTS FOR			PEDESTRIAN WRITTEN WARNINGS FOR		DRIVER ARRESTS FOR
	Intoxi-cation	Crossing against signal	Crossing between intersections	Crossing against signal	Crossing between intersections	Violation of pedestrian right of way
Over 500,000						
Baltimore, Md.	....	....	....	....	....	....
Buffalo, N.Y.	2,787	....	10	....	....	....
Chicago, Ill.	....	....	....	....	....	8,421
Cincinnati, Ohio	6,104	3,421	1,140	6,288	2,096	....
Cleveland, Ohio	3,946	4,784	7,054	....	....	588
Detroit, Mich.	10,488	37,026	34,553	....	....	3,594
New York, N.Y.	200,000	37,905	2,056	....	....	1,046
Milwaukee, Wis.	17,575	6,047	2,016	5,962	1,987	795
Pittsburgh, Pa.	8,741	....	....	....	....	299
Philadelphia, Pa.	41,059	....	....	8,256	2,748	1,526
St. Louis, Mo.	7,847	10,749	3,583	....	....	1,008
Los Angeles, Calif.	80,119	17,198	33,262	....	....	16,780
Seattle, Wash.	14,851	3,074	7,170	....	....	2,463
Washington, D.C.	47,950	1,002	457	18	7	320
200,000—500,000						
Columbus, Ohio	5,608	1,089	1,783	....	....	90
Dayton, Ohio	7,018	1,726	5,391	....	352	44
Des Moines, Iowa	4,454	551	184	....	....	....
Fort Worth, Texas	14,021	251	170	....	....	62
Indianapolis, Ind.	9,134	889	828	....	....	202
Grand Rapids, Mich.	1,454	48	148	2	6	62
Long Beach, Calif.	3,100	15	369	....	....	443
Norfolk, Va.	5,336	....	....	....	....	6,987
Albuquerque, N.M.	1,015	47	185	....	....	86
Portland, Ore.	8,400	7,804	9,635	....	....	433
Richmond, Va.	9,127	534	123	....	....	47
Rochester, N.Y.	3,650	799	503	....	....	50
St. Paul, Minn.	....	....	37	....	....	75
San Jose, Calif.	6,333	243	86	....	....	838
Syracuse, N.Y.	2,332	....	....	....	....	3
Tulsa, Okla.	5,252	50	16	....	....	9
Wichita, Kans.	1,587	56	793	....	....	296
Kansas City, Kans.	....	422	150	....	....	....

SOURCE: AAA Pedestrian Program Appraisal

Traffic accidents, especially pedestrian accidents, are usually more serious; fatal accidents are more frequent. The person on foot should be aware of these dangers and remain constantly alert to avoid them. Here are six good rules for pedestrians walking along rural highways:

1. Use highway sidewalks or footpaths where they are provided.
2. Walk on the *left* side of the roadway, facing oncoming cars.
3. Step off the road if cars are going to pass each other near you.
4. Wear something white at night or carry a light. (The white is seen at a greater distance if it is worn low on the body, as shoes, hosiery, or even a white band tied around the ankle.)
5. Always remember that drivers passing each other at night are apt to be blinded, or partially blinded, by headlights. They may not see a person on foot at all. He must protect himself by stepping well away from their paths.
6. Where a pedestrian overpass or underpass is provided, by all means use it! Many people have been killed because they failed to judge the speed of fast-moving vehicles.

Pedestrian-safety Programs Pedestrian safety must be planned. *Records show remarkable results from community-sponsored, planned programs.* It is a well-known fact that they save many lives and prevent many injuries. Since 1937, pedestrian deaths have been reduced 49 percent, while all other traffic deaths have increased a total of 37 percent.

181

Driver and Pedestrian Cooperation

We must share streets and highways when we walk and when we drive. Sharing is a part of civilized living. Sharing can be a pleasant experience if we understand others' shortcomings and, being truly mature, make allowances for them. We may then reasonably expect others to do the same for us; but we don't depend on it.

This is the important thing to remember: What difference "which hat we wear" at any one time—driver or pedestrian? Both need *cooperation!* It is merely a matter of intelligently cooperating with *ourselves.*

To Talk About:

1. During what hours and under what weather conditions should drivers be most alert for pedestrians?

2. How should experience as a driver help make you a better pedestrian? How will experiences as a pedestrian make you a better driver?

3. What seems to be the attitude of the average pedestrian in regard to vehicular traffic? Is he cooperative? Understanding? Does pedestrian attitude vary much with age? Give an example.

4. Discuss all the possible situations that could arise as the result of a driver carelessly getting out of his car on the traffic side, or even opening this door on a busy street without first looking.

5. In what situations should you expect that a child may run into the street?

6. What kinds of traffic signals, signs, crosswalks, or other means of protection do you have in your community to aid in pedestrian control and safety?

7. How do you account for the fact that most pedestrian accidents occur to those under fourteen years of age and those forty-five and over?

To Do:

1. Make a study of pedestrian practices in your community. Decide what the greatest faults are and plan a campaign to combat them and inform the public of existing pedestrian regulations.

2. Obtain information as to pedestrian traffic injuries and fatalities in your community. Tabulate these according to age groups: under fifteen, fifteen to twenty-four, twenty-five to forty-four, forty-five to sixty-four, and sixty-five and over. How do the results compare with national figures?

3. Make a study of hazardous pedestrian crossings in your community. See whether you can suggest ways to decrease the danger.

4. Have a local traffic officer talk to your class about the pedestrian problem. Discuss with him the results of any studies you have made.

5. Report all the things your community is doing for the control and protection of pedestrians.

6. Have someone in dark clothing stand on the curb, away from traffic, where there is little light. Knowing he is there, find out how close to him you must be (on foot) in order to see him. How fast could you be driving and still stop your car before hitting him? What should this indicate to the driver about alertness and speed? What should the pedestrian realize? Have the person put on something white and find out how much farther away you can see him.

7. Secure a copy of the traffic ordinances of your city. Compare provisions concerning pedestrians with the Model Traffic Ordinance. Are your city's provisions wise? Adequate? Too severe? What changes or additions do you think should be made?

Freeway—Thruway—Turnpike—Parkway—Expressway—the professional calls them *controlled-access highways.* They carry through traffic and have a limited number of appropriately designed "interchanges," which are the only locations of entrances and exits. To refer to them easily in this chapter, we shall call them all *freeways.* The "free" part of the word applies to the freedom and ease of movement, not to absence of tolls or motor fuel taxes. Movement is free and easy, yes, but whether freeway driving is enjoyable or not is largely up to you.

The basic principles and practices of Chapter 10, "Driving in the Country," also apply to driving on the freeway. Yet freeway driving is different; it involves some special features which call for additional understanding. These features, peculiar to the freeway or emphasized by freeway conditions, will be described in this chapter. If some time has passed since you studied Chapter 10, review it at this time. To that basic knowledge of driving on the open highway, add this special knowledge of the freeway. The well-prepared driver is at home on any road.

The Interstate System

In 1956, work was begun on the most important highway network in the world —a connecting network of 41,000 miles of freeways that will cover the country. It is known as the *National System of Interstate and Defense Highways*—or, in brief, as the *"Interstate System."* The Congress

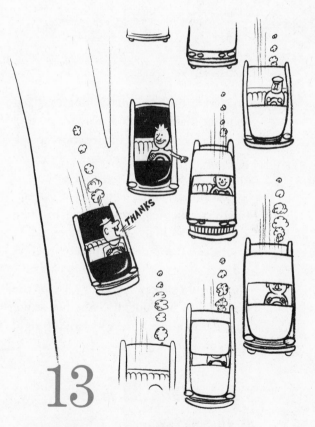

13
Driving on Freeways

Fig. 13–1.
The freeway
magic carpet
of the 1960s.

considered this one basic highway so important that it adopted a law providing that 90 percent of the construction cost is to be paid from Federal-aid funds. By contrast, not over 50 percent of cost is paid for on any other Federal-aid system. Moreover, the Congress gave this one road system so high an importance rating that the law provided for its completion by 1972.

Many other freeways also exist or are being built. Consequently, whether or not you are doing much freeway driving right now, you soon will be.

Special Characteristics of the Freeway

The freeway is designed for fast, uninterrupted movement of large volumes of through traffic and to minimize proba-

bility of accidents. Indeed, experience has shown that high-quality freeways usually have fatality rates (in terms of miles driven) which are considerably less than half those on the ordinary main highways. These results are achieved because of characteristics which affect the driver and which differ from those of older-type "through-traffic" roads. These are:

1. A limited number of interchanges at which vehicles may enter or leave the freeway. Except at interchanges, no adjoining land has direct access to the freeway.

2. No intersecting roads at the same level. No grade crossing with railroads. No stop and go signals.

3. Traffic moving in opposite directions is separated by a median strip of land, usually of considerable width. Neither crossing the median strip nor left turns are permitted.

DRIVING ON FREEWAYS

184

The freeway is destined to be the main through-travel highway of the future. The completed Interstate System alone will carry 20 to 25 percent of all U.S. traffic, even though it will comprise only a bit more than 1 percent of our road mileage. All drivers should know how to use freeways enjoyably, safely, and efficiently.

The basic principles of good driving are the same on freeways as elsewhere. We simply apply them to freeway conditions. Yet, the special characteristics of this type of highway create driving conditions that call for special preparation and knowledge.

Advance Preparations

Most airline trips today are fast, comfortable, and safe. One major reason is the tremendous amount of advance planning and preparation which has been done.

So it should be with freeway driving. You as a driver should have all the know-how and should be in good, wide-awake condition. You should know your intended route and the interchanges where you get on and off. Indeed, it's smart to know the interchange *ahead of* the one where you get off, as a "make-

Fig. 13–2. The Interstate System will form a network of modern freeways that will cover the entire country.

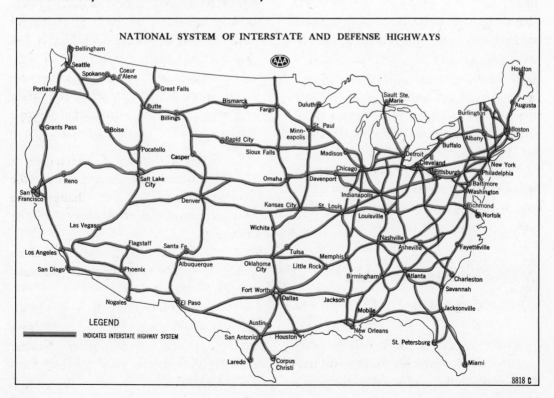

NATIONAL SYSTEM OF INTERSTATE AND DEFENSE HIGHWAYS

LEGEND
INDICATES INTERSTATE HIGHWAY SYSTEM

8818 C

Fig. 13–3. Planning the trip is both enjoyable and very useful.

the driver entering the freeway to select a gap and to gain speed *before* merging with the fast-moving traffic on the freeway. The ramp, with its acceleration lane, assures a safe, smooth entrance of vehicular traffic—*if both are properly used.*

One reason for this greater smoothness and safety is that the driver entering the freeway and the driver approaching can see each other. The former, while accelerating, should judge the speed of cars on the adjacent freeway lane, pick a gap in the line of vehicles, *signal,* and fit into the gap at about the same speed as that of vehicles on the freeway. Experts call this *accelerating into a gap.*

Most of the time on most freeways, the alert entering driver will have no trouble fitting in without causing much, if any, modification of speed by any vehicle in the lane into which he is merging. However, if traffic on the freeway is very heavy, it may be that no adequate gap will appear. Yet the entering driver may be approaching the end of the acceleration lane. The entering driver then *must* make the merge. It is desirable that he emphasize his electrical turning signal by extending his hand as though for a left turn (at the normal right-side ramp and acceleration lane). The affected freeway driver knows that he *must cooperate* and allow the merge; he does so by a momentary speed reduction to create a gap.

This driver already on the freeway should recognize that this is a special highway situation. It calls for the merging of traffic at high speed. When he sees another driver about to enter the freeway from an acceleration lane, he should

ready" reminder. It's a good idea, also, to decide in advance on rest stops or refresher breaks every hour or two.

The car, too, should be ready. A full gas tank is a good idea, since there are often long distances between filling stations. Check to make sure your tires are good, for freeway driving makes special demands on them. A sound fan belt is important: did you know that broken fan belts have caused many freeway breakdowns? Clearly, also, a freeway is no place for a car with steering trouble, lighting problems, or a need for oil.

Entering the Freeway

At the freeway interchange there should be a specially designed access ramp. This ramp leads into a long lane, which first parallels and then joins the freeway. Known as an *acceleration lane,* it permits

Fig. 13-4. Entering the freeway. The car in the foreground is on the acceleration lane.

recall one fact. He also is in that other driver's position at times. He also is the entering driver at times. He also needs cooperation from others on the freeway. It is in the interest of all, including himself, that this spirit of cooperation govern the actions of all drivers. Thus, freeway entry calls for increased alertness and at times a greater spirit of sportsmanlike cooperation than ordinary highway driving.

This special situation is not one a person would choose, but it does sometimes arise on very heavily traveled freeways, and it must then be dealt with. Beginners and timid drivers would do well to use other highways when they think such a heavy traffic situation may exist on the freeway.

The entering driver should not *stop* on the acceleration lane. For if he should stop, it would be necessary for him to make his entry from a standing start. If this should ever become necessary, it would be very hazardous unless traffic in the adjacent freeway lane was so light that a long gap would soon exist. Other-

wise an emergency situation would arise, with great likelihood of a multiple-car collision.

On entering the freeway, the driver should stay in the lane he first entered until he *knows* the whereabouts and speed of all other nearby vehicles.

Signal all lane changes well in advance and check your blind spots before moving over! And did you know that when you change lanes it is usually better to increase your speed a bit to catch up to a traffic gap than to wait for a gap to catch up with you?

Fig. 13-5. Signal lane changes well in advance.

Driving on the Freeway

Higher speeds, heavy traffic volume, and unique problems at interchanges combine to require emphasis on the need for special skill in freeway driving. Although this type of highway permits greater efficiency of travel, it also intensifies the need for sound driving practices.

The higher speeds mean that everything happens faster. They also call for longer clear spaces for passing and greater following distances. The heavy traffic volume means more closely bunched cars and more vehicles passing and changing lanes. Long, comfortable, and safe following distances are more difficult to maintain.

However, nature's laws are inflexible. Hence, your objective should be to maintain *more* than the usual following distance of "1 car length for each 10 miles per hour of your speed." When a passing vehicle cuts in too close in front of you, both he and you are in danger until the proper spacing is regained. To compensate for his error, you should drop back. Ordinarily you can do so without creating a new problem.

In very heavy traffic on freeways—usually in urban and suburban areas—you may find that if you create a really comfortable gap ahead of your car some other drivers will be constantly cutting into the space ahead of you. Such maneuvers involve substantially increased hazards.

What to do? You can leave the freeway. Or, you can reduce the gap ahead just enough to discourage others from trying to move into it. This, of course, never justifies "tailgating." Be sure you leave a sufficient distance ahead of you so that you are not creating a greater hazard than the drivers cutting in. Better, take this additional precaution to help retain a margin of safety: be alert to the changing actions of the second, third, and, if feasible, the fourth car ahead. You can ordinarily do this by looking through the rear windows and windshields of several cars ahead. Thus you can generally get advance warning of any change which might affect your peace of mind or your safety.

Bunching Hazard Why should your normal procedure be to avoid bunching, that is, following too closely one behind another?

Fig. 13–6. At freeway speeds, a longer following distance means a greater margin of safety.

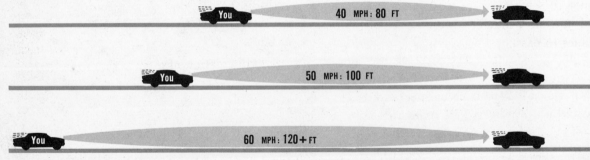

Bunching is not comfortable driving, for most of us. Moreover, bunching increases the hazard. Haven't you read or heard about large numbers of vehicles being involved in a "chain-reaction" accident? When such an accident happens, it is usually because drivers were following one another too closely, or bunching. In this situation, when a car unexpectedly decelerates sharply, all too often following drivers can't react fast enough!

Usually you can drop back to a reasonable, comfortable following distance—and it's an evidence of driving competence to do so!

Passing   When you are passing another car on a freeway, do so with *extra* care and concentration. Higher speeds require more alertness; they make passing judgments more difficult.

No Place for Loafing   With the bulk of freeway traffic moving at 55 to 65 miles per hour, a vehicle moving at a much slower rate is a serious hazard. Others are constantly overtaking it from behind, often having to slow down to await an opportunity to pass. When a number of following vehicles have to slow down rather suddenly, an accordion-type action results which can easily involve one or more crashes. Also, there is a constant merging of vehicles in the lane to the left of the slow-moving car as others shift lanes to pass.

Although it is true that no one should drive faster than he or she feels is safe, and some do fear high speed, the freeway is no place for a timid driver or a "slowpoke." Such persons should use other roads. As a matter of fact, many

Fig. 13–7. Slow drivers on freeways block traffic behind them and sometimes cause accidents.

freeways have a posted minimum speed limit.

Generally, a reasonable guide rule for sensible and safe freeway driving is to travel no slower than 5 miles per hour below the posted maximum limit, except when weather, traffic, or other conditions make this impossible or hazardous. Neither, of course, should one exceed the legal limit.

Darting   Observation of drivers who suddenly veer to one side or the other or who abruptly change lanes leads to the following very important rule for freeway driving. *Never* change your lane unexpectedly or suddenly! And *never* change

189

lanes without an adequate advance signal! Many fatal collisions have resulted from *abrupt* moves which forced other cars off the road. Some drivers, being forced into an emergency situation, have lost control, crossed dividing, or median, strips, and collided with oncoming vehicles.

Speed Checking Driving comfortably at high speed over a long period of time makes a person lose the feeling of moving fast. The freeway driver becomes so accustomed to his rate of travel that he is completely unaware of how fast the car is actually moving. Sixty miles per hour may seem no faster than thirty would on other roads. He should make it a habit to glance at the speedometer at regular intervals.

Keep an Eye on Other Cars   With many vehicles traveling at high speed, the driver must keep a sharp lookout, including to the rear. Glance in your mirrors, both inside and outside the car. Take appropriate action to avoid having "tailgaters" too close behind or anybody driving constantly in your blind spot. If a big truck is "tailgating" you, be especially concerned. For if you should have to decelerate sharply, the "big-rig" driver simply

cannot do the same. The reason is that his braking system is not nearly so efficient in reducing his speed as is that of a passenger car with brakes in good condition.

In such situations, you may decide to "get out of there"—or to slow down enough to encourage a "tailgater" to pass you. Whatever the action you take, it should be mature, responsible, and in accord with good driving practices. Be sure that you do nothing which would startle a nervous or inexperienced driver immediately behind you into any dangerous action. Also, make sure that you don't drive in another's blind spot any longer than necessary. While you are there, be ready for anything he may do, since he cannot see your car. This is especially important if you are driving a small car.

Since such defensive driving requires your full attention on a busy, fast-traffic freeway, a passenger with mature judgment can be of great assistance as "navigator." He or she can handle maps and keep track of highway signs while you concentrate on driving — yours and others'.

Fatigue and Monotony Are Dangerous

Absence of intersecting roads means freedom from normal intersection hazards and delays due to traffic signals and cross traffic. Also, the absence of customary roadside conditions eliminates other sources of interference and hazard. These and such other features as median strips

Fig. 13–8. Danger for the red car! One car is tailgating; the other is in a blind spot.

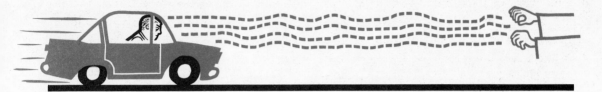

Fig. 13–9. Beware of "highway hypnosis"! At the first sign of drowsiness *act*.

to separate oncoming traffic are basic characteristics of freeways and are great factors in the excellent safety record of these highways.

Nonetheless, these very freeway characteristics also reduce the *obvious* necessity for constant alertness. They also tend to produce more boredom and monotony for the driver. Even if you start out wide awake, you may become drowsy, and drowsiness is more likely if you are tired, have eaten unwisely, or are not in excellent physical condition. You must remain particularly alert to recognize the first signs of drowsiness or sleepiness—or of what some imaginatively but usually inaccurately call "highway hypnosis" (see Chapter 4, "Physical Fitness and Safety").

What should you do when you feel the first signs of drowsiness? The best corrective is to get off the freeway and rest! But usually there is no rest area or interchange right at hand. So let lots more fresh air into your car—yes, even in bad weather, for it's better to suffer from the weather than to take the consequences of dozing. Take some new action: change your sitting posture, turn on the radio, talk or sing, vary your speed for short intervals as traffic permits, move your eyes to take account of the whole traffic situation. Remind yourself of the great danger of dozing—the *necessity* of remaining alert until you can reach a suitable rest spot. If, despite all such efforts, you find yourself still close to dozing, pull far off on the right shoulder, for you do indeed have a dangerous emergency situation.

Two Hazardous Moves The absence of frequent intersections also limits your ability to return to your intended course once you miss an exit. There is no opportunity to "go around the block." Watch the signs, be ready, and do the right thing the first time. In any case, never— *ever*—attempt to stop and back up for a missed exit.

Drivers of ordinary vehicles are prohibited by law from crossing a freeway median, or dividing, strip—even though special **U**-turn "slots" are provided in certain places for police, emergency vehicles, and maintenance crews. However, you will occasionally see a driver make such a turn. The act marks him as being not only irresponsible but also a very poor driver. Another car may smash into the rear of his car before he starts his turn, since such **U** turns can be made only at slow speed. Then, in addition to his difficulty in judging the speed of oncoming vehicles when he tries to enter the traffic stream, he isn't likely to realize how inadequate his acceleration will prove to be. He is a "sitting duck"!

1 Entering the Freeway (See page 186)

Where the ramp ends and the acceleration lane begins may well be termed the *point of decision*. Although slowing or stopping on the ramp should be avoided if possible, any necessary adjustment of speed to fit the freeway traffic situation should be made *before passing the point of decision*. Once on the acceleration lane, you should adjust your speed and position to permit steady acceleration so that you can merge into a gap.

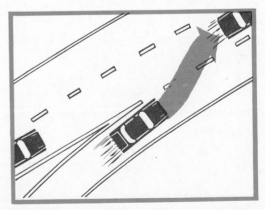

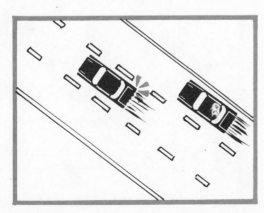

2 Lane Changing and Passing
(See pages 144–146 and 187–188)

The white tractor-trailer, which is not overtaking and passing, is in the right-hand lane. The driver of the dark tractor-trailer has 1. Looked in his left outside mirror (you would also check your inside mirror)   2. Signaled left   3. Looked again   4. Found a gap and 5. Moved left.

He will   1. Pass   2. Look right (using his mirror)   3. Signal right   4. Look again and 5. Move back into the right-hand lane.

3 Maintain a Safe Following Distance
(See pages 188–189)

The cars in this picture are well spaced. Of the *several* cars shown, only one may be said to be following too closely.

Can you identify that car?

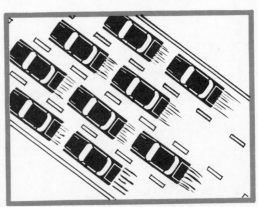

Too often, bunching occurs on freeways.

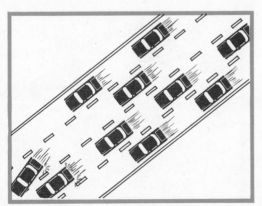

When a driver suddenly changes lanes in an unsafe way, all drivers behind him are affected.

4 The Urban Freeway

(See pages 188–189)

Driving in heavy traffic on urban and suburban freeways, with lane changing and passing, requires alertness to the movements of *several* cars ahead. At freeway speeds the need to drive ahead is especially important.

5 Driving Ahead (See page 138)

The white car in the right foreground was in the right-hand lane. The driver saw the car entering from the right and judged that his own speed would be greater for some distance past the point of merging. He looked, signalled, looked, and moved left to avoid conflict or unnecessary speed change. When the passing is completed, he will move right again.

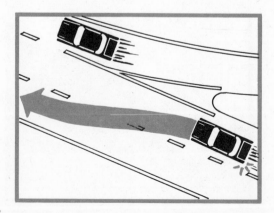

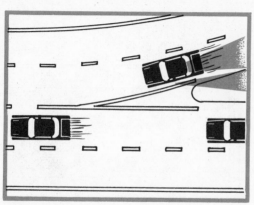

6 Merging on Multi-lane Freeways
(See page 28)

Because the fields of vision of car mirrors are not sufficient for merging on freeways, the driver must turn his head to look for conflicting traffic. The brief glance technique is safest.

7 Overhead Guides

Complex urban freeway interchanges often make specific lane use imperative. Overhead signs are posted to designate proper lane use. Heavy traffic makes it necessary to get into the proper lane as soon as you see the guide sign.

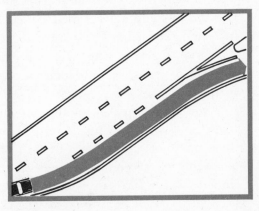

8 Leaving the Freeway (See page 194)

To leave the freeway safely, you should
1. Know your exit well in advance
2. Signal, and move into the proper lane, when you pass the "exit ahead" sign (or before, depending on traffic density)
3. Move into the deceleration lane early (do not slow down on the freeway)
4. On the deceleration lane, slow and check speed with brief glances at speedometer
5. Observe posted speed limits on the exit ramp. Be ready for possible sharp curves.

Motorist Services Limited

Limiting sharply the number of places vehicles can enter and leave the freeway to interchanges and rest areas has resulted in another special freeway characteristic. The abundance of roadside services— gas stations, restaurants, motels, and stores—common to other main highways is not found along the freeway. Keep this in mind when preparing for your trip.

The driver must rely on his own foresight and common sense, used *before* entering the freeway as well as on it. It is surprising how many people run out of gasoline between service stations. A practice of refilling the tank at the first gas station you come to after the gauge drops to "½" helps to avoid this. The "out-of-gas" stop—like any other stop—is both inconvenient and hazardous on the freeway or even on the shoulder of the freeway. Frequent, planned stops to get gasoline also refresh the driver.

Benefits of Advance Car Servicing No vehicle should be driven on a freeway unless it is in condition for high-speed driving and without any known breakdown possibilities. In addition to the hazards and inconvenience of the roadside breakdown, a considerable expense may be involved. It may mean a long-distance telephone call and an expensive towing charge to the repair garage serving that stretch of freeway.

Then there is the situation where a tire "can't take" freeway driving. Even if you have to drive some distance on a "flat"—and know you are ruining it— you *must* drive on until you can get your car well off onto a shoulder. Advance tire inspection might well have saved you considerable loss.

The Emergency Stop On most freeways, stopping other than for emergencies is illegal. But suppose something *does* go wrong while you are on the freeway. Suppose the car breaks down. It happens! What do you do then?

At the first sign of trouble, you check other traffic, signal, and move, if possible, into the lane nearest the outer edge of the road. Then stop well out on the shoulder. It may be necessary in some cases to use the center dividing strip, even though it is next to the fastest freeway lane. But, if possible, always move to the right-hand shoulder—it's a much safer location.

Then show a *distress signal*. Tie something white to the road-side door handle or radio antenna. Despite some disadvantages, many drivers also raise their car hood. Stay near your car, *on the side away from the freeway traffic*. Never attempt to walk along the freeway for help. The freeway is no place for pedestrians! Police and highway maintenance patrols are alert to help you. They can usually summon aid by radio quicker than you could by walking for help. There are also good Samaritan drivers who will take the message of your need to someone who will help you.

If you must stop at night, turn off your lights so that following drivers, seeing them, will not "follow into them." The tail lights of a vehicle stopped on the shoulder have, with surprising frequency, been mistaken for lights on a moving car.

Fig. 13–10. He forgot gasoline, but he did stop well off the pavement and knew how to signal for help.

Result: A following driver has steered over and hit the stopped vehicle! Some traffic specialists having extensive freeway experience insist that it is safer to keep all car lights off, all the time, in such circumstances. They point out that there is as yet no universally accepted *lighting* signal of distress. Authorities are aware of the problem, and a national committee is working on it (and other intervehicular signal needs). In the meantime, some favor turning on your right directional (electrical turn) signal and your dome light whenever a vehicle approaches.

The foresight to carry emergency flares, or a battery-operated flashing emergency light may prevent a serious accident. Be alert when putting these in place, however, and remember that for freeway speeds, they should be several hundred feet back of your car. Even when they are in place, do not put too much confidence in their effectiveness. The experience of freeway operational specialists shows that even with *multiple* advance emergency flares or flashers, vehicles have still crashed into stopped motor vehicles.

The "automatic," apparently effortless type of driving of the freeway tends to dull many a driver's alertness. This, combined with high speed, makes stopping on or close to the paved roadway an extremely hazardous act.

In summary, when it is absolutely necessary to stop the car, the following procedure should be carefully observed:

1. Check other traffic, signal, and move if possible into the lane nearest the outer road edge at the extreme right.
2. Signal a stop with left hand and arm extended downward. Flash brake lights on and off several times. (*Do not* brake sharply when another vehicle is close behind you.)
3. Check traffic in back and then pull as far off the main, traveled portion of the road as is safe *before* greatly slowing down.
4. Stop *well off* the traveled roadway.
5. Set up your distress signal.
6. Driver and passengers leave the car, but remain nearby on the side away from freeway traffic.

193

7. At night, or in conditions of poor visibility, avoid dangerous use of lights.
8. When reentering the traveled roadway, wait for a *very* long gap in traffic. This is doubly important where there is no smooth-paved road shoulder suitable for acceleration. Fast-moving vehicles will overtake you at an astonishing rate while you are gaining speed.

Leaving the Freeway

You must know where you are going and where to get off the freeway in advance. If the route is unfamiliar to you, obtain a road map or thorough instructions before you start your trip. Know your exit-interchange name, if any, and

Fig. 13–11. Leaving the freeway, slow down on deceleration lane (right).

the number of the route which you intend to use or the name of the nearby city which will show on signs as you approach your exit interchange. Also know how to identify the interchange just before yours.

Look for informational and exit signs well in advance. You can then signal and ease over into the proper lane and avoid abrupt and hazardous movements. Now a "repeat": if you find, at the last moment, that you are going past your exit, miss it! It is extremely dangerous to brake or swerve suddenly to reach the exit. It is worse yet to stop and try to back up! Remember, an oncoming vehicle a long way back will, at freeway speed, be "on you" in a flash. It is far better to go on to the next exit, even considering the delay and inconvenience.

Move into the *deceleration* lane if possible before slowing down to leave the freeway. Then slow down *much* more than seems necessary. Remember, you are accustomed to high speed—you are "velocitized." This means you are very likely misjudging your speed, moving too fast for that fast-approaching turn in the exit ramp. Give short, quick glances at your speedometer.

After leaving the freeway and its exit ramp, *keep checking your speedometer at frequent intervals.* Especially if you have been driving on the freeway for some hours, it will be difficult for quite some time to judge satisfactorily the lower speeds required on ordinary roads and city streets after leaving the freeway. You will also find that extra attention is needed to readjust for cross traffic, parked cars, pedestrians, driveways, signals, etc.

Remember and use *all* the good driving practices you have learned in Chapter 10, "Driving in the Country," both on the freeway and when you leave it.

In all, the freeway is a safe, efficient travel route for the good driver. Know about it and be ready the day you first start along that acceleration lane.

To Talk About:

1. Why do you think the Federal government has been so concerned with the construction of the Interstate System?

2. Discuss the advantages of freeway travel. When might it be better to travel on some other kind of road?

3. Summarize the special characteristics of freeway driving.

4. Discuss the safety features of freeways. The special hazards.

5. What do you think you would find most difficult about your first trip on a freeway?

6. Discuss ways in which a passenger can be very helpful as a "navigator" on a freeway trip. List special duties he can perform to aid the driver. Include also things he should not do.

7. Discuss conditions that may call for greatly reduced speeds even though maximum limits may be 60 to 70 miles per hour. In what ways can drivers be warned to reduce speed?

8. There is a device which can be connected to the carburetor of a car so that any given speed can be maintained without constant pressure on the accelerator. Stepping on the brake immediately disconnects the device. Discuss the advantages and disadvantages of using this device for freeway driving.

To Do:

1. On a map of your state, indicate where the Interstate System now exists and where it will extend when completed. Does it now, or will it in the future, affect traffic in your area? Discuss the advantages or disadvantages to your community.

2. Make a study of the various types of interchanges that may be found on freeways. Construct models or draw sketches; then indicate the flow of traffic on these interchanges. (See Chapter 19, "Traffic as You Want It.")

3. Plan a trip of at least 300 miles on freeways near you, if possible. What preparations would you make ahead of time and what would be your procedure along the way? How do these plans differ from those for a trip on an ordinary highway? What particular parts or units of your car would you want to have checked in advance? What extra equipment might you carry for emergency use?

4. Write an article that might be published in the local paper suggesting certain precautions and steps to be taken when driving on freeways.

5. Find out the accident rates for freeways as compared to some other main highway in the same area. Compare the number of persons killed and injured per mile of travel and the types of accidents.

14

Driving Under Adverse or Special Conditions

The professional driver gets to know every bump and hollow, every bend or turn in his route. His livelihood and possibly his life depend on it. The locomotive engineer not only knows his diesel locomotive but he also knows every foot of the roadbed over which he travels. The skilled airline pilot knows his plane intimately. He also knows weather, flying patterns, and emergency procedures. This knowledge enables him to recognize an abnormal or hazardous situation immediately. The lives of his passengers and crew depend on his ability to recognize danger quickly.

Similarly, the competent motor vehicle driver needs to know not only how to manipulate his vehicle easily but also how to keep it well controlled under a great variety of conditions. He must be able to keep it on roads with constantly changing contours—curves, turns, grades. He must be able to adjust to ever-changing and repeated hazards of the road—other vehicles, pedestrians, intersections, and blind areas. He must know how to control his vehicle when road surface conditions are hazardous. He must be able to adjust to difficult sight conditions, also.

When a driver suddenly meets adverse conditions, the element of surprise adds greatly to his peril. The expert driver, however, anticipates such conditions and is prepared to take appropriate action. Knowing when and where such hazards are most likely to occur is extremely important.

Conditions—the Expert Driver's Guide

Each year at the end of October some of our state motor vehicle records show a sudden sharp rise in the number and severity of highway accidents which occur between 5:00 and 6:30 P.M. Monday through Friday. No increase of vehicle speed is noted, and the actual snowy and icy weather hasn't arrived in most of the areas affected. Yet, we find this sharp rise in the number of accidents. Can you think of any sudden change in conditions at this time of year?

There are really two main reasons. First, some states revert from daylight-saving to standard time at this time each year. What change does that make in the *conditions* under which great numbers of people drive to and from their work?

The answer is this: darkness comes an hour earlier. And when it happens to combine with a hard rain, many moving car headlights, brightly lighted signs, and red and green neon signs that become confused with traffic signals, it means *dangerous* conditions.

Second, some drivers do not understand the need *always to drive in accordance with conditions.* Some continue to

Fig. 14–1. Night rain and bright lights may conceal danger.

travel at their normal speeds, even though the visibility is greatly lessened. You know the result!

The traffic expert and the superior driver have a better understanding of speed. They never think of speed only in *number of miles per hour*. They relate the speed limits *and* the driving conditions. "Driving too fast for conditions" may be reckless driving even when you are driving well within posted speed limits.

Under some conditions, on some roads, 60 miles per hour is a legal and reasonably safe speed. At other times, 25 miles per hour on the same roads may be reckless. As trained drivers, let's remember that word: *conditions*.

Fig. 14–2. What caused this skid?

Conditions That Mean Danger

Let us look at some of the factors which make driving hazardous and the steps we can take to lessen or eliminate the increased danger.

Skid Conditions the Year Round   Slippery surfaces are hazardous because some drivers allow them to become so. If forty-nine out of fifty drivers safely drive over a slippery road, should we blame the slippery road if one driver fails to make it? We often read, "Slippery road causes death of driver." Should we not ask, "In view of the fact that forty-nine drivers went along without trouble, what did the one driver do?" He did something which caused the tires of his car to lose traction and skid.

The taxi driver, the trucker, all the professionals know what the word "traction" means. They depend upon traction for their living and for their lives!

So we, as the trained drivers of the future, stop here a moment and look in the Glossary of this book. So we will never forget it, let's really *learn* the meaning of that professional term, *traction*. Then, let's learn what determines a car's traction on the road. What special conditions may we encounter that will decrease this traction, perhaps to the extent of threatening our lives? What can we do about these conditions?

On Dry Roads   The average driver thinks of skidding as a winter hazard. Yet, a great proportion of the most dangerous skidding and sliding of tires takes place on dry surfaces. The average driver does not think of the loud screeching of tires before collisions as the sound of skidding. This type of skidding is, however, as much a loss of control as the silent sliding into accidents which takes place on treacherous wet or icy surfaces. In fact, dry-surface skids kill and injure more people than slippery-surface skids.

Many tests of tire traction on dry road surfaces show that traction decreases as speed increases. Hence, at speeds of 65 to 70 miles per hour, it is not safe to "slam on" your brakes. If they are not adjusted equally, one or more wheels may lock, causing loss of steering control. The driver who must make a quick stop or suddenly slow down should use his brakes with caution. It is extremely dangerous to lock the wheels in braking.

Sand or Gravel on Roads   Traction on hard-surfaced roads is not improved by dry sand or gravel, as it would be on ice. On the contrary, dry sand or gravel acts the same way a quantity of buckshot or marbles under your wheels would act. Your tires cannot get a grip because they slide.

Gravel Roads   As you leave the concrete and asphalt highways and go further into the country, you often travel on gravel roads. Sometimes you find that these gravel roads continue for miles and miles. Gravel roads are fine when there is enough dirt and moisture to keep them packed down hard, with as even a surface as possible. When there is not enough of this binder to pack down the gravel, the road becomes rutted. Free gravel lies in

Fig. 14–3. A smooth stretch of gravel road.

the ruts and over the road surface. In such conditions, speeds of 30 to 35 miles per hour are dangerous. If the car's tread is a bit narrower or wider than the ruts, either the front or the rear end, or both, may jump clear of the rut and head for the ditch.

Gravel roads may extend for miles and be well packed. Suddenly there may be an unexpected stretch of loose, rutted gravel that will trick the unwary.

Wet Roads   Rain and fog do two things: they reduce visibility and they reduce traction. A very light rain or a heavy fog can wet the surface of a good, dry road and make it a dangerous, low-traction, wet road.

Worn tires decrease the traction still further. The traction is also reduced as speed increases. Tires which are worn smooth have no squeegee action to push water out from under their way. Water prevents the rubber tread from coming

Fig. 14–4. The rain-slick road is *slippery*.

into close contact with the pavement. In keeping tires and pavement separated, the water acts as a lubricant, and the tires slip or skid across the pavement.

It is strongly recommended that you always use tires with good treads. Taking chances with smooth tires is likely to result in a skidding accident, the cost of which would buy several sets of new tires. It could even result in a serious injury or loss of life.

The First Sprinkle When a shower comes up after a period of dry weather, the first raindrops make a fine, slippery mud of the dust and oil film on the road. The road surface becomes quite slippery until enough rain has fallen to wash it clean.

Mud on Pavements Wet pavements are made more slippery by even a little mud which may have been washed across a road by rain.

Oil Slicks The millions of motor vehicles passing over highways drop oil and grease. Each car drops only a little, but the oil and grease gradually collect on the road. In the course of a year, this can amount to as much as 1,000 gallons per mile (or about 1 gallon for every 5 feet of road). A little wet fog on this film of oil lowers traction just as though there had been a light snowstorm. Be aware of these conditions, especially when rain first begins to fall. You will be driving on a slippery road.

Wet Leaves In the fall, wet leaves make pavements slippery. When brakes are applied, the wheels often lock easily. Leaves gather in front of, and under, the locked wheels, causing them to skid. If you release the brakes for an instant, the wheels will roll over the packed leaves and will be back on clear pavement again. Releasing the brakes at short intervals may be necessary to keep free of wet leaves.

Wet Steel Rails Avoid wet trolley and railroad tracks. Steel traffic plates or steel gratings over bridges can be very treacherous when wet. They call for a 20- to 25-mile-per-hour speed—no more! When it is necessary to cross tracks, do so at a wide angle and a very low speed, watching out for nearby traffic.

Brick Pavements Brick pavement loses a little of its good traction quality when wet. It can be very slippery when icy. A skilled driver will reduce his speed when he encounters brick pavement which is not perfectly dry.

Wet or Frosty Planks Any wooden surface in which the planking is laid parallel to your direction of travel is dangerous when wet and exceedingly dangerous when covered with frost or ice. Planks laid crosswise on the road are ordinarily not dangerous unless covered with ice or frost.

Bumps or Rough Surfaces If either the gas or the brakes are applied too heavily, a bump or even a bumpy surface can throw a vehicle into a "bouncing skid." The skillful driver reduces his speed before reaching a bump or a bumpy surface. This is true in any kind of weather.

Action to Correct Skidding

Skidding is the result of a combination of sliding or spinning wheels and some outside force acting on the car, such as centrifugal force when driving through a curve.

The immediate remedy is to steer in the *direction in which the rear of the car is sliding.* Most drivers will turn their wheels in the direction the rear is sliding instinctively, but occasionally a driver will turn them the wrong way. The idea is to keep the vehicle rolling straight ahead as it normally does, not allow it to slide sideways.

Fig. 14–5. Turn the steering wheel in the direction the rear of the car is skidding.

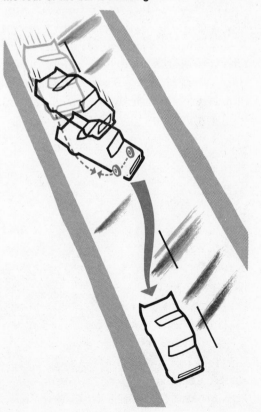

As soon as the car starts to straighten out the front wheels should be straightened to prevent a skid in the opposite direction. Brakes should not be used to control a skid.

Winter Driving

The automobile has become a year-round, dependable, and convenient means of transportation. There is little reason for your car not to serve as well in winter as it does in summer. Winter does, however, create some additional demands on its equipment. It is well to prepare your car adequately before the cold weather sets in.

The Committee on Winter Driving Hazards of the National Safety Council has conducted nearly twenty years of intensive research on driving safely during the winter. Here are ten items which the committee says deserve your attention and should be checked before cold weather starts:

1. *Antifreeze.* Have the cooling system flushed and put in antifreeze.

2. *Winter tune-up.* A properly tuned engine is essential to prompt starting in cold weather, and it helps avoid stalling. Difficulty in starting places a heavy drain on the battery when its output is lower because of the cold.

3. *Tires.* Install your winter tires before the first snowfall.

4. *Chains.* Always carry a pair of reinforced tire chains of proper size and in good repair.

5. *Defroster.* It is essential that this unit function properly to keep the windshield clear during periods of snow and ice. Know how to adjust the heater to keep down interior fogging.

6. *Windshield wipers.* Be sure the wiper blades are in good condition and have adequate arm pressure to sweep snow and sleet off.

Fig. 14–6. Winter driving is not easy.

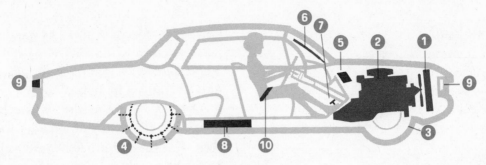

Fig. 14–7. Check points suggested to prepare for freezing weather.

7. *Brakes.* Brakes should be adjusted to uniform operation and relined if necessary.

8. *Muffler.* Be certain the muffler and exhaust system are tight and not leaking. Carbon monoxide can be a hazard in winter, particularly if you are stalled in traffic or a blizzard.

9. *Lights.* Be certain headlights, stop lights, tail lights, and electrical turn signals work properly.

10. *Seat belts.* Install and use seat belts. They are especially worthwhile under hazardous winter driving conditions.

Avoiding Sudden Action

You may find it difficult at first to make the change from your summer style of driving to that required for driving on snow and ice. In winter it is often dangerous to take any sudden action on slippery pavement. Even too fast release of the accelerator can cause a skid. By planning stops well in advance, it is possible to drive on slippery pavement with little use of brakes by permitting the engine to do the braking. Often, stops for traffic

signals at intersections, which are particularly likely to be icy, can be avoided by reducing speed gradually. This will allow time for the light to change to green and avoid the necessity of making a complete stop. Thus, traction can be maintained. In winter avoid the common tendency to *overpower, oversteer,* and *overbrake.*

Fig. 14–8. On a slippery road, any sudden action may trigger a skid.

ON AN ICY ROAD...

SUDDEN ACCELERATION OR OVERSTEERING OR OVERBRAKING

WILL CAUSE THIS TO HAPPEN

Fig. 14–9. On an icy road sudden acceleration, oversteering, or overbraking may cause this.

Overpowering Those who are not accustomed to driving when road surfaces are slippery have a tendency to apply power too rapidly. Foot pressure on the accelerator should be very light at first, then increased very gradually.

The seat should be so adjusted that the driver's foot presses as high on the accelerator pedal as possible, with his heel resting on the floor. This position allows maximum pedal control and helps to avoid sudden spurts of pressure that cause the rear wheels to spin.

Oversteering The steering wheel turns with very little effort when your car is on ice. It gives you the feeling that the front wheels are jacked up off the ground. Steering action doesn't feel firm.

The best turning power on ice comes with not much more than a 5-degree turn of the front wheels. This is equal to turning the rim of the steering wheel about 9 inches. Any sharper turn than 5 degrees *decreases* the turning force. Winter driving calls for steady, restrained steering.

Overbraking Overbraking locks wheels and may trigger a skid. On snow and ice, brakes should be applied *sooner and more gradually* than in normal operation. If the wheels lock, pressure on the brake pedal should be released *immediately* and then repeated more lightly and more gradually.

Starting on a Slippery Surface

Sometimes it is quite difficult to put a car into motion on snow or ice. The driver who is unable to move his car may have considerable trouble. He himself is delayed, and he may cause a long, embarrassing tie-up of other vehicles. His stalled car may cause an accident to himself or to others. Learning to start properly may save you from this situation.

Key Words—Gently and Gradually On any slippery surface, power should be applied *gently!* Sometimes, in starting a manual-shift car, it is easier to do this by starting in second gear and engaging the clutch very slowly. Sometimes you can start the car in low gear by "slipping the clutch," or engaging it at the friction point *very* gradually. In low gear there is more power to keep moving if it is required by such conditions as heavy snow.

Should a wheel start spinning as you are trying to start, traction has been lost. The gas pedal should be released immediately. Pressure is then resumed, *more gently and more gradually.* The spinning wheel makes ice more slippery. Try to get your start the very first time. In deep snow (or mud), a spinning wheel tends to dig the car in deeper. Very rarely does spinning a wheel help. It does help only when the ice or snow is so thin and soft, or brittle, that the moving tire wears through to bare ground.

Sometimes it is necessary to sprinkle a little sand or some ashes on a slippery surface to give the wheels traction. Many experienced drivers carry a shovel and a box of sand in the car trunk during the winter. Sand provides a rough, gripping surface when sprinkled on ice. There are times, however, when there is no substitute for tire chains.

"Rocking" the Car Sometimes, particularly in fairly deep snow, a car can be started by "rocking" it. Power is applied gently to move the car, usually backward over its own track first, for a foot or two. Then, just as the backward movement stops, forward power is *immediately* applied in the same manner. Again, *just as forward movement stops,* reverse power is applied. Avoid spinning the wheels under such circumstances.

With a little practice, a *rhythmic* back-and-forth motion can be achieved, increasing the distance covered and *lengthening the flattened track* with each movement. Finally, sufficient momentum is achieved to move the car in the direction desired.

Remember, keep the front wheels pointed straight ahead if at all possible! Use the car's own forward and backward flattened tracks as much as you can.

If the rhythm is broken even for a short time, it will usually be necessary to

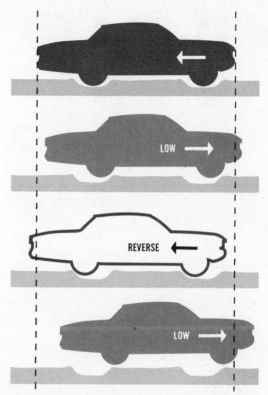

Fig. 14–10. Sometimes you can "rock" a mired car out of mud, snow, or slush.

start the process over again. Rocking is a driving skill in itself, and a little practice helps a lot.

Have Front Wheels Straight When Starting If the front wheels are turned, more force is required to start the car moving. If possible, steer straight ahead or straight back when starting the automobile on snow or ice.

If it is necessary to have the wheels cramped, apply power very gently and swing the steering wheel back and forth about half a turn. This helps to "iron out" a path for the front wheels. Sometimes starting from the curb can be aided by backing 2 or 3 feet first, clearing a path for the start.

Fig. 14–11. Putting on your tire chains.

Step 1. *Spread the chains on the ground behind the back wheels to remove tangles. Place the chain reinforcing bars so that they will not touch the tire.*

Step 2. *Put the end links of the side chains on the "applier" and push it on the tire, as shown in the first picture.*

Step 3. *Gather the chains up close to the tire. See the second photograph.*

Step 4. *Drive the car forward until the side chain fastener is near the fender. Remove the applier.*

Step 5. *Hook the chain together. Fasten the inside hook first, then the outside hook.*

Step 6. *After driving a few miles, stop and tighten the chains. This is important.*

Tire Pressures   The mistaken idea still persists that lowering tire pressure will help in starting. When tires required 40 pounds of pressure, there may have been some basis for this idea. Tests show that with today's low-pressure tires there is no improvement in traction from deflating tires below recommended normal pressures.

How to Keep Going

Your ability to start and to keep going is governed, of course, by your traction equipment. If you try to "get by" with well-worn regular tires, your ability to start and to keep going will be limited. You may become one of those who block the highways whenever there is a snowstorm.

If you anticipate driving in snow, it is better and safer to equip your car with snow tires before winter arrives. Have reinforced tire chains ready and, when conditions are appropriate, put them on *before* starting your trip. Remove them again as soon as the roads are clear. Driving on bare pavement will wear them out very quickly. Keeping chains tight will substantially reduce wear on them as you drive.

Avoid being a "road blocker" and delaying others. Have the necessary traction "plus." In many places today, snowbound cars are towed away at the owner's expense. Sometimes a heavy fine is imposed on the driver of the car for blocking traffic.

Uphill Grades   Although it is important that speeds always be held down to safe limits, controlled momentum as we start uphill is often necessary when traction is poor. We say that we "need a running start." Occasionally we see ahead a line of traffic blocked by one vehicle whose driver started up the hill too slowly and failed to reach the top.

If there are vehicles stalled on the hill and blocking traffic as you approach, it is usually best to stop some distance before reaching the hill to await clearing of the road. When the road is clear or traffic is moving freely, it is then possible to get a good moving start and to keep going.

Failing to wait and being forced to stop on the hill might mean being unable to get started again. Driving on the wrong side of the road to pass a stalled vehicle can be very dangerous. A car coming in the opposite direction on a slippery downgrade *may not be able to stop.*

When the expert driver approaches an ice-covered stretch of uphill road in a manual-shift car, he carefully gauges the length and steepness of the hill. He determines in advance whether his car will "make the hill" in high gear or whether it will require downshifting. If shifting to second gear will be necessary, he performs the shift *before* starting up the hill. He knows that when the road surface is very slippery the act of shifting gears on the hill and interrupting the steady application of power may cause his wheels to spin.

When driving on snow-covered roads, many problems are often avoided or lessened by the use of proper winter driving equipment—snow tires, or reinforced tire chains, etc. Trying to drive without chains when you really need them makes winter driving especially hazardous.

Icy Spots Following distances should be especially long in cold weather. A day or two after a storm, there may be icy spots on the road in such places as on bridges, under overpasses, or on shady stretches. If the driver ahead stops on bare road and there is any icy patch between you and him, you will be in trouble unless you have allowed plenty of following distance.

To pass another vehicle on icy, slippery roads, you require a much longer distance than you normally do. There is danger of sliding out of control if you accelerate too rapidly. It can be very dangerous, if not impossible, to move back into your proper lane quickly or to slow down quickly if you have to do either. It is wise to stay in line and be patient on slippery roads. Keep plenty of distance between you and the car ahead.

Fig. 14–12. Increase following distances when there are icy patches on the road.

Slippery spots are sometimes formed at intersections by the action of many tires slowing, stopping, and starting. Car wheels spinning on troublesome hills or sliding while slowing down for curves also cause slippery surfaces. Watch out for them. This rather common condition calls for you, as a trained driver, to slow down as you approach these areas.

Rear Wheels, Starting and Stopping

Inexperienced drivers sometimes do not understand how the rear wheels apply power to start the car. When a wheel starts spinning, they use sand or ashes under that wheel only or try starting with a snow chain or strapped-on "mud hooks" on that wheel. They are very surprised when, if that wheel then does not spin, the other may. When the rear wheels spin on a slippery road surface, it is usually necessary to increase the traction of *both* rear wheels. Remember to start gently and slowly.

It would be well for the new driver to know how power is transmitted to make the vehicle move. For winter driving, it is necessary that he know that if one rear wheel encounters less resistance to turning than the other, that one will spin while the other does nothing. It is only in recent years that some car manufacturers have designed differential systems to overcome this. These cause both wheels to turn under slippery conditions, even though one may have very little traction.

Stopping on Snow and Ice

One of the problems of stopping on any slippery road surface is that of applying brakes, yet maintaining steering control and avoiding a skid.

Research specialists have found, through years of testing, that the safest way to slow down or stop on ice is by rapid "pumping" of the brake pedal. Hard, steady brake pressure will lock all wheels, interfere with steering, and start or prolong skidding.

Pumping Apply the brakes quickly (lock them for an instant) and as quickly release them for an instant. Repeat this "on and off," "lock and roll" once or twice a second to a full stop. When this is done correctly, you feel a series of soft thuds. The effect is to give short intervals of four-wheel braking, alternating them with short intervals of effective steering while the brakes are released and the wheels are allowed to roll.

Downshifting Shifting down to lower gears and *using the engine as a brake* will help to slow the car down. There is one precaution to be observed. Shifting down too low on ice may cause the rear wheels to slide. To correct this, depress the clutch, shift to high, and put all four brakes to work by "pumping."

Effects of Temperature Changes

Temperature has a great deal to do with braking distances and available traction on snow and ice. As the temperature rises, ice and hard-packed snow become much more slippery—so much so that braking distances when the ice begins to thaw are twice those found at zero. Look at your outdoor thermometer when you start out. It gives a good clue as to what to expect. If it is approaching 32 degrees, it clearly says, "Caution. Take it 'slow and easy' today."

Hidden Change There are times during winter, in many areas, when the temperature ranges from well below freezing to well above. Temperature tends to drop at nightfall. Driving at that time and during the evening has a special meaning for the experienced, winter-wise, veteran driver. Any road which is wet, or gives the appearance of being wet, indicates danger

Table 14-1. How road conditions affect a driver's ability to stop in a given distance.

Driving conditions	Speed in mph at which driver can stop in 188 ft
Hard, smooth, dry, level, straight road, clear daylight; driver alert, car and tires in good condition. (Assume reaction time of 0.75 sec.)	50
Conditions as above, except that the car is going down a 5 percent grade.	49
Conditions as just above, except that the road surface is wet.	38
Conditions as just above, except that the car's tires are smooth.	36
Conditions as just above, except that fatigue has changed your reaction time to 1.5 sec.	32
Conditions as just above, except that you are driving on glare ice	17

when the temperature is near the freezing point. This is a road you check again and again. If you are moving at very slow speed, as you should under such conditions, an application of the brakes will "tell the story." The slipperiness of an icy or snowy road can easily be felt as you pump the brakes once or twice. On some road surfaces, night vision will not distinguish between a wet road and an icy road. In some cases, even a road that appears dry will be wet or icy. This is especially true when sleet is falling on the road.

Under the Car   There is one other special hazard occasionally encountered in this kind of weather. Snow and slush that accumulate under the front fenders of the car may freeze quite hard. If the car has been following a straight road for a considerable time, the forming ice may leave only a straight channel in which each front wheel revolves. *There may not be enough room to permit the wheels to be turned for steering.* Make sure that you do

Fig. 14–13. Snow and slush accumulating under front fenders may prevent turning the wheels to steer the car.

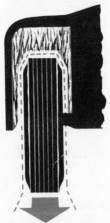

not allow this to happen to your car. Check for any icy formation which may interfere with steering the car effectively.

Visibility in Winter

Make every effort to see and be seen. Clear the snow off your car, cleaning windshield and side and rear windows so that you can see, *before you drive at all.* Just leaving the driveway or parking lot with snow-blocked windows has caused many people serious and unnecessary trouble.

Wiper blades and arms should be in good condition. Rubber blades, aged from the summer sun, are likely to streak the windshield. Even new blades will prove disappointing if the arm pressure against the glass is inadequate.

Be certain *you* can see. Do what you can to help *others see you.* Most cars today are equipped with defrosters and heaters. Use them and keep the car warm to aid defrosting. Keeping a window open slightly will lessen or eliminate "steaming" of the interior glass surfaces.

Use headlights on high beam to help others see you in *daylight* snowstorms.

Conditions of Low Visibility—All Year

Special driving precautions are necessary when visibility is poor. Car speed must be greatly reduced.

Approaching Bright Headlights Glaring headlights add to night driving hazards. Objects on either side, or beyond the approaching car, are very difficult to see. After a car passes, it is some time before your vision returns to normal. For safe nighttime driving:

1. Be sure that your headlights have been aimed properly. On a level road the depressed beams should reveal objects at least 100 feet ahead but be below the level of the oncoming driver's eyes. Make sure your headlights meet the standards of your state for light intensity and aim. Have yours checked.

2. Depress your headlights well in advance of meeting other cars and when closely following another car. The distance from an oncoming car at which you depress your lights is often prescribed by law.

3. Reduce speed when facing headlight glare.

4. Drive at the reduced speed until your eyes recover from glare.

5. Never drive blindly. Drive very slowly on the extreme right until the glare has passed.

6. When facing headlight glare, watch the right side of the road so that you do not stare into the approaching headlights.

Driving Toward the Sun When you are facing the sun, the light can be very deceiving, particularly if there is an accumulation of dust on the windshield. Oncoming cars may suddenly appear "from nowhere."

Similarly, if the sun is at your back, realize the limitations of sight now imposed on the *drivers coming toward you* and make liberal allowance for any surprise actions. *They may not see you.*

Twilight Twilight creates special visibility hazards. There is less light and visibility is poorer. Sharp line and color contrasts which make objects readily visible in the daytime are not seen at dusk. Reduced visibility calls for maximum alertness and slower speed. As soon as it starts to get dark, perhaps even before the sun has set, turn on your low-beam headlights so that other drivers can see your car readily. (Parking lights should be used only when the car is parked.)

Be sure you have your *headlights* lighted when you need them and at such times as they are required by law. This is usually from one-half hour after sunset until one-half hour before sunrise.

Rain Rain beating on the windshield makes it difficult to see ahead. *Reduce speed.* Even during daylight, heavy rain may make it advisable to use your low-beam headlights in order to be seen. The tail lights also will be lighted and the danger of rear-end collisions reduced.

For better vision in rainy weather, keep windshield, windows, and headlights clean and wipers in good operating condition. Mud, splashed by other cars from rain-soaked streets, spots the windshield and reduces visibility. This is especially true when so little rain is falling that the wipers cannot do a thorough job. Under these conditions, a windshield washer is of great help.

211

Even when the wipers do clean the glass they reach, smeared areas may remain on the rest of the windshield. These partial "blind spots" may very often hide persons or objects from your view.

Mud and dirt splashed up from the street sometimes cover your headlights. This should be wiped off to keep satisfactory lighting efficiency.

Fog Visibility may be at its worst in nighttime fog. The best rule for dense fog is: stay off the road unless the trip is absolutely necessary. Giving up the trip is better than the risk of giving up your life. Weigh that word, "necessary," carefully before starting out!

In dense fog, "creep." Drive with *low-beam* headlights, which throw the light down on the road where you need it, rather than out into the fog to be reflected back at you. Avoid any stop on the traveled road itself. Signal stops by slightly depressing and releasing the brake pedal to make your stop lights flash. Rear-end collisions are a special danger in fog.

Never assume a clear road ahead in fog. Drive according to the distance you can *see*. Usually that distance is very short. Drive in such a manner and at such a speed that you could stop within that visible distance, no matter how short it is! In dense fog, this means cutting speed to a "crawl"—the only intelligent way to drive under fog conditions.

If the fog lies in patches, slow down and *enter the patches at greatly reduced speed*. Patches of fog have led to multiple-car accidents. Drive as far as possible to the right of the center line. Watch the road edge carefully. Beware of pedestrians.

Fig. 14-14. Patches of fog spell "Beware."

Fig. 14–15. Mountainous country, beautiful scenery—and topnotch driving.

Fig. 14–16. Good advice for us all.

Driving Through Mountainous Country

Ours is a big country, with all sorts of topographical, or surface, features. Those who live and drive in mountainous areas learn to drive safely and efficiently in their own terrain. Others live where the country is flat. Experience teaches them about long, straight roads, high speeds, and the hazards involved. Many live in rolling country with hills and valleys. They, too, become used to their own areas. When any of these people drive in new territory, with different terrain, they have something to learn from the local folk.

Mountain driving, with downhill grades extending for miles, calls for driving that will not burn out brakes or damage other parts of the car. Sometimes it is necessary to shift to a lower gear or lower range and let the engine retard the speed of the vehicle. When this is done, vehicle speed should be kept down to approximately the same speeds as though driving normally in these gears. Letting the car gain too much speed under these conditions produces excessive engine speeds, which can seriously damage the engine.

Do not make the mistake of turning off the ignition to get more braking power. The engine will cool rapidly and continue to pull air and gasoline through the carburetor. This cold, unburned fuel will work down past the pistons. More than one novice driver has come to grief with an engine damaged by lubricating oil that has been thinned by gasoline. Explosion of the unburned gas in the muffler may also cause damage.

Use a steady application of the brakes, discarding the theory that if the brakes are applied and released intermittently they will cool off during the intervals when they are released. This obsolete practice is often called "fanning the brakes." Air cooling is very slow. If the brakes could be released for three or four minutes, they would cool appreciably. How fast would you be going, however, if the car were allowed to coast for three or four minutes? It would literally "run away" on any long, steep hill.

Again, if brakes were to be applied intermittently, the periods of application would have to be severe to make up for the periods of "no brakes." This would cause excessively high temperatures on brake drums and lining surfaces, possibly to the point of burning and destroying them. Tires may also suffer from heat.

Coasting Out of Gear   Occasionally, a long, straight downgrade may invite slipping the transmission into neutral or depressing the clutch pedal and coasting. Speeds may go much higher than you realize—high enough to whip out a drive shaft. The road may have a dip or two in it, a sort of "roller-coaster" effect, and you may lose control. Attempting to get back into gear can throw an excessive load on the transmission, clutch, or drive shaft, with serious damage. *Do not coast downhill out of gear. Do not hold the clutch pedal down and coast.* Generally, use the same gear going downhill that was required going uphill.

Some Special Care   Mountains, with their breath-taking scenery, are pleasant to drive through, but they do call for strict attention to the job of driving safely. Roads in the mountains are usually curved, steep, and narrow. Visibility ahead is often limited, and you take great risks in passing when going uphill or around a curve. Drivers who swing wide on curves, moreover, are liable to meet an approaching vehicle head-on. When driving in the mountains, stay in line and stay on your own side of the road unless it is safe to pass. When going downhill, remember that slowing-down and stopping distances are much longer for you and for everyone else. Uphill acceleration for passing will be slower, and the distance for safe passing will be longer. In other words, you have to readjust your habits of slowing down, stopping, accelerating, and passing.

Mountain driving often means much colder temperatures at high altitudes. In the early morning, you may find it foggy. You may even encounter a patch of ice when there is no sign of ice in the valleys.

Fig. 14–17. In rolling country, make certain there are no dips to hide oncoming cars before you try to pass.

On Rolling, Hilly Roads

In rolling country, roads often have short dips. A 6-foot depression is enough to hide a car from view as it comes toward you.

When you are about to pass another vehicle, you may suddenly find an approaching car rising into view from the dip in the road fairly close! It may appear suddenly, "from nowhere."

Main roads are usually well marked today for passing and not passing. Many have signs warning of dips in the road. There are some, though, where the driver's unaided judgment is the deciding factor in safety. There is no perfect substitute for good judgment!

To Talk About:

1. Discuss the statement, "Slippery roads do not cause accidents."

2. What reasons can you give for the fact that a greater number of accidents, and usually more severe ones, take place on clear roads in good weather than under bad weather conditions?

3. List places on highways that are most likely to be icy after a storm and where the wise driver will anticipate this possibility and slow down.

4. Driving too fast for conditions is a leading cause of accidents. List some conditions which demand reduced speeds, usually considerably below the legal speed limit.

5. What is meant by keeping a constant margin of safety? Illustrate how a driver would do this under two or three different driving conditions.

6. How many reasons can you give for slowing down when driving at night through a cold, pouring rain. If, under these conditions, you are traveling a stretch of road where 50 miles per hour would be a safe good-weather speed, to what do you think you should now drop your speed?

To Do:

1. Make a table of the various distances you might be able to see the road ahead in fog and figure the relative speed which would allow you a safe stopping distance in each case.

2. Make a list of all the things you can think of that might make a car skid. With each, state precautions and actions that would probably prevent skidding.

3. *Away from traffic,* at *low* speeds, on a straight, level, wet road without side ditches, experiment with different braking techniques. Do this with great caution. This practice is to show you how the car behaves under different braking conditions, to help you discover the kind of braking that gives you best control.

4. Describe driving situations with as many unfavorable conditions as you can imagine. List all of these conditions. State what you would do under each of these conditions to minimize the hazards.

5. Assemble clippings of accidents which you think were caused by driving too fast for conditions. How many different conditions are represented? Which is the most common?

Owning and Maintaining Your Car

Keeping your car running requires certain services. Whether performed by the owner or by a professional mechanic, proper maintenance procedures are necessary to the life of the car—and perhaps to the life of the owner.

When the automobile was engineered more simply than it is today, a great many owners did their own mechanical work. Rare today, however, is the owner who is sufficiently skilled to grind its valves or even to replace its distributor points. Most of us depend upon the skill of professional mechanics.

Let us, then, study our cars from a very practical viewpoint. Let us concentrate on what we really need to know about car features that to a certain extent determine our safety, our efficiency of transportation, our convenience, and our pocketbook. Chiefly it is a matter of *how to recognize* the need for skilled maintenance services—and of knowing where they can be obtained.

Knowledge of how the automobile runs permits an interesting insight into how man has applied science and ingenuity to an everyday need: transportation. Those having special interest will be fascinated as they study further the many engineering marvels of the modern motor vehicle.

The automobile is one of the major investments of the American family. It often constitutes one of the family's greatest financial responsibilities. There are many good maintenance procedures to be learned and many pitfalls to be avoided.

These are the very practical things we study in this section.

15

How the Automobile Runs

Those of us who enroll in driver education courses have two main goals: *safety,* and achieving as much all-round *operating efficiency* from our cars as possible. Beyond these two objectives, we can learn principles of good citizenship and respect for others, as well as something about automotive science.

However, there is so much to learn on the way to reaching our two principal goals that most of us cannot afford the time to study automotive mechanics in detail. Many of us simply would be confused by the mass of information a thorough study requires. The modern automobile is a highly complex piece of machinery. Few owners today perform extensive or intricate repairs on their cars. Unless an owner is unusually well trained and skilled, he should leave all such repairs to a competent and trustworthy mechanic.

There may be some students, however, who are interested in automobile mechanics as a hobby or a vocation. They may want very detailed information. For those advanced students, a list of references is given at the end of this chapter. Their hobby, or vocation, is a good one. By all means they should follow it!

How the Automobile Runs

Study the following pages of charts, including the summary page, and the story of how an automobile runs will unfold to you in clear and concise form.

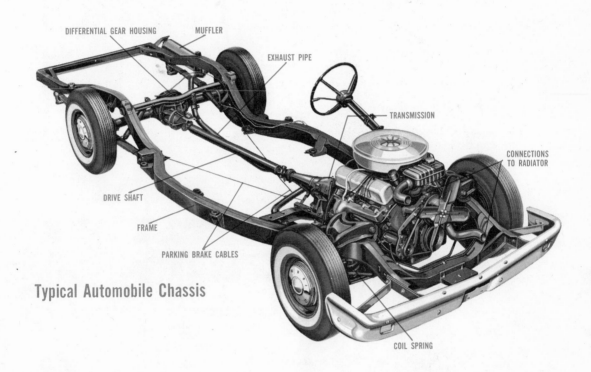

DIFFERENTIAL GEAR HOUSING — MUFFLER — EXHAUST PIPE — TRANSMISSION — CONNECTIONS TO RADIATOR — DRIVE SHAFT — FRAME — PARKING BRAKE CABLES — COIL SPRING

Typical Automobile Chassis

Automobile Engines

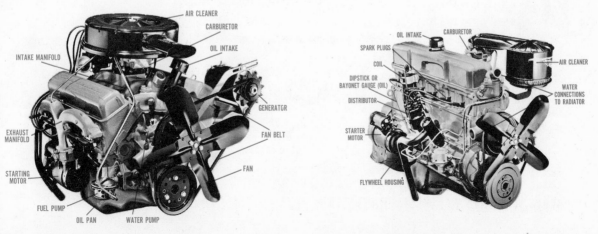

AIR CLEANER — CARBURETOR — OIL INTAKE — INTAKE MANIFOLD — GENERATOR — FAN BELT — EXHAUST MANIFOLD — FAN — STARTING MOTOR — FUEL PUMP — OIL PAN — WATER PUMP

OIL INTAKE — CARBURETOR — SPARK PLUGS — COIL — AIR CLEANER — DIPSTICK OR BAYONET GAUGE (OIL) — WATER CONNECTIONS TO RADIATOR — DISTRIBUTOR — STARTER MOTOR — FLYWHEEL HOUSING

V-8

Six Cylinders in Line

1 The Fuel System

CUTAWAY VIEW OF AIR CLEANER

1 The *fuel pump* forces liquid gasoline from the tank through the *gas line* into the carburetor.

2 Air enters the *carburetor* through the *air cleaner*.

3 Liquid gasoline and air are mixed in the *carburetor* to form *gasoline vapor*.

4 This gasoline vapor passes through the *intake manifold* to each of the *cylinders* of the engine.

The function of the carburetor is to mix liquid gasoline and air. This ready fuel, in the form of gasoline vapor, then goes to the *cylinders* of the engine.

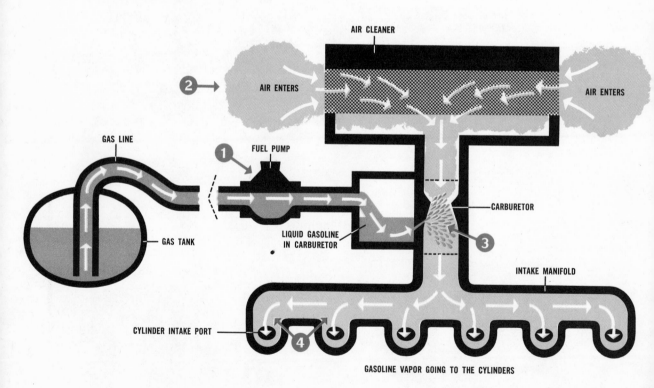

AIR CLEANER

2 AIR ENTERS

AIR ENTERS

GAS LINE

1 FUEL PUMP

CARBURETOR

LIQUID GASOLINE IN CARBURETOR

3

GAS TANK

INTAKE MANIFOLD

CYLINDER INTAKE PORT

4

GASOLINE VAPOR GOING TO THE CYLINDERS

Now We Have a Highly Inflammable Fuel in the Cylinder

2 The Electrical System

BATTERY

DISTRIBUTOR

SPARK PLUG

1 The *battery* supplies electricity.

2 Electricity flows through the *ignition switch* when you turn your ignition ON.

3 Electricity flows through the *coil*, where voltage (electrical pressure) is increased.

4 Electricity flows from the coil to the *distributor*.

5 The *rotor* (rotating arm) in the *distributor* rotates like the hand of a one-handed clock.

6 The rotating arm gets current from the coil (number 4, above) and distributes it *to each* of the spark-plug connections in *proper order*.

7 The spark plug is screwed into the engine so that the lower end is in the cylinder space where the gas-air vapor is compressed. As each plug receives current through wire cable from the distributor, a spark jumps a gap at the lower end of the plug. The spark ignites the vapor. The distributor is so made that it *times* the electrical impulse to each of the 4, 6, or 8 spark plugs *at the proper instant*. The spark plug fires when its piston is at the top of the cylinder as the compression stroke is completed. *Piston, cylinder,* and *compression stroke* are explained in Charts 3 and 4.

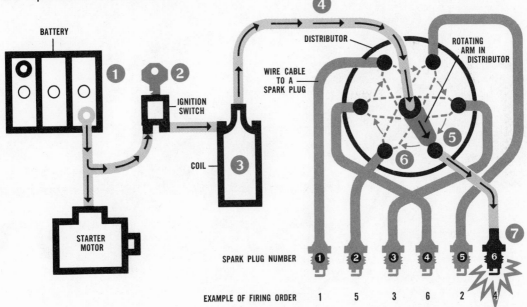

Now We Have Put a Spark to the Fuel in the Cylinder   **Result: The Mixture Burns with Explosive Force.**

3 The Power Stroke

How the engine harnesses the power of the gasoline-air "explosion," releasing energy that can be used to drive the car.

CUTAWAY VIEW OF CYLINDER AND PISTON

① The spark *ignites the gasoline-air mixture* which was brought to the cylinder by the intake manifold (Chart 1).

② The "exploding" gasoline-air mixture expands, causing pressure above the piston.

③ The only thing this pressure can move is the *piston,* so it presses it *downward.*

④ Like the bicyclist's foot, that downward pressure turns the *crankshaft* part of the way around.

⑤ *Like the bicyclist's other foot, other pistons push other* connecting rods downward, giving this first one the upward movement after it reaches the *bottom* of its path. There is always at least one cylinder "firing" and causing downward pressure somewhere along the crankshaft. Most cars have six or eight cylinders firing in a certain order to give continuous ("smooth") turning power to the crankshaft.

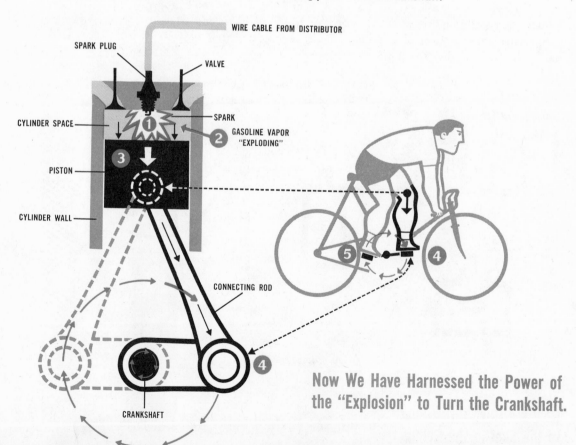

WIRE CABLE FROM DISTRIBUTOR

SPARK PLUG

VALVE

CYLINDER SPACE

SPARK

GASOLINE VAPOR "EXPLODING"

PISTON

CYLINDER WALL

CONNECTING ROD

CRANKSHAFT

Now We Have Harnessed the Power of the "Explosion" to Turn the Crankshaft.

Summary

Charts 1, 2, and 3 have presented the story of the principal factors of operation of the automobile engine. These should be well learned before you go on.

Remember 1.

Gasoline **+** air **=** gasoline-air mixture **=** fuel
This is mixed in the *carburetor* and passes to the *cylinders*.

Then 2.

The *battery* supplies electricity.

The *coil* increases the voltage of the electricity.

The *distributor* distributes and times electrical impulses to the spark plugs.

The electricity causes a *spark* at the base of the spark plug.

Then 3.

The spark ignites the fuel (gas-air mixture) in the cylinder.

This mixture burns with explosive force and

Pushes piston *downward* with *force*.

Piston and its connecting rod *act like knee and lower leg in bicycling*.

They push downward, giving *turning* force to the crankshaft.

Review 1, 2, and 3 thoroughly before going on.

Remember: We now have the crankshaft turning with power.

Be sure you know what a crankshaft looks like (a plain shaft would look like a solid round rod).

4 Getting the Fuel into the Cylinder and Exhaust Gases Out   OR   The Four-stroke Cycle

Now let us study the complete operation of a piston as it goes up and down in the cylinder. As you will see, there are four distinct actions which take place over and over again. Actions which take place in this manner make up a *cycle*. Since there are four actions, called *strokes*, in the automobile engine, we say that it operates on a *four-stroke cycle*.

1

INTAKE VALVE OPEN   EXHAUST VALVE CLOSED

Intake Stroke

The intake valve opens. The exhaust valve is closed. The piston moves downward, "drawing" the gasoline-air mixture from the intake manifold into the cylinder space above the piston (see Chart 1).

2

BOTH VALVES CLOSED

Compression Stroke

Both valves are closed. The piston moves upward, *compressing* the gasoline-air mixture into a small space.

3

BOTH VALVES CLOSED

Power Stroke

Both valves are closed. The spark ignites the gasoline-air mixture, and the explosion forces the piston downward, just as a bullet is forced out of a gun (see Chart 3, which shows this stroke).

4

INTAKE VALVE CLOSED   EXHAUST VALVE OPEN

Exhaust Stroke

The intake valve is closed. The exhaust valve opens. The piston moves upward, forcing the exploded gas out through the open exhaust valve. This exhaust gas goes through the exhaust manifold, exhaust pipe, muffler, tail pipe, and out of the car.

The four strokes comprise one complete cycle of a single cylinder. Each four-stroke cycle is followed by another and another in a continuous process in each cylinder of the engine. In turn, each piston transmits the power to the crankshaft.

We Are Still at the Point Where We Have a Crankshaft Turning with Power. We call this turning (or twisting) effort *torque*.

5 Transmitting Power from Engine to Rear Wheels: The "Power Train"

1 The turning crankshaft is connected to the transmission.

2 The transmission, automatic or manual gearshift, transmits the power of the crankshaft to the drive shaft. This power can be used for climbing steep grades at low speed or for traveling at freeway speeds. The driver selects the "speed" he wants. In manual-shift cars, this is done by meshing, or engaging, gears of different sizes, as described in Chapter 21, "Action: Automatic and Gearshift."

In manual-shift cars, the clutch is an important part of this power train. It permits the driver to connect or disconnect the engine from the transmission. When the clutch is in the connected, or coupled, position, power flows through it from the engine to the transmission. If the transmission is in gear, then power flows on through to the car wheels so that the car moves. Essentially, then, the clutch has the job of letting the driver uncouple the engine temporarily so that he can change speeds by shifting from one gear position to another.

The automatic transmission selects power and speed combinations as needed for various driving conditions. How the driver controls the automatic transmission is described in Chapter 21, "Action: Automatic and Gearshift."

Most automatic transmissions work on the principle of *fluid coupling*. Unlike a clutch, such a coupling connects the engine and the rest of the transmission through the action of one paddle wheel thrusting a heavy oil against another.

3 The turning of the drive shaft transmits the power to the differential.

4 The differential (through gears) conducts the power from the drive shaft through right-angle turns to the rear axles. The gear arrangement in the differential permits the rear wheels to turn independently of each other. The outside wheel, in turning a corner, travels farther than the inside wheel and thus must turn faster.

5 The axles, turning within their housings, carry the power to the rear wheels.

6 When the foot brake is applied, brake linings on all four wheels grip the brake drums to stop them from turning. Since the drums are fastened to the wheels, this pressure stops the wheels. The parking brake operates only on the rear wheels, or on the drive shaft, depending on the make of car.

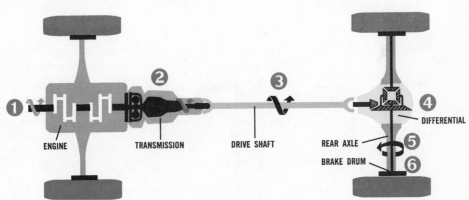

ENGINE   TRANSMISSION   DRIVE SHAFT   DIFFERENTIAL   REAR AXLE   BRAKE DRUM

The Power Developed in the Engine Has Been Transmitted Through the Power Train to Make the Rear Wheels Turn. The Brakes Slow Down the Wheels.

6 The Cooling System

When you burn a fuel such as gasoline in an enclosed place for some time, what do you get? *Heat*. Yes, and more and more heat as the burning process goes on.

Metal expands when heated. Excessive heating of the moving parts in your engine would cause them to expand, to "grip" each other, and to become immovable. Further heating might damage metal parts beyond repair. The engine, therefore, needs to have a method of keeping it cool. A typical cooling system is shown in the drawing below.

Surrounding the cylinder in which the gasoline is burned is a space like a pocket in the walls of the engine. Water circulates throughout this space, absorbing the heat which radiates from the gasoline-burning cylinders. This surrounding pocket for water is appropriately called the *water jacket*.

This water jacket is connected by two hoses to the top and bottom of the radiator. A pump keeps the water circulating through this system, as shown by arrows in the drawing.

The water in the water jacket, having absorbed heat in the engine, carries it forward to the top of the radiator. It passes downward through the core of the radiator, where it is cooled by the air passing through the core. The heat is passed off into the air. There are many little pipes in the core of the radiator. This increases the surface of the water in proportion to its volume, permitting maximum radiation of the heat.

The cooled water then passes through the lower hose, through the water pump which circulates it, and back into the water jacket of the engine. It then absorbs more engine heat, carrying it to the radiator in a continuing process.

The fan, aided by forward motion of the car, circulates the cooling air through the radiator and over the engine.

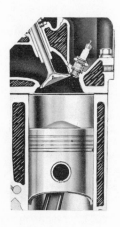

WATER IN JACKETS
AROUND CYLINDER

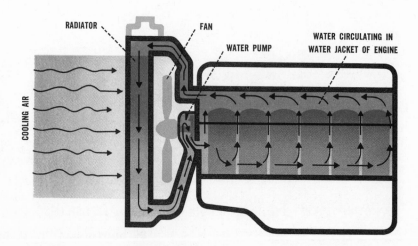

RADIATOR   FAN   WATER PUMP   WATER CIRCULATING IN WATER JACKET OF ENGINE

COOLING AIR

Power You Control, in Pictures

The color section preceding this page gives a picture presentation of how the automobile runs, and important parts of the car are named and shown. Scientific and technical terms are purposely limited; some are translated into more easily understood words and expressions. Those among you who are expert in such matters will note this, particularly in such terms as "explosion" of the gas, the description of the electrical system, etc.

Each set of photos and diagrams is accompanied by a condensed, step-by-step story of the action. You should always keep in mind that these actions are taking place at the same time. Each of these should be learned well enough so that you can recall it while learning the next. The parts of the car, the various "systems," and their actions are *interdependent*. Each one needs the others to keep the whole car operating.

A Challenge It has often been said that girls "can't learn" these facts about the car. It isn't true, of course, though there has been a marked tendency for girls to make much lower scores in this area.

The reason is that many boys already know by name the parts of the car and how they operate. When girls encounter the "new language," referring to so many unknown things, some become discouraged. To face a great mass of new detail, starting with so little knowledge or pertinent experience, would discourage anybody!

The illustrations and accompanying descriptions used herein are not difficult to grasp. Tackle this subject as you would a more difficult one in physics, mathematics, or some other academic field. Piece together the parts of the story. Make it a challenge. See whether the boys are "mentally superior" after all.

Allot Your Time Both boys and girls can make maximum use of their study time by following these suggestions:

1. Carefully study the illustrations and accompanying descriptions in Charts 1, 2, and 3. Learn each one before going on to the next.

2. Then use the summary to review the material covered in these three charts. If you find anything on this summary which you don't understand fully, review the appropriate chart.

3. Study Chart 4 for further details on the working of an engine.

4. Then study Charts 5 and 6, which contain important aspects of automobile operation.

There is another vital aspect of car operation which can be described in a few words. When two pieces of metal rub together, there is *friction*. This means wear, heat, and perhaps serious damage. Manufacturers of cars and other machinery put something between each two pieces of "rubbing" metal. They do it to reduce friction, wear, heat, or serious damage. What is the "something"? *Oil*, or grease. What do we call the process of applying oil or grease? *Lubrication.* How a driver keeps track of the lubrication of his engine and car body is dealt with in Chapter 16, "Taking Care of Your Car."

The engine, with a pump to circulate the oil, has a *lubrication system.* This use of oil and grease to reduce friction and its wear is the principle of one system. Now you know how one of the car's several systems works. You will find the other operating systems equally interesting and just as easy to understand if you study them carefully.

For the average driver, this is the story of the car you enjoy so much.

Further Study

This chapter is designed to give you an understanding of the principles by which the automobile runs. There are, of course, many other details familiar to a mechanic or an automotive engineer. These details rarely, if ever, concern today's drivers.

If, as a matter of interest or as a hobby, you feel that you would like to pursue the subject further, there are sources of information recommended under "To Look Up." For advanced hobbyists, there are many other specialized books and magazines in public and school libraries.

To Look Up:

Automobile Engine Rebuilding and Maintenance, H. T. Glenn, Chilton Company—Book Division, Philadelphia, 1958.

Automobile Power Accessories, H. T. Glenn, Chilton Company—Book Division, Philadelphia, 1959.

Automotive Mechanics, W. H. Crouse, McGraw-Hill Book Company, New York, 1960.

Automotive Mechanics: Principles and Practices, J. D. Heitner, D. Van Nostrand Company, Inc., Princeton, N.J., 1953.

Glenn's New Auto Repair Manual, H. T. Glenn, Chilton Company—Book Division, Philadelphia, 1961.

Automotive Electrical Equipment, W. H. Crouse, McGraw-Hill Book Company, New York, 1963.

Automotive Engines, William H. Crouse, McGraw-Hill Book Company, New York, 1964.

Motor Services New Automotive Encyclopedia, W. K. Toboldt and Jud Purvis, Goodheart-Willcox Company, Inc., Chicago, Ill., 1960.

To Talk About:

1. Why is the third stroke of the piston in a four-cycle engine called the "power stroke"? What keeps the crankshaft turning smoothly between power strokes?

2. Explain by what means the up-and-down motion of the pistons is changed to rotary motion.

3. What do you think are the advantages and disadvantages of an increased number of cylinders in automobile engines?

4. What might be the effect of faulty spark plugs or distributor points?

5. Discuss the idea that the clutch is the "connecting link" between the engine and the rear wheels of the car.

To Do:

1. If you are not familiar with the engine of a car, look under the hood and see how many of the following parts you can identify: air cleaner, carburetor, intake manifold, generator, battery, coil, distributor, spark plugs, exhaust manifold, radiator, fan, fan belt, starter (starting motor).

2. Write out the "life history" of a drop of gasoline from the time it is put into the tank at the filling station until it has been fully utilized by the car.

3. Find out how a "fluid coupling" works. How does it take the place of a clutch?

4. Bring to class some object containing a gear to see what it looks like and how it works.

5. Trace the "power train" from the engine to the rear wheels of the car.

6. Make a list of all the automobile parts mentioned in the chapter. Divide your study group into two sections, as in an old-fashioned spelling bee. Let the instructor assign the terms in the list as he would spelling words. If a student cannot explain the term satisfactorily, a point is awarded to the other side and the term goes to the other side. See which side can get the better score.

16

Taking Care of Your Car

History tells us of people of the past who were famous as horsemen and who depended for their lives on the strength and stamina of the horses they rode. Their reputations as horsemen depended, to a large extent, on the exacting care they gave to the well-being of their horses.

The veteran combat soldier or marine knows he has one possession that can guard his life—his rifle. He is constantly cleaning it and oiling it. He makes sure it is always clear of snow, water, mud, dirt, and rust.

This makes sense. It makes sense, too, that the modern civilian counterpart of these men efficiently maintains the machine upon which *he* depends. The average American lives with his car. His financial well-being and that of his family are closely tied to it. All their lives de-

pend on it, how it is driven, and how it is kept.

There are three main objectives of car maintenance: *safety, economy,* and *efficiency.* If a vehicle is kept in safe operating condition, its owner is performing a duty to society—to all of us. He is protecting himself, too. Beyond that, its economy and operating efficiency affect him and perhaps his family as well. To achieve these objectives, he must know a number of things about taking care of a car.

Car maintenance, then, can be divided into two categories: procedures necessary for safety, and procedures designed for economy and efficiency of operation. Good maintenance procedures help us to achieve all three of these important objectives.

Keeping the Car Safe to Drive

If a man suffers tooth decay, yet doesn't see a dentist, there is only one person to blame for the trouble that follows. That a man or woman driver cannot make mechanical repairs is not the slightest excuse for his not recognizing the *need*. ("I didn't know" has never erased a single accident. "I didn't have time" and "I couldn't afford it" excuse no one, either.) When we first take the wheel of a car, we assume full adult responsibility. From that moment on to the last day we drive, whatever a car does we drivers and owners are considered to have caused it.

Neither the dentist, nor the doctor, nor the expert mechanic can help you if you do not recognize signs of trouble and go to them for their skilled services. Our real responsibility today is not specifically to know how to repair mechanical defects but to *recognize* them and to take appropriate action at once.

In general, maintenance for safety deals with the tires, brakes, lights, steering mechanism, and safety accessories. In the paragraphs that follow, we shall discuss some of the details of their care.

Tire Care

One of the areas of maintenance in which safety and economy go hand in hand is *tire care*. All car owners and drivers should observe the following precautions:

1. Check tires regularly for underinflation (air pressure too low) or overinflation. Keep the air pressure as recommended by the tire manufacturer. Don't underinflate for driving on slippery roads (see Chapter 14, "Driving Under Adverse or Special Conditions," page 207) or for hot summer driving. In the latter case, the excessive flexing of the tire sidewalls generates *more* heat. It also tends to damage the sidewall fabric. You should also know that underinflation makes steering harder. Check for leaks if tire air pressure shows a definite drop.

2. Check regularly for excessive or uneven wear. A "bald" tire (one on which the tread is worn off) leaves a very small margin for safety. It skids more easily and there is greater probability of punctures or blowouts. A tire which wears unevenly shows that there is some "front-end" trouble in your car. Have it checked by a competent mechanic.

3. When turning in toward a curb to park, the car should be moving *very* slowly as it nears the curb. Have your foot on the brake. Park within the legal

Fig. 16-2. Every driver should know how to change a tire.

Fig. 16-3. When these symptoms appear, determine the cause and correct it.

OVERINFLATION

UNDERINFLATION

UNBALANCE

MISALIGNMENT

TIRE PRESSURE GAUGE

distance from the curb, but be sure your tires do not *forcibly* strike the curb. The sidewalls of tires are easily damaged. A damaged tire might blow out later from the increase in air pressure which accompanies fast highway driving. The consequence could be serious.

4. Rotate your tires after about every 5,000 miles of driving, or sooner if uneven wear appears. The rotation pattern to even up the wear is as follows: spare to left front, left front to left rear, left rear to right front, right front to right rear, and right rear to spare. Check the lug nuts after rotating your tires.

5. Drive sensibly. Don't be like the Show-off described in Chapter 2, "The Psychology of the Driver." He uses his tires as noise makers to call attention to himself when starting, stopping, and turning. How stupid a person is when he actually strips rubber off his tires to make a noise which means, "Look at me!" It also means, "See how brave I am." And it probably also means, "Father is not looking!"

6. Keep oil, grease, and gasoline from contact with tires.

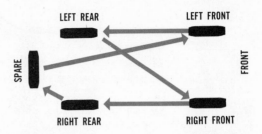

Fig. 16-4. Proper tire rotation lengthens the life of your tires.

Brake Maintenance

Your brakes are your chief mechanical protection when you are in your car. The foot brake operates on all four wheels. The application of brake power to the various wheels, as well as the reliability of the brakes, involves complex mechanical action (see Fig. 16-5). The day when most drivers adjusted their brakes by turning a nut at each of the rear wheels is gone forever. Brake adjustment is a job for a professional. The average driver should not attempt it.

The following procedure is characteristic of the mature, responsible driver and car owner:

Fig. 16-5. The braking system is a critical area of maintenance.

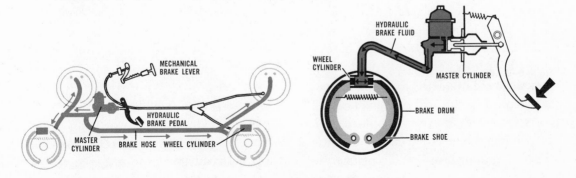

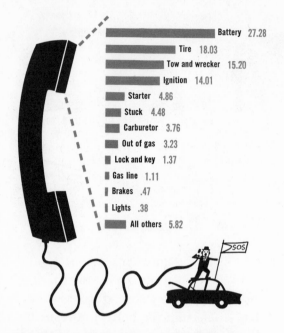

Battery	27.28
Tire	18.03
Tow and wrecker	15.20
Ignition	14.01
Starter	4.86
Stuck	4.48
Carburetor	3.76
Out of gas	3.23
Lock and key	1.37
Gas line	1.11
Brakes	.47
Lights	.38
All others	5.82

Fig. 16–6. Calls for assistance made to the American Automobile Association reveal the chief causes of highway breakdowns (shown as percentages).

1. Have your brakes inspected regularly and adjustments made as needed.

2. Have any badly worn or damaged parts replaced at once.

3. Have repairs made by a reliable mechanic, using only high-grade materials. An inferior grade of brake lining or fluid may bring disaster.

Mechanical failures have a way of occurring without regard for the timing of our periodic inspections. However, if a part shows wear at one of these times, a breakdown can be prevented. If the inspections are frequent and efficient, most mechanical failure will be eliminated.

When a breakdown is imminent, signs or symptoms of an ailing car often appear. These are things we must recognize. Just as we learn the meanings of traffic signs and signals, we should also learn when danger lurks in a mechanical weak spot.

"Trouble Ahead" This is the real message the alert driver gets when he notices:

1. The brake pedal, when depressed, is less than 1½ inches from the floor.

2. Continuous hard pressure on the brake pedal finds the foot moving down past the normal stopping point of the pedal. You must pump the pedal to make it "grip" at its normal stopping point.

3. The car "pulls" right or left when the foot brake is applied.

4. The brakes squeak or "chatter."

5. The brakes tend to "grab," or take hold violently.

6. Stop lights remain lit until you pull the brake pedal back.

7. *Any* abnormal action or "feeling" noticed during braking.

The driver who is interested in and knows mechanics will recognize one or more kinds of brake trouble indicated by each of these conditions.

For the rest of us—the great majority of drivers—they each mean just one thing. Have the brakes repaired. Now!

Wet Brakes After driving through water deep enough to soak the brake drums and linings, *try the brakes*. What happens may surprise you! Try them as soon as it is possible and safe to do so. Be ready. Your car just may not respond to your brake pressure. It is better to find that out safely and at once than when you are approaching the next intersection or when a pedestrian steps in front of your car.

Fig. 16–7. After driving through water, try your brakes and dry them *before* you need them.

You may find that your brakes do respond, but not evenly. Be ready, with a firm grip on your steering wheel, to counter a sudden brake pull to the right or left.

Brakes affected by being wet may be dried without much trouble. Gently apply pressure on the brake pedal while driving very slowly until the brakes respond properly.

Temperature Drop Sometimes, when driving on very wet roads or through water and slush, traffic conditions may require very little braking. If the temperature is falling, as it often does at nightfall, try the brake pedal lightly at intervals. Wet brakes can freeze while your car is running.

If you have parked your car under such conditions, or in a sleet storm, you may find your parking brake frozen when you try to start. Many times, when the car will not move forward, the brake can be freed by carefully backing the car a few feet.

Hints for the Wise Driver Do you remember how Nobody's Friend, the Show-off, drives? It would be worth your while to read about him again now. You can see that he is grinding down his brake linings as rapidly as he possibly can. Smooth driving, with just enough acceleration and a minimum of forceful braking, marks the skilled driver. He recognizes two kinds of waste in the hurry-up-and-slow-down type of driving. First, extra gasoline is consumed to develop unnecessary speed. Second, the additional braking made necessary by this speed wears out brake linings at a rapid rate.

In studying brake maintenance, there is an item about power brakes you should not miss. Read page 298 in Chapter 20, "Before You Start the Engine."

A final point: *Before* you put a ton or two of steel into violent motion among other human beings, you must control the only means you have of stopping it—your brakes.

The Steering Mechanism

Imagine yourself driving along a highway at 50 miles per hour. Coming from the opposite direction, passing within a few feet of you, is a stream of vehicles traveling at about the same speed. Now, think what will happen if one of those vehicles, immediately before reaching you, suddenly swerves to its left and strikes your car head-on. You would not have time to avoid it. The two cars would collide with an impact equal to that of a car going 100 miles per hour and hitting a stopped car.

Your first thought may be, "Well, who would do such a thing?" There are several possibilities, but one sure answer is this: "A man whose steering mechanism failed at just that moment: *he* would do it." He would probably be trying his best to steer away from you, but there would be one tragic flaw in his effort. He was trying to correct a situation he should have prevented. His effort came too late.

These things happen. Did he ever have a chance? He probably did. It is very probable that he experienced one of the following "feelings" in his steering wheel in the past:

1. *Too much "play" in the steering wheel.* He felt, when turning the wheel, that it would turn 2 or more inches before the front wheels began to turn.

2. *His steering wheel was hard to turn.*

3. *At certain speeds, his front wheels would "shimmy,"* that is, vibrate violently. Sometimes, when this condition is discovered, a driver will avoid those speeds but foolishly continue to use the car in that condition.

4. *His car "wandered,"* either persistently toward one side or from side to side.

5. He felt a click or bump in turning the steering wheel.

This is an imaginary case, of course. It is one way to picture the tragic result of neglect. It can happen and sometimes does. It can also be prevented. Regular checking of steering, brakes, tires, lights, and other equipment that affects safety is part of the answer. Immediate repair of anything found wrong by inspection, or in driving, will do the rest.

Fig. 16–8. The steering mechanism must not fail. Have any variation from normal checked at once.

TOO MUCH "PLAY" IN STEERING WHEEL.

FRONT-WHEEL "SHIMMY" AT CERTAIN SPEEDS.

Care of Car Lights

Good lighting is an absolute necessity for driving at night and under conditions of poor visibility. When car lights were far inferior to those we have today, and highway lighting was poorer, almost all headlights made visible the comparatively dark road ahead. A driver did not face glare comparable to that he faces now. Today, when great numbers of vehicles pass by, a car with inferior lights is a greater source of danger. If a car has poor lights, its driver's eyes adapt to the degree of illumination in front of other, oncoming cars. His eyes are not ready for immediate dependence upon the much weaker light from his own car after the other vehicles have passed. Neither can the driver distinguish his own poorly lighted side of the road when the opposite side is better lighted by much better and properly adjusted headlights.

At the same time, the more powerful headlights on cars today can be more blinding and more dangerous than ever before if not properly aimed.

Keep Them Clean The simplest and possibly the most common light trouble is dirt. Merely cleaning dirty headlights greatly increases the amount of light they beam, as well as night-driving comfort and safety.

Visible Danger It is easy to spot defects in your car's lighting equipment. Weak lights may result from dirt, poor connections, a weak battery, or corrosion on the battery terminals. A light that does not operate at all is a very obvious hazard. Check your lights frequently, including your stop lights and electrical directional signals. In most cases, failure of a car light can be corrected at very little cost by merely stopping at a service station. A burned-out headlight unit or bulb can be replaced in a few minutes with the proper equipment.

229

Fig. 16–9. Headlights should be checked for both light intensity and aim.

If all the car lights fail at once, it is probable that a fuse has burned out. This may happen anywhere, far from a service station. Learn, from your owner's manual, where the light fuse or fuses are on your car and how to replace one that has burned out. It is easy to do. Carry spare fuses in your glove compartment; they cost very little.

Headlights not only should be capable of supplying sufficient intensity of light but they also should be very carefully *aimed*. If they are too high, they blind other drivers; if they are too low, they do not give you sufficient visible distance ahead. Aimed too far to one side, they are obviously inefficient.

Many automobile-dealer service departments and repair garages have special equipment for testing your headlights. A good rule is to have them tested at least

Fig. 16–10. The front-end check may reveal a dangerous condition.

every six months. Some states require periodic testing of automobile safety equipment. Some make on-the-spot road checks where defects seem apparent. In any case, existing tests or their absence do not relieve any driver of the responsibility of keeping his car in safe condition.

Other Safety Equipment

The intelligent driver neglects no item of safety value. His horn, inside and outside rear-view mirrors, and windshield defroster are always immediately usable and working perfectly.

Windshield wipers occasionally need new blades or replacement wiper arms to press them against the glass. You will see when yours need attention.

The vacuum type of wiper tends to slow down, or even stop, as you apply power to drive up a hill. If you lift your foot briefly from the accelerator, the wiper blades will start again. You may have to do this occasionally in bad weather when driving up hills.

With the possible exception of cleaning lights and electrical connections and replacing wiper blades, few drivers repair safety equipment themselves. Most such repairs call for four things:

1. An honest, dependable service garage or service station
2. A skilled mechanic
3. High-quality, reliable parts
4. Most of all, a mature, responsible driver who recognizes trouble-in-the-making and takes action

Economy, Efficiency, and Your Car

You will learn in Chapter 17, "Buying, Insuring, and Operating Your Car," what the motorist's cost of keeping a car is. Who is the "average motorist"? Well, nobody. He is an imaginary person created to help us understand the mathematical concept of "average." Actually, there is a tremendously wide range of cost in owning and operating automobiles. One driver may pay three or four times as much per mile as another. Two drivers with the same make, model, and year automobile may pay greatly different costs. They may also get an entirely different quality of service from their cars.

Chart 1. Maintenance Tips on the Ordinary Gas Stop

Fig. 16–11. Little jobs your car needs each time you stop for gas.

Watch each procedure and understand it. Know what your car needs. Be sure it gets what it needs.

1. Choose the type of gasoline recommended by the manufacturer of your particular car.

2. Refuel before the tank becomes even nearly empty, preferably when the fuel gauge reads one-fourth or more full. There is less condensation of moisture in the tank, less chance of pumping sediment through your gas line, and less chance of running out of gas.

3. Have an under-the-hood check made. Watch the service station attendant. You may be more familiar than he is with the oil dipstick reading of your particular car and when it shows that oil should be added. Check the oil level every time you stop for gasoline.

4. Be sure that the water level in the radiator is correct. If you check this yourself, remove the cap correctly and carefully. The modern pressure cap permits considerable pressure within the cooling system. When the radiator cap is removed, hot water, and possibly steam in the case of overheating, may spout forth. To prevent scalding, loosen the cap slowly in a counterclockwise direction, preferably using a cloth. After you hear the pressure release, turn the cap the rest of the way and remove it.

5. Check the fluid level in your battery. Remove each cap and see that the metal plates of each cell are covered. If not, add soft, preferably distilled, water.

6. Keep the battery terminals covered with a light layer of grease. Do not allow deposits from corrosion to remain on them.

7. Inspect the terminals, connections, battery cables, and electrical circuits which are visible. This can be done with a quick look.

8. Notice the condition of the fan belt. A damaged belt may mean trouble and expense in the future. Look for any leaks in the cooling system.

9. Have your windshield cleaned, as well as any other glass that may need it.

10. Look for dirt on front and rear lights of the car. Clean them, if necessary. A light film of dirt impairs their efficiency appreciably.

231

Perhaps the most significant point is that of these two drivers, it is very probable that the one whose cost of operation is lower will get the better service. The difference lies in the way they take care of their cars.and the way they drive them.

The following hints are worth remembering. First, read your owner's manual and learn its contents, then:

1. Buy good service. Learn what materials and what services are necessary to the life of your car. Patronize the service station or garage which you *know* gives honest, reliable service. See and check for yourself. Ask for service that may have been overlooked. The vital car maintenance procedures every driver and car owner should follow are outlined in Chart 1. Learn them, remember them, and make them a habit—second nature to you. They "pay off."

2. Change the oil and lubricate (grease) the car as instructed in the owner's manual for your particular car. This should be done at such mileage intervals as are recommended (see Chart 2).

3. Follow all instructions in your owner's manual, including periodic checks of a new car at specified mileage intervals.

4. Do not "race" your engine. This wastes gas and causes unnecessary wear of engine parts.

5. Keep your speed moderate. Your gasoline mileage drops sharply above 40 to 50 miles per hour. (This does not, of course, justify low speeds on a 60-mile-per-hour freeway.) A car capable of 20 miles per gallon may deliver less than 5 at its top range of speed.

Chart 2. Oil Change and Lubrication Procedure

1. *Know the recommendations in your owner's manual. Change oil as often as it directs. Use the kind of oil recommended for your car. Watch the oil-changing operation at the service station. Know how much fresh oil your car needs and check that no mistake is made in putting it in. Do not put anything in the oil unless the owner's manual or a competent mechanic you know and can trust recommends it.*

2. *Learn the lubrication plan of your car and the mileage intervals at which the manufacturer recommends the car be lubricated. Watch the greasing job. See that all grease and oiling points are lubricated, including door hinges and locks.*

3. *Have the level of fluid in the transmission checked and some added, if needed.*

4. *Remember, the service station's business is greasing and oiling. Stay back so the operator will not have to watch you to protect your clothing from grease and oil. Do not stand under an elevated grease rack. Nevertheless, if conditions are appropriate, watch the job.*

   If the car is taken somewhere you feel you cannot go to watch the job, be sure the owner — and his assistants — can be trusted to do conscientious work. If not, there are many good places and conscientious people in the business. Find one.

Chart 3. For Spring and Summer Maintenance

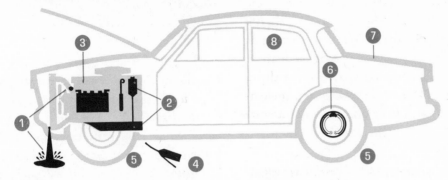

Fig. 16–12. When spring comes, prepare your car for the changed conditions.

1. *Drain antifreeze; if necessary, change thermostat. This prevents overheating. After one season's use, antifreeze rust-inhibiting ingredients weaken and lose their effectiveness—fresh antifreeze next winter may be far cheaper than a repair bill. Follow owner's manual.*

2. *Change oil and filter cartridge. This aids in proper lubrication. Winter oils are too light when temperatures increase. A new filter will help to remove winter oil sludge and prevent engine damage.*

3. *Engine tune-up. Cold-weather starting frequently leaves gas-stealing deposits on spark plugs. This, in turn, may cause rapid wear of other ignition parts. For peak summer efficiency and economy, check, adjust, or replace the plugs, points, condenser, coil, voltage regulator, ignition wires, automatic choke, battery, cables and connectors, idling speed, timing, and gas-air mixture.*

4. *Lubrication. Fresh lubricant will force out winter grease, which may be contaminated by salt, cinders, and sand.*

5. *Rotate tires and check alignment. Wintertime use of snow tires and chains often causes uneven tire wear. "Crisscrossing" or rotating tire placement extends their useful mileage (see Fig. 16–4, page 225). Improper front-end alignment (frequently caused by potholes and frozen ruts) causes very rapid, uneven wear of front tires. Have this checked, also.*

6. *Check, adjust, and/or replace brake linings. Safe brakes are vital in summer driving (at fast, sustained speeds). Check brake-fluid level—use only heavy-duty fluid. Check brake hoses for exhaust heat damage, cuts, and deterioration.*

7. *Wash and polish car. Wash off harmful winter and road deposits from paint and chrome. A good protective wax will help to prevent color fading and to maintain the paint's luster through hot weather.*

8. *Clean interior. Remove upholstery stains. Clean all carpeting (underneath also to remove corrosive deposits tracked in on shoes). Vacuum thoroughly, particularly near fresh-air vents to prevent grit and dust from circulating when air vents are opened.*

6. Shut off your engine while waiting for any length of time. An idling engine burns gas.

7. Keep your engine temperature as recommended in your owner's manual. Engine efficiency requires proper temperature. If the temperature reading of your engine, when warmed up, is not as recommended, have it checked by a competent mechanic.

8. Do not "ride the clutch" in a manual-shift car. This means that you do not let your foot rest on the clutch pedal as you drive along the highway. Excessive wear results.

9. Avoid "jackrabbit," "fast-getaway" starts. They are bad for the car and the pocketbook.

10. Avoid rust and deterioration of car finish, tires, windshield wiper blades, door-seal strips, and other parts by keeping the car sheltered from wet, dampness, ice, and hot sun. A garage is a good protection for your car. Washing and applying a good coat of wax protect the paint of most cars.

11. Prepare for seasonal changes. When winter approaches, be sure your car is ready. Read and learn the "getting ready" section in Chapter 14, "Driving Under Adverse or Special Conditions," page 202.

12. For the change to spring and summer driving conditions, follow the maintenance procedures in Chart 3, on page 233.

Chapter 20, "Before You Start the Engine," tells about the charge light or ammeter, the oil-pressure light or indicator, and the temperature indicator. Any of these may indicate a condition which requires repair by a skilled mechanic. In the case of overheating, there is one additional important point to note.

Hot Engine Remove the radiator cap with extreme care (see Chart 1, item 4, page 231). If the water level is low, let the engine cool off before adding water. Cold water may crack the cylinder block of a hot engine, and cylinder blocks are very costly.

When adding water, have the engine idling. Look for water leaks. Check the fan belt to see that the fan is turning properly. The cause of the overheating may be corrected easily. Occasionally it may result from difficulty in the ignition system.

Tune-up About every 10,000 miles, it is well to have your car checked over and your engine tuned, if the check-up so indicates. Sparks plugs, distributor points, and carburetor may require adjustment to give you efficient service. If the engine seems to be "missing," losing power, producing a "pinging" noise, or is in any way abnormal, have it checked.

Remember, a check-up or a tune-up is only as good as the mechanic who performs it. The results are only as reliable as he is. Learn the reputation of dealers' service departments, repair garages, or service stations. Ask your friends and acquaintances about their experiences with them. Compare jobs and prices. Try to have all your repair work done at a place you know. Do not leave repairs, or possible need for repairs, for the road on trips away from your home area. You may be lucky—but you cannot *know*.

Fig. 16–13. Checking the spark plugs is one way to measure engine efficiency.

The Invisible Necessity Airlines, the Air Force, railroads, bus, truck, or taxicab fleets, the military transportation services, the Navy, the Merchant Marine, and industrial organizations operating thousands of vehicles—all are absolutely dependent on one service: *careful maintenance.*

When you ride the plane, train, or bus, you rest more easily knowing that the service that you never see is efficiently performed. Your comfort, convenience, and safety depend on it.

As an intelligent owner-driver of a private vehicle, you take advantage of the lessons learned by the wide experience of all those institutions. Intelligent, safe, economical, and efficient maintenance really means just one thing to you: Taking Care of Your Car.

Fig. 16–14. Regular maintenance checks prevent troublesome emergency stops on the highway.

To Talk About:

1. Discuss things you have seen "show-off" drivers do that you know are harmful to a car or that result in needless expense.

2. Discuss reasons why it is unwise to "race" the car engine, particularly during the warm-up period.

3. At approximately what speed are you likely to get your best gasoline mileage?

4. What does it mean to "ride the clutch"? Why is this harmful?

5. Discuss the value, from the point of view of economy, of keeping the proper pressure in tires.

6. Why should you make sure that the man who lubricates your car attaches a sticker showing the mileage reading on the car's odometer?

7. What would you do if you noticed uneven wear on your front tires?

8. Why do experienced drivers try their brakes after driving through very deep puddles? What might you expect and what would you do about it?

To Do:

1. Summarize the mechanical defects which you think you would recognize from study of this chapter. Which defects do you think could be most dangerous and which most costly if neglected?

2. Examine the dipstick, or oil stick, on a car. Note the markings on it. What procedure should you follow to measure the oil level accurately? Where in the car is this oil stored? Where do you add oil when it is necessary to do so?

3. Does your state have compulsory car inspection? Find out how many states do. Try to obtain statistics from various states on accidents believed to have been caused by mechanical failure. Compare the statistics of those states having compulsory inspection with those that do not. Discuss your findings and decide whether or not you think this is an important part of the safety program of any state.

4. Find out just what items are examined on a car at an inspection station. How important is the proper functioning of each of these to safety? Which items could be defective without the owner's knowledge or without his being aware of the danger?

5. Study the owner's manual for your car and learn where the fuses are located. Get a supply of fuses and put them in the glove compartment for future emergency use.

6. Find several people who own the same make and model car. Compare the operating costs of each car and try to determine reasons for differences.

Once considered a luxury, an automobile is now thought by many families as much a necessity as a stove, a refrigerator, or a furnace. Some people even seem to "wear" it as a mark of success and prestige. The two-car family is no longer unusual.

The automobile is so commonplace today that we sometimes forget what it means in terms of cost to the individual and to the family. Many adults stay in debt most of their lives to pay for the cars they drive. These people do not realize that their mistakes and poor judgment as car buyers are responsible. This is the case, however, of thousands of individuals and families. If they were more careful, they would save a large part of their lifetime payments. What about you? What are the important points you *should* consider when you start thinking about buying a car?

Study the Buyer First!

The first and most important consideration is rarely recognized by the prospective buyer: himself! Those businessmen who sell things spend time and money studying the potential market—the buyer. The intelligent buyer should do the same. Take a good look at yourself. Recognize and frankly admit to yourself a human characteristic: When we want something very much, we are emotional about it. Car dealers are well aware of the emotional side of the buyer. As we learned in Chapter 2, "The Psychology of the Driver," emotions are a function of that

17 Buying, Insuring, and Operating Your Car

Fig. 17–1. When you want something very much, emotion may cloud your thinking. The real test is whether you genuinely need the article or not.

"older," "lower," powerful area of the brain, the brain stem. Our reason and judgment, centered in the "higher," comparatively "new" cerebrum, tend to be obscured. Those connecting two-way pathways can carry disturbing "messages" from the brain stem upward to cloud our judgment and reason. Want, one of our emotions, upsets our judgment. The car buyer is in a state of desire and want. It is not a weakness in you alone; it is a characteristic of the human nervous system. Recognize it and profit by knowing how to control it.

Be sure you have a good reason for buying a new car. Many buyers get "carried away" by arguments or statements that obscure the real situation. They think they are finding a good reason for buying a car when actually they are selecting superficial or silly reasons for doing so. This process is known as *rationalization.*

When any salesman gives you reasons for buying a car to replace one you have, be suspicious about his rationalizing, and be even more suspicious about your own rationalizing. Many times such reasons as "It needs new tires," or "It should have a new paint job," or "The engine will soon need a valve job," are merely attempts to justify a $1,000 expenditure. Think twice! Perhaps you can spend only $60, get the new paint job, or the new set of tires, or an engine tune-up, and continue to drive a perfectly good automobile. On the other hand, if your automobile is really worn out and you no longer have confidence in its safety features, then you may wisely consider buying another car.

Be equally suspicious of rationalization when you are thinking of buying your first car!

Determine Your Price Range Do your planning *before* you shop for a car. Wanting a car that you see may obscure your better judgment. Many dealers know that if they get people into their showrooms, the cars will "sell themselves," as they express it.

Before you look for a car, ask yourself these basic questions:

1. Exactly how much money can I afford to spend for a car? (Include the cost of insurance, registration, license tags, and sales tax in your calculations.)

2. Can I afford just these *average* annual costs? (based on 10,000 miles of travel)

Gasoline and oil	$261
Maintenance	68
Tires	41

Insurance	147
Operator's license	varies
Registration and tags	varies

3. Will I have a financial "cushion" for unexpected expenses such as a ruined tire? A faulty generator? Or . . . ?

4. Will this mean sacrificing something of greater lasting value? Time for study and grades in school, perhaps? These often lead to a lifetime of good things, including fine cars.

If the car is a used one and has gone 20,000 miles or more (about two years of average family use), you may expect mounting repair bills. A single one of them could exceed the estimated maintenance costs of $68.

If your answers to questions 2, 3, and 4 are favorable, you are financially ready to become a car owner.

Hold to Your Car-buying Budget   Now write down your answer to question 1, and make it a detailed budget. Can you pay all costs? How much can you give as a down payment? How much per month are you *sure* you can pay? This is your budget. Look only at cars within this price range. Don't be misled by a salesman's "only $12 more per month." These "slight" increases are the usual manner in which the buyer gets into budget trouble. Once you have set your budget, *hold to it!*

Plan Your Investment

Now you know your resources and about how much money you will need. If you can pay the full amount in cash, you are ready to start shopping. To pay cash is the cheapest and most satisfactory way to buy a car. If you will need to borrow money to finance the car, there are some very important points to consider.

Before choosing your car, know exactly how you will pay for it and how much it will cost. Under no circumstances go to the car lot or showroom, choose a car, and then hurriedly sign forms to finance it. If the dealer is unscrupulous, this is asking for serious trouble. Even though he is honest, it may still cause trouble if you haven't given enough thought to your own financial circumstances and the method of payment best suited to *you.*

Kinds of Car Loans   There are at least six kinds of financial institutions that lend money for the purchase of cars. Among some of them are both honest men and swindlers. If you haven't enough cash for the down payment required by a legitimate dealer, you can't possibly afford "loan-shark" charges! Now let us consider the way you finance a car.

You make a down payment in cash and borrow the balance to pay the car dealer all at once. Note that he gets all his money immediately. The amount of money you borrow must be paid back in monthly installments to the lender. This is called *buying on time,* or *installment buying.*

The loan may be obtained from:

1. A bank
2. Your life insurance company, if your policy has sufficient loan value
3. A credit union
4. An installment finance company or acceptance corporation
5. A personal loan company

Fig. 17-2. Buying a car is an enjoyable—and important—venture.

6. A pawn shop, if you have jewelry, cameras, silverware, or other items of value to leave as security

Cost Differences in Car Loans The cost of such loans varies widely: from about 6 percent interest with the bank or life insurance company to over 20 percent interest charged by some other lenders. Pawn shops are not recommended for the purchase of a car. The buyer who deals with dishonest dealers and "loan sharks" may find himself paying 100 percent or more for the loan!

If your credit is good because you have a steady job or can offer good security, such as stocks or bonds, you can obtain a bank loan. A regularly employed person who makes a substantial down payment can secure the loan from a bank with a chattel mortgage on the car itself. This means that the bank holds the title to the car until the amount borrowed, plus interest, is paid. Then the purchaser owns the car. Obviously, the lower interest rates charged by banks and by insurance companies on policies which have loan value are a big advantage to the borrower. Also, the integrity of these institutions is an excellent safeguard for him. In general, the better your credit standing and the greater the down payment you make, the better the arrangement you can make to finance your car.

Be sure you understand all the terms of any loan before you sign anything. You should know these even though the transaction is honest beyond all doubt. Ask the lending agency for exact, filled-in copies of all forms that you will be required to sign, and read them carefully.

Any reputable bank or insurance company will be glad to explain all terms in detail.

If you borrow the money elsewhere, make every effort to be sure that the lending institution is trustworthy.

Understand the Price If your car purchase is not your first and you have a car to trade in, check the turn-in allowance against the cost of the car you are thinking of buying. If a dealer allows you $100 more for your old car than his rival but charges $125 more for the same model you are buying, it is no bargain. Shop around, and figure your real costs. Be sure the contract you sign totals exactly what you verbally agreed to pay. If "optional equipment" has added to the total, investigate before you sign.

Sixteen Tips on Buying a Car As you learned in Chapter 1, "What Driving Means to You," some car buyers unwittingly find their way to the few unscrupulous dealers who live by trickery.

A car is perhaps one of the largest investments you will make. To protect you in purchasing a car, the following tips are offered. They are recommended by *The Washington* (D.C.) *Star*, the Better Business Bureau, a license enforcement agency, bankers, and executives of nationally recognized finance companies:

1. Be wary of "$1-down" promises. If you plan to get your car financed, you can't do it for $1 down or $5 down. One way or another, you are going to have to raise about one-third of the car's value before it can be financed.

2. Don't buy a car if you can't pay

one-third in cash, and don't borrow in order to meet the down payment. If you do, you'll have to pay off two loans at once—no matter what the dealer may tell you while he is trying to sell you the car.

3. Insist on test-driving the car yourself before agreeing to buy it. Better still, have a good mechanic with you, one whom you can trust. Make provision to pay for his time. Don't sign anything before you make that trial drive—even if the salesman tells you the paper is "just for insurance purposes," or to keep you from being "picked up by the police."

4. Don't sign any contract without reading it very carefully. Be sure that *every* blank is filled in with either a figure or the word "none." A thin line through a blank or an X can easily be turned into figures you did not agree to pay.

5. Don't make any down payment until you know what *all* the charges will be. A legitimate dealer will return the down payment if he can't get the balance financed. An unscrupulous dealer—no

Fig. 17–3. A hidden payment may cost the buyer his entire investment.

matter what he tells you in advance—*will not return the down payment.* If the dishonest dealer cannot get the contract financed on the down payment you offered, he will insist that you borrow more or accept a beat-up car that you do not want. Once he has your money, he is "in the driver's seat."

6. Don't be misled by small monthly payments. The finance company will finance the loan for only a specified period, depending on the age of the car. To keep the loan within that period and pacify you with small monthly payments, the lender will either require a large "pick-up payment," due within a few days, or add a "balloon payment," a large lump sum, after you have been making payments for two years. Either might cause you to lose your car and your entire investment.

7. Read carefully *all* the papers you are asked to sign, even if you are told they are simply duplicates of the original. If all the copies have not been filled in when you sign, any of them can become a costly contract. If you own a home, you may even be signing a mortgage on it!

8. Don't trust verbal guarantees. Even a written guarantee is only as good as the company that gives it.

9. Don't trust figures on a separate, unsigned sheet. They don't mean a thing unless they appear in the contract.

10. Don't authorize life, health, and accident insurance unless you want to buy it from the insurance company represented by the dealer. The same applies to choice of a finance company. You

Fig. 17–4. Don't trust verbal agreements.

don't have to do business with the company suggested by the dealer. You may get the necessary financing cheaper elsewhere, and you may not need as much insurance coverage as the dealer insists upon.

11. Don't sign your name or initials in the margin on the side of the contract unless it is immediately after something already written there or a change you yourself have seen made. An unscrupulous dealer can insert an extra "pick-up payment" if he has the space to do it.

12. Don't sign the contract if the price is different from the one quoted or if the payments are not what you agreed to. Be sure the contract specifies what the dealer is supposed to do and what you are able to do. Be sure all copies are exactly alike, including changes.

13. Don't pay a deposit to road-test the car. In business transactions, pay nothing without getting a receipt. Check engine number and body plate to see that the car numbers and description correspond to those on the contract, certificate of ownership, and registration. Be sure you receive all papers needed for registering the car; otherwise, don't buy it.

14. Insist on an exact copy signed by the dealer before you leave the used-car lot. Don't let the dealer put you off by saying he left it in the glove compartment or will mail it later. Look over each copy before you sign it, and be sure each is an exact copy of what you agreed to.

15. Beware of clauses in the contract that give the dealer the right to repossess the car if you take it out of the county or state or if you are twenty-four hours late with a payment.

16. Always have at least one witness with you who can read, write, and understand the contract. You need at least one witness at all times. Don't let the seller get your witness out of the room at the crucial moment. If you have been cheated and want to take legal action against the dealer, it is only your word against his written contract unless you have at least one witness to support your claim.

Don't Be Shy   A great many people are shy about asking questions and requesting time to read the contract and all papers concerned. They seem to feel that the dealer would resent it as evidence that they suspect his integrity. This is not the case. The legitimate dealer *wants* the buyer to know how to make a purchase intelligently. Knowing this, the buyer will not deal with a swindler but will go to an honest dealer and will recognize the fair treatment he receives. Don't be afraid to ask questions. The average person doesn't buy a car often and doesn't necessarily understand the business procedures involved in the transaction. The way the seller answers your questions may yield a clue as to his honesty.

Fig. 17-5. Since World War II, public-spirited automobile dealers have furnished 110,000 cars to schools for use in driver education courses. The value of these cars exceeds $240,000,000.

Where to Shop for a Car

You may have a friend who wants to sell his car. Knowing the strong and weak points of that car is, of course, very valuable to you. Most of us, however, have to "shop around."

Pick a reliable dealer. The new-car dealer who sells used cars he has taken in trade is usually a reliable businessman. He holds a franchise from the manufacturer which is too valuable to risk by shady dealings.

Ask Your Friends Some used-car dealers have been in business at the same location for many years. Ask people you know whether they have bought cars from these dealers. Find out what kind of service they received after the sale and whether the dealer in question has a service depart-

ment or guarantees his cars. The item of service and guarantee applies to new-car purchases, also.

Your town's Better Business Bureau or Chamber of Commerce may help you choose reliable dealers. If you find that you have been brought to a car lot by "bait advertising," leave immediately. This practice advertises extreme bargains, but when you get there, the salesman talks you out of buying the car advertised or claims it has been sold. If the salesman tries to switch you to another car, it is time to leave.

Avoid dealers who advertise or offer "repossessed" cars at bargain prices. If in good condition and cared for by the driver, such cars are as valuable as any. However, many reliable dealers say they are no bargain at any price.

Don't Hurry Take your time and shop around among the reliable dealers. Don't be hurried into a "bargain buy." As long as you, the buyer, have your money, *you* are in a position to pick and choose. There is an almost unlimited number of cars for sale in the United States!

How to Choose a Used Car

Study newspaper ads in advance of your intended purchase. You can learn a good deal about the market and current prices in this way. Remember your budget. Don't let a salesman talk you into "just trying out" something in a higher price range.

Try to have a good mechanic with you before you finally close a deal on a car —but not one recommended by the dealer who is selling you the car!

Don't let "style" dictate your choice. Performance is much more important. Don't be hurried into a purchase.

Learn the prevailing prices of the cars you consider buying. Most dealers get periodic issues of one or more booklets that report current retail selling prices.

Beware of Invalids on Wheels Remember that cars can be "doctored" so that they temporarily look and sound like bargains. The car you are considering may be a good one, but let a performance test prove it to you. If you are unable to obtain the services of a competent mechanic, or are mechanically inclined yourself, here are ten things to look into before you buy a used car:

1. *Car history*. Get the full history of the car, if possible. A reputable dealer will give you the name and address of the previous owner. Ask the former owner why he sold the car, what gasoline mileage he obtained, how much oil the car burned, and whether it had been in any serious accidents. If it had been, what damage was done? Ask when the car was last overhauled, how much it has been driven since overhauling, how old the battery is, and how many miles the tires have been used. Try to find out the total miles the car has been driven, for the odometers (see Chapter 20, "Before You Start the Engine," page 292) of used cars have often been set back, although this procedure is illegal in some states.

2. *Driving test*. Drive the car *yourself*. Drive far enough to warm the engine thoroughly and to loosen up the transmission and differential. Listen for unusual noises which may indicate the approach of serious trouble. Note the steering-wheel play. If it is a gearshift car, notice the clutch-pedal clearance, which should be from ¾ to 1½ inches before the clutch is released. The steering wheel should have no more than 2 inches of play at the outer rim when the car is standing still. Take note of how smoothly the gearshift lever and transmission operate *after* a few miles. Be sure the transmission does not slip out of any gear going up or down a grade.

3. *Search for leaks*. Look under the car after you drive it and see if there are any puddles or spots of oil, water, or gasoline. Such evidence could indicate serious leaks. Examine the wheel hubs—oil

Fig. 17–6. Search for leaks.

or grease showing around them may mean faulty bearing packing. Tap the muffler with a screw driver to see whether it has rusted almost through. While the engine runs, look over the exhaust and tail pipes to see whether there are leaks in the system. Find out whether the top, trunk, ventilators, or windows leak when it rains.

4. *The "follow-me" test.* Have a friend follow as you drive and notice whether the car "tracks" properly, whether the wheels wobble, whether the stop light

Fig. 17–7. The "follow-me" test tells a story.

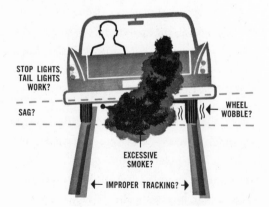

STOP LIGHTS, TAIL LIGHTS WORK?

SAG?

WHEEL WOBBLE?

EXCESSIVE SMOKE?

← IMPROPER TRACKING? →

and tail lights work, and whether an excess of blue-gray smoke comes from the tail pipe when you accelerate in low or second gear. Such smoke could mean excessive burning of oil and that the rings, pistons, and cylinder walls are probably badly worn. Or it could mean that the car has been driven more miles than you were led to believe. Improper "tracking" may mean a bent frame or bent or broken front- or rear-end parts, which could have resulted from a serious accident. Wheel wobble could be caused by a loose or bent wheel.

5. *Chassis inspection.* Does the car sag to one side? This could mean broken or damaged springs, faulty shock absorbers, a "sprung" frame, or a damaged front-end suspension. Even if the car shows no signs of aging, make a good inspection of all chassis parts.

6. *Tire inspection.* Examine the tires, including the spare. Front tires that are worn more on one side than the other indicate misalignment. "Cupped" tires may mean that the brakes do not take hold evenly, that the drums are badly and unevenly worn, or that the wheels wobble or are out of line. Look for bulges on tires. The sidewalls may be broken, and there may be only a boot between the tube and the outside of the tire to prevent a blowout.

7. *Body and finish.* Look under the fenders. Use a knife or screw driver to scratch away the dirt and rust. The fenders may be nearly eaten through. Do the doors rattle? Do the windows roll up and down smoothly? Is the upholstery worn through, especially near the door handles?

Is the paint worn off the door where the driver's arm rested with the window open? Are there "off-shade" patches of paint? Are the seat springs and upholstery in satisfactory condition? Look for clues to age and wear and tear.

8. *Car inspection record.* If there is compulsory motor vehicle inspection in your state or city, find out when the car last passed inspection. Inspection stickers are usually dated. If there is no sticker, insist that the car be inspected or have it done yourself before you buy.

9. *Radiator inspection.* Take the cap off and look into the radiator when the engine is running and thoroughly warmed up. Gas bubbles may show up when the engine is accelerated, indicating the possibility of a cracked cylinder block, leaky head gasket, or cracked head. Oil on the water is another indication of these defective conditions.

10. *Safety devices and accessories.* Check the accessories and safety devices. Try out the lights, horn, windshield wipers, sun visors, ventilators, foot and parking brakes, heater, defroster, and radio, if any. The foot-brake pedal should have a reserve of at least 1½ inches from the floor. Apply the brakes hard and notice whether you get a smooth, even stop with no swerving or lurching.

Even when you can afford to purchase a used car, you may find that the operating costs of such a car are well beyond your budget. Try to judge the soundness of critical parts, such as engine, transmission, steering assembly, brakes, and tires. A shiny exterior and beauty of design, together with clever salesmanship, must

not distract your attention from those parts that mean either economy in operation or serious expenses and loss.

Protect Yourself with Insurance

If the price and the payment plan are satisfactory, and if the car has passed its performance test, you have a car. But there is still another consideration. This may be the most important of all. Don't drive a car without proper insurance coverage! This could be, by far, the most costly error of all.

Case One, in Chapter 1, "What Driving Means to You," describes the tragic consequences of a lack of understanding of insurance protection. The person who owns or drives a car without having appropriate insurance is extremely vulnerable. No matter who is driving his car, he is in danger of losing his possessions and much of his future income if an accident should occur. Dependence on his own skill or careful driving does not guarantee against human or mechanical error or future legal complications. *Proper insurance is a virtual wall of protection around the family pocketbook, personal possessions, and around the home itself.*

An accident may result in damage to someone else's property or in injury to a pedestrian, driver, or passenger. In many cases, drivers' licenses are revoked following accidents when there is no proof of financial responsibility such as insurance brings. This occurs regardless of who was at fault and may be for a fixed time, such as a year, or until the case is settled. Frequently, a case of this nature will not be settled for a number of years, resulting in substantial legal expense, loss of time from work, and great mental anguish.

The only alternative is to post *security* as proof of your ability to pay a court-assessed claim. Such security may be: (1) cash, (2) stocks or bonds, or (3) a surety bond. In the event that security is posted by the latter means, you are held personally responsible to reimburse the carrier of the bond. Laws which require this are known as *security-type financial-responsibility laws.*

Your own car may be damaged or destroyed by fire, theft, vandals, wind- or hailstorm, or by being involved in an accident. Less serious than losing one's possessions and even future income, it is still not pleasant to lose your car or be faced with substantial repair bills. Should this occur, you must make full payment of any sum that you may still owe for its purchase, even though the car may be completely destroyed.

Classes of Automobile Insurance

There are three general classifications of automobile insurance. *Liability insurance* provides for injury or damage to others because of an accident wherein the policyholder is legally responsible. *Medical-payments,* or *medical-expense,* in-surance is not based on legal liability. This insurance pays all reasonable medical costs resulting from an accident up to the amount of the coverage purchased. *Physical-damage insurance* protects a car owner against damage to his own automobile.

Types of Liability Insurance From the point of view of personal responsibility and consequences, the type of accident that injures someone or damages another's property is the most serious. The type of insurance which protects you against claims for injury or damage to others is known as *liability insurance.* This protects you against all claims made against you, up to the amounts set forth in the policy. Liability insurance *pays you* no money, but it *protects you* against others' claims resulting from an automobile accident.

The types of coverage under liability insurance are:

1. *Bodily injury.* The insurance company pays, within stated limits, all court assessments against the insured after an accident involving injury or death.

2. *Property damage.* The insurance company pays, within stated limits, all court assessments against the insured as damages for the destruction of property. This includes loss of use of such property.

In addition to the liability limits assumed by the insurance company, they also agree to the following. They will defend any suit against the insured. They will pay the premium for bail and other bonds, within certain prescribed limits. They will pay the costs assessed against the insured in any suit. They also agree to repay the insured for all reasonable expenses, other than loss of earnings, incurred at the request of the company. The insurance company further agrees to pay the insured party's expenses for immediate medical and surgical relief to others as imperative at the time of, and resulting from, the accident.

A majority of states have adopted the "security" type of safety responsibility law. This requires immediate evidence of security to satisfy judgments in the event of a personal-injury or property-damage loss over a specified amount. Evidence of security must be filed by each person involved in an accident regardless of fault or negligence. Evidence of security may be in the form of cash, stocks or bonds, an appropriate surety bond, or by a certificate from an insurance company properly licensed to do business in the state. Obviously, the latter is the most convenient. Although states vary in the amounts of security required, most states will accept as evidence of your security a policy providing limits of $10,000 or $20,000 for bodily injury and $5,000 for property damage.

Limits of liability are generally expressed as "$10,000–$20,000–$5,000" or "$25,000–$50,000–$10,000." The first figure represents the insurance company's maximum liability for injury or death to one person. In other words, that is the highest amount the company will pay. The second figure expresses the company's maximum liability for injury or death to two or more persons for any one accident. The final figure reflects the company's maximum liability for damage caused to another person's property.

In many cases of personal injury or death, court judgments are for amounts several times the $10,000 and $20,000 limits. If a court awards any person or persons an amount larger than the limits of the policy, *you must pay the balance yourself.* Since coverage in greater amounts costs comparatively little, you may consider it advisable to purchase a policy of higher face value than the required "10–20 and 5." *Remember:* The insurance policy that you are required to buy when you purchase a car on time does not protect you against legal liability. It is usually only physical-damage insurance to protect the lender.

Medical-payments Insurance   The insuring company agrees to pay all reasonable medical expenses (up to the amount of the coverage purchased) incurred within one year from the date of the accident, as a result thereof. This covers each person, including the insured, his wife, children, and relatives, if residents of the same household, injured by an automobile accident. It does not matter whether these injuries were sustained as a pedestrian, occupant of a car, driver of a car, or otherwise. The coverage also extends to any person who suffers such injury resulting from an automobile accident involving the insured car while being used with the owner's permission.

Types of Physical-damage Insurance   Another general class of automobile insurance covers the car owner *for his own personal loss.* In this class we find three types of coverage.

1. *Comprehensive.* This pays you if your car is damaged or destroyed, or for loss by damage resulting from fire, explosion, windstorm, hurricane, tornado, hail, water and flood, earthquake, falling objects, theft and robbery, missiles, vandalism, riot and civil commotion, or broken glass. It will also reimburse you, under certain circumstances, for renting a car if yours is stolen.

2. *Collision.* This type of coverage pays you for accidental damage to your car whether or not the accident is your fault. The main purpose of collision insurance is to avoid a large loss which the insured person cannot afford, such as total destruction of the car. Since the majority of persons can afford a small loss, this coverage is generally written with a *deductible provision,* such as "$50 deductible" or "$100 deductible." The higher the deductible amount, the lower the cost of the insurance. The deductible provision requires that *you pay the deductible amount,* say the first $50, toward repair or replacement of your car, and the insurance company pays the balance. The $100-deductible policy operates the same way, except that you pay the first $100.

3. *Uninsured-motorist insurance.* Suppose you or members of your family are hurt in an automobile accident, either in the car or as pedestrians, and the other driver is to blame. You expect him to pay. *But* suppose he is a hit-and-run driver and is not caught. Suppose he owns nothing on which you could collect damages. Suppose he has no money with which to pay. Under those circumstances, the uninsured-motorist coverage pays

you. The amount would be that which you should have been able to collect from him for the bodily injury, up to the limit of the coverage specified in the policy.

Conditions That Affect Insurance Costs

When you buy an insurance policy, you are buying protection. For this protection, you pay the company a fee, called a *premium.* The cost, or premium, must be approved by the state. The premium you pay is based upon:

The type of insurance bought
The type of car that you own
The amount of coverage you buy
The amount paid in claims by insurance companies for your area
Whether a youthful male driver, generally under age twenty-five, will drive the car, and whether he has taken an approved high school driver education course

Sportsmanlike, accident-free driving can pay you real dividends by reducing the insurance premium you must pay. The major cost of insurance premiums is determined by the traffic-accident experience of all persons insured in a given area. If the number of claims paid for accidents increases, the insurance companies must pay out additional sums of money and automobile insurance costs go up. Some companies reduce premiums of drivers who have had accident-free driving records for a specified number of years.

If insurance companies continue to suffer heavy losses as a result of serious and repeated claims by a poor driver, they are reluctant to continue to insure such a person. This can make it extremely difficult for you to keep a driver's license *and may rule you off the road.*

Even when you are accepted as a good risk and hold a policy, an insurance company reserves the right to cancel it or to refuse to renew it if your driving or claim record should change.

Statistics show that youthful drivers have an extremely high percentage of accidents. While only 17.7 percent of the licensed drivers were under age twenty-five, they were involved in 30 percent of all accidents. They were also involved in over 29 percent of all fatal accidents. These statistics show clearly that accidents involving youthful drivers are generally more serious and more likely to result in death or permanent injury.

Many companies recognize that high school–trained drivers accept their responsibility to society and are interested in becoming safe and competent drivers. The result is that they charge a lower premium for those male drivers under twenty-five years of age who have completed an approved course in a high school.

Requirements for Reporting Accidents

If you are involved in an accident, certain reports must be made. The exact reporting system varies with states, communities, and insurance companies. Know what to do *before* anything happens. Know *what reports* are required by law in your state, *when* they must be submitted, and *to whom.*

The law requires you to file an accident report, but that is not your only responsibility. You must send a separate report to your insurance company within a specified time after an accident occurs. This is necessary under all types of car insurance, and you must send it to be protected.

Fig. 17–8. Accident records affect insurance.

Fixing Responsibility

A *civil court* is one in which a citizen would sue another for damages arising from an automobile accident. A *traffic court* is one in which a driver is tried for violating a traffic law.

The driver or owner of one car may not be solely at fault in case of an accident. A civil court may determine that two or more persons were to blame for an accident.

Sometimes a person is fined in traffic court for a violation of law which resulted in a motor vehicle accident. The same person may later be sued in a civil court by a victim of the accident to recover damages to pay for the results of the accident.

Businesses are held liable for damages resulting from accidents caused by drivers of their commercial vehicles while operating these vehicles on the business of their employers. These include taxi companies, trucking concerns, and bus lines. They set up training courses for their drivers. They know the advantages of driver education, as do the automobile insurance companies.

Insurance Protection— A Necessity

If your parents seem concerned about your driving the family car, be patient and understand why. Even if it weren't for the personal danger, there is a lot more than the cost of the car at stake.

A family without liability-insurance protection can be ruined by a heavy burden of debt for years. The savings of a lifetime can be taken with a single court action. For your own protection and the protection of your family and your future, don't drive without proper insurance. It is much better to wait than to face years of regret. Protect yourself and your family for the good years ahead.

To Talk About:

1. Discuss problems that have been encountered in buying used cars.

2. Suggest a number of ways in which a person might rationalize the necessity of buying a new car.

3. Do you think car dealers should be required to give more information as to the past history of used cars? What requirements would you set up for the protection of buyers?

4. Discuss the advantages to a car owner of having liability insurance. What, besides money, may he lose if not protected in this manner when involved in an accident? Can he afford *not* to have insurance?

5. Is liability insurance compulsory in your state? Do you think it should be? Is there any legal protection for those who are injured or whose property is damaged by uninsured drivers?

6. Discuss the types of car insurance you think would be a wise investment. What kind of protection does each type offer?

7. Compare the cost of owning and operating a car with other large family expenses, such as rent, taxes, mortgage payments, and food and clothing.

8. Why do you think accidents caused by drivers under twenty-five years of age result in a greater number of fatalities in proportion to the number of drivers than those involving other age groups?

BUYING, INSURING, AND OPERATING YOUR CAR

252

To Do:

1. Study the latest advertisements for a number of makes of new cars. List features which each is using as selling points. How many of these would be determining factors if you were to buy a car? How many appeal to the emotions? Could any of these fool you into buying something which you should not buy?

2. Figure out how much it would cost you to drive a car for a year. Include payments on the car if it is to be bought "on time," depreciation, taxes, and the other costs. How far would this money go toward a college education or payment for a home?

3. Set up a form on which to record the costs of operating the family car. Keep the record for a definite period. Determine the cost per mile for a two-month period. What annual costs are not included?

4. Find out how insurance rates in other parts of the country compare with those in your area. What are some reasons for the differences?

5. Find out the costs of different kinds of insurance on your family car. Does your insurance company charge a higher premium if a male driver under twenty-five years of age is using the car? How much does this cost your family? Will the company reduce this higher premium if that driver satisfactorily completes an approved high school driver education course?

6. Find out the different methods of buying a car on the deferred-payment plan. Indicate the difference in cost of the various methods.

7. Find out what percentage of accidents in your community and in your state are caused by drivers under twenty-five years of age. How do these figures compare with those for the country as a whole? How do they compare with the percentage of *all* licensed drivers?

8. Invite a local insurance agent to talk to your group about various types of insurance. Ask him why insurance companies offer to reduce rates to male drivers who have completed a driver education course. Find out what might cause his company to refuse to insure a driver.

9. Learn what kinds of reports must be filed in case of an accident in your state. Have a representative of the class obtain a copy of each kind. Select a newspaper clipping of an accident. Discuss each item of the accident report form in class. As a class project, fill out the report form for the accident described in the newspaper.

You in the Motor Age

"Once upon a time" the family farm was the basic unit, or "building block," of which America was formed. From the pioneer's log cabin to the Mount Vernon type of plantation, ours was an agricultural civilization. Each family unit could produce on its own land about all it really needed. Spinning, weaving, blacksmithing, and other essential work were often done right at home. Compare this picture with American life today!

Automobiles, trucks, and buses are the lifeblood of much of our country. Imagine a great city, with its sprawling suburbs, cut off from its farmland source of food. Or industry cut off from its incoming raw materials and outgoing flow of finished products by a stoppage of traffic. How would millions of workers reach their places of work without passenger cars and buses? They must travel from ever-expanding residential areas to locations of business that are also continually spreading out.

Yes, the highway transportation industry is one of our greatest. One out of every seven of our employed persons works in it or in a closely related activity. It is a vital part of our national life.

Also, as our motor vehicle traffic increases each year, the building and maintenance of modern highways becomes of even greater importance. Efficient, convenient, and safe *use* of our roads and streets is equally important. And so we must also have progressive traffic engineering and other activities productive of desirable traffic conditions.

These are needs of this, the Motor Age. These are *your* problems as a citizen. How well they are met will depend on you and other citizens.

Understanding these needs and what to do about them is the theme of *You in the Motor Age.*

255

Driving as Your Job

How often we hear remarks like: "He has a big job . . . lot of responsibility . . . important man. . . ." The leader of great corporations, the holder of high political office, the research scientist, the popular entertainer—all of them are part of America.

There are others, also—others whose names we don't know but who are no less important. We don't know them individually, but we do know that our country couldn't exist without them. Who are some of these people on whose services and responsibility we so greatly depend?

Did you ever ride, perhaps with fifty others, through a confusing mass of traffic, or over icy streets or roads, in an ordinary bus? Did you ever particularly notice the driver—and his job?

Did you ever stop to think that he is responsible for your life? The lives of all his many passengers depend on his skill, judgment, and courage. Many other drivers share the highway safely with this huge, rolling bulk of a bus, guided and controlled by one highly skilled man.

We entrust our money to the banker, our constitutional rights to elected officials, and our amusement to the entertainer. Our lives, though, and the lives of our children, are guarded by the men who wheel the "big ones."

What makes the strength of America? How long could our great cities live if shut off from the food-producing farm land? The highways are their arteries, the great truck fleets their lifeblood. Our country prospers as long as the wheels of the tractor-trailers roll.

"Men Wanted"

There are few sailing ships left in the world for young men to man. The old frontiers have been tamed. Those of us who perform routine daily jobs and retire to our homes each night seldom realize that there is plenty of adventure left. Taking one of the big trailer rigs over the mountains in snow, or across the country in violent summer storms, is active living.

While the rest of us sleep, the "big ones" keep rolling all night, as well as all day. Rare is the experienced, well-traveled automobile driver who hasn't been guided, or helped when in trouble, by the professionals of the highway.

Commercial driving is a "man's job."

Highway Regulars

We seldom think of some people as professional drivers. Actually, however, they must drive a great deal as a part of their jobs. No novices as drivers are policemen, firemen, physicians, visiting nurses, welfare workers, farmers, salesmen, postal employees, delivery men, real estate agents, and many others. Many of them are women drivers. Win-

ter and summer, in fair weather and storms, they must keep moving. They, too, are really behind-the-wheel professionals.

Commuters? Yes, uncounted thousands of them all over the country spend hours in their daily driving. Many persons could not keep their present jobs unless they drove to work. Other types of transportation are often not available or are inconvenient and time consuming. Millions of persons use their family cars as a method of transportation to and from work. In a study called *Travel Patterns in Fifty Cities,* the U.S. Bureau of Public Roads reported that nearly half of all automobile trips are for work and business purposes.

These daily to-and-from-work drivers become highly skilled, though perhaps not quite so skilled as the professionals. With their jobs depending on reaching factory or office without accident and without being late, they become competent and safe citizens of the highway.

Housewives also must use the family car, or a second car, for necessary transportation, for homemaking is a full-time job. The shopping center, the market, the station, and the bus line may all be some distance from the home. Taking small children to school or to the doctor or dentist requires use of a car. This is true in many rural areas and increasingly true elsewhere, as suburban developments spread out from our great centers of population. Driving is more and more a part of the housewife's job of keeping a home and raising a family.

257

**Those
who
drive**
as part of their
daily work
understand the vital
importance of safe,
efficient use of our
streets and highways.

Our
modern
world,
civilian or
military,
runs on wheels.

Driving Is a Business

Driving is a serious, dignified business to those who make it their life's work. They are not interested in showing off. It is not a game they play at like children. Nor is driving a competition to them. They make it a *cooperative* enterprise in which each man works for safety and efficiency on the highway. Anything else would be poor business indeed!

If you decide to become a professional driver, the first quality your prospective employer will seek is expressed in the adjective *safe*. You must be a *safe* driver or he will not employ you.

Your driver attitude, as shown by your driving record, will be his first consideration. Some young men who wanted and intended to become good commercial drivers never got the chance. A bad driving record, as Show-offs, before they became mature permanently killed their chances.

This is too bad, but that's the way it is. Truck and bus fleet owners cannot take chances on Show-offs or on any job applicants who *have been* Show-offs in the past. The professional drivers don't want to associate with them, either. One careless, immature driver can spoil the long-time low-accident record of any truck or bus fleet.

Mature, safe drivers who can handle a vehicle smoothly are wanted. Imagine the Show-off (in Chapter 2, "The Psychology of the Driver," page 22) operating a bus. After his passengers were thrown around on *one* trip, would he still have a job?

Do you want to wheel a "big one"? Imagine you are being tested for professional driving. Imagine a "tumbling cylinder," perhaps 2 inches in diameter and 6 inches high, on the floor of your car. (An ordinary milk bottle can be used.) Could you start, turn, and stop without upsetting it? An expert driver can. Anybody can push his accelerator pedal to the floor and brake or turn to make his tires squeal. Far fewer can drive smoothly!

If you are looking for a steady job, good pay, and travel—and some adventure, too—professional driving may be the answer. Prepare yourself well for it—in skill, mature attitude, and good record—from the first day you drive.

Drivers in Military Service

For those who may go into the military service, many opportunities exist in motor vehicle transportation. Drivers, motor-pool personnel, and others are trained specialists. Many girls in the services are full-time vehicle drivers. As in civilian life, good drivers are in demand.

Many kinds of vehicles are used by the armed forces. The government invests considerable time and money in choosing and training the men who are going to drive them. There are vehicles for rapid movement over highways and over rough country. There are armored vehicles. There are amphibious vehicles. Even the familiar jeep can be made to run under water, getting air through a long breather pipe. Modern military life, like civilian life, depends on wheels.

To Talk About:

1. The bus driver, carrying many people in his vehicle, must be highly skilled and must feel his responsibility. Compare his responsibility with yours as the driver of a passenger car. You are likewise responsible for the lives of many people, even though they are not in the vehicle with you.

2. What do commercial driving jobs offer with respect to opportunity? Stability of employment? Advancement?

3. What characteristics of applicants should disqualify them from commercial driving jobs?

4. What regulations would you set up to control the use of alcohol: (*a*) by operators of trucks carrying merchandise belonging to you? (*b*) By operators of buses and taxis?

5. Can truck and bus companies afford the costs of weeding out accident-prone drivers from their applicants for jobs? Support your statements with figures, if possible.

6. Name some jobs in which driving or experience in driving is essential.

7. Discuss situations you know of where truck drivers have aided motorists in some way.

8. Discuss jobs that require a great deal of driving skill which are open to women.

To Do:

1. Interview a bus or truck driver and find out in what ways his vehicle is checked before he begins a trip. Should it be any less important for a commercial driver, a salesman, a housewife, or any other driver to know the condition of his vehicle before taking on his responsibility as a driver?

2. Interview several drivers in well-managed bus or trucking fleets. Ask them what training they received before making their first runs alone. Contrast their training with that of the usual private-car driver. With that of an airplane pilot.

3. Find out how smoothly you drive. Place an empty milk bottle on the floor of your car and find out how far you can travel without upsetting it.

4. Report on tests used in selecting professional drivers. What are the licensing requirements for these drivers in your locality or state?

5. Find out about the requirements as to the physical condition of bus drivers. Is there a limit as to the number of hours per day or night they are allowed to drive? Are there rules regarding their use of alcohol or drugs? Do you think the regulations are strict enough?

6. Talk to a school bus driver and find out about any special safety requirements for school buses.

Today's motorists want streets and highways that provide safe and efficient transportation. They want pleasant, smooth travel; they want to get to their destinations without trouble and accident. These goals require carefully planned construction and carefully controlled operation. Knowing how streets and highways are planned, built, and operated is important to the motorist-citizen. As a driver he can make better use of them. As a citizen he can participate intelligently in making decisions affecting their future.

19

Traffic as You Want It

Planning Roads and Streets

In earlier days, rural roads were developed along Indian trails and the natural paths of travelers. In the western states, they went along property lines. City streets were laid out much the same way —following natural paths in the older sections and in a grid pattern in the new sections to divide the city into blocks. As automobile travel increased, certain roads and streets served different purposes and carried different volumes of traffic.

Highway Planning Planning modern highways for the present and the future is a job of a well-organized team of specialists under each state highway department administrator. The group of engineers under his direction are specialists in:

Locating and designing highways
Designing bridges
Developing and beautifying roadsides
Deciding on the need for traffic signs, signals, markings, and their proper locations
Arranging to buy land for new highways or for widening existing roads

The specialists must know how land to be served by the new highway is used —whether for residences, factories, large shopping centers, recreation, stores, farming, mining, or other purposes. This in- formation helps them to tell what kind of traffic is to be served (that is, what proportion of the traffic load will be passenger cars, trucks, and buses). They must know where traffic is coming from, where it is going, and how much traffic there is. They must know these characteristics of all present-day traffic. They must also forecast changes in the use of the land and in traffic for years ahead.

After gathering the important facts, they draw maps and charts showing where drivers want to go and the numbers of vehicles that will travel to various destinations. Then, comparing these charts with maps of existing highways and streets and knowing the capacity and physical condition of these roads, they determine where new highways are needed or old ones should be improved.

TRAFFIC AS YOU WANT IT

264

Planning for the Future   Highway planners agree that highways should be planned and built to meet future as well as present traffic needs. Different uses require different kinds of roads. Some roads must be designed to carry large volumes of traffic; others can be built for lighter traffic. Some need much heavier construction than others, because they serve great numbers of heavy trucks. Some important main highways connecting cities, states, and regions must carry large volumes of through traffic and serve certain local needs as well. Most roads, on the other hand, have the single job of serving local purposes.

The work of fact gathering and planning is carried out continuously by highway planners in the various state highway departments. In cities, the city planner, the city engineer, and the traffic engineer work together as a team to do a similar job. An important part of their work is keeping the public informed of their plans. In turn, as citizens and voters we want to understand the need for planned improvements. We can then support these specialists when decisions are being made on locating and financing streets and highways.

Financing the Roads

As traffic needs grow, roads have to be widened, straightened, paved, and improved. Sometimes old two-lane roads cannot carry increased volumes of traffic without being changed into four- or even six-lane arteries. Sometimes it is more practical and less expensive to choose new locations and build entirely new highways adapted to new traffic needs.

City, County, and State Roads   The responsibility for roads is divided among several governmental agencies. Most streets and county roads are the responsibility of their respective city and county governments. Cities and counties get some financial aid from state-collected motor vehicle revenues. The state is responsible for the limited mileage of state highways, which are roads connecting the major areas of the state. These roads usually carry a state route number.

The Federal-aid System   Some roads, which are part of the state road system and connect cities or cross state lines, qualify for Federal-aid funds. To plan, design, and construct these important roads, states may receive up to one-half of the construction cost from the Highway Trust Fund. State highway departments design these highways in the Federal-aid system and submit their plans to the U.S. Bureau of Public Roads. The plans must meet certain design standards that have been established for such roads. When they do, the states build the roads and then are repaid for the Federal-aid share of construction cost. These highways are marked with the familiar U.S. shield route sign (Fig. 19–2).

Another part of the Federal-aid system is the National System of Interstate and Defense Highways (see Chapter 13). Taxes collected from highway users by the Federal government are deposited in the Highway Trust Fund and then are used to pay 90 percent of the cost of planning,

Fig. 19-2. Shield route signs on Federal-aid highways.

designing, and constructing this system. These highways must meet certain requirements for control of access and other characteristics of high-capacity design. The U.S. Bureau of Public Roads sees that they do. The states pay the other 10 percent and all maintenance costs. When you see a distinctive red, white, and blue shield (Fig. 19-1), you know you are on the "Interstate System."

Fig. 19-3. We all pay for our highways.

Where the Money Comes From

Suppose you drive to a friend's house in a town about 15 miles from your home. Suppose, as well, that the road is the familiar two-lane type, with no special modern design features. Fifteen miles isn't far. One gallon of gasoline will take you that far. Of course, the round trip means 30 additional miles of wear on your car and the use of a certain amount of oil and grease. With each day, also, your car's value depreciates. The greater its mileage and the older it becomes, the lower its value will be. So the 30-mile visit to and from your friend's home will entail some dollars-and-cents cost. You are purchasing transportation.

But all your costs are not obvious. You are also helping to pay for an item which, though a necessity, is not usually thought of as the expense factor it really is: the highway itself. You and millions of your fellow citizens are paying for the roads you travel, including the road to and from your friend's home. You are also helping to pay for the thousands of miles of modern freeways now being built. It is worth thinking about how we pay for all these roads.

The next time you stop at a service station, look carefully at the price sign on the gasoline pump. Note how much of the total price you pay is the cost of the gasoline itself and how much of it is tax. This is one way we pay for our roads. Your car registration and driver's license

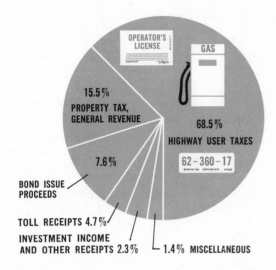

Fig. 19-4. Where the money comes from.

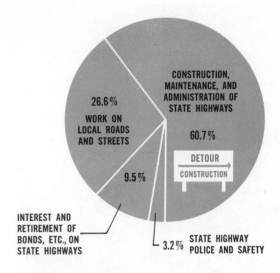

Fig. 19-5. How it is spent.

fees also help. Some of the money derived from various taxes and tolls may be used for road expenses. Figures 19–4 and 19–5 tell the story quite simply.

You and the rest of the American public own the roads of the country. We should all want to be sure that we continue to get our money's worth!

Modern Road Construction

The automobile and its changing needs have brought about great changes in road design and construction. Man has long known how to build roads that remain hard and reasonably smooth even in bad weather. Two thousand years ago, the Romans needed durable highways to connect their conquered territories and to move military forces without delay. They built sturdy roads with strong foundations in which great blocks of stone were closely fitted together. Many were so well built that they have weathered the centuries; some are used today. For example, tourists still drive out from Rome along the historic Appian Way. However, much more modern methods and materials are now used to build strong foundations and hard, watertight surfaces.

Foundations Buildings, trees, roots, vegetation, and topsoil are first removed over the route of a new highway. High spots are cut away. Low places are filled in and the roadway is properly graded. Adequate drainage is provided. Then a good, durable foundation is laid which may, in some cases, be many inches thick. Finally, surfacing is added.

Fig. 19–6. Modern equipment and skill are needed to build modern highways.

Surfacing   Road surfacing differs greatly, depending on the traffic for which the road is designed. Surfaces on some minor roads are of gravel, or gravel topped with a mixture of sand and clay. Some roads consist of layers of crushed stone, with large stones at the bottom and smaller ones above. They are then topped with stone chips. All layers are rolled solid, and asphalt or other bituminous material is frequently used to bind the surface of the road.

Heavily used roads must have both strong foundations and well-built surfaces to bear heavy loads, keep out water, and wear well. The surface may be of portland-cement concrete, bituminous concrete, sheet asphalt, or stone block laid in cement. Highway engineers are extremely interested in producing surfaces on which skidding is greatly reduced, despite effects of traffic wear.

Modern Road Design

Wider Highways   Increased speeds and greater numbers of wider commercial vehicles have brought about a need for wider traffic lanes. In heavy traffic, passing on two-lane roads (one lane in each direction) is difficult and dangerous. Where there is a large amount of traffic, these two-lane roads are inadequate. Therefore, more and more four-lane highways are needed, and all of them (except some city streets) should be divided so that traffic moving in opposite directions is separated.

Divided Highways   A center, or median, strip is now built into practically all new main highways. It separates the highway into 2 one-way roadways and greatly reduces head-on collisions, overtaking and passing accidents, cutting-in crashes, and sideswipes. Wide center, or median, strips also considerably reduce irritating and dangerous headlight glare.

Longer Sight Distances   The faster you drive, the farther ahead you must be able to see in order to stop or overtake and pass safely. Higher speeds make it dangerous to pass where hill crests, curves, and "dips" can hide approaching cars. Blind corners are also dangerous. Modern highway design therefore requires increased sight distances.

Road Crowns and Banking   Older paved roads were considerably "crowned," that is, much higher in the middle than at the edges, as illustrated in Fig. 6–6, so that water would run off promptly. Level sections of modern road surfaces slope off slightly to the side for the same reason.

Newer roads are now banked on curves according to the sharpness of the curve, making them safer and easier to negotiate. A banked road is illustrated in Fig. 6–6.

Other Improvements   Other improvements which have highway safety as their goal include:

Wider bridges—usually providing a paved roadway as wide as that on the rest of the highway, plus some extra width at the sides so that drivers have no feeling of a lack of width while crossing the bridge

269

Elimination of dangerous deep side ditches

Gentle side slopes to reduce roll-over accidents involving cars which run off the road

Wider, firmer shoulders which will support the weight of car wheels when necessary

Better guard rails to retain cars within road borders when driver control is lost

Elimination of culvert headwalls near the paved surface as dangerous obstructions

Continuation of road shoulders under and on overhead bridges as a margin for safety

An extra lane on steep upgrades for slow-moving vehicles

Special turnouts for loading or unloading buses

Bigger and more legible road signs of all types

Pedestrian and vehicle underpasses and overpasses

Improvements at Intersections Approximately one-half of all city traffic accidents occur at intersections. Even on rural roads, a great many accidents occur at road crossings. Hence, intersections are a problem to which highway and traffic engineers can apply their knowledge to save lives and prevent injuries.

To take care of heavy traffic, improvements such as the following are now used at intersections:

Traffic-control devices, such as signals and stop signs

More "rounded-off" corners with longer radii to make turns easier

Pedestrian islands

Channelizing islands to separate vehicles and guide them in proper paths

Longer sight distances

Special lanes for right- and left-turning traffic

Long, widened approaches and exits

Two special types of intersection design are commonly used in highway engineering: the traffic circle and the grade separation.

Traffic Circles Traffic circles are intersections where all vehicles move counterclockwise around a large central island, or circle. Drivers move around the circle until they come to the street they want and then turn right to leave the circle. Despite their name, not all such central islands are circular in shape. Recognizing this, the English call them "roundabouts."

Well-designed traffic circles are usually an improvement over the ordinary intersection. They help to decrease the problem of motorists having to stop and wait, for unless they become overloaded, they promote a steady traffic flow. When they are properly designed, they compel approaching drivers to slow down. They eliminate right-angle conflicts, reducing intersection crashes. But they are not suitable for roads with very heavy traffic, where the only adequate solution is to separate cross traffic completely.

Factors such as cost, grades, and available land have to be considered in planning a traffic circle. Circles require considerable land and pavement, and this makes them much more costly than the usual type of intersection. Furthermore, if there are pedestrian crossings at the circles, vehicular traffic is often delayed or interrupted. Like any other traffic aid, the traffic circle must be properly designed and used only where it is suitable.

Grade Separation   Where busy traffic arteries cross, the best type of intersection completely separates the traffic on the intersecting roads. This type is called a *grade separation*. In a grade separation, one road is carried over the other, just as a grade separation lifts a highway over a railroad. This keeps traffic moving and eliminates intersection collisions. Provision for turns sometimes makes this type of intersection seem complicated.

The complete cloverleaf design and the directional interchange design eliminate left-turn conflicts. To turn left at a cloverleaf, you go straight past the crossroad and make a right-turn loop (see Fig. 19–7). Study Figs. 19–7, 19–8, and 19–9, and trace out the paths that cars would use in making right and left turns. Notice how conflicts that frequently cause delays and accidents are eliminated. When traffic is heavy, over twice as much intersection traffic can flow without interruption where one road is carried over the other as can pass through an ordinary intersection.

A diamond grade separation, as shown in Fig. 19–9, is a good design where a main artery crosses a lesser road and where left turns are not heavy. Connecting roads or ramps roughly form a diamond, although obstacles, such as streams or hills, may somewhat change the shape. Left-turn conflicts remain, but they are moved from the main express artery to the crossroad.

A directional interchange, shown in Fig. 19–8, is generally thought best for heavy turning traffic and at very important intersections. You change to another route merely by moving into the proper lane or ramp. This design is generally more costly than other grade separation designs because of the numerous bridges and the amount of land needed.

Operation of Highways

A street or highway costs a lot of money. It is, therefore, important to see that the original investment is protected by keeping the road in good repair. Maintenance can be a preventive measure to avoid costly repairs. If cracks are sealed, holes filled, and shoulders graded on a regular basis, later costly damage is often prevented.

Even the best roads would be places of confusion and danger if there were not well-planned *operation* of the roadway network. This is accomplished by traffic engineering. The traffic engineer's job is to make the use of roadways safer and more convenient for the driver and for the pedestrian. Good traffic engineering and good driving give us orderly and efficient traffic flow.

Traffic engineering means planning the safest and most efficient use of streets and highways and of parking and loading facilities. It means applying knowledge of the way individual drivers and pedestrians act, of what safeguards and guides they need, and of the way large numbers of drivers and pedestrians move. It means

Fig. 19-7. A cloverleaf interchange. Note the path of a vehicle making a left turn without encountering cross traffic.

Fig. 19-8. A directional interchange. The path of a vehicle making a left turn is shown.

Fig. 19-9. A diamond interchange. Left turns are made as shown.

planning, not only for present needs, but also for those of the future.

Traffic engineering has proved valuable in many problems. At a rural junction of two important highways in Michigan, accidents decreased 65 percent after proper signs were installed. A properly installed signal system and improved parking regulations in the Chicago Loop district reduced accidents about 20 percent and speeded up traffic about 50 percent. Marked traffic lanes on a major artery in Philadelphia increased by about one-third the number of vehicles which could use the street in peak-load hours. The first year after a signal system was installed on North Broad Street in Philadelphia, fatalities dropped from twenty-three to eleven. We citizens get good results when our traffic problems are solved on the basis of *facts*.

Traffic Engineering in the City

Cities have many complex traffic problems. In the first place, a great many businesses, industries, apartment houses, and homes are crowded together. The number of people per square mile is much greater than in suburban and rural areas. There are large numbers of passenger cars, buses, and trucks on the city streets. The parking problem alone is very serious. These problems call for continuous work by traffic engineers.

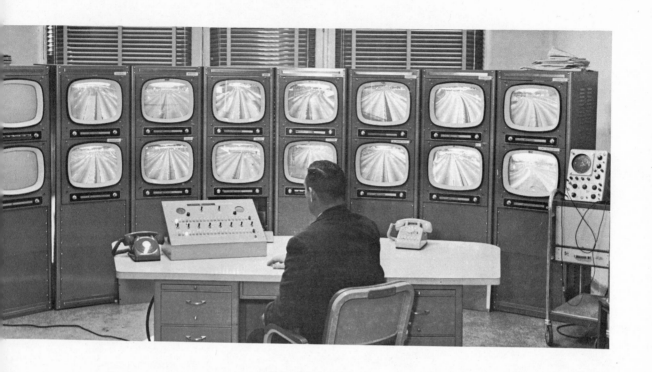

Fig. 19–10. This experimental television installation in Detroit relays traffic information to a control center, where an operator can regulate lane utilization, vehicle speeds, and the opening and closing of entrances to, and exits from, the freeway. The object is to prevent or reduce traffic congestion and delays, to increase the traffic-carrying capabilities of the freeway, and to make it safer. The circle in the lower photograph surrounds one of the cameras used in the installation.

Accident Prevention   A city traffic engineer makes use of accident records. One of his jobs, for example, is to correct conditions that cause many accidents at the same locations. He first finds out where the worst accident locations are. Accident "spot maps" help him to do this. A cluster of spots on this kind of map graphically indicates places where accidents are frequent. Accident reports also help when they are filed according to the location of each crash. After a time, a "worst-corner" chart is prepared.

After a "worst corner" has been located, the question is, "Why does this intersection have so many crashes?" Clues to the answer must be found. The intersection is observed and studied. A "collision diagram" is made, showing the directions of movement of vehicles and pedestrians involved in the accidents, the times of day or night, the times of year, and a number of other helpful facts. All these facts are then analyzed for clues to the trouble. Often one cause stands out; or a few types of cases predominate.

After the causes of the accidents are found, the traffic engineer works out remedies. A sight obstruction, such as a high fence, shrubbery, or billboard, may be removed. One or more stop signs may be installed. In certain places, stop-and-go signals may be needed. The best remedy is the one which corrects the situation with the least interference to traffic movement and at the least cost.

Accident facts also help police officials assign their men where they can be most effective in moving traffic and preventing accidents. Accident analyses may indicate the need for changes in traffic regulations. Drivers and pedestrians who prepare accurate reports when involved in traffic accidents help in such accident prevention work.

Traffic Signs   Traffic engineers determine the need for signs. They decide what types of signs should be used and how such devices should guide or control traffic. Installation is the next step.

Fig. 19–11. These tell the engineer a story.

ACCIDENT SPOT MAP

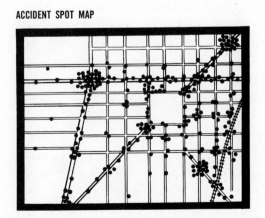

COLLISION DIAGRAM

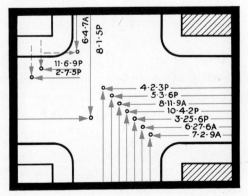

Signs cause confusion if they are not standardized or if they are set up in the wrong places. Only standard signs should be used. Those needed in night driving should be fully visible at night. They should be placed only where facts show that they are really needed. They should be installed in standard positions. Signs that are hidden by branches, too high, or not properly installed are often of little use—they may be harmful.

Traffic Signals Traffic-control signals or stop-and-go lights can help conditions at intersections or they can cause needless delay, irritation, and accidents. If installed where they are not warranted by traffic conditions, they are likely to fail to reduce accidents or to improve traffic flow. Indeed, studies have shown that in many cases signals installed at intersections without the services of competent engineers and without proper study of facts have actually *increased* accidents.

Signal Controls The traffic engineer should also decide the method by which the signal is controlled. There are two main types of signals:

1. Those operated by electrical timers, or "clockwork"
2. Those operated by the traffic itself

Most signals are of the first type. The length of one complete sequence of green, yellow, and red lights is determined by an electrical timing device, or clock. These devices permit the traffic engineer to change the lengths of the STOP and GO periods to meet changing traffic needs at different times of the day.

Some signals are controlled by the passing of vehicles over, under, or between devices known as *detectors*. These are *traffic-actuated* signals. Such devices regulate GO intervals according to the traffic at the time. At some locations, pedestrians can bring about a GO interval for their use by pressing a push button.

Properly engineered traffic signals greatly help drivers. Have you ever driven or ridden as a passenger through a "progressive" signal system, where each signal changes to green as you approach? This is easily done, provided that you drive at a speed for which the system is timed, as described on page 158. Sound traffic engineering made this possible.

Pedestrian Signals The traffic engineer plans traffic-control signals to fit the needs of pedestrians as well as drivers. Signal "faces" which apply to pedestrians are placed directly in the pedestrian's line of vision. The order of signal changes and the length of time each signal in the cycle shows take pedestrians' needs into account. The law should and usually does require obedience to pedestrian signals in the same manner as it requires drivers to obey traffic signals.

Where pedestrian traffic is heavy only at certain times, such as at schools, factories, or sports centers, signals are sometimes used which permit a pedestrian to bring about a green, or WALK, signal which would not otherwise appear. The pedestrian pushes a button on a post at the curb. In due time, taking account of vehicular traffic, the signal changes in the pedestrian's favor. After allowing time for pedestrians to cross the street, the signal automatically changes back in favor of motor traffic, pending the next pedestrian request.

Through Streets and Stop Signs   A "through street" is normally a major artery, at the entrances to which side street traffic must stop. A sound through-street plan requires careful study. A traffic-flow map is made to show which streets carry the most vehicles.

In planning a sound through-street system, traffic engineers consider such factors as traffic volumes, bus routes, street widths, road-surface conditions, the number and speeds of vehicles on cross streets, and how to help through traffic bypass congested sections. Not only local residents but also out-of-town drivers who want to get through a city quickly and conveniently appreciate good through-street planning. Careful routing of such through traffic also helps reduce congestion in busy city areas. Traffic which has its destination in the city must also be taken into consideration. Planning a through-street system is a job that can be adequately handled only by trained traffic engineers.

A driver should never assume that he is on a through street because it is busy and looks like a "main" street. Too often someone on a similar, intersecting street has the same idea and a crash occurs.

Engineering Intersections   Traffic engineering is needed in designing and redesigning intersections. The best solution for a particular location can be found only after an engineering study. An unfamiliar, irregularly shaped intersection can badly puzzle a driver. Such intersections cause

Fig. 19–12. Channelizing islands guide the traffic.

confusion, delay, and accidents. Good traffic engineering avoids or corrects bad intersection design.

Channelizing islands often help at intersections. Notice in Fig. 19–12 that left turns can be made only around islands. When such islands are properly located and designed, the correct way is the natural and safe way to turn. Well-planned channels reduce the number of points where turning cars could come into conflict with other vehicles and pedestrians.

Crosswalks   Crosswalks are provided to encourage pedestrians to cross only at carefully selected locations. They are usually marked by paint, buttons, or pavement inserts. Crosswalks are usually about as wide as the sidewalks of which they are extensions. At busy crossings, they may be somewhat wider.

At a few places, traffic engineers find it necessary to mark mid-block crosswalks.

Fig. 19-13. Pedestrian barriers prevent dangerous jaywalking.

Such crosswalks, where used at night, must be marked clearly and well illuminated. Then drivers who do not ordinarily expect crosswalks in the middle of the block can see them well in advance.

Barriers of chain, pipe, or rope are sometimes erected along curbs to assure use of marked crosswalks and to prevent "jaywalking." Notice the barriers in Fig. 19-13.

Pedestrian Tunnels and Overpasses

Traffic engineers sometimes advise construction of a pedestrian tunnel or overpass where heavy pedestrian traffic conflicts with heavy vehicular traffic. Either plan completely removes the danger of pedestrian crossings if the pedestrians cooperate by using it.

Pedestrian tunnels and overpasses are costly, but the expenditure at certain locations can be justified by the prevention of pedestrian accidents and the reduction of traffic delay.

The Planned Community

Figure 19-14 shows parts of the plan of a residential community designed for the Motor Age. The wide, central, general-traffic artery (A) serves through traffic. Secondary arteries (B) serve traffic to and from the residences. In some cases, small "turn-around" islands (C) also serve residences. They also permit traffic to turn around on "cul-de-sac," or dead-end, roadways. All through traffic should be bypassed around residential areas and business districts.

Good community engineering such as this means safety, convenience, and beauty. It preserves property values in residential areas. Houses front on private parklike areas with foot paths conveniently located. No vehicular traffic roars by. Children go to school or playgrounds on pedestrian walkways with underpasses and overpasses to avoid crossing vehicular roadways. This is the kind of modern planning in residential areas that citizens of this Motor Age should encourage.

Places for Play

With today's traffic conditions, street play is extremely dangerous. Most child-pedestrian deaths and injuries occur to youngsters playing in streets or entering the roadway while at play. An important part of the remedy is to provide attractive play areas off the streets.

Children under six need parent-supervised play yards in their own block. Older children need larger well-supervised play areas, such as playgrounds and parks.

Progressive traffic engineers and city planners encourage play yards and community playgrounds designed and equipped for suitable play. Play areas should be located where they can be reached with a minimum of danger, and barriers should be installed to prevent children from running carelessly from playgrounds into streets.

Street Lighting   Traffic engineers encourage and often help design proper street lighting. Many studies show that street lighting has a close relationship to nighttime accidents, both pedestrian and vehicular. Lighting engineers have studied the problem and know what kinds of lighting installations are warranted for differing conditions. They use scientific methods to determine how efficient existing lighting is on any street and how nearly it approaches recommended standards.

Too few of today's city streets measure up to satisfactory standards of lighting. Those streets which carry heavy traffic especially need effective modern lighting that is properly installed under the supervision of trained engineers.

Parking—a Major Problem   Finding a suitable place to park a car is difficult in many communities. As vehicular traffic grows heavier and heavier, there is less and less street space available for parking. More and more is needed for loading and unloading trucks and the movement of the great volume of vehicles. Even where curb parking is still permitted, parking time is carefully controlled so that the best use can be made of what space there is.

Fig. 19–14. Good engineering designs a community for the Motor Age.

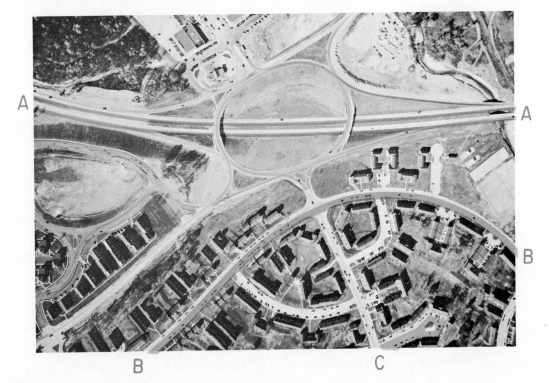

Storage space for vehicles is now provided in lots or garages *off the streets*. The number of multilevel parking structures is increasing. Two such parking garages are shown in Figs. 19–15 and 19–16. These provide car storage space on several floors. Communities which wish to develop off-street parking facilities should be guided by recommendations made by traffic engineers.

Adequate parking facilities are of great value to merchants, property owners, the city, and the general public. "Downtown" districts which provide convenient and reasonably priced parking attract customers who otherwise would shop elsewhere. This helps maintain downtown property values. Much of the total property tax receipts in many cities comes from downtown properties. Hence, this aspect of the total parking problem is an important matter, warranting constant expert attention. Citizens should not let it merely drift along.

Traffic Engineering in Rural Areas

Traffic engineers are needed in rural areas as well as in cities. They collect facts, determine how accidents can be reduced, erect traffic signs and signals, apply pavement markings, determine no-passing zones and special speed zones, and provide advice on highway design problems.

Thousands of pedestrians are killed and injured on suburban and rural roadways.

Well-engineered sidewalks help safeguard pedestrians. Such walkways are needed in the outer sections of cities and towns, near schools located near the edges of town, and wherever there is heavy traffic along the road. Sidewalks should have hard, smooth surfaces, and they should be kept clear of snow, mud, leaves, and trash.

Rural danger points where accidents occur, or are likely to occur, should be hunted out and remedied to reduce accidents. No-passing zones need to be carefully located and clearly marked. After speed zoning is worked out scientifically (see Chapter 8, "Traffic Laws Made by Man"), speed-limit signs that are clearly visible both day and night should be put up. Intersections and other rural road improvements should be planned and guided by engineers.

Research Is Needed

State highway departments, the U.S. Bureau of Public Roads, cities, counties, and the Highway Research Board collect facts, conduct research, and develop improved road-building and traffic-handling methods. This highway research helps highway administrators and city officials get the most out of the highway dollar. New facts and better methods are constantly being sought on all road and traffic subjects.

Leading universities now maintain centers which not only train specialists but conduct extensive research in all related areas. They comprise an important source of much-needed new knowledge.

Fig. 19–15. Modern multifloored parking garage.

Fig. 19–16. Some cities have underground parking facilities.

In recent years, states have been making thorough studies of their highway needs. They study their total road system in cities, suburbs, and country areas in cooperation with local governments. Their objective is to learn what roads and streets are needed to take care of present and estimated future needs.

States also study the way their highways are now financed and how they should be financed in the future to be fair to everyone. Studies are important in helping to decide what roads are needed, what governmental agency should be responsible for them, and how much money should be spent on them.

State and Federal highway officials have developed techniques for origin-destination traffic surveys. Residents of an area are interviewed to learn *from where, to where,* and *by what route* they traveled during a certain period. This information aids in forecasting potential future use. Engineers use the findings to help them select routes for new or improved roads and streets so they will best serve the largest number of people.

Just as industry uses research to improve products and methods, so states and cities can employ it constantly to improve highway transportation. More knowledge is needed. Constant research is applied to improved road-building materials and construction and maintenance methods. Further analysis of new traffic-engineering techniques and devices is required.

One of the greatest needs in highway transportation is a vast increase in research. Industry is spending over 3 percent of its income in this way. In the highway field, about .5 percent of the amount spent in one year for highways is spent for research. If as great a percentage of highway income were spent on research as industry spends in this way, highway research expenditures would amount to about $375 million instead of the current $60 million. Many more research specialists are needed to solve important and perplexing highway transportation problems, and these specialists must be provided with adequate funds to carry on this important work.

Highway Transportation as a Vocation

The people engaged in highway transportation should be highly trained and experienced. The public loses greatly unless it insists that highway planning, design, construction, and operation be done by experts.

The continuing large-scale need for better roads and streets, with its challenge to man's ingenuity and ability, makes highway transportation an outstandingly attractive field for a life work. Every dollar of the billions now annually going into highways should be spent on the basis of engineering know-how. There are not enough highway and traffic engineers today—or in sight. Shortages of such specialists exist in state, city, and county organizations, in consulting firms, and in related industries.

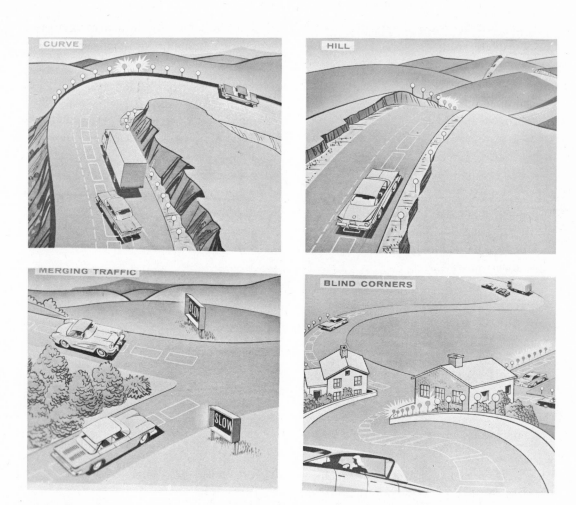

Fig. 19–17. Electronics may become a significant factor of highway operation and traffic safety in the future. Note roadway installation to activate warning devices.

For young men and women of ideas, highway transportation provides an excellent future. The challenge of Motor Age problems offers unsurpassed opportunities for a stimulating career. If you like difficult problems involving motor vehicles, highway transportation engineering may be a stimulating and challenging career for you.

Highway engineering is offered at a number of engineering colleges as a part of their civil engineering course. Many universities now offer special courses dealing with traffic engineering. Other universities and colleges offer regular courses and short courses to give specialized traffic engineering training for engineers who are already at work.

To Talk About:

1. Discuss the interest of the Federal government in developing a highway system. Can you justify Federal aid for highways?

2. What new roads have been built in your area or what old roads have recently been modernized? What improvements have been built into these roads?

3. What recent improvements in traffic control have been made in your community? Discuss what was done and in what ways it has contributed to safety and efficiency of traffic movement.

4. What problems may be encountered on a high-crown road in such situations as (*a*) driving straight ahead on dry pavement; (*b*) driving on slippery pavement; (*c*) turning onto such a road; (*d*) pulling over to a curb to park?

5. What problem may be encountered in using traffic circles? In what ways is a grade separation safer and more efficient?

6. Discuss "traffic-actuated" or "pedestrian-actuated" signals in your community. How do these work and why were they put at those particular intersections? Are there other locations where you think these would be helpful?

7. Discuss the advantages and disadvantages of through streets in cities.

8. As future citizens, how can you keep informed on traffic problems and related research? What active part should you take in promoting improvements in your community and state?

9. Are the school children in your community properly protected when going to and from schools? When at play? Discuss the need for better protection and control at certain actual locations. How can faster progress be made in protecting children in your community?

10. As a future voter and taxpayer, consider what you should know about parking problems. What is being done in your community to provide off-street parking areas? Loading zones for trucks? In what ways is parking restricted?

11. Discuss parking meters and the extent to which they improve parking conditions.

To Do:

1. Find out what important traffic studies your community has made in the last few years. What were the findings and recommendations? What has been done about them?

2. Make a study of several busy intersections in your community. Consider any problems in connection with each and offer suggestions for improvement.

3. Find out who must authorize STOP signs, YIELD signs, and traffic signals at corners in your community. On what basis is a decision made to put up such traffic controls? Are there some dangerous corners which, for various reasons, are left uncontrolled?

4. Make a study of traffic conditions on rural roads in your area and write a report containing recommendations based on the improvements suggested in this chapter.

5. After studying Figs. 19–7, 19–8, and 19–9, list the hazards that have been eliminated at these types of intersections and the hazards that still exist.

6. Make a report on any traffic signs or signals you can find that may not be fully visible because of their location.

7. Write an editorial for a local newspaper urging property owners to cut hedges and remove bushes and other obstructions which cause blind corners. If tree branches hide STOP signs and signals and interfere with vision at intersections, this might also be mentioned.

8. Study street lighting in your community and decide whether it is efficient. If not, what recommendations would you make?

9. Build a model or make a drawing of an irregular street intersection in your community to show: (*a*) dangers to both motorists and pedestrians; (*b*) the way in which these dangers have been, or could be, lessened (for example, by installing islands). Invite an appropriate city official to come and discuss this with your group.

10. Have several interested students look into various aspects of traffic engineering as a vocation and report to the class. Consider where proper training can be obtained, what it involves, and some of the job possibilities. Look in college bulletins in the guidance office or library for this information.

11. Design and draw a plan for adapting some undeveloped area of your city to suit the Motor Age. Reduce pedestrian and vehicular conflict as much as possible. Plan for adequate playgrounds and traffic-control devices.

12. Assemble clippings from local papers on the subject of new roads, road improvements, parking problems or solutions, or appropriation of funds for any of these purposes. These may be factual news items or editorial comment. Discuss these from the standpoint of what you have learned in this course.

PART TWO In the Car

You in Control

For countless years man labored with only the strength of his own body. Then, somewhere in prehistoric times he learned to use beasts of burden as a source of physical power greater than his own. The horse served man for thousands of years, giving not only greater strength but also wider horizons and more speed and endurance in travel.

Greater power came through the discovery of coal and development of mechanical devices through which steam could be harnessed. The flow of our rivers became another important source of increasing power. Indeed, much of our progress has been tied to such increasing development of power.

All this time there lay beneath the earth's surface reservoirs of power beyond man's imagination. Finally, he discovered this great energy source—petroleum. After some years, he learned how to make crude oil into products such as gasoline, a ready source of power. He learned how to build an engine which could harness that power and propel a vehicle with it. The automobile, the truck, the bus, the diesel locomotive, the oil-burning steamship or motorship, and both piston- and jet-engined planes all "live" on petroleum products.

Harnessed in the engine of the motor vehicle, this earth-born power easily moves tons of steel at man's desired speeds. Your car means both power and speed beyond the dreams of men who came before us—with *you in control.*

20

Before You Start the Engine

You are almost ready to start driving—almost, but not quite. There are a few important things that every good driver must know well.

Like the pilot of a plane, you must be familiar with the positions of all instruments and controls of the vehicle. You must be able to manipulate many of them automatically. In many instances, you may have time for only a swift glance at the instrument panel. You must learn to feel for a switch or a control lever with your hand or foot, without taking your eyes off the roadway.

The purpose of this chapter is to explain the functions of the various instruments, controls, and safety features within the driver's reach. Various makes and models of cars locate similar instruments and controls in different positions. Before attempting to drive an unfamiliar car, study the owner's manual.

Predriving Habits

In preparing to drive, it is essential to develop certain predriving habits, since many driving skills are employed automatically and from habit. Predriving habits that should be developed by each driver before starting the engine include those that follow.

Adjusting the Driver's Seat This seat is provided with an adjustable mechanism. It can be moved forward or backward to fit the leg length of each driver. In some cars, it can also be moved up and down. This is quite important when several persons of different heights drive the same car. The seat should be adjusted to allow the operator to sit comfortably in a relaxed position but still to be able to reach all pedals and controls easily.

Locking the Doors The driver should see that all doors are locked from the inside. This serves two purposes:

1. In case of an accident, the doors are less likely to spring open from impact. There is much less chance of occupants being thrown from the vehicle. A person who remains inside the car during a crash is not so likely to be seriously injured as one thrown out of a car.

2. People inside the car are protected from persons who may try to enter the car when it is stopped for a traffic light or sign.

Adjusting the Rear-view Mirror It is essential that the rear-view mirror be adjusted for *each driver*. In today's high-speed traffic, it is almost as important for the driver to see the traffic pattern behind him as that in front. Each driver should adjust the inside mirror so that he can see the traffic directly behind through the rear window. If the vehicle is equipped with outside mirrors, they should be adjusted to cover as many blind spots as possible. (The *blind spots* are those areas which cannot

Fig. 20-1. The front seats of all cars may be adjusted forward and backward. Some move up and down.

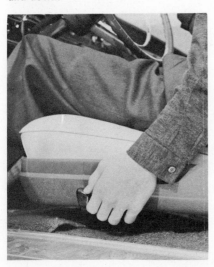

Fig. 20-2. Adjust the rear-view mirror before you start the car.

WITH A REAR-VIEW MIRROR...   WITH A SIDE-VIEW MIRROR...   WITH BOTH MIRRORS...

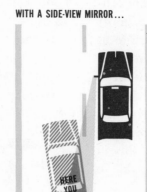

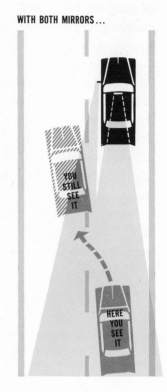

Fig. 20–3. An outside mirror reduces the area otherwise invisible to the driver which is called the "blind spot."

be seen by looking in the inside rear-view mirror. They are directly to the right rear and the left rear of the vehicle).

Using an Outside Mirror By all means *do* have one on your car. It supplements the range of vision of your regular rear-view mirror. Using both, you can move to the next lane to pass on multilane highways much more safely than with only one. You can see whether another vehicle is overtaking you to pass before you make your move left. You do not have to take your eyes away from the picture ahead in heavy, fast-moving traffic. Your field of vision includes the road ahead while you glance in the inside and outside mirrors.

But be sure that your outside mirror is mounted below or above your eye level. If located *at* your eye level, it would make a *permanent blind spot* to your left and front.

A common plea following some serious accidents has been, "I didn't see him." Frequently, the driver cannot understand *why* he did not see the other car—even when questioned some time after the accident. Unless an investigator his size sits in the driver's seat, no one may ever know.

This is a point that is not well known among drivers. You can help by passing it on as a friendly tip.

BEFORE YOU START THE ENGINE

290

Fastening Seat Belts   This is an action well known to people who fly. If a car is equipped with seat belts, the driver should suggest that his passengers fasten them. In case of a collision, they may prevent occupants from striking the instrument panel or the windshield. A seat belt may also prevent a person from being thrown out of the car.

Adjusting Ventilation   Before the engine is started, windows and side vents should be adjusted for the passengers' comfort. In cars equipped with air conditioners or vented heaters, this may not be so important as in the past. However, there should always be some fresh air entering the car to prevent its occupants from being affected or overcome by carbon monoxide.

Informational Devices

The only way you can *know* that the car is running smoothly and efficiently is by the use of instruments. You must be familiar with the information obtainable from the instrument panel. Even your judgment of the speed at which you are traveling can be very unreliable. Now is the time—*before* you start driving—to learn what instruments do and how to use them.

Speedometer   This unit indicates the miles per hour at which the vehicle is traveling. (It actually indicates how fast the rear wheels are turning.) It is a good driving habit to check the speedometer frequently.

Fig. 20–4. A seat belt may prevent serious injury in event of a collision.

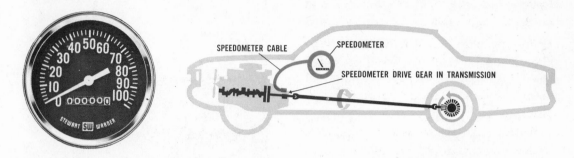

Fig. 20–5. The speedometer translates the drive shaft revolutions per minute into the car's miles per hour. The odometer records the total distance traveled.

Speedometer error is not uncommon. Suppose you drive regularly at, or within, posted speed limits and still consistently pass most other vehicles. Your speedometer may be slow. Have it checked. "My speedometer must have been slow" has often been hopefully recited to a police officer by a speed-limit violator. It is not recommended as a legal defense.

Odometer This instrument is usually located very close to the speedometer. It shows the total distance the vehicle has traveled. It is helpful in determining

when oil changes and grease lubrications are necessary. It can be used to record the number of miles traveled during a day or on a trip. It can also be used for figuring gas mileage.

Ammeter or Generator Charge Light The ammeter indicates the number of amperes of electricity being sent to, or withdrawn from, the storage battery. When the charge light is on it shows that current is being withdrawn from the battery. The latter is sometimes referred to as the "heart" of the car.

The charge light will glow if the ignition is turned on and the engine is not running. Sometimes it will also glow when the engine is running very slowly. The battery may discharge for short periods without serious damage to the electrical system. If the charge light glows or the ammeter gauge shows discharge after all switches have been turned to the

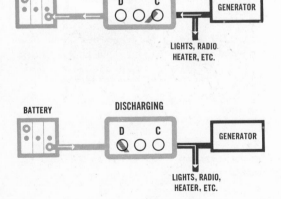

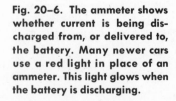

Fig. 20–6. The ammeter shows whether current is being discharged from, or delivered to, the battery. Many newer cars use a red light in place of an ammeter. This light glows when the battery is discharging.

OFF position, have the system checked at once. If the instrument indicates discharge with the engine running rapidly, there may be trouble in, or failure of, the generator or the voltage regulator. If these conditions exist, a mechanic should be consulted.

Battery maintenance is very important. Its water level should be checked regularly to avoid damage. The plates of the battery should be covered with water. If the top of the plates are exposed, you should add water to each cell. Distilled or "soft" water is preferable. Do not overfill the battery, however.

Oil Pressure Light or Indicator The oil pressure gauge shows the amount of pressure with which oil is being pumped throughout the engine. It varies in different makes of cars. This gauge does *not* show the *amount* of oil you have in the engine!

In many modern cars, this gauge, like the ammeter, has been replaced by the *oil pressure light*. When the light glows, it shows that the oil pressure is low. A condition dangerous to the engine may be developing. If the glow persists when the engine is running at normal road speed, stop, turn off the ignition, and have the car checked by a mechanic.

It is natural for the light to glow when the engine is idling very slowly. The oil pump, activated by the slow-turning engine, is merely not turning fast enough to develop much pressure. When you speed up the engine, the light should go out.

Temperature Indicator The normal operating temperature for each make of car is shown in the owner's manual. The driver should

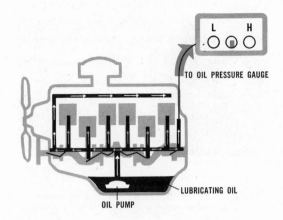

Fig. 20–7. The oil pressure gauge indicates the pressure at which oil is being pumped to the moving parts of the engine. Many new cars have a light that glows when the oil pressure falls below normal.

keep track of the reading of the temperature indicator to avoid damage to the engine. If the temperature rises too much, it will cause loss of water from the cooling system. The engine could become hot enough to cause serious damage.

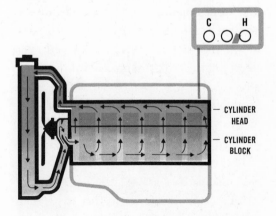

Fig. 20–8. A thermometer in the engine water jacket is connected to a gauge on the instrument panel.

There are a number of causes for excessive engine temperatures, including:

1. Clogging of water lines in the cooling system
2. Loose or broken fan belt
3. A breakdown in the lubricating system
4. Ignition trouble

Running too cold, although an infrequent condition, decreases engine efficiency. Any variation from the normal temperature range, shown by the gauge while the engine is running, calls for investigation.

Fig. 20–9. An electrical device attached to a float in the gas tank registers the fuel level on the instrument-panel gauge.

Fuel Indicator   The fuel indicator shows the approximate amount of gasoline in the fuel tank. It is usually expressed by the marks of EMPTY, ¼, ½, ¾, and FULL. Keeping the tank reasonably full is a good practice. It prevents embarrassing situations, reduces condensation, and promotes safer use of the highway. The latter is true because the stalled car can be a hazard.

High- and Low-beam Indicator Light   This instrument is located on the instrument panel, usually directly in front of the driver. A small light, usually red, glows when the headlights are on high beam and is off when the lights are on low beam.

Operating Switches

Ignition   This switch is controlled by the ignition key. When it is turned ON, electricity from the battery is delivered to the engine, enabling it to operate. This switch must be turned on before using the starter. The ignition switch is usually located on the instrument panel within easy reach of the driver.

Starter   Both the type and the location of this switch vary with makes and models of automobiles. You may have to find it with the help of your owner's manual. It may be a dash button, a button on the floorboard, or part of the accelerator pedal mechanism. It may also be built in as a part of the switch-key assembly. Operating this switch causes the powerful electric starting motor to engage and turn the flywheel of the engine.

As soon as the engine starts, the switch should be released. Do not engage the starter while the engine is running, as there is danger of damaging its mechan-

Fig. 20–10. The ignition key operates a switch in an electrical circuit between battery and engine.

ical parts. If you are in doubt as to whether the engine is operating, depress the accelerator pedal and listen for the sound of the engine. A glance at the oil pressure gauge and the ammeter or the indicator lights can also tell you whether or not the engine is running.

Auxiliary Switches or Controls

The electrical lighting system of the modern automobile is quite elaborate. Among other things, it provides light for operating the car at night or during bad weather. Your lights also warn other drivers of your presence.

The switches that control the car's lights are easily accessible to the driver. Inasmuch as he must frequently operate them when it is dark, he should be thoroughly familiar with their location and operation.

Exterior Lights The circuits for exterior lights are so wired that the driver can obtain different combinations of these lights. They consist of headlights, tail lights, parking lights, brake lights, and back-up lights.

There are two circuits in the headlights: the high and low beams. After the master switch has been closed, these two circuits are controlled by a high- and low-beam switch. It is located on the floorboard at the left side of the driver's area.

The high beam is used when driving on rural roads or highways. When meeting an oncoming car, you should change the

HIGH-BEAM LIGHTS

LOW-BEAM LIGHTS

Fig. 20–11. Headlight beams are elevated or depressed by a foot switch.

lights to the low beam by tapping the switch with your left foot. The lights can be returned to high beam when desired by again tapping the floor switch. In some cars, a photoelectric cell operates a switch automatically when it receives a certain amount of light from oncoming headlights. It changes headlights from high to low beam, stays on the low beam until after the vehicle has passed, and then changes back to high beam.

State laws require that a driver lower his headlights to low beam when meeting another vehicle. This should be done far enough in advance of meeting to prevent blinding the other driver. It is important to know that the high beam *can* momentarily blind an approaching driver. The low beam should be used when driving on urban streets so as not to blind other drivers or pedestrians. It also should be used when following another car. This avoids blinding the driver of the other car with the reflection of your lights in his rear-view mirror.

The tail lights glow when the master light switch is set for use of either headlights or parking lights. In either case, they help others to see your car from the rear. However, parking lights must not be used when headlights are required by law.

Brake lights operate automatically when the brake pedal is applied. They inform drivers who are following you that you are reducing speed or stopping the car.

Back-up lights to help a driver back safely at night are sometimes installed on the rear of the car. They light automatically when the gearshift or selector lever is placed in reverse position.

Interior Lights   The instrument panel is illuminated at night. Intensity of this lighting can usually be controlled by turning the master light switch.

The dome light in most cars switches on automatically when a door is opened. An additional hand-operated switch permits lighting it without opening a door. It should not be used when the car is in motion at night because it interferes with the driver's ability to see outside the car.

Windshield Wiper Control   Two types of automatic windshield wipers are the vacuum-operated and the electric-operated. The control for this accessory is usually located on the instrument panel.

A windshield washer unit consists of a water container, two spray nozzles, or jets, and a control mechanism. It is used to spray fluid onto the windshield to aid the wipers in keeping the glass clean. This is optional equipment.

Horn Control Button or Ring   The switch button for sounding the horn is located on the hub of the steering wheel. The horn ring is just inside the rim of the wheel. Pressure on the button or ring will sound the horn.

The horn is a safety warning device. It should never be sounded except in the interest of safety. Unnecessary sounding of the horn is a violation of law in many places. No good driver is a "horn tooter."

Operational Control Devices

The control devices are made up of types of levers. Safety and efficiency in driving depend upon the driver's knowledge and use of these levers.

Steering Wheel   The steering wheel is used to guide the vehicle. Imagine that it is numbered like the face of a clock. Hold the rim of the wheel with your left hand where the 10 would be. Hold it with your right hand at 2 (some drivers prefer 10 and 4). These are the best places for your hands.

Controlling the wheel from the 10-and-2 position permits maximum use of the top half of the steering wheel. This enables you to concentrate upon developing one set of skills for turning the car. Mixing top and bottom handling of the wheel involves hand movements in opposite directions for identical turns of the car. This makes learning to steer more complicated. In addition, in case of sudden emergency, steering action might be confused. Hands at 10 and 2 also permit maximum application of strength to offset wheel pull resulting from a blowout or a soft road shoulder.

Clutch Pedal   The clutch pedal is operated with the left foot. Cars with automatic shifts usually do not have clutch pedals. The purpose of the clutch is to engage

Fig. 20–12. Hold the wheel firmly at "10 o'clock" and "2 o'clock."

and disengage the engine from the transmission when stopping the vehicle or in shifting gears. The clutch should be disengaged when starting the engine.

Gearshift Control The gearshift lever is usually mounted on the right side of the steering column. In a few cars it is located on the floor of the vehicle to the right of the driver. Its purpose is to change gears to fit the varying requirements for power, speed, and forward or reverse travel.

With an automatic transmission, the selector lever is mounted on the right of the steering column. It serves the same purpose as the gearshift lever—selecting the desired gear ranges. If a car has a push-button selector, it is usually mounted on the instrument panel.

Whatever type of control the car has, it should be in the NEUTRAL or PARK position when the starter switch is engaged.

Accelerator Pedal This device controls the amount of the gas and air mixture that enters the engine through the carburetor. It regulates the speed of the vehicle. The pedal is operated with the right foot. The heel should rest on the floor, close to the pedal. To feed gas, exert pressure on the pedal with the ball of the foot.

Foot Brake The brake pedal is located to the left of the accelerator. Its purpose is to stop or slow down the car. The amount of pressure applied controls the amount of braking force exerted on the brake drums.

There are five types of braking systems: (1) mechanical, (2) hydraulic, (3) air, (4) vacuum, and (5) electrical. Hydraulic brakes and, in a few instances, mechanical brakes are the most popular systems used on passenger cars. The others are designed primarily for use on trucks, buses, and tractor-trailers.

...es do not decrease the vehicle's ...tance. They only make the ... of the brake pedal easier. ... pressure is required. *Changing ...ar having one type of brake to a ...ving another requires extreme cau-...f your power brakes fail*, press the ... pedal down as far as it will go and ...n exert increasing force. The emergency foot-brake "reserve" should stop the car efficiently. It just requires much more pressure. Have power brakes and the emergency reserve checked regularly.

Parking or Hand Brake   This brake may be a hand lever or a small foot pedal. The latter is usually located to the left of the steering column. The hand lever may be located at either side. The purposes of the hand brake are to keep the car from rolling when it is parked and to hold the car when starting on a hill. It operates independently of the foot brake and will help in an emergency if the latter fails. It must be released fully before moving the vehicle. If it should be only partly released, there is danger of damaging the brake linings by overheating.

Additional Safety Features

Turn or Directional Signals   Most states have legalized the use of flashing lights to signal change of direction. Some states have laws requiring that a vehicle be equipped with this device. Electrical turn signals inform other motorists in advance of the direction of an intended turn. The

Fig. 20–13. Can you locate the following: speedometer, horn ring, clutch pedal, foot brake, accelerator pedal, parking brake, high- and low-beam floor switch, gearshift lever, directional signal lever?

lever for this device is mounted on the steering column just below the steering wheel—usually on the left. To indicate a right turn, the signal lever is moved clockwise; for a left turn, counterclockwise. In other words, the lever is moved in the direction the steering wheel is to be turned.

After using the signal, the driver should make a habit of checking the turn indicator lights on the instrument panel. He should make sure that the signal lever returns to the OFF position. If it does not return automatically, the lever should be returned manually.

Sun Visors These devices can be tipped to the front or side to prevent blinding effects from the glare of the sun. Care should be taken in their use to prevent the driver's view from being obstructed, for example, so that he cannot see overhead traffic signals. It is best to reserve sun visors for their proper use, not to load them with odds and ends.

Defroster Defroster slots are built into the top of the instrument panel just below the windshield. Hot air is blown through these slots against the windshield. This prevents accumulation of ice or snow on the outside and fogging of the glass on the inside.

Padded Dash This is another safety feature in the modern car. Its purpose is to serve as a cushion in case the occupants are thrown forward against the instrument panel.

Practice Makes a Good Driver

After studying the instruments, controls, and additional safety features of the car, practice using them while the car is parked. Become so thoroughly familiar with the instruments and their positions that you can locate and read them at a glance. Be able to locate the controls without having to look or fumble for them.

Practice until you feel confident and at home with them. Practice until you are ready for—action!

Fig. 20–14. Skill is a product of practice.

To Talk About:

1. What causes the reading on your temperature gauge to rise when you stop the car and let the engine idle and then return to a normal reading when you begin to move again at a normal rate of speed?

2. Explain how a glance at the oil pressure light or gauge or at the generator charge light or ammeter may let you know whether or not the engine is running?

3. Some drivers install a device on their cars which causes a buzzing sound when they exceed the speed for which the instrument has been set. Do you think this is a wise thing to do?

4. What is the advantage of back-up lights, other than to light a path in back of your car?

5. Under what circumstances is it illegal to sound a horn? Why?

6. What is the importance of always having fresh air in the car?

7. Discuss the merits of seat belts. See whether anyone can tell you what he thinks of them from personal experience. Decide whether or not you would install them in your car.

8. What safety precautions should the driver take as soon as he gets behind the wheel?

To Do:

1. Make a drawing of the instrument panel on your car, showing the markings on each of the gauges and switches. Explain briefly how each gauge works and how it should read. How does each switch work?

2. Compare the gauges and safety and control devices on an old-model car with those on the latest model of the same make. List the major changes. Why do you believe these changes have been made?

3. List some things that might be wrong with your car that would cause the engine to overheat. Look under the hood and see how many of these you could check yourself to find the trouble.

4. Make a list of all additional car devices of which you have heard. Which would increase safety and which are merely "gadgets"?

5. Sit in the driver's seat of any car. Look about you in all directions. Then, facing forward and with the aid of the mirror or mirrors, locate the directions of the blind spots. Make a drawing showing the areas near the car that you cannot see.

6. While in the driver's seat, note the advantages of an outside mirror.

317

20, 21, 22, 23.

Action: Automatic and Gearshift

The two general types of automobile transmissions are automatic and gearshift. Both serve the same purpose: selection and use of the driving gears best suited to the conditions of the moment. In general, automatic transmission models are gradually replacing gearshift models. It is well, however, to read and learn as much as you can about both. A driver never knows when an emergency may require him to drive an unfamiliar car.

Preparing to Drive

Before beginning practice driving, a fourfold checkup is in order:

1. *Check the car.* Your owner's manual gives valuable information. Study it.

Refer to it whenever you are in doubt about the best way to care for your car. With its aid, check your tires, radiator, oil, battery, gasoline, lights, mirrors, horn, and windshield wipers. Do this now, at regular intervals, and at the start of each long trip.

Be sure that any books or packages are safely stowed in the car before taking your place in the driver's seat. You don't want your arm movements restricted by books on the front seat or a spare gym shoe under your brake pedal when you need to stop. Books on the back window shelf may obstruct vision. In a sudden emergency, they may become dangerous missiles.

2. *Check yourself.* Sit in the driver's seat. Review your predriving habits, described in Chapter 20, including careful

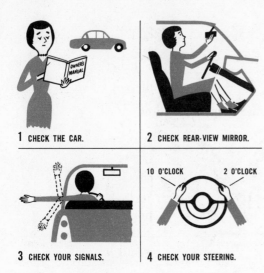

1 CHECK THE CAR.

2 CHECK REAR-VIEW MIRROR.

3 CHECK YOUR SIGNALS.

4 CHECK YOUR STEERING.

10 O'CLOCK   2 O'CLOCK

Fig. 21–1. Make this predriving check.

seat adjustment. Use a good, firm seat cushion, if necessary, to see over the steering wheel. Close your eyes and reach for each of the operational control devices. Be sure you can locate them without fumbling around the driving compartment. Now check the speedometer with a quick glance. Locate the horn button or ring quickly, and find the headlight-beam floor switch.

3. *Check your signals.* Be sure you know how to give hand signals (see Fig. 10–6). Practice them a number of times, holding the wheel with your right hand. The law requires that you know them. Someday, moreover, your electrical turn signals may fail while you are driving.

Practice using your electrical turn signals (they operate only when your ignition is turned on). Notice the flashing light on the instrument panel, usually accompanied by a clicking sound. The light and the sound indicate that your signals are operating.

Be ready when your instructor tells you to signal when you move away from the curb, change direction, slow down, or stop.

4. *Check your steering.* As you prepare to drive, you will practice the basic elements of driving. With this in mind, you will do well to learn just the first steps in handling the steering wheel. As you progress with certain basic skills, you will widen your practice activities. You will then learn more advanced turning movements, as described in Chapter 22, "Maneuvers."

Do you remember that in Chapter 20, "Before You Start the Engine," the steering wheel was compared with the face of a clock? The recommended grip on the wheel has the left hand at ten o'clock and the right at two o'clock. The knuckles of each hand should face outward from the rim of the wheel.

Most people find learning to steer easy. If this and other beginner skills seem to come easier to another student than to you, don't be discouraged. Past experience with bicycles, toy vehicles, and perhaps farm vehicles may be the reason. Most beginning drivers can become skillful *with practice.*

Moving the car forward or backward, you soon learn to steer *by feel.* You won't have to think, "Now I turn the wheel clockwise," and so on. Basic skills must become automatic for you so that you can devote your full attention to traffic and road conditions.

If you have never steered a bicycle or toy vehicle of any kind, remember this at first: The car turns in the direction the

CLOCKWISE

COUNTERCLOCKWISE

Fig. 21-2. Whether moving forward or backward, the car turns in the direction you move the top of the steering wheel.

top of the steering wheel moves. This is true moving forward or backward.

Practice with the steering wheel, brake, accelerator, and turn signals, *keeping your eyes on the road.* The only exception now will be a quick glance at the selector lever. Later, there will be similar very quick glances at the speedometer and other instruments. Now, only when changing selector positions on an automatic shift car do you very briefly take your eyes off the road. In a gearshift car, it should not be necessary.

The various makes and models of cars have different mechanical features and require different operating procedures. The best source of information is your owner's manual. In your driver education car, your instructor will teach you the best methods of operating that car.

Because the principles of operation are the same for most cars, the following directions are for cars in general. Your family car, however, may require some different procedures.

Driving Cars with Automatic Transmissions

Development of the automatic transmission has made driving easier and learning quicker. The gearshift lever and clutch pedal, requiring a much more complex coordination of hand and foot movements, have been replaced by a single lever.

The Selector Lever   The selector device in automatic transmission cars is usually on the steering column, just under the steering wheel (see Fig. 21-3). On some cars, it is a series of push buttons, usually on the instrument panel.

There are four or five positions on the selector quadrant, depending on the make

Fig. 21-3. Using the selector lever.

of car. These positions are marked by letters. As you move the selector lever, an indicator moves with it to show the new position. With the push-button type of selector, you can see which button is engaged by its depressed position. Quadrants and buttons are illuminated for night driving.

The selector positions indicate the following conditions in the transmission machinery of the car:

N *Neutral position*
Transmission gears are disengaged.
The engine cannot drive the rear wheels of the car.
When starting the engine, the lever must be at **N** or, in some cars, at either **N** or **P.**

D or **Dr** *Driving position*
Most forward driving is done in this position.
The lever is placed in this position after you start the engine and are about to drive the car forward.
In most cars, the engine cannot be started using this position. Remember this if you ever suddenly find that your starter "doesn't work." It may be only that you forgot. (Changing to **N** will "fix" your starter quickly.)

L or **Lo** *Low position*
In this position, the car uses only low-ratio gears for maximum power at low speeds.
The position is used for climbing very steep grades.
It is used for driving in mud, sand, or over extremely rough road.
It helps braking on long, steep downgrades by letting the engine compression help hold the car back.

R *Reverse position*
This position is used for backing the car.
The lever must be slightly raised to move it to the **R** position.
On some Hydra-Matic cars, this is the parking position when the engine is stopped.

P *Parking position*
In this position, the transmission is locked so that the car cannot move.
The engine can be started in this position in some cars.

The positions of selector levers are different on cars of different makes, even though the functions of the levers are identical. A person accustomed to one selector pattern may be confused when he drives a car with a different pattern.

Note the **R**, or reverse, position. Obviously, an unintentional shift to **R** when the driver intended **D** might prove hazardous and destructive. Carefully examine the selector on every automatic transmission car before you drive it, and keep the positions well in mind when driving.

Starting the Engine The first step in actual driving is to start the engine:

Step 1. *Check to be sure that the parking brake is firmly set.*

Step 2. *Place the selector lever at* **N** *or leave it at* **P** *if your engine will start in this position.*

Step 3. *If the engine is cold, press the accelerator pedal to the floor once to set the choke and then release it.*

Step 4. *Turn on the ignition switch.*

Step 5. *Engage the starter and release it the instant the engine starts. (In many cars, steps 4 and 5 are ordinarily performed in one continuous turning motion of the ignition key.)*

If your car has an automatic choke, the engine will start more readily when cold if you include step 3 to set the choke. If your car has no automatic choke, omit step 3 and use the manual choke. If the car has a starting device operated by the accelerator pedal, omit step 3, as it may cause carburetor flooding.

Do not pump the accelerator pedal when starting the engine unless the owner's manual advises it, and do not "race" the engine. Some engines run at a fast enough

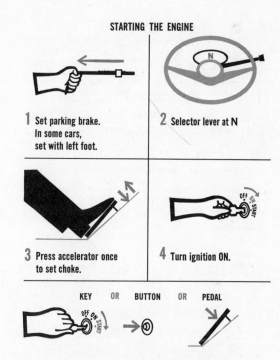

STARTING THE ENGINE

1 Set parking brake. In some cars, set with left foot.

2 Selector lever at N

3 Press accelerator once to set choke.

4 Turn ignition ON.

KEY OR BUTTON OR PEDAL

5 Use starter and release instant engine starts.

Fig. 21–4. Your first action as a driver.

idling speed when cold without using the accelerator pedal. If your engine does not start and run after following this procedure, press lightly and steadily on the pedal. Don't pump it.

If the engine fails to start, it may be for any of the following reasons:

1. Lack of gasoline.

2. Engine flooded with gas. (Hold the accelerator pedal tightly to floor while using the starter.)

3. Failure to turn on the ignition switch fully.

4. Moisture on spark plugs, wires, or other ignition parts which can be wiped off. (Be sure the ignition is turned to OFF.)

5. A clogged fuel line.

PUTTING THE CAR IN MOTION.

1 Apply brake with right foot and hold through Step 5.

2 Place the selector lever in D position.

3 Release parking brake.

4 Check rear-view mirror.

5 Signal and check traffic to left and to rear.

6 Accelerate.

Fig. 21–5. **You begin to drive.**

6. A broken or disconnected wire in the ignition system.

7. Fouled spark plugs.

8. Improper carburetor adjustment.

It would probably take a mechanic to remedy the more complicated troubles, such as mentioned in 5 to 8.

Putting the Car in Motion Before you drive a car, you should certainly know how to stop it. To stop the engine, turn the ignition key to the OFF position. Without the engine running, practice using the brake pedal. For your first actual driving, you should have a wide, quiet, level street or road away from traffic. You may have marked-off practice areas.

Start and warm the engine. Then follow these steps in order:

Step 1. *Apply the brake pedal with the right foot.*

Step 2. *Set the selector lever in the* **D** *position,* holding the brake pedal down firmly.

Step 3. *Release the parking brake.*

Step 4. *Check traffic conditions in the rear-view mirror.*

Step 5. *Signal. Look back over your left shoulder immediately before allowing the car to move. Make steps 3, 4, and 5 firm habits so that you couldn't start off in your car absent-mindedly without first doing all three.*

Step 6. *Move your right foot to the accelerator pedal and press it down gradually. The car is now under way, and you must concentrate carefully on your steering. When you want to pick up speed, press down gradually a little harder on the accelerator pedal. Most of your driving will be with the selector lever at* **D.**

WHEN CAR IS STOPPED AND YOU PUSH BUTTON OR SELECTOR LEVER TO MOVE...

BE SURE YOU PRESS DOWN ON THE BRAKE PEDAL.

Fig. 21–6. **Observe this rule.**

Some automatic transmission cars tend to move faster than expected as soon as the selector lever is at **D** and the parking brake is released. For this reason, form the following habit: *Always hold your right foot on the brake as the first step in starting the car.*

Be careful to press down on the accelerator pedal very gently and gradually.

Stopping the Car Practice the following smooth-stopping techniques. Steps for brief stops in traffic on a level road are:

Step 1. *Check traffic in the rear-view mirror.*

Step 2. *Give the stop signal.*

Step 3. *Ease up on the accelerator pedal.*

Step 4. *Apply the brake pedal until the car comes to a full stop.*

Applying gradual pressure and *easing up slightly* on the pedal just before the car comes to a full stop gives smoother stop-

5 When fully stopped move selector lever to P, or R in cars without P position.

6 Apply parking brake (in some cars with the left foot).

7 Turn off the ignition, remove key, and lock car when leaving it.

Fig. 21–7b.

ing and avoids the jolt that marks the unskilled driver.

To learn to stop smoothly, practice until you are skillful in using the correct pressure on the brake pedal. Practice until you can stop your car at any exact spot you choose. Pick out practice stopping spots in advance—by a pole, tree, or other mark. Then practice until you can stop every time with the car's front bumper exactly even with the spot you chose.

For long "parking" stops, follow through steps 1, 2, 3, and 4, above. Then continue with three additional steps:

Step 5. *Move the selector lever to **P**, or to **R** in cars without the **P** position. (Always stop the car completely before moving the selector lever to the **P** or **R** position.)*

Step 6. *Apply the parking brake.*

Step 7. *Turn off the ignition, remove the ignition key, and lock the car when leaving it.*

STOPPING THE CAR

1 Check rear-view mirror.

2 Give the stop signal.

3 Ease up on the accelerator pedal.

4 Apply brake pedal until car comes to a safe stop.

Fig. 21–7a. There is a correct method of stopping.

Right- or Left-foot Braking   As owners began to change from manual gearshifts to automatic transmissions, the question arose as to which foot is better to use in braking. After several years of experience driving both types of cars, most driver education teachers have come to favor use of the right foot for all highway braking. Although this is the opinion of professional people, it does not mean that other procedures are necessarily wrong.

The following braking procedure is recommended for use in cars with automatic transmissions:

1. In braking on the traveled portion of streets and open highways, the right foot is preferred. This has several advantages:

    a. It prevents "freezing" on the accelerator under stress of emergency.

    b. It uses the right-foot braking skill which most drivers learn from the beginning.

    c. When a driver switches between automatic and gearshift cars, it prevents errors of habit. Hitting a power brake with the left foot using the force habitually applied to a clutch will lock wheels. This force may also lock ordinary brakes.

2. There are two exceptions to the principle of using the right foot on the brake. The left foot may be used to advantage:

    a. When "inching" a car forward, as to the wall of a garage or into a tight place. At this slow speed, there is no danger of a sudden, screeching stop. With the right foot you can feed a little more gas than necessary to move the car, while keeping it from moving with the left foot on the brake. Then, little by little, you can release pressure on the brake pedal, letting the car move very slowly and smoothly. Hold the accelerator pedal stationary. Alternately depress and release the brake pedal, keeping smooth control.

    When backing the car in a limited space, the same technique as described above may be used.

    b. To hold the car from rolling back while stopped on an upgrade, make the stop itself with right-foot braking, as described in Chapter 22, "Maneuvers."

Using the Selector Low Position   All ordinary driving is done with the control lever at **D**. The **L** position is used for such purposes as to:

Start on very steep upgrades
Pull slowly through sand, mud, or snow
Descend very steep grades
Rock the car back and forth between **L** and **R** in deep sand, mud, or snow

Practice using the **L** position under the following conditions:

1. *Starting the car in low*. Set the selector lever at **L** and start the car the same way you would with the lever at **D**. When your car is under way, change the lever to **D**.

If the car is started under slippery road conditions, better traction is available with the lever at **D**. The wheels have less tendency to spin than when **L** is used.

2. *Climbing steep upgrades in low.* Move the selector lever from **D** to **L** if you are slowed down behind a slow-moving truck or line of cars on a steep upgrade.

Changes to **L** should never be made on wet or slippery roads until car speed is reduced to barely moving. Otherwise, the car can be thrown into a skid by the suddenly introduced braking power of the engine.

3. *Using low on steep downgrades.* If you are on a long, steep downgrade and need a lower ratio than can be had in the **D** range, slow down to the speed recommended in the owner's manual and move the lever to **L**. This change prevents building up momentum and saves brakes by letting the engine serve as a brake. Don't change the selector-lever position on wet or slippery roads without first bringing the car nearly to a stop.

Never change from a driving range into **N** and coast. This is hazardous and can damage the transmission.

4. *Using low for heavy pulling.* Think of the **L** position as one that gives you heavy pulling power for the rough, slow going required by bad weather or road conditions. It increases power and lessens strain on the engine.

5. *Using low to "rock" out of deep sand, snow, or mud.* To rock out of sand, snow, or mud, move the selector lever back and forth between **L** and **R**. Use gradual acceleration to avoid spinning the wheels (see Chapter 14, "Driving Under Adverse or Special Conditions," page 205).

Downshifting   On automatic transmission cars, downshifts to lower gear ratios take place automatically with decreasing car speeds. They do not occur automatically when a downgrade requires engine braking action. Manual downshift is then necessary.

On some cars, you can force a shift to lower gear ratios at higher speed than occurs automatically, if you want extra-fast pickup. This is sometimes called

Fig. 21–8. A situation for the forced downshift.

PRESS PEDAL TO FLOOR

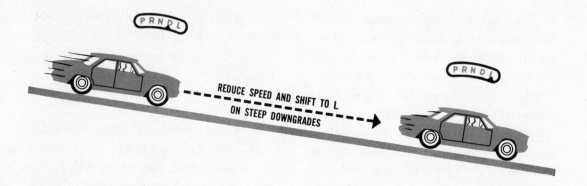

Fig. 21–9. On steep downgrades, let your engine assist in braking.

making a *kickdown* shift. This shift is used, for example, if you are back of a slow-moving car on a hill, have a clear, long view ahead, and need a sudden spurt of speed and power to pass.

Press the accelerator pedal quickly all the way to the floor. The downshift rapidly occurs, and you can pull around the slow-moving car. Your car automatically returns to a higher range as soon as you ease up on the accelerator and return to usual driving conditions. For each make of car, there is a top speed above which this forced downshift cannot be made. Study the owner's manual for your car to learn at which speeds forced shifts can be made to lower gears.

Cars with Manual Gearshifts

If you are going to drive a gearshift car, there are different operating techniques to learn. You must learn to use the gearshift lever and change gear ratios manually as needed.

The Gearshift Lever With this lever you select the different-sized gears in the transmission to give you various combinations of speed and power. Study Fig. 21–10, until you can visualize perfectly the five positions of the gearshift lever with your eyes shut. The positions are *low, second, high, reverse,* and *neutral.* Then, hold one end of a pencil with your left hand and practice shifting the other end from neutral to low, to second, and then to high with your right. Repeat this, low to second to high, until you are sure of it.

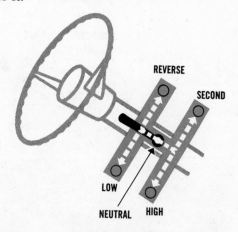

Fig. 21–10. Gearshift movements follow an H pattern.

Never move the gearshift lever without first pressing the clutch pedal *all the way down* with your left foot. Keep the pedal firmly depressed until you finish shifting the lever to the new position. This is very important. Pushing the clutch pedal down completely disengages the clutch. It disconnects the engine from the transmission until the shift is made to gears of a different ratio. If the clutch pedal is not depressed completely, there will be a loud grinding of gears; the gear teeth can be broken.

Starting the Engine

Before you start the engine, be sure the parking brake is set. Now practice starting the engine.

Step 1. *Depress the clutch pedal as far as it will go with the left foot.*

Step 2. *Be sure the gearshift lever is in neutral position.*

Step 3. *Set choke. Turn on the ignition.*

Step 4. *Engage the starter. Be sure you release it the instant the engine starts running.*

The engine is now running. You can slowly release the clutch pedal. Never touch the starter device when the engine is running.

To stop the engine, turn the ignition key to the OFF position. Start and stop the engine until it is easy for you to remember the four steps.

If the engine fails to start after you have used the starting device several times, release the starter and look for the cause. Check the list of causes for the engine's failure to start; the list can be found on page 305.

STARTING THE ENGINE

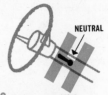

1 Depress clutch pedal all the way with left foot.

2 Be sure gearshift is in neutral position.

3 Turn ignition ON.

4 Use starter. Release it the instant engine starts.

Fig. 21–11. How the engine is started in the manual-shift car.

Putting the Car in Motion

Know exactly where the brake pedal is and how to stop the car. Then, after you have started and warmed the engine, follow these steps:

Step 1. *Depress the clutch pedal.*

Step 2. *Shift to low gear; keep your palm up.*

Step 3. *Release the parking brake.*

Step 4. *Check the rear-view mirror.*

Fig. 21–12. Shift to low gear, palm up.

PUTTING THE CAR IN MOTION

1 Depress clutch.

2 Shift to low gear.

3 Release parking brake.

4 Check rear-view mirror.

CLUTCH AT FRICTION POINT

5 Signal before you move. Look back, check blind spot to left rear.

6 Press accelerator. Release clutch to friction point.

7 Slowly let clutch pedal come up. At the same time,
8 Increase pressure slightly on accelerator.

Fig. 21-13. Starting the manual-shift car.

Step 5. *Signal. Look back over your left shoulder just before you start to move the car, checking the blind spot.*

Step 6. *Let the clutch come up very slowly until it reaches the friction point— the point at which you can feel it*

taking hold. Hesitate, or hold it at that point, until the car is moving ahead, and then

Step 7. *Increase pressure slightly on the accelerator, and at the same time*

Step 8. *Slowly let the clutch pedal come up the rest of the way.*

In step 6, you are harnessing the engine for its work of moving the car. So you must accompany it with steps 7 and 8 and give it gas to do the work. If your car moves with jumps or jerks, you have not released the clutch pedal properly or your foot is "bouncing" on the accelerator. Depress the clutch pedal immediately and practice releasing it more gradually until you can start smoothly. The secret of a smooth "take off" is proper clutch control.

Drivers who shift gears noiselessly and smoothly, without jumping the car, stalling the engine, or grinding the gears, have learned to sense and use the friction point of the clutch. At the instant you reach this point—where the clutch takes hold and your car begins to move—press lightly on the accelerator pedal. Then, while you let the clutch pedal come farther up, gradually feed more gasoline.

If you feed gasoline too late, or after the friction point is reached, the engine does not have enough speed and power to pull the car, and there will be a series of slow, bumpy jerks. The engine may even stall.

When you have carried out the above steps, your car will be moving in first, or low, gear, and you must attend closely to steering.

Stopping from Low or Second Gear These are the steps for stopping the car correctly:

Step 1. *Check traffic through the rear-view mirror.*

Step 2. *Signal for a stop.*

Step 3. *Depress the clutch pedal.*

Step 4. *Release the accelerator pedal. In low gear, take your foot off the accelerator pedal just slightly later than you press down on the clutch pedal. This prevents jerkiness.*

Step 5. *Apply your right foot to the brake pedal and gradually press down, stopping the car.*

Step 6. *Shift to neutral. (Follow the path of the arrow shown in Fig. 21–14.)*

Step 7. *Apply the parking brake and remove your feet from pedals.*

In step 5, ease up slightly on the brake pedal just before you bring the car to a full stop. This gives you smoother stopping.

After step 7, keep the gearshift lever in the neutral position until you are ready to move again. This practice is recommended at all times and is especially important at traffic lights, STOP signs, and places where there are pedestrians. Serious accidents have occurred where a car has been kept in gear while standing and the driver's foot has slipped from the clutch pedal.

Shifting from Low to Second Gear When your car is running smoothly in low gear and you are ready to change to second gear, keep your eyes up and:

313

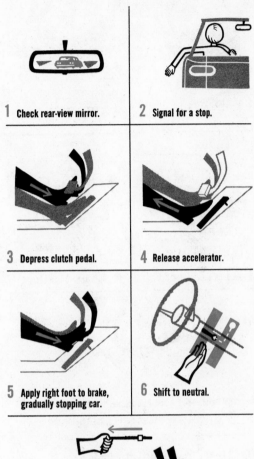

1 Check rear-view mirror. 2 Signal for a stop.

3 Depress clutch pedal. 4 Release accelerator.

5 Apply right foot to brake, gradually stopping car. 6 Shift to neutral.

7 Apply parking brake and remove feet from pedals.

Fig. 21–14. The order of these steps should be carefully noted.

Step 1. *Press the accelerator until the car is running approximately 8 miles per hour.*

SHIFTING FROM LOW TO SECOND

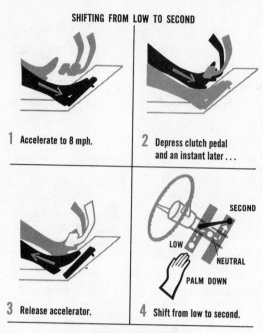

1 Accelerate to 8 mph.

2 Depress clutch pedal and an instant later...

3 Release accelerator.

4 Shift from low to second.

SECOND

LOW

NEUTRAL

PALM DOWN

CLUTCH FRICTION POINT

5 Release clutch pedal slowly. Hesitate at friction point.

6 At almost same time, gradually press accelerator.

Fig. 21–15. Your first shift with the car in motion.

Fig. 21–16. Shift to second, palm down.

Step 2. *Depress the clutch pedal, and just an instant later*

Step 3. *Release the accelerator pedal. In shifting, the clutch movement precedes the accelerator movement by a very brief instant. This is the secret of good, smooth shifting.*

Step 4. *With your palm down, move the gearshift lever forward to the position of neutral; then push it downward, then forward into second.*

Step 5. *Release the clutch pedal slowly. Hesitate an instant at the friction point. At almost the same time,*

Step 6. *Gradually press the accelerator pedal.*

In step 1, you are giving your car enough speed so it can run on momentum while the clutch is disengaged during the shifting of gears.

In step 4, the slight pressure away from the steering wheel keeps the lever from moving past the neutral position into reverse. Follow the path of the arrow shown in Fig. 21–15. Notice the hesitation point and practice observing it.

Shifting from Second to High Gear To shift into high gear, have the car running smoothly in second gear, and then, with your eyes up:

Step 1. *Press down gradually on the accelerator until you reach a speed of about 15 to 20 miles per hour.*

Step 2. *Depress the clutch pedal.*

Step 3. *Release the accelerator pedal.*

314

Fig. 21-17. Shifting from second to high.

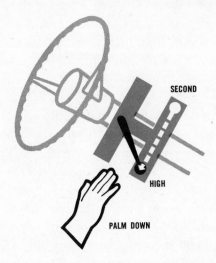

Step 4. *Shift to high gear, palm down (see arrow in Fig. 21-17).*

Step 5. *Let the clutch pedal come up smoothly, and at the same time*

Step 6. *Gradually press the accelerator pedal.*

Step 7. *Move your foot from the clutch pedal to the floor.*

Fig. 21-18. Shift to high, palm down.

In step 1, you give your car sufficient speed—approximately 15 to 20 miles per hour—to carry it along while the engine is disengaged during the shifting of gears. This speed also keeps the engine from laboring when it first moves the car in high gear.

You are now driving the car in high gear. You will find the steering easier because of the increased speed. Keep on the right side of the practice street. Keep your eyes on the road.

Stopping from High Gear When stopping from high gear, there is a change in the order of steps:

Step 1. *Check traffic in the rear-view mirror.*

Step 2. *Signal for a stop.*

Step 3. *Release the accelerator pedal gradually.*

Step 4. *Press the brake pedal, slowing your car to approximately 10 miles per hour.*

Step 5. *Depress the clutch pedal.*

Step 6. *Continue braking, easing up slightly just before you come to a full stop.*

Step 7. *Move the gearshift lever to neutral (as shown by path of the arrow in Fig. 21-10).*

Step 8. *Apply the parking brake and remove your feet from the pedals.*

Notice that steps 4 and 5 are different. Stopping from high gear, you use the foot brake before you depress the clutch pedal.

As you take your foot from the accelerator pedal, the engine slows down and helps brake the car. If you depress the clutch too soon when in high gear, you lose this braking power of the engine.

Shifting from High to Second Gear Sometimes, on hills, turning corners, or slowing down in traffic, it is necessary to shift from high gear to second.

Always shift into second if you feel you can keep your car under better control by doing so or if the engine is laboring under its load. Such a shift, if necessary, should be made *before* turning a corner or crossing railroad tracks, for example.

For this shift, you need greater engine speed to match the car speed. This is how you make the shift:

Step 1. *Release pressure on the accelerator and use brake if necessary to reduce speed, while you*

Step 2. *Depress the clutch pedal.*

Step 3. *Shift from high gear to second (reversing the direction shown in Fig. 21–17).*

Step 4. *Press the accelerator pedal to increase the engine speed.*

Step 5. *Release the clutch pedal slowly, and at the same time*

Step 6. *Increase your pressure on the accelerator pedal.*

Step 4 is necessary to increase the speed of the engine because second gear requires a faster engine speed than high gear for the same car speed. Practice gives you the feel of proper engine speed.

If you shift from high to second on an upgrade, make the shift quickly enough to maintain momentum and avoid a stalled engine. A shift from high to second should usually be made only when the speed of the car has dropped to 15 or 20 miles per hour.

Sometimes a downgrade proves steeper than it looks. A shift to second should have been made before starting down. However, if the shift was not made, then the problem is how to make it while on the downgrade. The procedure is:

Step 1. *Press on the brake pedal with your right foot to check speed.*

Step 2. *Depress the clutch with your left foot.*

Step 3. *Shift to second gear.*

Step 4. *Increase your engine speed to match your car speed by pressing on the accelerator.*

Step 5. *Release the clutch pedal, moving through the friction point very slowly.*

Step 6. *Remove your foot from the accelerator and use the brakes as needed.*

Much well-guided practice away from traffic brings results. When the driving operations described in this chapter become easy, you are ready for the more complex maneuvers.

To Talk About:

1. When turning the steering wheel, some beginners place one hand inside the wheel with the palm facing out, rather than on the outside with the knuckles facing out. Why is this a bad habit?

2. Some automatic transmission cars tend to move as soon as the selector lever is placed at any driving position. How should this fact affect your driving habits?

3. Explain the importance of the friction point in getting a gearshift car moving smoothly. Tell exactly what happens to the car mechanism when this point is reached and why the car will jump or lurch if you do not hesitate at this point in letting up the clutch. Why does it often stall after lurching forward?

4. When stopping from low speeds, you depress the clutch just before you brake, whereas in stopping from higher speeds you brake first. What is the reason for this? Why must you depress the clutch before the car comes to a stop?

5. List all of the situations you can think of in which it might be wise to shift from high to second gear.

6. Explain why you must never shift gears without fully disengaging the clutch and keeping it disengaged until the shift is completed.

7. Why, during shifts to higher gears, must the car be going fast enough to run on momentum?

8. When a driver who normally drives a gearshift car changes to an automatic transmission car, what changes in his driving habits must he expect to make? If the situation is reversed?

To Do:

1. Get a piece of cardboard 5 inches long and 3 inches wide. Cut a ½-inch "track" in this in the shape of an "H" that is 4 inches long and 2 inches wide. Insert a pencil in this track and practice moving it with your right hand as you would a gearshift lever, while you hold the cardboard with your left hand. Be sure to have your hand in the proper position for each shift that you make.

2. Make a list of all the switches and levers on your car and indicate which hand or foot controls each.

3. Study the owner's manual for your car, then check your tires, radiator, oil, battery, gasoline, lights, mirrors, horn, windshield wipers, and brakes.

4. Talk with several drivers experienced with automatic transmission cars. Discuss in class what they say about the ease of learning to drive these cars, the ease with which they drive, special precautions they take with this type of car, driving habits they have to break temporarily when driving another car, and care of their cars.

22 Maneuvers

In athletics, man has learned precisely which movements are the most efficient in each sport. Consistent success in competition has been the test. What would you say is the common expression for these time-tested, *most efficient* movements?

They are called "good form," aren't they?

In just the same way, there is good form in driving a car. It consists of the tested, most efficient manner of performing each act.

The beginner in a sport and the new driver should both remember this. Good form, learned from the very beginning, has three distinct advantages:

1. The learner profits from man's past trial-and-error experience.

2. He achieves greater skill in a shorter time.

3. He avoids the time-consuming and often dangerous formation of bad habits. These may or may not be "unlearned" later. If they are, it is usually "the hard way."

This is why road instruction in the car under a trained teacher is so important. We begin with certain basic maneuvers, *using the proper form from the start.*

Handling the
Steering Wheel

When it is necessary to turn the steering wheel more than about half a turn, one form is better than others. One hand grips its own side of the steering wheel and pushes it up and over the top. It continues the motion, pulling the wheel part way down on the opposite "side" of its own circumference. The other hand, meanwhile, is free and crosses over that hand to get a new grip to pull the wheel. It pulls and continues the wheel motion. The pushing, crossing over, and pulling movements are repeated as long as necessary. This is known as "hand-over-hand" turning of the steering wheel (see Fig. 22–1).

Always hold the rim of the wheel *from the outside.* We tend to follow our usual habit patterns of movement when an emergency arises. Some drivers make the mistake of reversing one hand and grasping the wheel from the inside. If you develop this habit, you are very apt to follow it in a fast emergency turn. Should your fingers collide with a spoke of the wheel in doing this, you may lose control.

Notice that each hand makes a substantial movement with each gripping of the wheel. *Avoid the habit of "walking" the wheel.* This means moving each hand only a few inches and passing the wheel around in short, jerky movements.

Recovery   When the car has completed the turn, its front wheels will usually be attempting to return to a straight-ahead position. You may let them do so, but

319

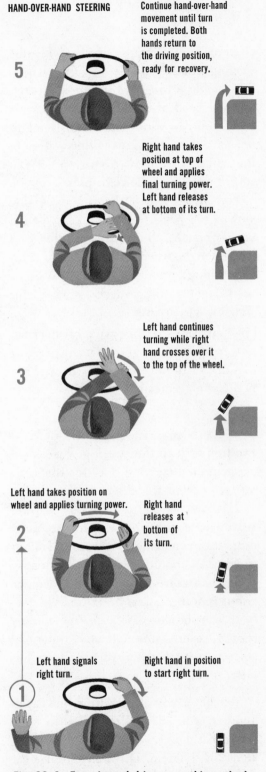

HAND-OVER-HAND STEERING

5 — Continue hand-over-hand movement until turn is completed. Both hands return to the driving position, ready for recovery.

4 — Right hand takes position at top of wheel and applies final turning power. Left hand releases at bottom of its turn.

3 — Left hand continues turning while right hand crosses over it to the top of the wheel.

2 — Left hand takes position on wheel and applies turning power. Right hand releases at bottom of its turn.

1 — Left hand signals right turn. Right hand in position to start right turn.

Fig. 22–1. Experienced drivers use this method.

continue light hand contact with the steering wheel. Never let go of the wheel. Let it slide through your hands, *controlling* its speed of movement. At the same time, you can slide your hands back to normal position, following the contour of the wheel. In this way, you are able to stop it exactly at the right point.

Sometimes, when the car is moving slowly, the wheels return too slowly and you oversteer. Be ready for this and straighten the wheels, if necessary. Learning to judge the exact moment to begin to straighten the wheels is vital for smooth, safe driving.

Power Steering In this type of steering, power from the engine is used to assist the driver in turning the wheel. Four points to remember are that power steering:

1. Requires considerably less physical exertion to turn the steering wheel than conventional steering does for the same degree of front-wheel movement

2. Gives the driver more power to resist the side pull from a front-tire blowout or from having run onto a soft or rough road shoulder

3. Does not function when the engine is not running

4. If it should cease to operate for any reason, reverts automatically to manual steering, which requires more "force" to make turns

Whenever you change from one car to another, you are called upon to have skills that may be either slightly or considerably different. Drive any strange car slowly, allowing an extra margin for safety

in every maneuver. You can no longer rely on automatic skill actions. You must think of each movement as you perform it, just as you did when you were first learning to drive. To the highly skilled driver, a strange car is a challenge. He carefully modifies his every movement to drive it *smoothly.*

Driving Forward To maintain a straight or nearly straight course, you must make a continuous series of slight turning movements of the steering wheel. These correct for steering-wheel play, road crown, bumps, unequal tire pressure, and cross winds. These movements should be made with a continuous, steady grip on the wheel. Move your hands *with* the wheel; do not "walk" it. Beginners sometimes correct too late, which results in their oversteering. They then zigzag down the road.

Right Turns When you are about to make a right turn, there are a number of things you must keep in mind. Each is important, and you should learn these five steps well:

Step 1. *Check other traffic, especially behind you and to your right.*

Step 2. *If you are not in the right-hand lane, signal for a right turn, check to see that the lane is clear, and move into it.*

Step 3. *Give the correct signal for a right turn.*

Step 4. *Be sure you are about 3 to 5 feet from the curb when you start to turn.*

Step 5. *As you start to turn, carefully note all other traffic in the intersection.*

Fig. 22–2. The right-turn signal.

It is important to remember that your position in the roadway is often more obvious to other drivers than your signals. They see the car but are apt to miss the signals. *Be sure to get into proper position sufficiently in advance of any turn.*

Start turning the steering wheel when your front wheels are opposite the point where the curb begins to curve. Starting the turn too soon will cause the right rear wheel to strike, or "jump," the curb.

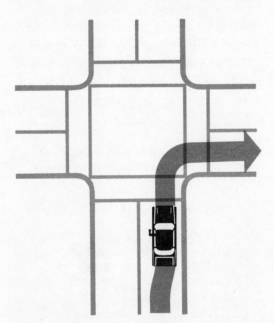

Fig. 22–3. Making a right turn.

Starting too late will take you into the wrong lane when you complete the turn. Either movement can be quite dangerous to you and to others. Always watch for pedestrians.

Follow the general curve of the curb as you turn. Arrive in the right-hand lane of the street or road into which you are turning.

Left Turns Start left turns from the lane nearest your side of the center line. On one-way streets, turn from the lane farthest to the left.

In preparing for a left turn:

Step 1. *Check traffic conditions, especially to the left and rear.*

Step 2. *If you are not in the correct lane, give the proper signal and move into it.*

Step 3. *Give the proper signal for the turn.*

Step 4. *Just before turning, check traffic ahead and both left and right.*

Step 5. *Be sure any driver following you has not missed your signal and is about to pass on the left as you turn.*

Start the turn as your front wheels reach the pedestrian crosswalk. Turning too early or too late may place you in an embarrassing or even dangerous position. Follow the pattern in Fig. 22–5. After the turn, arrive in the lane on the cross street which corresponds to the lane you left.

Where the turning lane is marked or where signs require a certain turning procedure, the course must be followed as directed.

Fig. 22–4. The left-turn signal.

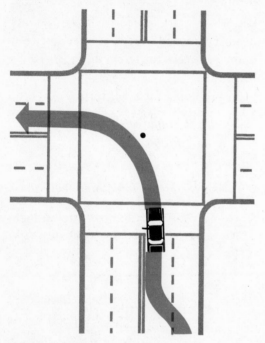

Fig. 22–5. Making a left turn.

Caution Beware of "fading right" just prior to your left turn, and vice versa. Another driver, following you and failing to note your signal, may be misled by your movement. He may try to pass you on the side to which you are really turning. This preliminary movement to the opposite of the direction of your turn is often unconsciously made. It is necessary only when entering a very narrow passageway. If you find it necessary, be sure any

following driver sees your signal and knows what you are going to do. In some situations, it may be wise to use a hand signal as well as a directional signal to make sure that your intentions are clear to other drivers. This is a good thing to do *any time* you want to make your planned movement absolutely clear to other drivers.

Backing the Car

This skill is needed in many common driving situations. The driver must be in complete control and able to stop at any instant.

First, be sure the backward path is clear. Your visibility to the rear is limited, so you must be very careful in backing. If you have approached your car from the front, take a look in back *before entering.* The ground just in back of the car is never visible from the driver's seat! A child may be playing there. Near a shopping center, a neighboring driver may have left a shopping cart there.

Fig. 22–6. "Fading" to the left when making a right turn or vice versa can cause accidents.

To steer the car in reverse, you move the top of the wheel in the direction you want the rear of the car to go. Turning the wheel clockwise steers the car to the right. Turning the wheel counterclockwise steers the car to the left. This direction of turning is something you learn by *doing*. Practice enough that steering the car in reverse is so natural that you don't have to think about which way to turn the wheel.

Get Set Before starting to practice backing, find a firm position—one from which you can both steer and see. Be sure you can work the foot pedals in this position. Normally, you should turn your head and body to the right so that you look out the back window. Don't try to steer by the very limited vision of a mirror. In general, when backing to the left you should look over the left shoulder. Whenever there is a hazard on the side opposite your turn, continue glancing in that direction until you have cleared it, remembering that the front of your car will swing in the opposite direction.

When you have achieved a good backing position, the next step is to practice the backing movement itself.

Check These Points In performing any car maneuver such as backing, it is very valuable to develop a habit pattern of appropriate procedures. Practice these *now and as long as you drive:*

1. Take your time. Back the car slowly.
2. Check traffic conditions, vehicular and pedestrian, in all directions. Be aware of any intersecting street or driveway to the left and rear.

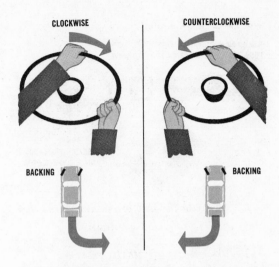

Fig. 22-7. **When you back the car it turns in the same direction that you turn the top of the steering wheel.**

3. Steer carefully and stay in your lane. Give quick, short glances in all directions.
4. Avoid backing into main streets, highways, and pedestrian crosswalks.
5. Practice backing in a place free of other vehicles and pedestrians.

Backing Cars with Automatic Transmissions Always be sure the car is stopped before shifting between forward and reverse gears.

With the car completely stopped and the parking brake set, practice these steps in backing:

Step 1. *Apply the foot brake.*

Step 2. *Move the selector lever to the* **R** *position. You may have to lift the selector lever a little for this position.*

Step 3. *Release the parking brake.*

Step 4. *Check traffic conditions in all directions.*

Fig. 22–8. A good rule!

WHEN CAR IS STOPPED AND YOU
PUSH BUTTON OR SELECTOR LEVER TO MOVE...

BE SURE YOU PRESS DOWN
ON THE BRAKE PEDAL.

Step 5. *Release the foot brake and press the accelerator down* gradually.

Step 6. *When the car starts, release accelerator-pedal pressure slightly.*

Steer carefully and be ready to brake at any instant. Control the car by alternately using the accelerator and brake pedals. Move the car *slowly* when backing.

Practice these steps in stopping from reverse when backing cars with automatic transmissions:

Step 1. *Lift your foot from the accelerator pedal.*

Step 2. *Apply the foot brake and stop the car.*

Step 3. *Move the selector lever to neutral.*

Step 4. *Apply the parking brake and move the selector lever to* **P** *or* **R** *if you are leaving the car.*

Practice starting, steering, and stopping the car in reverse on a well-marked course. Do this until you can steer and stop exactly where you want to. Drive in a straight line and also turn left and right while backing. In a protected practice area, reversing in a "figure 8" is a good way to turn by "feel."

Backing Gearshift Cars   Practice in a place away from other vehicles and pedestrians. Check traffic in all directions and then practice these steps:

Step 1. *Depress the clutch pedal.*

Step 2. *With your palm up, raise the gearshift lever toward the steering wheel. Press it forward, maintaining a slight upward pressure, into reverse gear.*

Step 3. *Slightly increase pressure on the accelerator pedal, and at the same time*

Step 4. *Slowly release the clutch pedal to the friction point, that is, the point at which the clutch begins to take hold.* NOTE: *Control in backing gearshift cars depends largely on skillful use of the friction point of the clutch. Learn to back with the clutch held at the friction point. This allows you to control the speed of the car, stopping the reversing power by slightly depressing the clutch.*

FRICTION POINT
OF CLUTCH

Fig. 22–9. When backing gearshift cars, hold the clutch at the friction point and increase pressure on the accelerator. Slightly depress the clutch to control reverse speed.

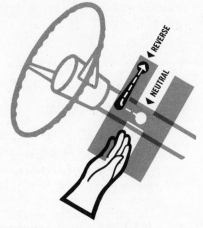

NEUTRAL TO REVERSE (PALM UP)

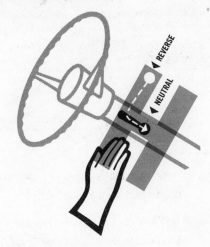

REVERSE TO NEUTRAL (PALM DOWN)

Fig. 22–10. Path of shift between neutral and reverse.

Beginning drivers tend to feed gas too quickly. They then release the accelerator pedal too suddenly in an effort to correct the error. Avoid this by holding the clutch at the friction point. Hold the accelerator as steady as possible with the engine running slightly faster than idling speed.

A gearshift car moving in reverse requires the following steps to stop smoothly:

Step 1. *Depress the clutch pedal.*

Step 2. *Release the accelerator pedal an instant after you push the clutch pedal down.*

Step 3. *Apply the foot brake.*

Step 4. *Shift the gears to neutral.*

Key Word: Slowly Backing a car should always be done at a slow speed. It is much safer—and wiser, for the driver must realize that all the time he can possibly save by fast backing throughout his life will be a very few minutes.

Turning Around

This maneuver is becoming increasingly difficult as traffic gets heavier. Before deciding to make a full 180-degree turn, a driver should carefully consider all conditions at that particular time and place. There are many situations where going around a block would be simpler and far safer.

Intersection Turn Occasionally, visibility and traffic conditions permit using an intersecting street to turn around. Figure 22–11 shows the path which the car should follow. This type of turn should be made only with excellent visibility and no fast or heavy traffic near. Plan your turn carefully, making the safest use of the intersection.

U Turns Sometimes you will want to make a **U** turn, that is, a turn in one complete sweep. Be sure it is in a place where **U** turns are permitted; in many places they are illegal. If you are doubtful of having enough room to turn in one

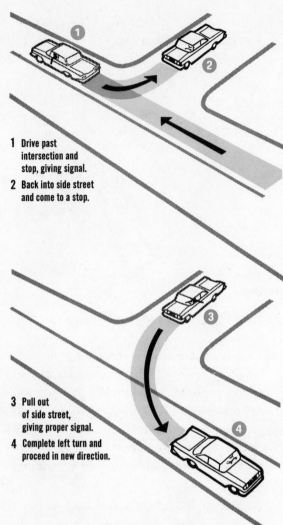

1 Drive past intersection and stop, giving signal.

2 Back into side street and come to a stop.

3 Pull out of side street, giving proper signal.

4 Complete left turn and proceed in new direction.

Fig. 22–11. Very light traffic conditions may permit this turn.

movement, be sure there is time for backing and turning.

When **U**-turning on country roads, be sure you are not near a hill crest, curve, or intersection. A fast-moving vehicle may come upon you suddenly. On city streets, make sure no vehicles, pedestrians, playing children, or animals are close. When the way is clear, turn slowly and be ready to stop instantly. Never cross double solid lines.

These are the steps:

Step 1. *Stop the car close to the right-hand curb.*

Step 2. *Check for oncoming traffic (also look at the rear-view mirror).*

Step 3. *Signal for a left turn.*

Step 4. *Look back over your left shoulder immediately before starting to turn.*

Step 5. *Turn the steering wheel rapidly left, moving the car slowly.*

Step 6. *When the turn is completed, straighten the car's front wheels to proceed in the proper lane.*

Step 7. *Check and fit in properly with the traffic pattern.*

Turning Around on a Narrow Street When the width of the street does not permit a **U** turn, another method of turning may be used. Some people call this a *three-point* turn.

Before turning, note carefully the following points:

1. Be sure you are not near an intersection, curve, or hill crest. Caught facing across the road by a suddenly appearing, fast-moving car, you would be helpless.

2. Notice the height of the curbs. The front and rear ends of cars extend well over a curb before the tires touch it.

3. Pick a spot without trees, telephone poles, fire hydrants, etc., near the curb. They are hard to keep in sight while maneuvering the car, especially in backing and turning!

4. Move the car *slowly* and the wheel *rapidly*.

Eight Steps

Practice turning the car around, using the following steps:

Step 1. *Stop close to the right-hand edge of the pavement.*

Step 2. *Check for a clear path both ahead and behind.*

Step 3. *Signal for a left turn.*

The next five steps are illustrated in Fig. 22–12.

Step 4. *Go forward in* **D** *or low gear, turning the steering wheel to the left to bring the car to position 2.*

Step 5. *When the front wheels are about 4 feet from the curb and the car is still moving slowly ahead, turn the steering wheel rapidly to the right and stop just short of the curb or road edge.*

Step 6. *Back slowly, turning the steering wheel to the right to bring the car to position 3 and turning the wheel to the left just before stopping.*

Step 7. *Go forward slowly, completing the turn to the left, bringing the car to position 4. Check traffic and proceed.*

Step 8. *Repeat the action of Steps 6 and 7 if necessary to complete the turn.*

Practice   In some states, the driver's license examination requires you to demonstrate the three-point turn on a narrow roadway without touching the curb either in backing or going forward. Practice this until you can do it correctly every time.

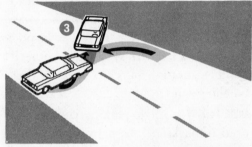
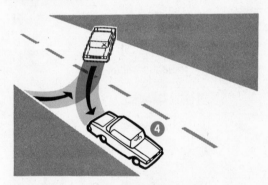

Fig. 22–12. Many people call this "the three-point turn."

The turning method you use at any time depends on such circumstances as traffic and the width and layout of the street. Choose the method which permits clear, unobstructed vision and causes the least interference with traffic.

Turning around is not permitted on many streets, where the turn may be hazardous or delay traffic. Remember that many times the simplest and best method is to drive around the block.

Parking

The ability to park is a necessary driving skill. Many drivers find parking in a limited space at the curb the most difficult maneuver to learn. How well you park shows your driving *control*.

At first, practice parking away from traffic. Set up markers at each end of the parking space to represent parked cars. Every time you touch a marker in practice, score a bent fender against yourself! Practice until you can park without touching one.

Angle Parking Angle parking is commonly used in parking lots, shopping centers, and (in some cities) especially on wide streets, at the curbs. On the street, it adds to traffic congestion and is hazardous.

Angle parking may be "head in" or "back in." Both are simple operations, but they require practice.

"Head-in" Parking Although this is the easiest of the parking maneuvers, correct procedure will make the movements much easier and much safer. When entering a "head-in" parking space on your right:

Step 1. *Observe traffic conditions both ahead and behind.*

Step 2. *Signal your intention to slow down.*

Step 3. *Move your car to the left at least 5 feet from the parked cars, bringing the rear of your car in position to clear the parked cars. Signal and be sure that any driver following you knows what you intend to do!*

Step 4. *Steer sharply to the right, centering your car in the parking space as shown in Fig. 22–13.*

Step 5. *Continue forward slowly until the front wheel barely touches the curb. Do not hit the curb.*

Step 6. *Place the gearshift lever in reverse or the selector lever in P or R.*

Step 7. *Apply the parking brake.*

Before backing out of a "head-in" parking space, look in all directions. If you have approached your car from the front, walk around and look directly in back of it before entering. Move your car slowly and carefully, because it is very difficult to see approaching traffic. Be sure no approaching car is close in the

Fig. 22–13. "Head-in" parking.

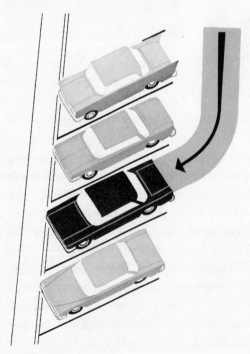

lane into which you are backing. If pedestrian traffic is heavy, as on some parking lots, tap the horn as an extra precaution.

When you can see past the tops of the adjacent cars, stop and look about again. Look for other drivers who may be ready to pull out at the same time, including any in the line of parked cars directly in back of you. Be sure that the front of your car, which swings *opposite* the direction of your turn, has clearance. Then back slowly until the left front wheel passes the rear bumper of the car parked on the left. Then turn the steering wheel sharply to the right. Straighten the wheels quickly as your car comes back into the line of traffic.

"Back-in" Parking Backing into a parking stall is more difficult than heading in. However, it is easier and much less hazardous to drive out forward after backing in.

Step 1. *Drive slowly past the vacant stall, B–C, in Fig. 22–14.*

Step 2. *Signal, and stop with the right end of the rear bumper opposite the center of stall C–D.*

Step 3. *When traffic permits, back slowly, turning the steering wheel to the right as far and as fast as necessary to place the car in position to back straight in. In backing and turning right, the tendency of most beginning drivers is to start turning the wheel too late.*

Step 4. *Ease in very slowly until the rear wheels barely touch the curb.*

Fig. 22–14. "Back-in" parking.

CAUTION: Remember, when you back and turn, the front end of your car swings in the opposite direction. Look out for other traffic!

Parallel Parking Moving your car into a small space at the curb requires special skill. Practice until you are skillful and confident in your ability to park.

Learn first of all to judge whether or not the space left along the curb is sufficient for parking. A rough rule is that you need at least 5 feet more than the overall length of your car to park easily.

Assume that you are in car A in Fig. 22–15, and that each of the other vehicles mentioned below is of standard passenger-car wheelbase length. Some allowance may be indicated when compact or long vehicles are involved. You are going to park at the right-hand curb

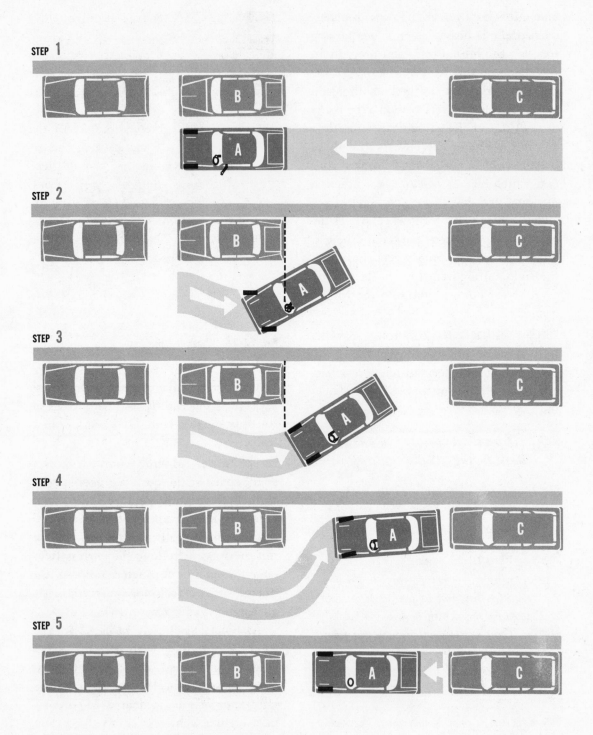

Fig. 22–15. A guide to skillful parallel parking.

between cars B and C. Take these steps in order:

Step 1. *Signal for a stop. Drive alongside, and parallel to, car B, with about 2 feet of space between. Stop when the rear bumper of your car is beside the rear bumper of car B. This beginning position is extremely important.*

Step 2. *Back very slowly, steering sharply to the right, until your car is at nearly a 45-degree angle to the curb. Your steering wheel should now be opposite the rear bumper of car B.*

Step 3. *Straighten your front wheels. Continue backing into the parking space until the right end of your front bumper is opposite the left end of the rear bumper of car B. The right rear wheel of your car is then about 1 foot farther from the curb than the right wheels of car B.*

Step 4. *Turn the steering wheel rapidly to the left as far as it will go, while backing slowly into the parking space. The rear wheel should be close to the curb but should not touch it. Just before stopping, turn the wheel to the right.*

Step 5. *Then go forward slowly and finish turning the steering wheel to the right to bring the car parallel to the curb. Stop the car, after centering it about an equal distance from cars B and C.*

Be Accurate Parking regulations in cities require both the front and the back wheels of a parked car to be from 6 to 18 inches from the curb. Check your state and city provisions for the exact distance. If the wheels are too far from the curb, you have failed in one or more of the above steps. In that case, swing the car carefully out and follow through all steps again. If there is enough space in front, you can go forward slowly, turning the wheel first to the right and then to the left and finally backing parallel and closer to the curb.

Parking too close to the curb, with your car's wheels "frozen" against it, makes it very difficult to get out of the space. There is also a danger of scraping fenders on high curbs or damaging tires. Avoid, as far as possible, turning the steering wheel when the car is standing still, as this strains the steering mechanism and wears tires. If the car does not have power steering, this also tires you.

If you park at the left-hand curb on a one-way street, follow all the steps above, reversing all right and left directions. Practice parking at the left-hand curb until you can do it as easily as you can on the right-hand side. One-way streets are becoming more common, so this maneuver is more often required.

Leaving When leaving a parked position at the right-hand curb, first look back. Move slowly back until your car nearly touches the bumper of car C. As you back, turn the wheel right as far as you can without scraping the curb with your right rear wheel.

Before starting out from a parked position, always do three things. Make them a habit so you practically cannot start without doing them:

Step 1. *Start your electric directional signal operating for a left turn. If another vehicle behind yours obscures your rear directional signal, use your hand signal also until your move is obvious to drivers approaching from the rear.*

Step 2. *Look in your rear-view mirror to see what is behind you.*

Step 3. Then, immediately before starting out, look over your left shoulder for traffic not visible in your mirror. *(Never pull out from a curb or open your driver-side door without this over-the-left-shoulder look first.)*

Move slowly forward, steering rapidly left. Try to pull out at an angle of about 45 degrees. When your steering wheel is opposite the rear of car B, start turning your wheels right to move in the direction of traffic. Check the position of car B, being sure not to scrape it on the way out. Keep a sharp lookout for approaching traffic, especially from the rear.

Careful The chief responsibility for avoiding a collision lies with the driver who is leaving a parking space. If there is a stream of traffic, wait for a gap. If there are no gaps, edge your way into the traffic stream by "nosing" out little by little. Signal your intention all the time. Give approaching drivers time to see what you are doing and to adjust their actions to yours. Many times, another driver will stop or slow down so you can pull out.

Safeguards in Parallel Parking on Hills

To prevent an accident caused by, or involving, a runaway car, certain safeguards are necessary in parking on a grade.

To park on a *downgrade*, the following procedures are used:

Step 1. *Bring the car to a normal parallel-parked position.*

Step 2. *Move forward slowly, turning the wheels sharply left.*

Step 3. *Turn the wheels sharply right as you continue moving forward very slowly toward the curb.*

Step 4. *Stop the car when the right front wheel is just touching the curb (see Fig. 22–16).*

To remove the car from this parking position, it is necessary to back up enough to straighten the front wheels.

On an *upgrade*, follow steps 1 and 2, above, moving about 5 feet in step 2. Then stop the car. In this case, further procedures will be carried out as follows:

Step 3. *Using reverse gear, back the car very slowly while turning the wheels the rest of the way left.*

Step 4. *Hold them left and continue slowly backing until the right front wheel is just touching the curb (see Fig. 22–16).*

When parking on an upgrade where there is no curb, turn the wheels to the right instead of the left; on a downgrade, turn them right.

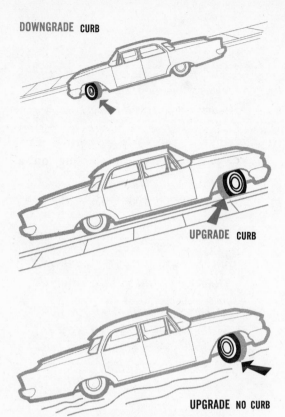

DOWNGRADE CURB

UPGRADE CURB

UPGRADE NO CURB

Fig. 22–16. Position of front wheels when the car is parked on grades.

If the hill is sufficiently steep, the clutch pedal may be depressed, permitting the car to roll back (in reverse gear). Speed is controlled by the foot brake.

This parking position can also be achieved by backing in as described under "Parallel Parking" on page 331. Steps 1 through 4 are followed except that, in step 4, the wheels are turned and kept all the way left until the right front wheel just touches the curb.

In *all* cases of parking on a hill, the hand brake should be firmly set and the selector lever set at **P** after the car is parked. In gearshift cars and in automatic transmission cars which have no **P** position, *reverse* is used.

Starting on an Upgrade

Sometimes you have to stop momentarily on an upgrade and then move on. Learn to start on the grade without letting the car roll back even slightly. This skill is another high mark of driver control.

In Automatic Transmission Cars The method you use for starting on upgrades with automatic transmission cars may depend on several things. Your state licensing authority may require one specific method in their license tests, such as using the parking brake. This is done in the following steps:

Step 1. *Stop the car with your right foot on the foot brake.*

Step 2. *Set the parking brake firmly.*

Step 3. *When ready to move with the selector lever in* **D**, *press your right foot on the accelerator, with your hand ready to release the parking brake.*

Step 4. *At the same time, as the engine speeds up for sufficient power, release the parking brake. (It is not necessary to race the engine. Practice will give you the ability to judge how much to depress the accelerator.)*

For momentary stops, the selector lever may be left at **D**.

Some drivers, experienced in automatic transmission cars, use still another method satisfactorily. They stop the car with the right foot on the foot brake. They then hold down the foot brake with that foot while they place the left foot beside

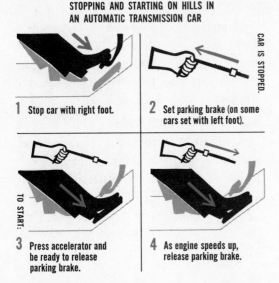

STOPPING AND STARTING ON HILLS IN AN AUTOMATIC TRANSMISSION CAR

CAR IS STOPPED.

1 Stop car with right foot.

2 Set parking brake (on some cars set with left foot).

TO START:

3 Press accelerator and be ready to release parking brake.

4 As engine speeds up, release parking brake.

Fig. 22–17. This maneuver can be learned quickly.

it on that brake. The left foot then takes over pressure on the brake and the right foot is moved to the accelerator. The driver then feeds gas while he releases the foot brake and drives ahead.

Sometimes, the hill may be so slight that you prefer simply to hold the car with your right foot on the foot brake, moving quickly to the accelerator when ready to start. There is less tendency for cars with automatic transmissions to roll back or stall than there is with gearshift cars.

In Gearshift Cars The best method for up-hill starting of gearshift cars is to use the parking brake and the accelerator pedal in combination.

The steps in stopping and starting are:

Step 1. *Stop the car with your right foot on the foot brake, depressing the clutch to prevent stalling.*

Step 2. *Set the parking brake fully (if this requires moving your left foot, shift to neutral to free this foot).*

Step 3. *Shift to low gear.*

Step 4. *Have one hand on the steering wheel and the other in position to release the parking brake at the instant desired.*

Step 5. *Press the accelerator pedal for sufficient power for the uphill start. Avoid racing the engine.*

Step 6. *Slowly release the clutch to the friction point. (You will often feel the car "try" to move ahead as the clutch engages. At that point, the engine begins to labor and slow down.)*

Step 7. *As the clutch begins to engage, release the parking brake gradually and feed more gas.*

Step 8. *Fully release the parking brake and fully engage the clutch as the car moves ahead.*

Step 9. *Continue in low gear until your car has gained enough momentum to permit shifting to a higher gear.*

If your engine stalls on an upgrade in a gearshift car, apply the foot brake quickly and depress the clutch. Set the parking brake and shift to neutral. Restart the engine. Then follow steps 3 through 9 again.

Practice away from traffic until you have this skill well learned and have confidence.

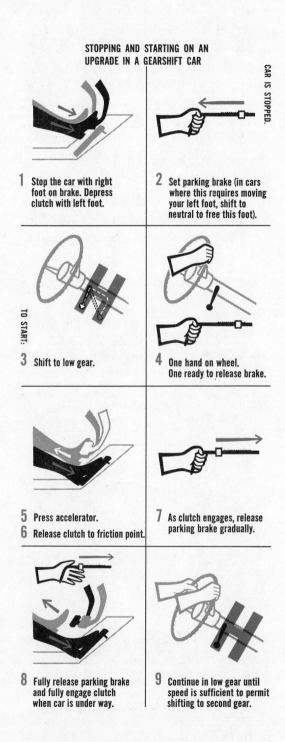

CAR IS STOPPED.

1 Stop the car with right foot on brake. Depress clutch with left foot.

2 Set parking brake (in cars where this requires moving your left foot, shift to neutral to free this foot).

TO START:

3 Shift to low gear.

4 One hand on wheel. One ready to release brake.

5 Press accelerator.
6 Release clutch to friction point.

7 As clutch engages, release parking brake gradually.

8 Fully release parking brake and fully engage clutch when car is under way.

9 Continue in low gear until speed is sufficient to permit shifting to second gear.

Fig. 22–18. This maneuver requires more practice.

Additional Points   Some cars have a device to prevent rolling back or stalling on uphill grades. To get a car moving again requires more power. Therefore, it is necessary to press down on the accelerator harder than when starting on level ground.

A different method for starting on a hill uses only the foot brake. It is good only on a slight grade where the car will not easily roll back and when the stop is a brief one, such as at a traffic signal. Stop the car and hold it firmly with the foot brake. Shift into low gear. Let the clutch pedal back to the friction point. Then move your right foot quickly from the brake to the accelerator pedal. Release the clutch pedal slowly while feeding gas to move forward.

Use this method with care and only after you become experienced. Unless your movements are exactly coordinated, the car may roll back or you may stall the engine.

Never attempt to hold your car on a hill by "slipping" the clutch. This causes excessive clutch wear and, when not perfectly done, results in stalling or rolling back. Always use either the foot brake or the parking brake when you are holding the car on an uphill grade.

Starting to Back Uphill   The procedure for starting to back up a grade is the same as starting forward, except that reverse gear is used.

The same procedure also applies when backing out of a downgrade stopped position. Always use either the foot brake or the parking brake to hold the car.

Push-starting Your Car

If your car battery fails and will not start the engine, the best plan is to have it started with a garage booster battery or a "jump cable" from another car with a battery of the same voltage. If neither is available, the car should be pushed to start the engine, never towed. There is danger with a towed car that, when the engine starts, speed will pick up so rapidly that it will crash into the car doing the towing. Study the owner's manual to learn what procedure the manufacturer recommends.

Automatic Transmission Cars   Some cars cannot be push-started. Some manufacturers recommend starting with the selector lever at **D**; others, with the lever at **L**. They differ also as to the speed the car should be going when the ignition is turned on.

To push-start an automatic transmission car, follow these steps:

Step 1. *Place the selector lever at* **N.**

Step 2. *Push to a speed of from 30 to 35 miles per hour.*

Step 3. *Turn on the ignition switch.*

Step 4. *Move the selector lever to the position recommended in the owner's manual.*

The driver of the car being pushed should be cautioned of one particular danger. When his engine starts, his car may "jump" ahead violently. He should be alert and should allow himself sufficient clearance of all objects nearby to assure safety. He *should not* exert pressure on the accelerator greater than necessary in ordinary operation at about 25 to 30 miles per hour.

Cars with Clutch Pedals   It is quite easy to start such cars by pushing them, when it is necessary to do so. Both drivers should understand perfectly both the procedure they will use and any special signals.

TO PUSH-START A CAR WITH CLUTCH PEDAL:

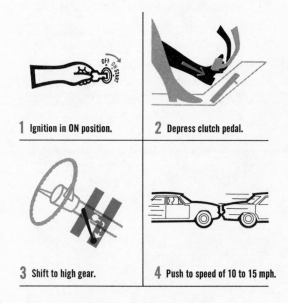

1 Ignition in ON position.   2 Depress clutch pedal.

3 Shift to high gear.   4 Push to speed of 10 to 15 mph.

5 Release clutch fairly slowly.

Fig. 22–19. Push-starting your car.

To push-start a car with a clutch pedal, follow these steps:

Step 1. *Put the ignition switch in the* ON *position.*

Step 2. *Depress the clutch pedal.*

Step 3. *Shift to high gear.*

Step 4. *Push to a speed of from 10 to 15 miles per hour.*

Step 5. *Release the clutch pedal fairly slowly.*

The engine should then start. If it fails to start, depress and slowly release the clutch pedal several times until the engine starts. Sometimes it is easier to start the engine when in second gear. If it does not start within a half mile of pushing, do not continue to try a push start. There may be some serious difficulty, and you might damage the transmission.

Towing an Automatic Transmission Car

Study the owner's manual for your car to learn how it should be towed, in case towing proves necessary. It is possible to damage automatic transmissions seriously by improper towing. This may involve expensive repairs.

Cars must always be towed with the selector lever at **N**, never at **D** or **L**. Tow at low speeds and only for very short

distances unless the drive shaft is disconnected or the rear wheels are elevated. It is safest always to tow automatic transmission cars with the rear wheels elevated.

Are You Ready?

When you have successfully mastered these skills in maneuvering and have. acquired confidence, you are on your way to becoming a topnotch driver. Remember: the better your skill, the less *conscious* attention to each movement is needed. The more of that attention you can devote to traffic and highway conditions the better for you—and for other highway users. Practice well!

Remember when you first played basketball? Look at a beginning player now. He doesn't do behind-the-back dribbling, pivot in either direction, and make hook shots with either hand. He has all he can do to bounce the ball with his eyes "glued" to it, and he looks for someone to pass to only after stopping. His full attention is needed for each move he makes. No wonder he occasionally passes the ball to an opponent! He simply hasn't had enough practice to be able to perform the skilled movements while he looks around and decides on his next move.

The new driver faces the same problem. His job is to practice the fundamental skills until he has mastered them. Whether athlete or driver, it is then—and *only* then—that he is ready.

To Talk About:

1. The process of trial and error is not an efficient, satisfactory method of learning any skill. Why is it a particularly poor way to learn to drive a car?

2. Choose several maneuvers and for each one discuss bad habits that a beginner might form if not corrected.

3. What will happen if you do not fully stop the car before shifting to reverse?

4. Talk about actions of drivers preceding turns which cause confusion. Can you depend upon a driver's signal? What is the importance of being in the proper lane for a turn?

5. Explain the proper position of your car at a "stop" intersection if you wish to make a right turn. A left turn.

6. As a part of the road test for a driver's license, in some states you are required to turn around in a narrow street. Discuss all the conclusions an examiner can make about your driving efficiency from watching you make this turn.

7. List all the situations you can think of in which it would not be wise to attempt to turn your car around by means of a U turn or three-point turn.

8. As you drive down a street with angle parking, what warning signals may you have that a car is about to back out?

9. Discuss courtesies you can show to drivers who have indicated to you that they wish to parallel-park or pull out from parking.

10. How should a driver signal his intention: to slow down; to come out of a parked position; that he is going to pull over to the curb?

To Do:

1. As you ride with some untrained drivers, note how they perform some of the maneuvers in this chapter. List the poor or inefficient habits they have developed. Along with your criticisms, tell how each maneuver could be more efficient.

2. Secure permission to paint a line 100 feet long and 4 inches wide on a practice roadway. Then test your steering skill. Drive forward, keeping the left front tire on the line. Repeat the same maneuver, keeping your right front tire on the line. Have someone check your performance.

3. On a blackboard, draw four diagrams of street intersections. Show on each of the four 1 car approaching the intersection. Have it approach from a different direction in each diagram. Assume in each case that the driver wishes to make an "intersection turn." Tell which turns would be wise and which unwise. What factors at any given time might change this and make your "wise" choice unwise?

4. If you have spaces marked on the street for parallel parking in your community, note how many cars are not parked *in* them but are too far forward or back from their lines. Why do you think this happens? Find a way to judge, from inside the car, when you are in exactly the right spot and explain it to the class.

5. Draw a design for an off-street area for practice-driving purposes. Include crosswalks, center lines, angle-parking lines, parallel-parking lines, such signs as CAUTION, SCHOOL ZONE, STOP, RIGHT TURN, RAILROAD CROSSING, etc. Indicate the procedure a driver should follow in order to include as many maneuvers as possible.

Advanced Driving

23

the Superior Driver

During the next several years you will have the opportunity to make yourself into the kind of driver you want to be: the highly skilled, obviously superior driver, the run-of-the-mill driver whose passengers frequently endure discomfort, embarrassment, and often risk life and limb, or the ridiculous and rather pitiful show-off who has little respect for the rights of others and whose every action loudly cries, "Look at me."

There is a widespread belief that a person suddenly changes from a learner to a superior driver on the day he passes his license test. This erroneous impression is very unfortunate. Sometimes the newly licensed driver's attitude toward learning changes and he closes his mind just at the time when there are many learning situations to be met. Or he may become careless and may not drive as well as he knows how. He becomes satisfied with careless performance. This attitude is definitely reflected in the disproportionate number of 18- to 20-year-old people involved in traffic accidents. Ironically, too, almost all people convicted of moving violations have the opinion that they are above-average drivers.

Ask a doctor, lawyer, tradesman, businessman, or professional athlete if he stopped learning on the day he received his diploma or first contract. Ask a good driver whether he stopped learning when he got his license. The final ceremony of school life is called commencement. Although it is the end of one part of your life, it is only the beginning, or commencement, of another. You have finished the first stage of becoming a superior driver—an important stage, of course, but only the first.

In the driver education course you receive a basic preparation for the future, just as the army recruit learns the fundamentals of being a soldier in basic training. Like the soldier, you now face a new way of life, a new road ahead. Both the soldier and you are now ready to acquire what might well be called advanced training, that is, experience.

Years of experience and perhaps a hundred thousand miles of driving are needed to make you a really superior driver. Even though they may drive hundreds of thousands of miles, however, some people never become good drivers. You will need many things in addition to

339

experience, including the will to learn, in order to become a superior driver.

Your driver education course up to this point was your basic training. This part of your book is a plan for your advanced training. These are some of the things you must learn, know, and do as you drive the many miles in your future. Only you can choose the road that will enable you to become a superior driver.

The Driver's License

You may have to wait a few weeks or months between the day you finish your driver education course and the day you can take the state license examination. Your behind-the-wheel road instruction is the time in which you learn how to learn how to drive. The completion of your driver education starts with your prepa-

Fig. 23–1. Your license examination is an important step in your driving career.

ration for the driver's license examination and may continue for 100,000 miles of driving. Your learning should continue as long as you drive.

Permit and Partner   In most states you need a learner's permit to practice driving before you obtain your license, and you must have a driver licensed in that state beside you on the front seat. The best plan is to have an experienced adult accompany you. Before your first practice session, ask your licensed partner if he would like to see what your driver education course was like. If he says he would, you might loan him your textbook, driving guides, and state driver's manual. Ask your driver education teacher to give you a list of the items that are checked on a road test. This list will help your partner by giving some suggestions to help you review and practice.

If at all possible, practice in the same car you will drive for your license examination. Even in cars of the same make, model, and year, there are often little differences in the feel of brakes, accelerator, or steering. Make a list of the various skills and procedures that you had trouble with in your driver education course. Spend extra time on the items that gave you the most trouble.

Examination   Before you take the driver's license examination, you should know what items are generally included. Review the booklet provided by your state. It will save your time, the time of the person who will accompany you, and the time of the state examiners if you wait to schedule the test until you and your partner are sure you are ready for it.

It is psychologically as well as practically wise to be accompanied by an adult. Be sure you have all the necessary material with you when you go for the test; take the car registration, your learner's permit, your partner's driver's license, and anything else that may be required by the licensing authority in your state. The best way to avoid being nervous is to be ready for the test; you should be confident that you can do better than the minimum required by the examiner. Your car must be in good operating condition; in some states the car is inspected before the license examination.

You Passed!   When you obtain your license you reach a crossroad in your driving life. The state has examined you and found that you have the *minimum* qualifications as a citizen of the driving world, a world of vehicles and drivers, of highways, of travel, and, sometimes, of tragedy.

In driving, be ever conscious of the limitations of your own experience. Don't become overconfident at this point! Hit at least that 100,000-mile mark before you class yourself with even the least experienced of the professionals.

You may ask, "What more is there for a driver education graduate to learn about driving?" There is much more, much

that simply could not be squeezed into the time available for the course. There are also a great many things that you weren't ready to learn until you gained additional driving experience.

Defensive Driving

We share our highways with millions of other drivers. All drivers must defend each other. No driver is alone. While you defend one driver, another driver is defending you. Defensive driving should mean a little more than defense against reckless drivers; a little more than what the law requires; a little more than minimum courtesy. The superior driver protects himself and his passengers and in turn enjoys the protection of others in his own class of drivers. Defensive driving is cooperation at its best.

Protecting Others   You are driving past some parked cars. There is a car following fairly closely behind you. Ahead of you, you notice a man on the traffic side of a parked car, changing a tire. What do you do? If he seems not to be aware of your approach and possibly apt to step in front of your car, you would warn him with a light tap on your horn. This is obvious, but what else?

Fig. 23–2. To help the driver of car B, the driver of car A moves left well ahead of the hazard.

A really superior driver will edge left before reaching the parked car to let the driver in the car behind see the man in the roadway. Occasionally, too, a person works under his car with his feet and legs extending out toward traffic. As foolish as this is, it does happen.

Another example might be a case in which a car is stopped, stalled, or even double parked in the lane ahead. Noting a car following him closely, and seeing that he will be able to move left and go around the stopped vehicle, the superior driver signals that he will move left. This does not, however, warn the following driver of the hazard ahead. If the first driver waits until the last moment to drive left, as many drivers do, the following driver may be too close to stop when he does see the hazard. The superior driver moves his car left well in advance of a hazard to permit following drivers to see the danger. The first move should be well in advance of the final move left to go around the stopped car.

Courtesy   You are approaching an intersection. A small child is standing at the curb on the near right corner, waiting for an opportunity to cross the street. You stop, either for cross traffic or for a stop sign. What do you do then? As a superior driver, and therefore a courteous driver, you keep your car standing and wave the child across in front of you.

Good, but one thing might be wrong. A superior driver would first look in his inside and outside rear-view mirrors, and glance back over his left shoulder. Is there a car in back of yours? Is there a car approaching from behind which might pass you? In passing you, the driver would have the child screened from his view by your car. Is there any turning vehicle which may endanger the child? Be careful never to encourage another driver or a pedestrian to drive or walk into a hazardous situation.

You Have Company   On today's busy highways a driver is rarely alone. The superior driver not only recognizes areas of potential danger, but makes sure that he knows what other vehicles are present on and entering the road ahead.

Suppose you see a car in a driveway or parking lot on the right side of the road some distance ahead, about to pull out

Fig. 23–3. Driver of stopped car checks for approaching cars before waving pedestrian across.

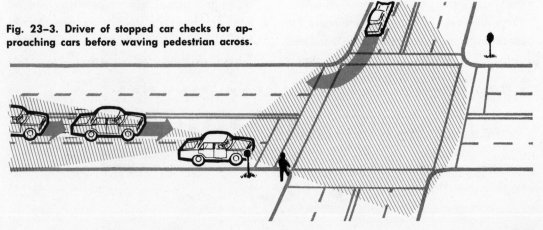

Fig. 23-4. When approaching an area of potential hazards, a superior driver looks both ahead and behind.

in front of you as you approach. Or you may see a bus stopped at the curb, or children about to dart out into the road. You are in the right lane on a four-lane street. What would you do? Do you concentrate all your attention on the potential hazard as you approach it?

If you are a really superior driver, you don't. You glance in your inside and outside rear-view mirrors to learn whether any vehicles are overtaking you—cars which may be either passing you or following you closely when you reach the danger area.

If one vehicle is overtaking you, it is wise to slow down a little so it will be past well before you reach the potential hazard. *Well* before, rather than immediately before, because in the latter case your car would hide the hazard from the other driver right up to the last moment.

If you reach the danger area free of the other vehicle, you have room for movement left and right. You can move quickly left if you see that such a move is desirable. If you reach the danger point just

as you are being passed by another vehicle, you will not be able to move left to avoid an accident.

If there is a line of vehicles overtaking you, and you see that you will not be able to move left, or even to time your reaching the hazardous area so that you will be alone, you must slow down enough to permit an easy stop. You will want to know if someone is following you closely and whether anyone will be passing you when you reach the danger area. In these cases you will want to give warning well in advance that you may have to stop. A hand signal and a few flashes of your brake lights should warn anyone following you. If the car following is too close, however, beware of using the brake lights as a warning (see page 190).

In short, when a superior driver sees a potential danger area ahead, he makes the conditions under which he will enter it as favorable as possible. Too many drivers rely on the hope that a potentially hazardous situation will work itself out all right.

Errors of Assumption

A frequent cause of trouble can be called the error of assumption. Here are two common examples:

1. You are stopped, about to turn left into a 55-mile-per-hour divided highway. There is another vehicle stopped in front of you, also about to turn left. As a gap in the traffic from the left appears, the driver ahead of you starts to turn left to enter the lane beyond the median strip. You start also, assuming that he will keep going. He sees a vehicle approaching from his right, and decides to wait and let it go by, meanwhile stopping in the intersection space in the median strip. You also must stop. Because of the position of his car and the width of the median strip, your car is now stopped across the travelled lanes of the highway, with cars

rapidly approaching you from your left.

The error here is one of assumption, in that you assumed that another driver would take a particular action, in this case that he would keep going. Obviously, you should have waited until he cleared the intersection before you started.

2. You are approaching the entrance to a shopping center on your right. You are in the right-hand lane. There is some traffic in the lane to your left, proceeding in the same direction. An oncoming car makes a left turn through a gap in the traffic some distance ahead of you. It is about to enter the shopping center parking lot on your right. You adjust your speed so that you will just clear the turning car without changing lanes. A car is overtaking you on your left and may be alongside you about the time you reach the turning car.

Fig. 23–5. The driver of car B is now in a dangerous position because he *assumed* that the driver of car A would complete his entry into the far lane of traffic.

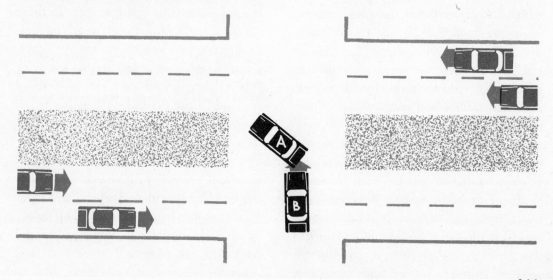

Suddenly the driver of the car which is about to enter the lot brakes to a stop in front of you. Your speed is too great to allow you to clear him as you had intended. You must brake strongly. Remember, he is facing your right and needs no braking distance in the direction you are moving. You do. The interval behind you and the reaction distance of the one or more drivers behind you become vital. Your error here is that you assumed that the oncoming driver would not stop in your lane.

Beware of a similar error of assumption when a driver in front of you, proceeding in the same direction, is about to turn right into a driveway. He may stop suddenly.

Adverse Weather Conditions and Judgment

There are people who pride themselves on their boast that bad weather never stops them from driving. This is silly, of course, and a sure sign of lack of experience. There are weather conditions in this country in which no vehicle moves, and many conditions in which wise drivers choose not to drive.

There are some conditions (extremely heavy fog, wet glare ice, etc.) under which *no* person can control his car, however highly skilled he may be. Then there are less adverse conditions under which most drivers believe they can control their cars. But many drivers have been involved in

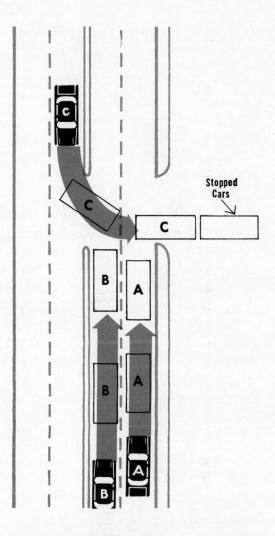

Fig. 23-6. The driver of both car A and car C are in a hazardous situation because driver A assumed that the driver of C would continue into the parking lot and driver C assumed that he would be able to enter the parking lot without stopping.

accidents because of the simple fact that while they could control their own cars, they could not control *other* vehicles on the highway—vehicles driven perhaps by poor drivers.

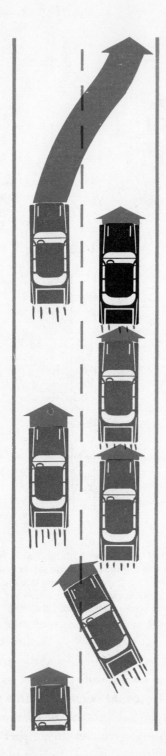

Fig. 23–7. Differences in speed cause dangerous freeway situations.

The Speed Differential

Traffic moves most safely when all vehicles move at about the same speed, a speed which is reasonable for existing conditions of visibility, weather, and road surface. Some vehicles may move at faster or slower speeds than the average speed of all vehicles on the road. This creates what is called a speed differential. Such a speed differential causes drivers to overtake and pass, to change lanes, to speed up and slow down, and to cut in. All of these maneuvers result in situations which increase the possibility of an accident.

If a driver drives at the speed of other traffic, he is not constantly slowing down, speeding up, changing lanes, or watching for tailgaters. If the proper following distance is maintained, a relatively small speed differential (about five miles per hour) would mean roughly equal stopping distances for all vehicles. The probability of rear-end collisions, the most common type of accident on freeways, would be lessened considerably.

A superior driver adjusts his speed so that there is little difference between the speed of his car and that of other vehicles moving in his traffic lane. However, he does not exceed the posted speed limit just because other drivers may do so.

Speed Tolerance

How fast does a superior driver feel that he is entitled to drive? Have you ever heard people say that police allow you to drive five (some say ten) miles over the speed limit? This is a widespread idea and some people drive under the delusion that when they are five or ten miles over the speed limit they are within the law. They aren't. (See page 33.)

This tolerance theory is used by some enforcement people on the basis of the fact that speedometers are not always accurate. Very few car owners ever have their speedometers calibrated. The vast majority of car owners do not know the amount of the error in their speedometers. Even if a driver were to check his speedometer at 60 miles per hour, covering a measured mile in one minute, this would not be a guarantee that the readings at 30, 40, or 50 mph would be correct also. Speedometer error is not uniform at all speeds.

Suppose the speed limit is 50 miles per hour. Suppose, also, that you depend on a 5-mph tolerance which someone told you the police observe. You drive with your speedometer indicating 55 mph. One of four things may happen:

1. You may not have an accident, and you may not be arrested for speeding.

2. Your speedometer may, by chance, be fast. If it is 5 mph fast at 50 mph you will actually be traveling at 50 mph and will not be exceeding the speed limit.

3. Your speedometer may be correct at 55 and the police can legally and properly arrest you for speeding.

4. Your speedometer may be slow. If it is slow by 5 mph at that speed, you are actually traveling at 60 mph, 10 mph over the speed limit. In some states this constitutes grounds for revocation of your license.

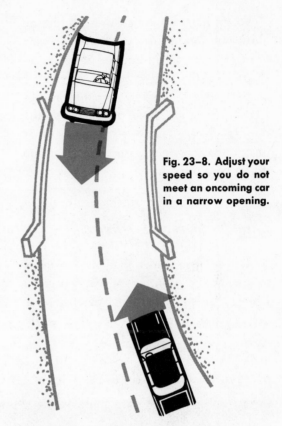

Fig. 23–8. Adjust your speed so you do not meet an oncoming car in a narrow opening.

Meeting a Vehicle in a Narrow Opening

The obvious procedure to follow in a situation similar to that shown in Fig. 23-8 is to slow down or speed up, to time the meeting either before or after going through the narrow space. Some drivers, however, refuse to change speed, feeling that any hesitancy would show a lack of confidence in their ability to judge car width and to drive accurately through a narrow opening. The fact is that people who know they're superior drivers don't worry about proving their abilities as drivers. Efficiency, not display of ability, is their aim.

You don't know anything about the ability of another driver coming toward you. He may misjudge and take three-quarters of the roadway or he may panic and shy away from your car into an object on his right. Don't let your pride drive your car. Time the meeting so that only one car is in the opening at a time if you possibly can.

The New Road Ahead

As you gain experience in the years following the granting of your driver's license, be sure that you pattern your driving practices on those of a really superior driver. It is foolish to follow the examples of show-offs, habitual law violators, or other immature bad-risk drivers.

Continuing effort to improve your driving performance will enable you to have the most satisfying career possible as a driver. In addition, your performance and attitude as a superior driver will win the respect of your family, friends, and fellow motorists.

As you drive, continue to acquire the outlook of the superior driver. Cooperate with other superior drivers. Make allowances for immature drivers. Drive defensively, confidently, and in the sportsman-like way.

Fig. 23–9. There's a new road ahead.

Reference List (Compact Model)

	Chapter references
Accident Facts (annual publication), National Safety Council, Chicago, Ill.	1, 3, 4, 5, 10, 11, 12, 13, 16
Action Program, The President's Committee for Traffic Safety, Washington, D.C., 1962.	8, 9, 19
Automobile Facts and Figures (annual publication), Automobile Manufacturers Association, Detroit, Mich.	1, 18, 19
Careers in Highway Traffic Safety, National Commission on Safety Education, National Education Association, Washington, D.C., 1958.	18, 19
Digest of Motor Laws (annual publication), American Automobile Association, Washington, D.C.	3, 8, 9, 10, 11, 13, 17, 19, 20
The Federal Role in Highway Safety, 86th Cong., 1st Sess., H. Doc. 93, 1959. (Purchase from U.S. Government Printing Office.)	8, 13, 19
Manual on Uniform Traffic Control Devices for Streets and Highways, U.S. Bureau of Public Roads, 1961. (Purchase from U.S. Government Printing Office.)	8, 10, 11, 12, 13, 19
Model Traffic Ordinance, National Committee on Uniform Traffic Laws and Ordinances, Washington, D.C., 1962, Revised.	8, 10, 11, 12, 19
Motor Carrier Safety Regulations of the Interstate Commerce Commission, Code of Federal Regulations, Title 49, Parts 190–198: Safety Regulations. (Purchase from U.S. Government Printing Office.)	
Motor Truck Facts (annual publication), Automobile Manufacturers Association, Detroit, Mich.	18
State Motor Vehicle Code (procure from your state motor vehicle department).	3, 4, 5, 6, 8, 9, 10, 11, 12, 13, 16, 17, 18, 19, 20, 21, 22
Uniform Vehicle Code, National Committee on Uniform Traffic Laws and Ordinances, Washington, D.C., 1962, Revised.	3, 4, 5, 6, 8, 9, 10, 11, 12, 13, 16, 17, 18, 19, 20
Vehicles, Roads, People, Automotive Safety Foundation, Washington, D.C., 1960.	1, 2, 8, 9, 12, 16, 19

PHOTOGRAPH ACKNOWLEDGMENTS

Acknowledgment is gratefully made to the following for the illustrations as listed below:

Acme Newspictures, New York, page 6

American President Lines, Ltd., San Francisco, Calif., page 6

American Red Cross, Washington, D.C., page 260

American Trucking Associations, Inc., Washington, D.C., page 258

Andersen-Roeney Operating Co., Tulsa, Okla., Fig. 19–15

Armin Jacobs & Co., New York, Fig. 3–7

Asphalt Institute, College Park, Md., No. VI in color section following page 191 (freeways)

Automotive Safety Foundation, Washington, D.C., Figs. 11–11, 16–14

Bureau of Public Roads, U.S. Department of Commerce, Washington, D.C., color section following page 110, Nos. II and IV in color section following page 191 (freeways), Figs. 3–15, 4–8, 8–7, 8–9, 10–10, 13–1, 13–4, 13–5, 13–11, 14–8, 14–14, 14–15, 19–1, 19–3, 19–7, 19–8, 19–14

California State Highway Department, Sacramento, Calif., Fig. 19–9

Callander, Don, Washington, D.C., pages 3, 5, 8, 259, Figs. 1–10, 3–6, 3–7, 3–13, 3–14, 4–2, 4–3, 7–5, 8–5, 8–11, 9–2, 9–3, 9–5, 9–12, 11–6, 11–7, 11–9, 12–10, 12–11, 12–12, 12–15, 14–1, 19–2, 20–1, 20–2, 20–10, 20–12, 20–13, 21–3, 21–12, 21–16, 21–18, 23–9

Cal-Pictures Photographic Association, San Francisco, Calif., Fig. 19–16

Canadian Government Travel Bureau, Ottawa, Canada, Fig. 14–3

Central Railroad Company of New Jersey, New York, Fig. 10–16

Chamber of Commerce, Eureka, Calif., page 3

Chrysler Corporation, Detroit, Mich., Fig. 20–4

City of Detroit, Mich., Fig. 19–10

City of Miami (Fla.) News Bureau, Fig. 12–9

Department of Transit and Traffic, Baltimore, Md., Figs. 11–2, 19–12

Douglas Photographers, Arlington, Va., page 259

Ford Motor Company, Dearborn, Mich., Fig 17–2, color section following page 218 (chassis)

General Motors Corporation, Detroit, Mich., color section following page 218 (engines)

J. Al. Head, U.S. Bureau of Public Roads, Washington, D.C., No. VII in color section following page 191 (freeways)

Harold C. Meyers & Co., New York, Fig. 8–8

James T. Jenkins, Jr., Editor, *American Road Builder,* Washington, D.C., Nos. I and V in color section following page 191 (freeways)

Kalec, George, Washington, D.C., Figs. 3–4, 3–10, 8–2, 9–7, 12–13, 14–2

Markel Service, Inc., Richmond, Va., Fig. 7–6

Marshall J. Robb, Milwaukee, Wis., Fig. 13–3

Maryland State Police, Pikesville, Md., Figs. 5–4, 9–8, 9–14, 13–10, 23–1

Maryland State Roads Commission, Baltimore, Md., page 260

Motor Vehicle Research, Inc., South Lee, N.H., Fig. 6–11

National Highway Users Conference, Washington, D.C., Figs. 16–9, 16–10

New Mexico State Tourist Bureau, Santa Fe, N.M., page 4

New York State Dept. of Public Works, Albany, N.Y., No. VIII in color section following page 191

North Carolina State Highway Patrol, Asheville, N.C., Fig. 8–6

Ontario Department of Travel and Publicity, Toronto, Canada, page 4

Packwood, Dave, Fig. 1–11

Radio Corporation of America, New York, Fig. 19–17

H. Armstrong Roberts, Philadelphia, Pa., Figs. 2–8, 7–3, 14–4, 19–6

Route 17 Association, Inc., Binghamton, N. Y., No. VIII in color section following page 191 (freeways)

Safe Winter Driving League, Chicago, Ill., Fig. 14–11

South Dakota State Highway Commission, Pierre, S.Dak., Fig. 6–10

State of Colorado Advertising and Publicity Department, Denver, Colo., Fig. 14–15

Sun Valley-Union Pacific Railroad, New York, Fig. 2–5

Texas Highway Department, Austin, Tex., No. III in color section following page 191 (freeways)

The Pennsylvania State University, University Park, Pa., Fig. 9–1

U.S. Air Force, Department of Defense, Washington, D.C., Fig. 2–10

U.S. Army Photo, Department of Defense, Washington, D.C., Figs. 1–8, 4–6, page 260

U.S. Post Office Department, Washington, D.C., page 259

Virginia Trailways, Washington, D.C., page 260

Warren, George T., Fig. 11–11

Washington (D.C.) *Post,* Fig. 14–6

Glossary

Acceleration An increase in speed.

Acceleration lane A special traffic lane that permits vehicles entering a highway to gain speed before merging with fast-moving vehicles already on the highway.

Accelerator (pedal) The foot pedal near the driver's right foot that is used to regulate the amount of fuel passing into the cylinders, thereby affecting the speed of the engine.

Access ramp A turning roadway at an interchange that permits traffic to move from one highway to another on a different level.

Accident prone (said of a person) Having a tendency to more than a normal number of accidents.

Antifreeze A chemical preparation used in an automobile cooling system to lower the freezing point of its fluid.

Arm pressure (of a windshield wiper) The pressure of the wiper blade against the windshield.

Arterial highway (or street) Any major street or highway designated by the authorities having jurisdiction over it as being part of a major street or highway system.

Arteriosclerosis "Hardening," or loss of elasticity, of the arteries.

Asphalt A substance refined from petroleum and commonly used in building roads and roofing.

Audiometer An instrument to test hearing.

Bill of sale A document prepared by the seller to serve as legal evidence of a sale.

Binder A material used to hold other substances together.

Biochemical Pertaining to the chemistry of living things.

Biological scientist A scientist who studies living things.

Bituminous An adjective used to describe materials containing bitumen, such as asphalt from petroleum and tar from coal.

Blind spot An area outside a car not visible to the driver even with the aid of his rear-view mirror.

Brake drum A steel drum or shallow cylinder which forms the inner portion of the wheel assembly; used in braking.

Brake lining A material used as efficient friction surface between brake shoe and brake drum.

Brake shoe A part of the brake which is forced toward the brake drum when the brake is applied; this creates friction and converts kinetic energy (of the car) to heat.

Bureau of Public Roads (U.S.) The part of the United States Department of Commerce that directs the Federal highway program.

Camshaft A shaft having cams, or eccentric pieces, which open and close the intake and exhaust valves of an engine.

Carbon monoxide A poisonous, colorless, odorless, and tasteless gas.

Channelizing islands Traffic islands that guide streams of traffic into definite channels.

Chassis The frame and mechanism of an automobile; does not include the body.

Choke A device for limiting the amount of air entering the carburetor, thus enriching the gasoline-air fuel mixture.

Coasting Driving a car with clutch depressed and/or in neutral **(N)** gear, disconnecting the engine from the rear (driving) wheels.

Code (e.g., state vehicle code) A law, or a group or set of laws.

Coefficient of friction Skid resistance—the force required to drag an object over a surface divided by the weight of the object.

Coil A part of the electrical system that increases voltage to the spark plugs; consists of copper wire wound around an iron core.

Collision diagram A diagram of an area of roadway or intersection with arrows showing the paths of cars colliding in an accident.

Color perception The ability to distinguish colors.

Combustion chamber An enclosure in which fuel is burned (*see* cylinder).

Compensate Make up for.

Condenser An element for storing electricity for a short period.

Connecting rod A metal rod which connects a piston to the crankshaft in an automobile engine (also in marine and other engines).

Contract An agreement, usually in writing.

Control devices (*see* Traffic-control devices)

Cramped (wheels) Front wheels turned to the extreme right or left position.

Crankcase The lower portion ("oil pan") of the engine; it contains the bulk of the oil.

Crankshaft The specially shaped shaft to convert downward thrust from pistons and connecting rods into torque, or rotary power.

Crown (road) The highest part of a convex road surface.

Cruising speed A normal car speed for which the engine is designed to be run without overworking.

Culvert A drain, or drainpipe, passing under (across) a road.

Cycle (engine) A complete series of movements ending at the starting position.

Cylinder The chamber in which the gasoline-air mixture burns; the piston moves up and down within the cylinder.

Cylinder block The main body of the engine, bored for the pistons.

Damages Compensation imposed by law for a wrong or injury caused by violation of a legal right.

Dealer (legitimate) One who sells in accordance with the law. The term usually implies conformance to business ethics.

Deceleration lane A special traffic lane adjoining the regular traffic lanes which permits vehicles leaving the highway to slow down to a safe speed outside the main traveled portion of the roadway.

Deed of trust A document putting property in trust to guarantee the payment of money.

Deflate Let air out (of).

Defroster A device for thawing ice and snow on the windshield, usually by means of a stream of warm air.

Degenerative changes Changes for the worse in quality; the organism becomes inferior.

Depressant That which lessens activity, makes less vigorous.

Deteriorate Grow worse.

Diaphragm (of a camera) A shutter which changes the size of an opening, permitting control of the amount of light reaching the film.

Diesel (engine) A high-compression engine which uses oil as fuel; now used in most railroad locomotives, many trucks and buses, etc. The high compression causes the fuel to "explode" without the use of spark plugs.

Dimmer switch The switch on floor in front and to the left of the steering column that lowers and raises headlight beams.

Dipstick Also known as a *bayonet gauge.* A long, flat, removable metal strip extending downward into the crankcase, or oil pan, of an automobile engine. Used to measure the level of the oil.

Directional interchange An interchange, generally having more than one highway grade separation, with direct connections for major left-turning movements.

Downshift A shift of gears from a higher to a lower gear.

Drag racing Timed racing from a standing start over a set, short distance.

Drive shaft A steel shaft which forms part of the power train between the transmission and the differential.

Dual-control car A car equipped with additional controls for a driving instructor (usually a clutch and a brake; sometimes there is a button switch to shut off the ignition).

Egotist A self-centered person; the term implies vanity.

Electronic eye A device that reacts to a beam of light, usually used to activate an electric circuit.

Emergency brake The parking brake of a car, sometimes called a *hand brake,* which usually operates on the rear wheels only.

Enforcement Acts performed by legally constituted officials with the object of causing obedience to law, including acts of apprehension of violators. Includes imposition of penalties on traffic-law violators.

Engage (the clutch) To allow the clutch pedal to come back so that the friction surfaces of the clutch come together.

Engine block See cylinder block

Engineer One professionally educated in engineering.

Engineering The science of designing and building or skillfully managing.

Exhaust Waste gases from an engine.

Fan belt A flexible belt driven by the engine to turn the fan.

Flooding A condition in which too much gasoline in proportion to air is admitted to the combustion chamber; the mixture will not ignite.

Fluid coupling A means of transmitting power through motion of a fluid.

Flywheel A heavy metal wheel on the end of the crankshaft to steady its motion; it has an external gear to mesh with the cogs of the starting motor.

Fog lights Headlights of a type designed to serve in fog, usually amber in color and mounted low on the vehicle.

Foot-candle   The intensity of light cast by a standard candle on a surface 1 foot away.

Front-end suspension   The parts (springs, and so on) which support the front end of the car on the front wheels.

Fuse   A device in an electrical system which will melt and break the circuit if the current exceeds the limit of safe operation.

Gauge   An instrument showing quantity or measure.

Gear   A cog wheel with teeth. In the automobile, a certain combination of such wheels engaged to transmit power to the rear wheels.

Gearing down   Shifting to a lower gear, as for a steep downgrade, to aid braking (*see* downshift).

Gear ratio   The number of times a small gear turns for 1 revolution of a larger gear with which it is meshed.

Gearshift lever   The lever with which the driver selects the desired combination of gears in the transmission in shifting gears.

Generator   A device, driven by the engine, which produces electricity.

Grade crossing (railroad)   An intersection of a roadway and a railroad track on the same level.

Grade separation   Vertical separation of roadways so that one passes over the other.

Grade, Gradient   A stretch of road that is not level, or the degree of variation from the horizontal.

Head (of engine)   The top portion of engine fitted to main engine block.

Highway casualty   A person suffering fatal or lesser bodily injury in a highway accident.

Hill crest   The top, or highest part, of a hill.

Hit-and-run driver   A driver who illegally leaves the scene of an accident in which he was involved without identifying himself.

Horsepower   A unit of power; the power needed to raise 33,000 pounds at the rate of 1 foot per minute.

Hydraulic   Operated by means of power transmitted through a fluid.

Idling speed (of engine)   The rate of speed at which the engine is adjusted to operate without use of the accelerator.

Illegal   Contrary to law.

Inching   Moving a short distance slowly, "an inch at a time."

Inertia   That property of matter by which it tends, when in motion, to continue in motion in a straight line, or when at rest to continue to be at rest unless acted upon by an outside force.

Inflate   Put air into.

Internal combustion   The combustion of fuel in a closed space such as a cylinder, with the result that the expanding gases move the piston.

Intersection   A junction of two or more streets or roads.

Interstate Commerce Commission   An agency of the Federal government having jurisdiction over commercial vehicles transporting passengers and goods across state lines.

Intoxication   State of being drunk.

Jaywalkers   Pedestrians who cross streets outside the regular crosswalk areas.

Judgment (law)   An obligation created by a decision of a court of law.

Legislation   Law.

Liability   Responsibility to pay.

Locked (wheels)   Wheels stopped by a strong application of the brakes.

Lubricate   To add a lubricant (such as oil or grease) to lessen friction.

Maintenance   The process of keeping a vehicle (or highway, etc.) in proper condition.

Manifold, exhaust   A tubelike arrangement which conducts the hot exhaust gases from the cylinders to the exhaust pipe.

Manifold, intake   A tubelike arrangement which conducts the gasoline-air mixture from the carburetor to the cylinders.

Manslaughter   Generally, as applied to an automobile accident case, the unintentional killing of a person.

Medial strip, Median strip   Nontraveled area separating traffic moving in opposite directions.

Mileage (gasoline)   Miles traveled per gallon of gasoline used.

MPH   Abbreviation for miles per hour.

Missing (of engine)   Its failure to ignite fuel and obtain power in all cylinders.

Mortgage   A contract pledging property (such as a house or car) as security for a loan.

Motor skills   Acts requiring dexterous movement of parts of the body.

Muffler   A device in the exhaust system for minimizing noise from explosions of gasoline.

Muscular contraction   Shortening and thickening of a muscle which causes a part of the body to move.

Nervous system   The intricate network of nerves which exists throughout the human body.

Neuromuscular   Refers to action involving nerves and muscles.

No-passing zone   A section of road on which vehicles are forbidden to pass others proceeding in the same direction.

Oil filter cartridge   Removable strainer, with filtering material, found in the oil filter of an automobile engine. Removes dirt and other impurities from the oil.

353

Oil slick   A film of oil on a roadway surface.

Ophthalmologist   One who deals with the structure, functions, and diseases of the eyes; an eye specialist.

Optional equipment   The equipment and accessories of an automobile not included in the listed purchasing price.

Optometrist   One who examines the eyes for the purpose of prescribing glasses.

Origin-Destination traffic surveys   Studies in selected areas of the origins and destinations of trips, vehicles and passengers using the roads being studied.

Overdriving headlights   Driving at a speed at which the car could not be stopped within the distance ahead which is visible in the headlight beams.

Overpass   A bridge which allows one road to pass over another.

Parallel parking   Parking with the car parallel and close to the curb.

Pattern of behavior   A tendency to act consistently in certain ways.

Pedestrian islands, isles of refuge   Defined areas between traffic lanes, sometimes raised, for pedestrian refuge; vehicles are excluded.

"Peeling rubber"   A slang expression used to describe excessive acceleration which causes tires to squeal or screech. "Peeling" refers to the damage done in stripping rubber off the tire when power is suddenly applied.

Peripheral vision   The ability to see to the sides while looking straight ahead.

Piston   A steel cylinder having the appearance of an empty can with the bottom removed; it moves up and down within the cylinder of the engine.

Play (of steering wheel)   The amount the steering wheel will turn before affecting the position of the front wheels of the car.

Policy (insurance)   An insurance contract between the company and the insured person.

Premium (insurance)   A payment to an insurance company for a policy.

Premium reduction   A lowering of the cost of an insurance policy.

Primary road   A main highway.

Prosecuted   Brought to trial in court.

Psychology   Study of the mind.

Radar   An electronic device to detect the presence of objects; also used to measure motor vehicle speeds.

Rate (insurance)   Basis for determining premium, usually based on accident costs in a given area, qualifications of the driver, and type of vehicle he drives.

Rear-end collision   A collision in which a vehicle strikes the rear of the vehicle ahead.

Reflectorized   Treated or covered with a substance which will reflect light; becomes luminous (glows) in the dark when struck by light beams.

Refraction   The deflection of light rays from a straight line.

Registration certificate   The official certificate of title to a motor vehicle issued by the state.

Repossessed cars   Cars which were sold and later legally confiscated (seized) for failure of the purchaser to fulfill his part of the contract; usually for failure to make payments when due.

Restricted license   A driver's license which imposes special conditions on the driving privilege.

Revocation (of license)   Cancellation of the privilege of driving.

RPM   Abbreviation for revolutions per minute.

"Riding" the clutch   The practice of driving with the foot touching the clutch pedal. Results in excessive wear of clutch surface.

Rings (piston)   Metal rings with outward spring pressure which fit into grooves in the outer walls of pistons. They press outward, sealing the space between piston and cylinder wall.

Roadbed   The graded portion of a highway upon which the road base, shoulders, and median are constructed.

Sealed-beam headlight   A headlight unit including the permanently enclosed filament, lens, and reflector; replaces the (older-type) separate bulb, lens, and reflector.

Seat belt   A belt fastened about the waist to prevent driver or passenger from being violently thrown forward by collision or sudden stopping of the car. The belt is firmly anchored to the car frame.

Settlement   Payment.

Shimmy   A violent shaking of the front wheels of an automobile.

Shock absorber   A device to lessen the bouncing of a car.

Shoulder   The outer portion of a roadway adjacent to the traveled portion.

Skills   Ability to perform acts of dexterity, to do things that require specific training.

Slipping of the clutch   Holding the clutch at the friction point so that the power from the engine is only partly transmitted to the wheels. It is practiced to hold the car from rolling back on a hill and sometimes to start the wheels in motion very gradually. Since it causes abnormal wear, it should be used only when necessary, as in deep snow, etc.

Snow tires, Snow treads   Tires with special treads for maximum traction in snow.

Social   With regard for society, humanity, people.

Social drinkers   Term used to denote those who drink alcoholic beverages to a lesser degree than those who become intoxicated, or drunk.

Speed zoning   Establishing maximum (and sometimes minimum) speed limits for a section of roadway by means of an engineering study.

Spring(s) (car)   A flexible steel coil, flat leaf, or bar which permits the wheels of a car to bounce up and down while the body of the car stays fairly level.

Squeegee   An action involving squeezing or wiping water off a surface.

Stanchion   An upright post or device to mark a location or boundary.

Starter, Starting motor   An electric motor operated by the car battery to turn the engine in starting.

Statistics   Numerical facts pertaining to a subject.

Stimulant   Something that leads to greater activity; enlivens, makes more vigorous.

Stimuli (nerve)   Electrochemical impulses traversing, or moving along, a nerve or a nerve fiber.

Summons   An order to appear in court.

Sun visor   Adjustable visor, or sun shade, near the top of the windshield.

Suspended sentence   A court-ordered sentence which will not be enforced unless some further act warrants its enforcement.

Tailgating   Following another car too closely.

Tail lights   Red lights on the rear of a car that are turned on automatically when the headlights or the parking lights are turned on.

Thermostat   A control device actuated by heat; controls the rate of flow of liquid through the radiator, thereby controlling the temperature of the engine.

Through street   A street at whose intersections traffic on the cross streets is required by law to stop or to yield the right of way to vehicles on the through street.

Ticket, Traffic ticket   A notice to appear in court or post collateral (money or property) for a traffic violation.

Tire pressure   The pressure of the air within a tire.

Toe-in   The position of the front wheels when the extreme fronts of the tires are closer to each other than the backs of the tires.

Torque   Rotary, or twisting, force.

Tracking (of tires)   The manner in which the paths of the rear tires follow those of the front tires.

Traction   Friction of a tire on a road surface.

Tractor-trailer   A truck-type vehicle consisting of pulling unit (the tractor) and detachable load-carrying unit (the trailer).

Traffic-actuated signal   A traffic signal operated by impulses from approaching vehicles.

Traffic artery   A major highway primarily for through traffic.

Traffic-control devices   Traffic signs, signals, and markings.

Traffic island   A defined, restricted area in a roadway which physically separates traffic streams with different destinations.

Tranquilizers (drugs)   Drugs having the effect of calming people and relieving nervous tension.

Transmission   An arrangement of gears serving as part of the power train that permits the driver to select various combinations of power and speed.

Tread (tire)   The surface of a tire grooved for traction.

Turnout lane   A special lane of limited length separate from through traffic lanes, for use by vehicles making brief stops.

Two-way radio   A combination sending and receiving radio set.

Uncontrolled intersection   An intersection having no traffic-control devices.

Underpass   A grade separation where one highway passes under another, or under a railroad.

Universal joint   A type of joint which permits the ends of two rotating shafts to be joined at an angle.

U turn   A continuous 180-degree turning movement on a street or roadway without backing.

Vacuum (operation)   Operated by a piston which moves because air pressure has been reduced on one side.

Valve   A device for opening and closing a vent or opening.

Vapor lock   Heat vaporizes gasoline in the carburetor, preventing a normal amount of gasoline from passing through the carburetor.

Velocitized   Having become accustomed to speed and therefore not fully conscious of it.

Violation   An act of breaking or disobeying a law.

Voltage regulator   A device for controlling the amount of current produced by the generator to meet the needs of the moment.

Index

A

Exhaust system, faulty, and night vision, 49
    function, color section following p. 218
    inspection, in purchasing car, 246
    (*See also* Carbon monoxide poisoning)
Expressways (*see* Freeways)
Eyeglasses, tinted, 49–50
Eyesight, 38–53, 55–56
    acuity and tests, 38, 40–42, 55–56, 69
    adjustment to light conditions, 46–47, 49
    and age, 57
    blind spot, 11, 290
    color vision and tests, 43–45
    controlled eye movements, 28
    distance judgment and test, 45
    effects of alcohol on, 66
    effects of drugs on, 73
    eye fatigue, 48–49, 51–52
    field of vision and test, 42–43
    minimum corrected vision, 42
    night vision and tests, 46–51, 69
    parts of eye, 46
    20/20 vision, 40–41

F

Fan, color section following p. 218
    condition of belt, 186, 231, 234
Fatigue, 28–29, 59–62
    driving on freeway, 190–191
    and drugs, 72–73
    eyes, 48–49
    highway hypnosis, 60–61, 190–191
    and night driving, 50
Federal-aid funds, 183–184
Federal-aid system, 265–266
    (*See also* Roads)
Field of vision, 42–43
Financial responsibility, 114–115, 118, 249
    security type, 248
Fines (*see* Violations)
First aid, 113–114
Flares, 146, 193
Flashing emergency light, 193
Florida pedestrian studies, 171
Fog, 212, 214
    visibility and traction in, 199–200

"Follow-me" test, 246
Following distances, 101–103, 157
    bunching hazard, 188–189
    bus or truck, 162–163
    on freeway, 188, 190
    rule, 101, 157, 188
    winter driving, 208
Force of impact, 85–88
    cushioning, 87–88
    and speed, 85–86, 96
    and stopping distance, 85–88
    and weight, 88
Foresight, value to driver, 14, 29–31, 138, 161–163, 171–178
Fountain of youth, 57
Freeways, 183–195, color section following p. 191
    acceleration lane, 186
    access ramp, 186
    deceleration lane, 194
    design of, 269
    fatality rates on, 184
    interchanges, 184, 186–187
    Interstate system, 183–185, 264
    median strips, 184, 191
    roadside services, 192–194
    safety factors, 184–185
    special characteristics of, 184–185
    (*See also* Driving on freeways)
Friction, 79–83
Friction point, 312, 324–325, 334–335
Fuel, economy of, 232, 234
    indicator, 294
    system, color section following p. 218
Fuses, 229

G

Garages (*see* Parking)
Gasoline, mileage, 232
    refilling tank, 192, 231
    service stations and freeways, 186, 192
    tax, 266–267
    type to use, 231
    use in engine, color section following p. 218
Gears, **D** or Drive, 304–309
    high, 310, 314–316

Overpowering in winter, 204
Oversteering, 160, 320
Overtaking and passing (*see* Passing)
Owner's manual, 232

P

Padded dash, 87–88, 299
Parked cars, bicyclist passing, 178–179
  driving near, 159, 177
Parking, 328–333
  angle, 328
  "back-in," 329, 333
  garages, 280–281
  "head-in," 328–329
  on hills, position of front wheels, 332–333
  off-street, 280–281
  parallel, 329–333
    on hills, 332–333
    leaving parked position, 331–333
  in rural areas, 280
  and tires, 223–224
  in traffic, 163
  and traffic engineering, 279–280
Parking brake, freezing of, 227
  purpose, 298
  use in starting car on upgrade, 333–334
Parking lights, 295–296
  use at twilight, 211
Parkways (*see* Freeways)
Passengers, blocking view of driver, 15
  knowing driver, 15–16
  as navigators, 190
  sudden actions of, 14–15
Passing, 143–146
  in city traffic, 160
  commercial vehicles, 149
  cooperation in, 145–146
  on icy roads, 208
  on hill crests, 148–149
  markings on pavement, 145
  mathematics of, 144–145
  mountain driving, 214
  no-passing zones, 280
  precautions, 145

Passing, return to proper lane, 145
  on right-hand side, 161
  on rolling, hilly roads, 215
  and sight distance, 144–151
  stopped vehicles, 162–163
Pavement, brick, 201
  dry, 198–199
  edges, 150–151
  gravel road, 199
  icy spots, 208
  kinds of, 269
  markings, color section following p. 110, 139–
    140, 145
  mud on, 200
  smoothness of, 81, 201, 320
  and stopping distance, 90, 100
    table of, 209
    variations in, 100
    wet, 199–200
  wet leaves on, 201
Pedestrian "paths" (*see* Crosswalks)
Pedestrians, 166–181
  accidents, 11, 14, 280
    at night, 172–173
    by age groups, 168–169, 174
    causes, 169–176
      alcohol, 173
      table of, 171
    on city streets, 169–170
    danger signs, 177–179
    likely to cause death, 166–167
    percentage of fatalities, by cities, 168
    rural areas, 280
    statistics, 166
    and visibility, 172, 174, 176
  arrests for intoxication, 180
  barriers, 288
  and city traffic, 162–163, 177–178
  cooperation with drivers, 181
  driver responsibility for, 166
  enforcement of ordinances in 32 cities, table
    of, 180
  on freeways, 192
  illegally crossing streets, table of, 180
  limitations of, 167–168
  overpasses and underpasses for, 181, 278

INDEX